Lena Frit

The Body as a Screen: Japanese A

Studien zur Kunstgeschichte

Band 192

Lena Fritsch

The Body as a Screen: Japanese Art Photography of the 1990s

Georg Olms Verlag
Hildesheim · Zürich · New York
2011

Lena Fritsch

The Body as a Screen: Japanese Art Photography of the 1990s

Georg Olms Verlag
Hildesheim · Zürich · New York
2011

Umschlagmotive:
Izima Kaoru, *Otsuka Nene Wears Tuzigahana # 213–214* (1999).
C-Prints. Courtesy of the artist.

Zugleich: Dissertation, Rheinische Friedrich-Wilhelms-Universität Bonn 2010

Die Deutsche Nationalbibliothek verzeichnet diese Publikation in der Deutschen Nationalbibliografie; detaillierte bibliografische Daten sind im Internet über *http://dnb.d-nb.de* abrufbar.

∞ ISO 9706
Gedruckt auf säurefreiem und alterungsbeständigem Papier
Umschlaggestaltung: Inga Günther, Hildesheim
Herstellung: Goldener Schnitt, 76547 Sinzheim
Druck: Strauss Druck GmbH, 69509 Mörlenbach

Printed in Germany

www.olms.de
ISBN 978-3-487-14679-9
ISSN 0175-9558

Acknowledgements

Numerous individuals and institutions have provided help, advice and inspiration for this thesis, and it is impossible to name all of those to whom I owe a debt of gratitude. However, above all, I would like to thank my supervisor, Prof. Dr. Anne-Marie Bonnet from the Art History Department of Bonn University, who let me work independently in Tokyo and London but was always there for me when I needed help. I am also grateful to her for suggesting Morimura Yasumasa's 'self-portraits' as a topic for my Master's thesis when I asked her for advice back in 2004 – our conversation was to become the very beginning of this project.

Prof. Dr. Melanie Trede from the Centre of East Asian Studies of Heidelberg University was terrifically generous and helpful in providing extensive advice. Deep thanks go to her for spending her precious time reading my thesis as the second advisor.

Without a PhD scholarship by the German National Academic Foundation (Studienstiftung des Deutschen Volkes) over a period of almost three years (10/2007–08/2010), and a scholarship for research in Tokyo by the Alexander von Humboldt Foundation in 2008, it would have taken much longer and been much more difficult to write this thesis. I am truly grateful for the generous financial and academic support.

For giving me inspiring interviews and helpfully providing me with information and images, I should like to express my gratitude to the artists this thesis is concerned with: Ishiuchi Miyako, Izima Kaoru, Mori Mariko, Morimura Yasumasa, Yamanaka Manabu and Yanagi Miwa.

For patiently answering my questions about Japanese art and photography, I am grateful to: Fukagawa Masafumi (curator at the Kawasaki City museum), Iida Shihoko (curator at the Tokyo Opera City Art Gallery), Isshiki Yoshiko (art consultant in Tokyo), Kasahara Michiko (chief curator of the Tokyo Metropolitan Museum of Photography), Kitamura Junko (curator at the Utsunomiya Museum of Art), Kokatsu Reiko (chief curator of the Tochigi Prefectural Museum of Fine Arts) and Nanjô Fumio (director of the Mori Art Museum).

Furthermore, this thesis has benefited from information and visual material provided by the following artists, galleries, museums, temples etc.: Andreas Binder Galerie in Munich, Araki Nobuyoshi, Byôdôin Temple in Uji, Craig Emmott with his homepage www.taleofgenji.org, Kudlek Van der Grinten Galerie in Cologne, Linden Museum Stuttgart, Museum of Fine Arts Boston, Museé d'Orsay Paris, Nara National Museum, National Research Institute for Cultural Properties Tokyo, Robert Mapplethorpe Foundation in New York, Sprüth Magers gallery in London, Stux Gallery in New York, Tenri University

Library in Nara, The Third Gallery Aya in Osaka, Tom Kelley Studio in Los Angeles, Galerie Wohnmaschine in Berlin, Yakushiji Temple in Nara, and Zoe Leonard.

For providing help as diverse as recommending literature, giving me intellectual input and critical feedback, providing information on Japanese law, or writing letters of recommendation, I would like to thank the following individuals, without whom this work would not have taken the shape it has: Prof. Dr. Jacqueline Bernd, Chad Fahs, Dr. Maren Godzik, Eva Hegge, Prof. Dr. Peter Pantzer, Krestina Skirl, Prof. Dr. Rainer Stuhlmann-Laeisz, Tachi Daiko, Wakita Mio and Carola Wanke.

Various native speakers helped me with my English writing: Lisa Caripis, Sonia Chang, Sinéad Cooper, Penny Elvy, Barry Freedman, Richard Klimpke, Louise Kessack Dear and Lucy Sorell. I am thankful not only for the proof reading but also for feedback and new ideas. For helping me with my Japanese, I owe a debt of gratitude to Sugino Kayoko.

Last but not least, I would like to thank my dear parents: I am grateful to my mother, Prof. Dr. Ingrid Fritsch, for her brilliant help and advice especially in the field of Japanese studies. Deep thanks also go to my wonderful father, Prof. Johannes Fritsch, who passed away shortly before I could finish this project and whom I think of every day: Rest in Peace.

Contents

Notes to the Reader

The spelling, grammar, punctuation and style of the English used in this thesis follow the conventions of British English as explained in the *Oxford Style Manual.*[1] Japanese words are italicised; their spelling follows the Hepburn system. Japanese names are written in Japanese order: the surname followed by the 'first name'. The Japanese calendar counts years according to the reignal years of the Tennô emperor. When mentioning a Japanese period for the first time, I include the equivalent of the 'Western' calendar in brackets; in addition, a list of Japanese periods is included on this page.

When referencing information from my interviews with artists and curators, only the first (direct or indirect) quotation includes a footnote with the date and place of the interview. Throughout this thesis, all following quotations by the same individual will refer to the same interview if not stated otherwise in the footnote.

All unattributed translations from Japanese, German or French into English, including direct quotations in quotation marks, are my own; footnotes reference the original text. In a few instances, I use other scholars' translations; the translators are mentioned in the bibliography.

List of Japanese Periods

Japanese Periods	Western Calendar
Heian	794–1185
Kamakura	1185–1333
Muromachi	1333–1573
Azuchi-Momoyama	1573–1603
Edo	1603–1868
Meiji	1868–1912
Taishô	1912–1926
Shôwa	1926–1989
Heisei	1989–ungoing

[1] RITTER, Robert M. (ed.) (2002): *The Oxford Style Manual*. Oxford: Oxford University Press.

Introduction

1. Choice of Topic and Artists

The main aim of this study is to examine the human body as a motif in Japanese photographic art of the 1990s, with particular reference to socio-cultural issues. Furthermore, my study seeks to explore the specifically Japanese context of the artworks, such as the historical foundations of 'art' and 'photography' in Japan, the structures of the 1990s art system, and the presence of Japanese photographs in a 'Western' art market.

Why 'body' and why 'photography'? During the last two decades, the plethora of virtual body images, worldwide debates on new reproductive technologies, the increasing blurring of biological gender boundaries and people's (re)design of their bodies through fitness training and cosmetic surgery have made questions on the human subject and his or her body increasingly pertinent. As well as being the subject of extensive discourse in the natural sciences, cultural studies and the media, the body has also been featured increasingly in art images, as evidenced by a large number of exhibitions.[1] At the same time, the medium of photography has been re-evaluated within the art system, and has been increasingly exhibited in art museums and galleries on a par with the traditional medium of painting. The canon of master photographers has been expanded; the large scale of photographic works has started to compete with the scale of paintings, and prices on photographic works of art have 'skyrocketed'. In light of these considerations, it is not surprising that increasing numbers of photographic works of art have expounded problems surrounding the human subject, one's body and identity.

Not only 'Western' but also Japanese artists have emphasised the body in their photographic work. In the 1990s, major travelling exhibitions of Japanese art toured North America and Europe bringing audiences and curators into contact with recent art and photography developments in Japan.[2] Interest in Japanese photography has grown in 'the West', resulting in galleries and museums hosting solo shows for Japanese artists. Morimura Yasumasa has attracted

---

1 The touring exhibition *Post Human* in Europe (1992/1993), *L'Âme Au Corps* at the Grand-Palais in Paris (1993/1994), *Andere Körper* at the Offenes Kulturhaus Linz (1994), *feminine-masculin* at the Centre Pompidou (1995/1996); *Spectacular Bodies* at the Hayward Gallery (2000) etc.

2 The touring exhibition *Against Nature: Japanese Art in the Eighties* in the USA (1989/1990); the touring exhibition *A Cabinet of Signs* at the Tate Liverpool etc. (1991); *In die Felsen bohren sich Zikadenstimmen* at the Kunsthaus Zürich (1993); the touring exhibition *Japanese Art After 1945: Scream Against the Sky* at the Guggenheim Museum in New York etc. (1994–1995); *Prospect'* 96 at the Schirn Kunsthalle Frankfurt (1996), *Desire and Void* at the Kunsthalle Wien (1997); the touring exhibition *The History of Japanese Photography* at the Museum of Fine Arts in Houston etc. (2003).

attention for his large-sized 'self-portraits' – photographic appropriations of 'Western' paintings or images of popular culture, featuring himself in different roles. Similarly, Mori Mariko in her early photographic work has presented herself as female figures reminiscent of images from Japanese popular culture. Miwa Yanagi has also created large colour photographs; her digitally altered images focus on young females and, for instance, their roles in Japanese society or their dreams of the future. In his series *Landscapes with a Corpse*, Izima Kaoru is concerned with the aesthetic of the female 'corpse' which is presented in elaborately-staged settings. The female subjects are models and actresses wearing designer clothes of their choice; the series can be linked with Crime Scene Photography as well as Japanese 'death' aesthetics. Yamanaka Manabu's black and white analogue photographs differ from these works: they present us with images of homeless people or naked old women, i.e. with body forms that contrast with popular media images. Ishiuchi Miyako has focussed on the human body in highly stylised close-up photographs featuring, among others, naked males and scars. In this thesis, I will analyse the body as a motif in the 1990s work of these six artists.

The images used in this study have been chosen primarily because they feature (clothed or unclothed) human bodies. The featured artists come from different backgrounds within Japan: their age, gender, family situation and artistic environment vary. For instance, Ishiuchi Miyako, who was born in 1947, has been influenced by the politically critical, feminist Zeitgeist of the 1960s, whereas Mori Mariko, born twenty years later into a famous and wealthy family,[3] started to take photographs in the prosperous era of the 1980s. However, the photographic images are of more interest to me than the individual artists with their biographies; the artist's personal background will only be reflected on when relevant for the understanding of the examined artwork. I use their photographic works of the 1990s as critical lenses through which various issues concerning Japan's culture and society can be considered.

Furthermore, the featured works of art have all been presented in the 'Western' art world and written about in exhibition catalogues, newspapers and magazines. By discussing ten images in a detailed and critical way, my thesis aims to provide a counterbalance to these predominantly short and commercial texts. My intention is to present readers with essential information on both the content and the context of ten Japanese photographs that they might have seen within the 'Western' art system.

---

3 The Mori family is one of the wealthiest and most influential families in Japan: Mariko's uncle Mori Minoru is a well-known property developer, heading the Mori Building Company, and Mori Akira is the chief executive of the Mori Trust. Their father, Mori Taikichirô, was listed the world's wealthiest man on the Forbes list in 1991 and 1992. Both Minoru and Akira are billionaires.

My thesis neither sets out to be representative of contemporary Japanese art nor aims to present an exhaustive overview, or a unified theory, of Japanese photography of the 1990s. It does, however, reflect a surge in interest among Japanese artists to examine the current structures of Japan in relation to attitudes to the body. They use the body to present different gender issues, identity problems and religious ideas. My goal is not only to identify these issues but also to link them to their historical, social and cultural context. In other words, this thesis offers an opportunity to gain insight into various socio-cultural problems broadly relating to the human body in 1990s Japan through the analysis of photographic works of art.

2. Definition of Terminology and Formalities

In order to avoid misunderstandings, some key terms of this thesis should be defined. Firstly, what is a 'body' and why is it a 'screen'? Following postmodern theories, including works by Michel Foucault, Judith Butler and Elisabeth Grosz, I view the 'body' as a changeable surface, inscribed and coded by social meanings of various regimes of discipline and training. The 'body' is more than animate material composed of flesh and organs; it is also a flexible concept, an idea, an image. In order to express this complex notion of the 'body', I will hereafter put quotation marks around it. This thesis interprets photographic body images as reflections of a 'real' world; each image is viewed as a 'screen', revealing inscriptions on the human body. Moreover, the 'screen' is used as a flexible 'umbrella term' since it covers inscriptions on the 'body' on three different levels: inscriptions by Japanese society, by the referenced artists, and by myself as a subjective viewer. A more detailed explanation will be given at the beginning of Part 3.

'The West', 'Western', 'Japan' and 'Japanese' are used as geographical terms as well as functional-notional categories representing images within the space of a 'Japanese' or 'Western' consciousness. When using 'the West' or 'Western' as a geographical category, I refer to North America and Europe. However, this reflects my consciousness as a 'West European' on the one hand, and a 'Japanese' viewpoint on the other. As such, geographical and subjective categories are often intertwined. I will hereafter put the terms 'the West', 'Western', 'Japan' and 'Japanese' in quotation marks in order to highlight their subjective denotion. What is an 'art photograph'? At its most basic level, a 'photograph' is a picture obtained by the medium of photography. However, any photograph is dependent on a series of historical, social, and cultural contexts which establish its meanings as an image and sometimes also its value as a work of 'art'. In Graham Clarke's words, a photograph is a 'distinctive cultural product ... As a means of representation, it says as much about the world it "mirrors" as it does about the world which produced the images in the first place.'[4] As the title of this thesis indicates, my project is concerned with 'art photography'; photographs taken for documentary purpose will be excluded. However, like 'documentary photographs', 'art photographs' say something about the world they 'mirror' while, at the same time, being socio-cultural products. Consequently, I view a 'photographic artwork' as an image which 'talks' to me about a human subject as its motif as well as about its own socio-cultural circumstances.

The '1990s' in this thesis refers to more than the last decade of the 20th century; it also stands for a notion of change. As I will explain in Part 1, the 1990s in Japan have been called the 'Lost Ten Years'; however, with regard to Japanese art as well as socio-cultural issues related to the 'body', they brought considerable change. In my interpretations, I will focus on the 1990s but also consider historical backgrounds and recent developments. Furthermore, I will include Yamanaka Manabu's *Arakan* series in this project although the photographs were taken between the years 1983 and 1988. This is due firstly to the series being stylistically linked to his 1990s work, secondly to the series being exhibited during the 1990s for the first time, and thirdly to my subjective viewpoint that it would have been a pity to exclude these interesting photographs.

3. Literature Review

In the last fifteen years, growing numbers of conferences and publications have addressed problems surrounding 'non-Western' art within a 'Western' art system which is under the influence of both colonial history and an increasingly globalised present.[5] Furthermore, conferences and publications have questioned alternatives to the traditionally Eurocentric discipline of 'art history', debating 'visual studies', 'world art history', 'global art history' etc.[6] However,

---

4 CLARKE (1997): 25.

5 For instance, the conferences *The Interplay of Art and Globalization* at the IFK in Vienna and *Where is Art Contemporary* at the ZKM in Karlsruhe in 2007; the conference *Contemporary Art and the Global Age* at the ZKM in 2009, the session *Imperial Tensions: Visual Cultures of Coercion, Silence and Display* at the annual conference of the Association of Art Historians in Glasgow in 2010 and the interdisciplinary conference *Veiled Orient, Unveiled Occident?* at the University of Zurich in 2010; publications include WEIBEL (1997) and VOLKENANDT (2004).

6 The concept of an art history which overcomes the cultural, chronological, and object-related restrictions and hierarchies of a traditionally 'Eurocentric' art history can already be found in George Kubler's 1962 essay *The Shape of Time*. Kubler suggests an explicitly interdisciplinary strategy by adapting not only genuine art historical methods like formal analysis but also approaches from historical studies and cultural anthropology. However, it was in the late 1990s that an alternative 'art history' became a topic of popular academic debate, for in-

few studies have been concerned specifically with the presence of contemporary Japanese art in the 'Western' art system. In addition, no publication has yet examined the structures of the art system in 1990s Japan, let alone the complex context in which Japanese photographic art is situated.

The 'body' has become a key problematic in the humanities of the late 20th century; this is indicated by the proliferation of books and journals, conferences and graduate schools dedicated to the analysis of the 'body' from various viewpoints. One example of a multidisciplinary approach to the 'body' is *Fragments for a History of the Human Body* (1989), a three volume collection of essays, which was edited by Michel Feher. The forty-eight academic essays examine the history of the human body in relation to social and cultural concepts; they show how different societies at different times have constructed the 'body' by adapting it to contemporary circumstances. Each volume focuses on a particular perspective: volume one explores the human body's relationship to the divine; volume two is concerned with human emotions; volume three investigates body parts and their functions, considering both the human and the social body. The anthropological, philosophical and historical focus as well as the quality of the essays vary to a great degree;[7] however, most of the essays show convincingly that the 'body' is, in Feher's words, 'thoroughly historicized'.[8] It is this demonstration of the 'body' as a socio-cultural artefact which makes *Fragments for a History of the Human Body* a model for a multidisciplinary collection of academic 'fragments' concerned with the 'body'.

---

stance: SUMMER (2003); VOLKENANDT (2004); BONNET, SAUERLÄNDER, SCHMIDT-LINSENHOFF and WYSS (2004); KEMP, LOCHER and PRANGE (2004); BOEHM (2004); BELOW and VON BISMARCK (2005); ELKINS (2007); VAN DAMME and ZILJMANS (2008); BELTING and BUDDENSIEG (2009). In addition, Leiden University and the University of East Anglia in Norwich already teach the subject 'World Art Studies'; Heidelberg University teaches 'Global Art History'.

7 For instance, Mario Perniola's essay *Between Clothing and Nudity* in the second volume could be criticized for not questioning, but rather stabilizing, the classic Western opposition of a male heterosexual gaze and a female body. Perniola analyses the relationship of clothing and nudity in the figurative arts, in striptease acts etc. across various centuries, linking it with philosophical concepts by, for instance, Plato and Heidegger. However, by not mentioning any homosexual contexts, he leaves his own perspective unexamined, reinforcing a Western heterosexual male perspective as the normative. In contrast to this, LaFleur's essay *Hungry Ghosts and Hungry People* in the first volume, which examines somaticity and rationality in medieval Japan, sets an example as the author openly acknowledges it was born out of a Western postmodern belief system, differing from the system of medieval Japan. LaFleur's willingness to present his own perspective as being bound to a certain culture and time, results in a refreshingly honest as well as informative essay on the 'body' in medieval Japan. As such, the essays in *Fragments for a History of the Human Body* vary in their quality and academic vantage points.

8 FEHER (1989): 11.

In the field of contemporary art history, Amelia Jones has analysed the 'body' and its representation in 'Western' artworks of the late 20th century, including performance art, photographs and videos; her interpretations are based on a critically postmodern and feminist approach. Her book *Body Art: Performing the Subject* (1998) is essential for two main reasons: firstly, Jones offers persuasive interpretations of works of 'body art' in relation to concepts of the 'subject'; these are grounded in descriptions of individual artworks, as well as in documentation and discourses which have framed the works historically. Secondly, she openly embeds her interpretations within both her own experience and contemporary thought while, at the same time, offering clear and logical argument.[9] Although Jones' study includes a section on Lyle Ashton Harris' photographs, it concentrates on art performances, e.g. by Vito Acconci, Carole Schneemann or Hannah Wilke. The book re-evaluates persuasively 'body art', especially of the 1970s, in relation to philosophical and political discourses; however, it does not offer any analysis of Japanese photography of the 1990s. In *Picturing the Self* (2005), Gen Doy has examined the 'body' in past as well as contemporary images in relation to philosophical theories of the self. Using Descartes' notion of the subject as a starting point, Doy analyses how ideas of the self in Western culture have changed since the 17th century and how these complex and often contradictory concepts are embodied in works of art. The book's focus on 'Western' images as well as its philosophical methodology differ from the subjects of analysis of my thesis and my approach of linking works of art to socio-cultural contexts. There are more examples for a new art historical interest in the 'body', which could be defined as a 'body turn'.[10] However, a detailed examination of the 'body turn', both in the field of art and the academic discipline of art history, do not appear relevant for this study, which is clearly confined to representations of the human body in Japanese photographic art of the 1990s.

A new concern with the 'body' can also be found in the academic field of Japan. However, as an essay on Japanese socio-cultural publications on the 'body' by Ingrid Getreuer-Kargl makes clear,[11] and as my own literature research corroborates, most publications are not concerned with photographic

---

9 See, for instance, her detailed analysis of Vito Acconci's work. JONES (1998): 103–150.

10 The term 'body turn' was coined by Anne-Marie Bonnet and used as the title of her presentation at the *iconclash* conference at the ZKM in Karlsruhe, Germany, in 2002. Bonnet used the term in reference to the 'iconic turn', highlighting the complex relationship of bodies with images especially in the context of the 1990s art scene. According to Bonnet, the human identity crisis (e.g. the post-human discourse) has made the 'body' appear to be the last resort for selfhood. Here, I use the term in a different context: not only in the arts but also in the academic field of the late 20th century, there appears to be a 'body turn' – a new interest in the body as a subject of analysis.

11 GETREUER-KARGL (2001).

images. Furthermore, some publications should be viewed within the *nihonjinron* discourse ('discourse on the Japanese') and are precarious in their focus on Japanese 'uniqueness'; for example Ban Yoshitaka's work *Anata no shintai wa nihonjin desu* (Your Body is Japanese), published in 1990, which analyses the 'Japanese body' without defining this notion of 'Japaneseness'.

Consequently, most texts used for this thesis were *indirectly* linked to the 'body' in 1990s Japanese photographs, for instance by analysing the 'body' in Japanese society and art history, or by examining gender and identity issues. For instance, Yorô Takeshi's *Nihonjin no shintaikan no rekishi* (The history of Japanese people's bodily feeling) (1996) has shown how various social developments, such as the introduction of Western medicine, have influenced the way that many Japanese people view their bodies. A symposium on the 'body' in Japanese history, chaired by Kuriyama Shigehisa in 2000 has resulted in an interesting essay collection on Japanese imaginations of the body in historical contexts.[12] Furthermore, Iida Yumiko's extensive sociological study on identity issues, *Rethinking Identity in Modern Japan* (2002), and other works of sociology and cultural studies were relevant for this thesis; I have tried to find overlaps and tensions between the 'body' in images and the socio-economic, political and cultural contexts of modern and contemporary Japan.

In addition, various interdisciplinary publications on Japanese 'visual culture' have been vital to my project: for instance, the essay collection *Consuming Bodies. Sex and Contemporary Japanese Art*, published by Fran Lloyd in 2002, and *Gender and Power. In the Japanese Visual Field*, published by Joshua S. Mostow, Norman Bryson and Maribeth Graybill in 2003. Both publications examine the multiple ways in which works of Japanese visual culture act as reflections on issues of gender, sexuality and national identity. These essay collections are concerned with how culturally-constructed notions of gender and sexuality are linked with political power and social circumstances; the publications were especially important for Part 3 of my thesis. Similarly, the 2008 publication *Performing "Nation". Gender Politics in Literature, Theater, and the Visual Arts of China and Japan, 1880–1940* by Doris Croissant, Joshua S. Mostow and Catherine Vance Yeh includes essays repeatedly cited in the third chapter of this study. For instance, Jacqueline Berndt's essay *Nationally Naked?,* with its convincing analysis of the nude body in Japanese oil paintings and posters of the late 19th and early 20th century, was essential for my study of the naked body.

Melanie Trede and the Institute of East Asian Art History of Heidelberg University organised a workshop entitled *Gender and Art History in a Global Context* in 2007, and a workshop series linked to the cluster *Asia and Europe in*

---

12 Kuriyama (2000).

a Global Context in 2009. The events featured various issues surrounding 'body' and 'gender' in a global art market; the lectures and discussions on Japanese art encouraged me in the gender section in this study.

With regard to literature on the work of the six artists of this thesis, most publications are concerned with Morimura Yasumasa's work. In 1995, Norman Bryson published an essay in *Art and Text*, offering three different viewpoints on Morimura's photographic 'self-portraits'. Although just a short article, Bryson's persuasive interpretations have inspired my project in the way they link Morimura's 'masquerades' with issues of gender and national identity. In 2000, Joonsung Yoon published his insightful PhD dissertation *The Emperor's New Clothes*, which relates both Morimura's and Cindy Sherman's photographic self-portraits with photographic and psychoanalytic theories. However, the psychoanalytic approach, with its emphasis on concepts of the self, does not address the role of socio-cultural issues reflected in Morimura's work. In the following year, Ruth Wright Jasinowski published her PhD thesis focussing on Morimura's work created between 1985 and 1991. Although defining her study as 'cross-cultural observation',[13] the author is not familiar with Japanese language and culture. As a result, the thesis remains a collection of short and rather superficial essays mirroring a 'Western' perspective on Morimura's work; the reader senses the complexity of Morimura's photographs but does not get any in-depth explanation. In 2008, Shimizu Akiko published a book comparing and contrasting Morimura Yasumasa's and Cindy Sherman's work, interpreting both as a 'representational practice of the "lying body"'.[14] Similar to Yoon's study, which Shimizu does note appear to have been aware of, the book investigates how the self is represented in Morimura's and Sherman's photographs, drawing on psychoanalytic theories, e.g. by Lacan. In short, most publications are not directly concerned with the socio-cultural contexts surrounding Morimura's photographic 'body images'. Moreover, there are no studies examining the 'body' in the work of the other five artists this thesis is concerned with.

In light of these gaps in the research on Japanese photographic art, my thesis has two principal objectives: firstly, to describe the context of art photography in 1990s Japan, and secondly, to outline the various ways in which specific works featuring the 'body' reflect socio-cultural issues. It is the purpose of this thesis to uncover the richness of artistic expressions within the medium of photography in 1990s Japan, using the human 'body' as a 'screen' for different contemporary problems.

---

13 WRIGHT JASINOWSKI (2001): 3.

14 SHIMIZU (2008): 6.

4. Thesis Structure and Methodology

With regard to the structure of this thesis, Part 1 starts from the premise that artworks are not autonomous but produced through and against specific historical conditions, and that these conditions are central to an understanding of their form, reception and positioning within society. The first chapter will examine the deeper historical, cultural and social forces which have engendered Japanese 'art' and 'photography'.

The second and third chapters are concerned with concrete works of art. Part 2 begins with a short introduction to the work of the individual artists, followed by an analysis of one or two artworks as case studies. Following this, I will offer brief comparisons with similar or contrasting works. Japanese artists active in the 1990s were working within a global network of ideas and images, and were mostly familiar with 'Western' art. It is thus appropriate to also consider 'non-Japanese' counterparts and equivalents.

Part 3 will relate the analysis of Part 2 to issues of class, power, gender, and religion. The first sub-chapter will introduce relevant body theories and explain the idea of viewing 'the body as a screen'. The second sub-chapter will move on to analyse the photographs which feature naked subjects, relating their nakedness to (art) historical backgrounds. The third section is organised around the themes of Japanese history and national identity while the fourth looks at bodily representations and 'social codes'. Following this, the fifth sub-chapter will raise different questions related to gender issues. The sixth section will be concerned with the 'body' as a 'screen' for religion and religiously-influenced culture, opening the way for the final section, in which the photographs will be linked to different photographic discourses.

In short, the thesis' main 'body' can be divided into two components, namely the first chapter focussing on the 'context', and the second and third chapters analysing the 'body' as a photographic motif. The conclusion reviews and extends my overall arguments.

As the literature review has shown, few English publications are concerned with the contexts of Japanese (photographic) art of the 1990s; hence, I have chosen to base Part 1 on Japanese literature, my own observations and in-depth interviews with Japanese artists and art specialists. The interviews were conducted between October and December 2008; they took place at various locations in Japan, such as the artists' studios or curators' offices. I e-mailed my questions to the interviewees before meeting them. The order in which the questions were asked was fixed; however, depending on the interviewees' answers, new questions were sometimes added. Hence, the interview method could be defined as 'semi-structured'; the interviews were 'designed to obtain information about people's views, opinions, ideas and experiences'.[15]

The one-to-one interviews were all conducted in Japanese and recorded digitally; the outcomes range from a 30-minute conversation to a three-hour discussion. The participating 'art specialists' were Fukagawa Masafumi (curator at the Kawasaki City museum), Iida Shihoko (curator at the Tokyo Opera City Art Gallery), Isshiki Yoshiko (art consultant in Tokyo), Kasahara Michiko (chief curator of the Tokyo Metropolitan Museum of Photography), Kitamura Junko (curator at the Utsunomiya Museum of Art), Kokatsu Reiko (chief curator of the Tochigi Prefectural Museum of Fine Arts) and Nanjô Fumio (director of the Mori Art Museum). In addition, all of the six artists which this thesis is concerned with agreed to give me an interview. I could not meet Mori Mariko in person; however, she answered my questions by filling out my questionnaire.

All interviews have been transcribed; excerpts of the interviews with the artists have been translated into English and are included in the appendix. Since Japanese syntax, semantics and style differ so much from the English, some compromises were inevitable. Where the original passage is linguistically central to the argument, e.g. when it includes a pun, the translation tends to be more literal. Where the passage concerns factual backgrounds, the translation is often freer.

The interview questions covered a range of issues. However, I am aware of the fact that the interviewee's persona as an artist, gallery employee or museum director are closely intertwined with the answers. Furthermore, every interview is, as the sociologist John Rex has emphasised, 'an interaction' and an 'interactive process'.[16] My personality and identity as a Caucasian young woman as well as social characteristics that the respondents attributed to me surely had an influence on the results. Hence, I have used the interviews carefully as a means to confirm and complete my impressions on the 1990s art context. The interviews were relevant for Part 1, in order to obtain answers to a series of questions relating to the 'art world' in Japan. I also asked questions on 'body' issues. However, the answers were less important for my interpretations of the photographic works of art than the results of my descriptions and formal analyses; I believe that the photographs 'speak' for themselves. This brings me to Part 2 and Part 3.

For Part 2 and Part 3, I have grounded my interpretations in the formal analysis of ten photographs, linking them with knowledge and data from different sources. I am persuaded by the multidimensional nature of artworks as well as of art historical studies: my multiple readings deliberately combine interpretations with observation from different disciplines and historical back-

15 ARKSEY and KNIGHT (1999): 96.
16 REX (1974): 85.

grounds. For instance, I have analysed the 'body' in a work by Morimura Yasumasa by firstly referencing its appropriation of 'Western' art historical traditions in the second sub-chapter of Part 3, then by considering it in light of post-colonial theories in the third sub-chapter and finally by regarding it from a gender viewpoint in the fifth. In addition, there are artworks which are interesting in reflecting ideas of photographic discourse, for instance by Roland Barthes. However, this thesis does not attempt to adopt any 'theory of photography'. Firstly, there is still no 'theory of photography' with a methodology peculiarly its own; the best known texts on photography, for instance by Susan Sontag or Roland Barthes, offer no 'theories' in a methodological sense. Secondly, I am an art historian intrigued by individual artworks and their socio-cultural context rather than a philosopher of photography.

In light of these considerations, it could be concluded that I attempt to follow an approach which has been described as 'bottom-up' interdisciplinary: as W. J. T. Mitchell has written, 'bottom-up' interdisciplinarity is always determined by a certain topic;[17] my choice of sources, theories and academic disciplines always depends on the individual artwork and the questions it raises surrounding the 'body'.

As previously mentioned, Part 1 will introduce the background of Japanese 'art photography' in the 1990s, while Part 2 and 3 will focus on ten images. As such, 'context' comes before 'content'. This ordering happened unintentionally at first: the 'context' and 'content' parts are two distinct and yet related concerns of this project. However, the arrangement also symbolises this thesis' interest in those Japanese photographs which are present in a 'Western' art context. The 'context' presented in the first chapter indirectly defines the 'content' of the second and third chapter; in this study, 'art' is examined as something which is institutionalised and mediated through the 'art system'. The analysis of Japanese art photographs which are not present in the 'West' would be a relevant topic for further research; it is surely necessary to examine photographic art which is only known in Japan. Furthermore, it is relevant to explore the complex reasons for certain photographers being known and others being unknown in the 'West'. However, in this particular project, I have chosen to focus on those artists whose works are exhibited and sold within the 'Western' system; my concern is to finally start an academic analysis of their works independent of commercial interests.

I make no claims to methodological originality in this thesis. Yet, what is offered here has not been attempted before; there are few academic works on Japanese art photographs of the 1990s, let alone on their representation of the 'body' in relation to socio-historical issues. As both a 'Western art historian'

---

17 MITCHELL (2003): 41.

and somebody whose personal history is influenced by the Japanese culture and language, I attempt to 'interpret' Japanese artworks to 'Western' readers. At the same time, I will present contexts and viewpoints which have not yet been examined by Japanese scholars either and thus, might also be interesting to a Japanese audience.

5. Two Principles for an Analysis of 'Non-Western' Art

Against the background of current discussions within the discipline of 'art history' on a move towards 'global art history', it could be asked if this thesis presents anything in its methodological approach which adds to this discourse, whether directly or indirectly.

First and foremost, the debate on a 'global art history' or 'world art history' seems relevant in representing a serious academic interest in 'non-Western' art and a need to expand the borders of our discipline. It is a fact that the field of 'art historical' study has become, as Anne-Marie Bonnet has written, 'wider, deeper and more complex' and hence, 'new methods of capture, thought and speech are necessary'.[18] Indeed, this thesis seeks to represent such an expansion of 'art history'. However, as Hans Belting has written, 'art on a global scale does not imply an inherent aesthetic quality, which could be identified as such, nor a global concept of what has to be regarded as art'.[19] As this quotation shows, a 'global art history' can only work as a flexible category; it should not claim to offer a universal model but rather constantly reconsider and define its understanding of 'art'. At the same time, Belting's statement alludes to one main problem of 'art history', whether 'global' or not, namely the precarious decision of inclusion or exclusion in the name of 'art'; I will return to a similar problem with regard to the 'Western art system' in Part 1. However, I certainly agree with Kitty Zijlman, who has suggested a 'multicultural point of view' in order to 'reinterpret the past' as well as a 'work toward the writing of art histories' rather than holding on to a single 'Western' art history.[20] Whether these approaches are to be realised within the academic field of 'art history', 'world art history', 'global art history' or 'visual cultural studies' is beyond the scope of this thesis. Rather, my intention is to demonstrate how an analysis of 'non-Western' works within any discipline of 'art history' or 'visual culture' at a 'Western' university can be insightful as long as two principles are followed.

The first principle is an awareness and clarification of one's research position. Examining 'non-Western' art, including Japanese photographs, as a

---

18 BONNET, SAUERLÄNDER, SCHMIDT-LINSENHOFF and WYSS (2004): 84.

19 BELTING (2009): 40.

20 ZIJLMANS (2007): 293.

'Western' scholar is precarious since the study tends to become exotistic. However, as long as one is aware of one's cultural 'starting point', the 'Western' perspective does not need to be a disadvantage. An outsider is able to present a viewpoint which is less socially or psychologically bound by the visual conventions of a society; the distance might even help to clarify the view. In addition, as Norman Bryson has written, works of art have a potential for meanings generated by different 'frames'[21] – as a researcher I both interpret and create 'frames'. I have tried to stay aware of my 'frame' – its advantages and limitations – throughout this study. Shifting between the 'outsider' position of a 'Western' art historian and an 'insider' perspective due to my personal biography being intertwined with a Japanese context since an early age, my research attempts to present a complex view on 1990s Japanese art. My alternations between distance and proximity might help to somewhat 'objectify' my analysis. At the same time, however, I am aware that this thesis will tell the reader as much about me as it will about the photographic images, 1990s Japan and any other circumstances under scrutiny.

The second principle is intertwined with the first: I believe it is necessary to interact with 'non-Western' scholars and 'art specialists'. Chino Kaori has stated persuasively that in the study of foreign cultures we should make use of our 'ability to make contacts and learn from others, and understand our own biases, and thus gradually correct our own scholarship'.[22] Nanjô Fumio has emphasised a similar point: 'when people from overseas ask me how they could understand Asian artists' perspective, I tell them that they should ask their Asian colleagues, curators and artists. They should talk to them... And then, they can develop their own viewpoint'.[23] As previously mentioned, I had the opportunity to meet most of the artists this thesis is concerned with as well as Japanese art specialists. As this thesis will hopefully show, I have 'gradually corrected my own scholarship' and developed my 'own viewpoint'.

This viewpoint is constantly shifting between a 'Western' distant position on the one side, and a 'Japanese' proximal position on the other. Hence, if categorisations were necessary, my thesis could be labelled as an experiment in 'Western-Japanese art history'; however, I would prefer to concentrate on specific art contexts and individual artworks rather than categorisations of academic discipline.

---

21 BRYSON (1994).

22 As cited in KANÔ (2003): 26.

23 NANJÔ, Fumio, conversation with the author, 03. 12. 2008 in the Mori Art Museum in Tokyo. All subsequent quotations by Nanjô are from this interview, unless otherwise stated in the footnote.

Part 1:
The Japanese Context

1. Introduction

In this thesis, artworks are considered in a historical, social and cultural context. Thus, the first part of this chapter will examine social and political issues of the 1990s, the historical background of 'art' in Japan and the contemporary 'art system', in order to understand the background of the Japanese artists and their work. The 'art system' consists of artists, critics and art historians as well as the art market, art collectors, curators and museum visitors. Since the structures of this system and its historical background are issues too broad to be explored in detail, I will focus on those aspects which are most relevant for the photographs featured in this thesis.

Since the 1990s, there has been a great acclaim for Japanese photographic art in the 'Western' art world. However, Japanese artists have created their works in an environment that should not be compared with that in the U.S. or Europe. Kasahara Michiko has stressed the importance of this context for an understanding of the photographs:

> In "contemporary photography", we have entered an age in which the photographers must take responsibility for, as well as be self-consciousness [sic] of, the venue for exhibiting their works, the method of distributing them, how will they be used, what meaning they carry, etc. What context the work was made in is in fact itself an integral part of the work.[1]

The second part of this chapter will explore this 'context' of photographic works from various viewpoints, such as the photography business, education system, debates surrounding the status of photography as 'art', and infrastructure developments. It will not provide an overview of Japanese photography;[2] only those historical movements and photographers that seem important in the context of Japanese photographic art in the 1990s will be considered.

---

1 KASAHARA (2001): xi.

2 For a historical overview on Japanese photography see WILKES TUCKER, FRIIS-HANSEN and RYÛICHI (2003).

2. The 1990s in Japan – the 'Lost Ten Years'?

The 1990s in Japan are often referred to as the 'Lost Ten Years'. This expression is related to the crash of the 'Bubble Economy': the enormous growth of the economy in the 1980s had been driven by a financial mania centred on inflated stock and property markets. Within ten months in 1990, Japan's Nikkei index lost almost 50% of its value and land prices dropped dramatically. This 'bursting' of the 'Bubble' led to a decade of prolonged stagnation as well as a wave of economic, political and social reforms. It also exposed a series of scandals linking figures from politics, finance, and the criminal underworld. In 1993, demands for reform led to the defeat of the Liberal Democratic Party, whose conservative majority had governed Japan for thirty-eight years.

The death of the emperor, Tennô Hirohito, in 1989, which marked the end of the Shôwa period (1926–1989), coincided with the economic and political collapse. The Shôwa period spanned sixty-three years of modern Japanese history – from the rise of imperialism to its defeat, from the post-war years of the American occupation to the success of Japan's economy. The early 1990s were marked by unprecedented criticism of the Tennô's role in society. A re-evaluation of the Shôwa era and the will to challenge social taboos surrounding the Tennô were increasingly evident in contemporary media and academia.

The media news was dominated by negative incidents, such as economic stagnation, the earthquake in Kobe, the Sarin gas attacks by the AUM Shinrikyo sect, and child abuse scandals. The term *anzen shinwa* ('myth about Japan being a secure country', a popular term within the 1990s) reflects how Japan's national pride had evaporated and how the population had lost faith in its country. Iida Yumiko has corroborated this by describing the 1990s as a decade characterised by a 'multifaceted breakdown of the political, economic and socio-cultural bases that had been the source of stability in previous decades'.[3] For instance, traditional business practices based on the idea of life-long loyalty to one company were now considered a cause of the economic problem.

Moreover, the erosion of conventionally held values and moral principles as well as problems of national and individual identity intensified. Gunji Pegio-Yukio has used two terms to illustrate the most relevant identity problems of the 1990s: *buru sera*,[4] i.e. young girls selling their used school uniforms and underwear to men for sexual stimulation, stands for indifference and nihilism, whereas the AUM sect stands for people's escape into religion and extremism.[5]

---

3 IIDA (2002): 209–210.

4 *Buru* comes from the English 'bloomers' and *sera* from 'sailor' and is used in *buru sera* as an abbreviation for school uniforms in sailor-style. *Buru sera* shops sell girls' used school uniforms and underwear, sanitary napkins and urine. The clothes are often accompanied by photographs of the girls.

5 GUNJI (1998): 172–173.

In this social context of the 1990s, searching one's own identity became important for many people in Japan.[6]

The negative expression 'The Lost 10 Years' suggests that the decade has been 'lost' and spent in vain. However, the 1990s could also be seen as a time of social and political alteration as well as a decade of new developments in Japanese art and culture.

3. The Concept of 'Art'

When discussing Japanese art, as Sawaragi Noi has pointed out, the most difficult issue is the concept of 'art' being 'an enormous paradox'.[7] This is connected to the fact that the notion of 'art' was for the first time introduced into Japan with the influx of 'Western' culture in the Meiji era (1868–1912); in pre-modern Japan a general word for 'art' had not existed. The introduction of 'art' was a politically motivated action; public exhibitions were connected to the government's aim of encouraging economic development. In an effort to make Japan a modern nation with military and industrial strength to equal the industrialised 'West', the regime undertook widespread reforms not only of the Japanese political system but also of its culture.

The beginnings of the Japanese art system were strongly shaped by the American Ernest Fenollosa (1853–1908), who was appointed professor of philosophy and political economy at the Tokyo University in 1878. Together with the art historian Okakura Tenshin, he collected and inventorised artworks; in addition, he participated in the foundation of the Imperial Museum in Tokyo (today Tokyo National Museum), becoming its director in 1888. One year later, the Imperial Ministry also opened a museum in Nara and Kyoto.[8]

As the art historian Satô Dôshin has pointed out, the new art concept caused conflicts with old conventions. Calligraphy masters rejected exhibitions, stating they would be 'too Western' and it would not be appropriate to display the calligraphies like in rarity cabinets. Having connections to politicians and educated people from 'high society', numerous calligraphy artists exhibited their works at exclusive meetings.[9]

In order to comprehend the 'paradoxical' Japanese art concept, three terms will be explained briefly: '*bijutsu*', '*geijutsu*' and '*âto*'. The term '*bijutsu*' was coined in the Meiji era. Satô Dôshin and Maren Godzik both highlight how the characters '*bijutsu*' are connected to the Meiji government's reforms: with '*bi*'

---

6 KAWAI (1998): 252.
7 SAWARAGI (1992): 388.
8 SATÔ (1996): 170–214.
9 SATÔ (1999): 168.

meaning 'beauty' and '*jutsu*' meaning 'technique', the term '*bijutsu*' mirrors the government's aim of combining economy and art.[10] Hence, '*bijutsu*' could be interpreted as symbolising the motto of uniting a 'Japanese spirit with 'Western' techniques' (*wakon yôsai*).[11] The terms '*hakubutsukan*' (literally 'house with various things') for 'museum' and '*bijutsukan*' ('house with beautiful things') for 'art museum' were also coined during the Meiji modernisation since such institutions had not existed before.[12] The term '*bijutsu*' was used for the first time in 1872 when a German article written for the Vienna World Exposition was translated into Japanese.[13] The German words 'Kunstgewerbe' ('applied arts'), 'Bildende Kunst' ('fine art') and 'Kunst' ('art') were all translated as '*bijutsu*'. This is of note because it provides evidence that the Japanese language at that point had not differentiated between 'applied arts' and 'fine art'. Hence, the term '*bijutsu*' represented 'art' in a general sense. Today, it is mainly used for 'fine art', while '*geijutsu*' stands for 'the arts' in general. However, as the arbitrary use of '*bijutsu*' and '*geijutsu*' by artists and curators in my interviews shows, as well as the translations in Japanese-English dictionaries, they can both be used for 'art' in general.[14]

The word '*geijutsu*' essentially means 'techniques to create something cultural, decorative, or entertaining.' It was already used in China as a general term for the aristocratic 'six skills' (*rikugei*), which included music, calligraphy, math and horse riding.[15] The character *gei* can be used for 'high art' as well as for 'popular art'; it is used in both the terms '*geijutsuka*' ('artist') and '*geinôjin*' ('entertainer'). Kinoshita Nobuyuki has pointed out that artists in Japan had been ranked alongside entertainers until the 'performing arts' (*geinô*) and 'art' (*geijutsu*) were separated during the modernisation process.[16] Kinoshita's argument can be corroborated by a quotation by Morimura Yasumasa: 'Art is basically entertainment. Even Michelangelo and Leonardo da Vinci were entertainers. In that way, I am an entertainer and want to make art that is fun.'[17] Considering the etymological background, Morimura's statement can be interpreted as a pun, referencing the etymological unity of 'entertainers' and 'artists'. Morimura is not an 'entertainer' in a 'Western' sense; the complexity of his works indicates serious artistic concerns. However, he often appears in

---

10 GODZIK (2007): 55–56.

11 SATÔ (1999): 166.

12 PUSTOLLA (2006): 14.

13 KITAZAWA (2005): 8–10.

14 The *New Concise Japanese-English Dictionary* by Sanseido (1985) defines '*geijutsu*' as '(an) art' and '*bijutsu*' as 'fine arts, art'; the *Senior English-Japanese Dictionary* by Obunsha (1968) translates 'art' with '*bijutsu, geijutsu*'; the *New Nelson Japanese-English Character Dictionary* (1997) translates '*geijutsu*' with 'art, the arts' and '*bijutsu*' with 'art, fine arts'.

15 SATÔ (1996): 43.

16 As cited in ÔNISHI (09. 11. 1999): 5.

17 As cited in DIPIETRO (1998): unnumbered.

public presentations or on TV, humorously telling anecdotes about his art production. Morimura has explained this double role by comparing himself to Kitano Takeshi.[18] Kitano is acknowledged in the 'Western' world as a film director, but mainly known as a TV comedian, producer and ex-*manzai*-star in Japan;[19] he creates 'high art' *and* popular entertainment. In addition, his popular 1990s TV show *Takeshi No Daredemo Picasso* (Takeshi's Everybody is a Picasso) featured autodidacts and entertainers, and at the same time artists, such as Kusama Yayoi and Murakami Takashi. Kinoshita has commented on the programme, stating that Japan does not have a class society like 'the West'. He has concluded that the Japanese population does not need high art; 'entertainment coming from the population is more real.'[20] Kinoshita's statement is precarious, however, considering the etymological background of 'art', Morimura's presentations and Kitano's show, it emphasises the concept of 'art' being closer to applied arts and popular entertainment than in Europe or North America.

Nowadays, the term '*âto*' (coming from the English 'art') is often used instead of '*bijutsu*' or '*geijutsu*', as it sounds more modern and international. As Godzik has pointed out, the word '*âtisuto*' (coming from the English 'artist') is increasingly getting popular in the Japanese language, whereas '*bijutsuka*' ('artist of visual art') sounds old-fashioned especially in spoken Japanese.[21] The terms '*âto*' and '*âtisuto*' not only exemplify the increasing usage of English words in the Japanese language but also symbolise how Japanese artists have positioned themselves in a global art market. However, in my interviews it became clear that 'art' and 'artist', as well as the art system today, are still seen as concepts originally introduced into Japan by 'the West'. Kitamura Junko, curator at the Utsunomiya Museum of Art, has summed this up nicely when saying, 'art is a Western concept, there are no rules for this game in Japan yet'.[22]

---

18 MORIMURA, Yasumasa, conversation with the author, 03. 07. 2005 in the MEM gallery in Osaka.

19 *Manzai* is a traditional stand up comedy, which has been popular in Osaka since the Meiji era. The fool (*boke*) presents puns and anecdotes, while his 'serious' counterpart (*tsukkomi*) harshly criticises him. Today, the production firm Yoshimoto Kôgyo in Osaka trains newcomer *manzai* comedians, whose performances are often broadcasted on TV.

20 As cited in ÔNISHI (1999): 5.

21 GODZIK (2007): 43.

22 KITAMURA, Junko, conversation with the author, 07. 11. 2008 in the Utsunomiya Museum of Art. All subsequent quotations by Kitamura are from this interview, unless otherwise stated in the footnote.

4. Art Education

The Kôbu Bijutsu Gakkô (Art School of the Ministry of Industry) was the first art academy in Japan. It was founded during the Meiji Restoration in 1876 and was part of the Tokyo University of Technology. Italian art academies were used as models and Italian artists were hired to teach painting and sculpture techniques.[23] The Meiji government sought a synthesis of industry and culture as a means to improve economic development. Therefore, as Kurahashi Shigefumi and Ôtsuka Haruo have pointed out, art techniques useful in economy were supported more than others;[24] for instance, artists were needed to draw product designs or maps for military use. In other words, the practicability of art was considered more important than concepts of self-expression or creativity. This again mirrors the traditional connection of arts and crafts in Japan.

The Tôkyô Bijutsu Gakkô (Tokyo School of Fine Arts), founded with the support of Ernest Fenollosa in 1887, has become one of the major art universities in Japan. In 1949 it merged with the Tôkyô Ongaku Gakkô (Tokyo Music School) and was renamed the Tôkyô Geijutsu Daigaku (Tokyo University of the Arts).[25] At the beginning, the art school only taught *nihonga* ('Japanese painting'). However, *yôga* ('Western painting', oil paintings) was added to the Curriculum in the 1890s. Ever since, not only art education but also the whole art system have been divided into a 'Japanese' and a 'Western' branch. Students have had to decide between studying *nihonga* or *yôga*, the former being a distinct category within the annual Nitten exhibitions at the National Art Centre in Tokyo. Still mostly male, the exponents are grouped in hierarchical cliques; the hierarchies are strongly influenced by the artists' schooling and art academy membership. *Nihonga* are seen as *kokumin kaiga* ('national paintings'), using 'Japanese' materials, picturing 'Japanese' subjects and dominating the Japanese market.

This *nihonga* and *yôga* separation has not only influenced the Japanese art world but is also relevant for the understanding of photographic art. In my interview, Kitamura has stressed that in the 1980s and 1990s, photography was usually not taught at art schools and if it were, it would not be part of the Fine Arts but of the Design branch. Only in recent years, new media have been introduced to Japanese art academies; in 2005, a Graduate School of Film was opened at the Tokyo University of the Arts, in 2008 there followed a Department of New Media. There have always been independent arts and crafts

---

23 SATÔ (1996): 51.

24 KURAHASHI and ÔTSUKA (1997): 233–234.

25 TOKYO UNIVERSITY OF THE ARTS (2009): unnumbered.

schools focussing on photographic techniques, however, they are not seen as part of the art system. Their role will be explored in 8. in this chapter.

Although there were few photography departments in art academies, photography centres offered equipment and training, which enabled students to photograph their works. Hence, it is not surprising that most Japanese artists who worked with the photographic medium in the 1990s did not have a photographic education but started as students of other genres. Morimura Yasumasa and Ishiuchi Miyako both studied design, Yanagi Miwa learnt traditional crafts and *kimono*.

5. Art History and Alternative Research Interests

'"Japanese art history" did not begin with Japan's origin or a long time ago, but in the Modernist Era.'[26] When stating this, Kitazawa Noriaki does not mean that there were no artworks in Japan before the Meiji era, but that there was no concept of 'art' and therefore no 'art history'. When the notion of 'art' was brought to Japan, Ernest Fenollosa and Okakura Tenshin acknowledged various works from the past as 'art'. They documented temples and shrines and raised an inventory of art treasures. In order to demonstrate that Japan was a modern state with its own culture, the government systematically established a Japanese 'art history'. In 1900, before the World Exposition in Paris, the Ministry of Agriculture and Trade published the book *Histoire de L'art du Japon* as the first written document about Japanese art history. Europeans were the target group, and information about the artworks and crafts were provided to support the art trade. The symbolic meaning of the book was more important than its content – Japan presented its art history to the 'Western' world.[27]

Japanese art history is a risky topic. Firstly, its concept was intertwined with the governments' intention to present Japan as a modern state. Secondly, the division of *yôga* and *nihonga* has led to an artificial separation of Japanese art as well as to an academic focus on 'Western' art and the 'Westernisation' of Japanese art. In 1989, the art critic Chiba Shigeo pointed out that the history of modern art in Japan should be reconsidered:

> … we need a radical break from Eurocentricism at one extreme, pure nativism at the other extreme, and eclecticism in the middle (i.e. trying to determine an appropriate blend of the Western and the vernacular). In other words, we must denounce and repudiate the established practices of

26 KITAZAWA (2005): 48.
27 SATÔ (1999): 126–128; 144, 147 or KITAZAWA (2005): 46–48.

> art history and criticism in Japan which have wantonly applied the yardstick of Westernization to Japanese art.[28]

Chiba's wish to re-examine Japanese art history has to a certain extent come true. In the last fifteen years, Japanese art has raised more interest, and publications have started to focus on domestic developments in Japan. Prominent art historians Kitazawa Noriaki and Satô Dôshin represent this trend. Kitazawa has argued that the role of *nihonga* should be reconsidered with regard to its position between traditional crafts and art.[29] Furthermore, both Kitazawa and Satô have examined the terminological and institutional foundations of modern 'art history' in the Meiji period.[30]

With the exception on *onna-e* research,[31] the role of women in Japanese art was not a topic of much interest to Japanese art historians before the late 1980s. The 'watershed year' for feminist art history in Japan was 1992, when translations of works such as Joan W. Scott's *Gender and the Politics of History* and Rozsika Parker and Griselda Pollock's *Old Mistresses: Women, Art, and Ideology*, appeared alongside original essays such as Suzuki Tokiko's *Feminisuto no bijutsushi* (Feminist Art History) and Chino Kaori's *Nihon bijutsu wo kangae naosu tame ni* (Toward Rethinking of Japanese Art).[32] Female art historians, such as Chino Kaori, Ikeda Shinobu, Wakakuwa Midori and Kokatsu Reiko, have played an important role in developing a new gender focus.[33] In 1995, the research association Gender and Image was established, which has held annual symposiums on different topics relating to feminism, female artists and gender issues.

Since the mid-nineties, there have also been exhibitions on gender topics, such as *Yureru Onna/Yuragu Imêgi. Floating Images of Women in Art History* at the Tochigi Prefectural Museum of Fine Arts, curated by Kokatsu Reiko in 1997. Kokatsu has explained that the exhibition was 'heavily criticised by Japanese critics arguing that gender studies were a Western invention and unnecessary in Japan'.[34] This statement is corroborated by Kanô Ayako, who has mentioned a heated debate between defenders of gender studies, such as Kokatsu

---

28 CHIBA (1989): 388.

29 KITAZAWA (2003).

30 SATÔ (1996); SATÔ (1999); KITAZAWA (2005).

31 *Onna-e* are literally 'women-pictures'; the word already appears in documents from the Heian period (794–1192) and functions in contrast to *otoko-e* ('men-pictures').

32 MOSTOW (2003a): 4.

33 Publications reflecting this new gender focus include: SUZUKU, CHINO and MABUCHI (1997a); SUZUKU, CHINO and MABUCHI (1997b); CHINO and KUMAKURA (2001); WAKAKUWA (1995); KOKATSU (2007).

34 KOKATSU, Reiko, conversation with the author, 07. 11. 2008 in the Tochigi Prefectural Museum of Fine Arts. All subsequent quotations by Kokatsu are from this interview, unless otherwise stated in the footnote.

and Wakakuwa Midori, on the one side and anti-feminists, such as Sanda Haruo, the arts editor of the Mainichi newspaper and the art critic Ueda Takahiro, on the other.[35] The debate started in 1997 when Sanda rejected gender studies as '*karimono*' ('borrowed things') from 'the West', concluding that they were not needed in a Japanese context.[36] Kanô has summarised the main arguments brought forward by anti-feminist art historians: firstly, 'feminist critique could become stifling', secondly, 'feminist critique is a foreign import' and thirdly, 'there is a realm of art that cannot be touched by criticism'.[37] Kitahara Megumi has written at length about her concern with a heightened Japanese nationalist presence in the arts, citing the different writings of Sanda and the art historian Inaga Shigemi. Both men's articles openly display a rift between the Japanese art establishment and those curators, art historians and artists who espouse feminism and multiculturalism.[38] Feminist curators and the discipline of gender studies in Japan have had to fight harsh criticism. Furthermore, as Kasahara Michiko has pointed out, gender studies met a backlash when 'distorted images of them in the mass media as frightening, inflexible doctrines took on a life of their own and repelled the general population.'[39] Chino's statement in 1999 that gender studies will continue to face criticism in the future but should try to somewhat change this 'harsh reality', reflects the Japanese resistance to accept gender studies as an academic discipline.[40] Furthermore, it shows how gender studies in Japan are generally not associated with an analysis of gender issues but rather with a feminist critique of women's discrimination.

In short, various publications and exhibitions in the 1990s reflect alternative research interests and advances in the academic field. However, it is only now that these trends have started to gain momentum. The area of gender still remains a minor field; as Kokatsu said, 'gender studies in Japan remain unpopular, especially in art history.'

6. Art Critique

According to Nakajima Masatoshi and Tomii Reiko, it is a misconception that there has been no viable art critique in contemporary Japan. Moreover, they state that art critique has played an important role in the field of literary criticism since the Meiji era.[41] However, with regard to art criticism in art maga-

---

35 KANÔ (2003): 31.
36 SANDA (1997); CHINO (1999): 123.
37 KANÔ (2003): 28–29.
38 KITAHARA (1998): 96–107; INAGA (1999): 170–173.
39 KASAHARA (2007): 99.
40 CHINO (1999): 300–301.
41 NAKAJIMA and TOMII (1994): 380.

zines, newspapers and books, articles meeting a high academic standard are rare. Although there are an overwhelming number of art magazines, and artists give presentations on their work in galleries or museums, both the articles and presentations are rather descriptive. There are only a few exceptions in magazines, such as *Bijutsu Hihyô*, *L&R* or *Bijutsu Techo*. Melanie Robert's opinion of Japanese exhibition reviews as being 'rather superficial' is supported by articles on Morimura Yasumasa's exhibitions: there is a great number of Japanese articles describing Morimura's artworks and their production process but they do not examine them critically.[42]

In my interview, Kasahara has explained that the lack of art critique is related to the Japanese art market being so small: 'you can't make a living by being an art critic in Japan. Even if you had your own column in the newspaper Asahi Shinbun, you would only get about 50.000 Yen or so each time. You can't make a living through that'.[43]

According to Nanjô Fumio, the lack of art critique is one of the reasons why artists, such as Morimura Yasumasa or Mori Mariko, have become famous in the 'Western' art world first: 'in Japan there is neither a basis for art criticism nor a system, therefore artists are criticised in the West first. When the West reacts positively, many Japanese follow that criticism. In other words, there are few people in Japan who judge art from their own viewpoint.'[44] This phenomenon is reflected in the way that Morimura became 'successful' in Japan; I will return to this in the following section.

7. Contemporary Japanese Art

7.1 Contemporary Japanese Art and the Japanese Art System

Due to Japan's economic growth and a 'Western' interest in Japanese contemporary culture, a large-scale internationalisation of contemporary art started in Japan in the 1980s. The founding of municipal and private museums, such as the Museum of Modern Art Saitama in 1982 and the Yokohama Museum of Art in 1989, as well as the opening of new art galleries brought financial opportunities for artists, enabling them to pursue independent projects.

---

42 ROBERTS (2001): 43; articles on Morimura's work include: BIJUTSU TECHO (1989): 199; FUSE (1991): 159–165; SHINOHARA (22. 4. 1998): 34; FUSE (06. 08. 1999): 10.

43 KASAHARA, Michiko, conversation with the author, 11. 12. 2008 in the Tokyo Metropolitan Museum of Photography. All subsequent quotations by Kasahara are from this interview, unless otherwise stated in the footnote.

44 NANJÔ, Fumio, conversation with the author, 03. 12. 2008 in the Mori Art Museum in Tokyo. All subsequent quotations by Nanjô are from this interview, unless otherwise stated in the footnote.

Nanjô Fumio has pointed out that the popular lifestyle magazine BRUTUS featured artists and galleries and presented contemporary art to a wider audience; 'employees started buying Andy Warhol posters'.

This rise of the contemporary art scene ended with the crash of the 'Bubble Economy'; a great number of art galleries went bankrupt. However, in the middle of the 1990s, young gallerists such as Koyama Tomio and Koyanagi Atsuko founded galleries featuring newcomers, and museums planned during the economic growth opened. In 1995, the Museum of Contemporary Art Tokyo and the Tokyo Metropolitan Museum of Photography were opened. Since then, an increasing number of exhibitions in and outside of Japan have reflected an interest in contemporary Japanese art.

The 1980s and 1990s were a time of change in the Japanese art world with new museums and galleries established and exhibitions held inside and outside the country featuring contemporary Japanese art. However, it was only during that period, that the museums' infrastructure started to develop and it was still difficult for Japanese artists to have a career in Japan. Consequently, all artists featured in this thesis living in Japan have not only been active as artists but also worked in other fields: Izima Kaoru worked as a director of TV commercials and as a fashion photographer; similarly, Yamanaka Manabu has taken a great number of commercial photographs. Although to a lesser extent, Ishiuchi Miyako, Morimura Yasumasa and Yanagi Miwa have collaborated with magazines and the fashion industry.[45] In addition, Morimura and Yanagi taught art history, while Ishiuchi Miyako worked in an office for many years. Yanagi has published essays in newspapers; Ishiuchi and Morimura have both written essays and books. One reason for these activities is connected to the fact that it is extremely difficult for artists to make a living through their art. Kasahara Michiko emphasised that the low social and economic status of artists in Japan cannot be compared to their standing in Europe or America. Kokatsu Reiko has stated that art museums do not attract a sizeable audience; by publishing art books or photographs in magazines many artists try to make their art known.

Another point to consider is the public pressure on museums: although many curators would prefer to show contemporary art, they have to display classical modern 'Western' art or works by local artists since those are most popular among visitors.[46] Some museums have compromised by having a permanent collection with popular 'Western' works of the 19th century and special exhibitions of contemporary art.

---

45 Ishiuchi took photographs for the design label Comme des Garçons in 1993; Morimura designed clothing for Issey Miyake in 1996; Yanagi worked with the designer Issey Miyake on his spring/summer 2001 menswear campaign.

46 PUSTOLLA (2006): 48.

In 1990, the curator Yamamoto Kazuhiro complained about the 'lack of a modern system of economic support for the contemporary arts in Japan today'.[47] This deficiency is linked to few Japanese galleries featuring contemporary art, especially until the mid-nineties. Hence, many artists had to rent gallery rooms; at the end of the 1990s, almost half of Tokyo's galleries in the Ginza-Yûrakuchô-Kyôbashi district were rental galleries.[48] Morimura and Yanagi have both stated that in the Kansai area the only option to present contemporary art was to use rental galleries, which provided rooms for usually one or two weeks.[49] Yanagi has pointed out how paradoxical the situation was for artists in Kyoto since there were five art schools but no galleries featuring contemporary art: 'young artists in the Kansai area couldn't do anything but exhibit their works in rental galleries. I did not even know commercial galleries existed and that it would be possible to sell my works. The first time that I sold an artwork was in Frankfurt.'

Overall, the market for contemporary art in Japan in the 1990s was small. A quotation by Nanjô stresses that although there have been changes, the market is still minor today: 'out of let's say 500 galleries in Japan, there are about twenty featuring contemporary art'. Iida Shihoko has emphasised her hope for reforms in the future: 'we have a basis now but the structures are not well organized and sometimes ineffective. Only few galleries are present in an international context, many interesting artists have not been discovered by the art market.'[50] Furthermore, Japanese museums are forced to concentrate on economic efficiency, making it difficult to feature artists who are not expected to draw a large audience or even to collect new works. This situation is an important reason why many Japanese artists, such as Morimura, have become known in the 'Western' art market first. As Isshiki has stated, 'in the 1990s there was an art market in America and Europe, but not in Japan.'[51]

It would be unthinkable to hold an exhibition of contemporary art in Japan (or abroad) without including women artists. However, as Linda Nochlin pointed out in 1971, a female artist 'must in any case have a good strong streak

---

47 YAMAMOTO (1990): unnumbered.

48 LLOYD (2002): 20.

49 MORIMURA, Yasumasa, conversation with the author, 13. 12. 2008 in Morimura's studio in Osaka. All subsequent quotations by Morimura are from this interview, unless otherwise stated in the footnote; YANAGI, Miwa, conversation with the author, 11. 11. 2008 in Yanagi's studio in Kyoto. All subsequent quotations by Yanagi are from this interview, unless otherwise stated in the footnote.

50 IIDA, Shihoko, conversation with the author, 13. 11. 2008 in the Tokyo Opera City Art Gallery. All subsequent quotations by Iida are from this interview, unless otherwise stated in the footnote.

51 ISSHIKI, Yoshiko, conversation with the author, 05. 11. 2008 in Isshiki's art consultancy office in Tokyo. All subsequent quotations by Isshiki are from this interview, unless otherwise stated in the footnote.

of rebellion in her to make her way in the world of art at all, rather than submitting to the socially approved role of wife and mother.'[52] This quotation describes the situation of Japanese female artists even in the 1990s: firstly, the post-war division of men working and representing the public, and women doing the household and representing the private, has led to an expectation of women to be housewives and mothers. Secondly, the 'Western' concept of artists as male genius, adopted into Japan in the Meiji era, has made it difficult for women to be accepted in the art world. However, the role of female artists in Japan in the 1990s is a topic too broad to be explored in this thesis.[53]

7.2 Censorship

Censorship has played an important role in the Japanese art system: all interviewed curators and artists could name situations when 'obscene' artworks were either confiscated by police at exhibitions or blocked by Japanese customs. Firstly, Article 175 of the Japanese Penal Code, enacted in 1907, prohibits the public display of 'obscene' images. Until the 1990s, photographs showing the pubic area in erotica magazines, such as *Playboy*, were censored by airbrushing or scratching over by hand. Even pubic hair was not publishable. Secondly, the import and export of 'obscene' material is prohibited under Article 69–11 (vii) of the Japanese Tariff Law. Isshiki has pointed out that there are problems with customs blocking the import of 'Western' art and the export of Japanese art. According to Yamanaka Manabu, his *Gyahtei* series with photographs of naked old women often does not get through customs.[54]

Since the 1990s, the interpretation of Article 175 has increasingly been eased and the display of pubic hair has become accepted. As Nanjô Fumio has explained, the law has not been changed; however, it has become easier to exhibit photographs showing pubic hair: 'the law is still the same, but the way the police judges has changed.' One reason for the moderation in the government's reading of the law might be an awareness of 'Western' museums exhibiting nude photographs. Another reason is perhaps connected to Araki Nobuyoshi's work; his photographs of naked women caused scandals in the 1980s and 1990s, however, due to his commercial success in 'the West', his work is now exported overseas and also shown in exhibitions in Japan. Kokatsu Reiko and Iida Yoshiko have pointed out in my interviews that the reaction of the police nowadays also depends on the individual museum and its audience. The Tokyo

52 NOCHLIN (1971): 170.
53 The role of female artists in Japan in the 1950s and 1960s is explored in GODZIK (2007).
54 YAMANAKA, Manabu, conversation with the author, 06. 11. 2008 in Tokyo. All subsequent quotations by Yamanaka are from this interview, unless otherwise stated in the footnote.

Opera Art City Gallery attracts a rather young and metropolitan audience; they are more used to seeing nakedness in art images. Hence, in a Wolfgang Tillmanns exhibition in 2004, the gallery decided to exhibit a small close-up photograph of male genitalia, which might have caused trouble in another museum. The Tochigi Prefectural Museum of Fine Arts does not attract a large audience like museums in Tokyo. Therefore works that could not be displayed in Tokyo are sometimes exhibited in Tochigi without causing problems since they receive less public attention.

Pubic hair in magazines, videos, as well as in art photographs and woodblock prints is not considered illegal anymore.[55] However, images showing female or male genitals are usually censored. As Yamanaka has emphasised, his photographs of old naked women in the *Gyahtei* series cannot be exhibited in public museums or galleries in Japan. When the artworks were featured in a TV programme only the upper part of the women's bodies was filmed. Nanjô has stated to have thought about sending the *Gyahtei* series to the Singapore Biennial in 2008 but decided against it because of censorship reasons in both Singapore and Japan.

Various Japanese artists have mocked the censorship law in their photographic art. For instance, Araki has photographed female genitalia in a monochrome close-up too extreme to show any pubic hair.[56] Izima Kaoru has published a book titled *Hairmode* (1994) with images ironically accentuating women's pubic hair. In 2001, the group exhibition *A Kiss in the Dark* at the Tokyo Metropolitan Museum of Photography featured male nude photographs by Takano Ryûdai. Each of the large-sized works is composed of an upper and a lower shot, mounted together with a thin gap between them. The genitals are cut out so that the censorship law is skirted. The missing sections of the photographs were pasted on the backs of the prints so that they could not be seen in the exhibition. Kasahara, who was responsible for displaying Takano's photographs, has persuasively criticised the equalisation of genitalia exposure and indecency. She has argued that on the one hand not every photograph of genitals is 'obscene' and on the other hand, there are also indecent artworks *not* showing genitalia; 'the interpretation of the law is precarious – not those who *display* the artworks can judge if something is obscene or not but those who confiscate them.'

---

55 Joshua Mostow has explained how the victory against censorship in the early 1990s 'created a bonanza for Japanese publishers' in the field of *shunga* ('spring pictures', explicitly sexual images, mostly woodblock prints): *shunga* could now be republished in unexpurgated form (MOSTOW 2003a: 5). Among the flood of publications, Timon Screech was the first who analysed *shunga* in its social context and as a tool for onanism in his *Sex and the Floating World* and *Shunga: kata-te de yomu Edo no e* (Shunga: Edo Pictures Read With One Hand).

56 BORNOFF (2002): 60.

Overall, censorship of photographic art was still an issue in the 1990s and remains so today. As Fukagawa Masafumi has concluded, 'a true Mapplethorpe exhibition can not be realised in Japan'.[57]

7.3 Contemporary Japanese Art and the 'Western' Art System

Globalisation has increased the circulation of artworks produced outside of Europe and North America within the 'Western' cultural system. Contemporary Japanese art was featured in various exhibitions and art fairs in the 1990s.[58] How was Japanese art dealt with in the 'Western' art system? How did Japanese artists use the 'Western' art market?

One of the reasons for the 'Western' market featuring Japanese art might be connected to Japan offering 'easy access': although being part of Asia, Japan is, in Kasahara's words, 'somewhat mentally Americanised'. This is due to Japan's adaptation of 'Western' culture since the end of the 19th century and its strong economic relationships with the USA and Europe since the 1950s. In the 1980s and 1990s, Japan was the only Asian 'global player' with a 'Westernised' mentality that easily adopted EuroAmerican ideas. A quotation by Kumagai Isako, curator at the Museum of Contemporary Art Tokyo, emphasises the importance of Japan's economy. She stated in 1995 that 'Japan has attracted special interest because of its great economic success. Yasumasa Morimura, Tatsuo Miyajima, and Toshikatsu Endo showed in the Aperto exhibition at the 43rd Venice Biennale in 1988, and the innovative work of these young Japanese proved attractive [sic] an international audience.'[59] In addition, Fukagawa Masafumi has explained how the growth of the Japanese art infrastructure in the late 1980s led to more cooperation between 'Western' and Japanese curators.

'Western' art institutions and art critics have been in a precarious situation when exhibiting and interpreting Japanese art; it is the 'Western' world that decides which Japanese objects are attested the status of 'art' by exhibiting them within its art system. Peter Weibel has described the art system in 'the West' as a place of 'inclusion and exclusion' and thus as a 'colonial discourse': the

---

57 FUKAGAWA, Masafumi, conversation with the author, 26. 12. 2008 in the Kawasaki City Museum. All subsequent quotations by Fukagawa are from this interview, unless otherwise stated in the footnote.

58 In 1991, *A Cabinet of Signs. Contemporary Art from Post-Modern Japan* at the Tate Gallery Liverpool; in 1993, *In die Felsen bohren sich Zikadenstimmen. Zeitgenössische japanische Photographie* at the Kunsthaus Zürich; in 1994, *Japanese Art After 1945: Scream Against the Sky* at the Guggenheim Museum in New York and the San Francisco Museum of Art; in 1996, *Prospect'* 96 in the Schirn Kunsthalle Frankfurt; in 1997, *Japanese Photography. Desire and Void* in the Kunsthalle Wien etc.

59 KUMAGAI (1995): 37.

'Western' cultural system draws lines between its own culture and other peoples, races and religions.[60] Susanne Boecker has offered a persuasive description of this situation by using the metaphor of the 'green card'.[61] Only those artists who possess a 'green card' are allowed into the system: artists whose work is 'Western' enough for the art market but at the same time associated with characteristics 'typical' of their country of origin. In order to be interesting for a EuroAmerican audience, Japanese art has to meet a paradoxical expectation: it has to be 'Western' *and* 'Japanese' at the same time.[62]

It is striking how 'Western' authors have continued to simplify Japanese art by viewing it from a somewhat Orientalist perspective. Boecker has criticised Heinz Spielmann's book on Japanese photography of 1985, written in German, finding it full of clichés.[63] Indeed, Spielmann talks about 'the naturalness' of the Japanese aesthetic,[64] and explains that 'the Japanese man understands more with his eyes than with his ratio, his intelligence is connected to looking', hence assuming that the photographic medium suits 'the Japanese character'.[65] Expressions like 'der Japaner' ('the Japanese man') or 'die japanische Wesensart' ('the Japanese character') are dangerous: they provide generalisations of all Japanese and imply that people are homogenous. Another example for an interpretation mirroring a somewhat 'exotistic' perspective are David Streiff's comments on Ishiuchi Miyako's photographs in an exhibition catalogue in 1993: in the series *1·9·4·7*, the Swiss curator sees a 'Japanese' and 'more natural relationship with the feet than in 'the West' where feet are put in shoes all day.'[66] However, as Ishiuchi has explained convincingly, 'showing women's bare feet is rather considered a disgrace in Japan. It is the absolute opposite of a natural relationship – when I took photographs of women's feet, two husbands of the photographed women protested.'[67]

It is noticeable that certain ideas, such as 'naturalness' or the idea of 'Zen' in contemporary Japanese art, are often only found by 'Western' viewers. Interestingly, in the same exhibition catalogue that Streiff's essay is published

60 WEIBEL (1997): 11.

61 BOECKER (2004): 193.

62 This is relevant for any 'non-Western' artwork within the 'Western' cultural system. For instance, Ole Oguibe has examined how African artworks are treated as cheap 'pornographic' objects in the 'Western' market, being priced much lower than comparable works by 'Western' artists. Furthermore, 'the West' is seeking to find 'African' characteristics in African works, 'symbols of difference' in order to distance them from White 'Western' culture (OGUIBE 1995: 93–96).

63 BOECKER (2004): 193.

64 SPIELMANN (1985): 125–126.

65 IBID: 10.

66 STREIFF (1993): 9.

67 ISHIUCHI, Miyako, conversation with the author, 02. 12. 2008 in the Meguro Art Museum in Tokyo. All subsequent quotations by Ishiuchi are from this interview, unless otherwise stated in the footnote.

in, Fukagawa Masafumi stated the following: 'if the audience of this exhibition feels and discovers something typically Japanese in the artworks, then I think the key to this is not only to be found in the cultural heritage but also in a specific way of reception.'[68] This quotation indicates that there are general motifs that the audience repeatedly notices and interprets as an attribute of another culture. With the intention to understand the artworks and perhaps also to separate them from their own culture, 'Western' viewers tend to discover aspects that are already known as 'typically Japanese'. In my interview, Fukagawa has also referenced the example of 'Zen': 'the West, especially Germany, loves to relate Japanese art to Zen, although Japanese people have almost forgotten about it. Zen does not reflect anything like a Japanese spirit'. With regard to Araki Nobuyoshi's art, Fukagawa went as far as saying the following:

> Araki's success is based on a misunderstanding: 'the West' has adopted a certain image of a Japanese erotic world, which is related to *ukiyo-e* woodblock prints. There is a Western market for *ukiyo-e* and it is extremely easy to connect them to Araki's photographs... I think an important reason for Araki's success is that the Western world already had a certain exoticism code, which made the interpretation easy.

Not only Fukagawa but also numerous other curators are critical of how 'Western' art critics and museums still look at Japanese art from a simplistic, Orientalist viewpoint. Sawaragi Noi has compared these critics and curators with Ernest Fenollosa, 'who projected his own desire onto "Japan as Other" and prescribed the representation of "Japan" to Japanese people'.[69]

However, at the same time, there are also cases in which interpretations by 'Western' art critics and art historians have added profound insights to Japanese art. Morimura Yasumasa is a good example of an artist who has been interpreted differently in the 'Western' and Japanese art world. In Japan, his art has been seen as connected to the entertainment culture of his hometown Osaka and more often been interpreted as 'fun',[70] whereas in 'the West' he has been viewed in a rather political 'postcolonial' light.[71] Appropriating mainly 'Western' culture, Morimura gave 'Western' art specialists topics that they were familiar with. Both viewpoints seem important when examining Morimura's art; its complexity can only be understood when both perspectives are considered.

---

68 FUKAGAWA (1993): 14.

69 SAWARAGI (1992): 388.

70 BIJUTSU TECHO (1989): 199; YAMAMOTO (1991): 17; FUSE (1991): 165; MITA (26. 09. 1994): 6; MORIMURA (2001c): 18; KASAHARA (2002): 93.

71 LEACH (1994): 8; BRYSON (1995); BRUNETTI (1998); HOFFA (2000); WRIGHT JASINOWSKI (2001); WALTON (2004).

But how did Morimura become known in the 'Western' art world? According to Nanjô Fumio, he saw Morimura's photographs in a gallery in Kyoto in 1986 when doing research for the American exhibition *Against Nature*. Nanjô suggested to his colleagues in New York that they include Morimura's work in the exhibition, which then was held in the Grey Art Gallery in 1989. In addition, as a jury member of the Japanese section at the Venice Biennale in 1988, Nanjô included Morimura in the Apertus newcomer section. As such, Morimura was introduced to Europe in 1988 and one year later to America. In other words, a Japanese curator was included in the marketing process. Morimura's case demonstrates that although it is the 'Western' art market deciding if a Japanese artist gets the 'green card', there have been members of the Japanese art world who define the circumstances under which a Japanese artist is introduced to 'the West'.

Morimura's exhibitions in 'the West' made it easier for Japanese curators to exhibit his art in Japanese museums – he now could be sold as 'a Japanese artist who succeeded in the West'. The opinion of 'the West' played an important role in a Japanese art system that found it difficult to appreciate its own contemporary art. This has started to change since the late 1990s, especially with the international commercial success of Japanese gaming and *manga* culture, and its invasion of contemporary Japanese art, particularly evident in the work of Murakami Takashi (∗1962).[72] Murakami's works certainly represent Japan's new self-confidence, born out of the enormous popularity of Japanese popular culture in 'the West'. However, in the 1990s, many Japanese people still had a 'complex' towards Western art and music; this is connected to the fact that since the Meiji era, public education in Japan has emphasised 'Western' culture, often relegating traditional culture to the shadows.[73] Hence, many artists and curators were more familiar with European than Japanese art, even though their knowledge was based largely on reproductions. Kokatsu Reiko has used her personal experiences as an example: 'when I curated the first gender exhibition in 1997, I still focussed on 'Western' art. It is only after that exhibition that I started to shift focus to Asian art'. This emphasis on 'Western' art may be an important reason why Morimura's adaptations of 'Western' masterpieces seem rather shocking to some Japanese viewers. As Kumagai Isako has written, for 'older people who have accepted European art as a cultural stan-

---

72 This is most evident in Murakami Takashi's success in the 'Western' as well as 'Japanese' art market and in *manga* exhibitions in art museums, e.g. the 1998 exhibition *Manga no jidai* [the Era of Manga] in the Museum of Contemporary Art Tokyo. The influence of *manga* and other Japanese 'low' culture on Japanese 'high' art would be an interesting topic for research. However, since this development only started in the late 1990s it is beyond the scope of my study.

73 I will examine the historical reasons for Japan's 'complex' towards 'the West' in the third chapter of Part 3.

dard, it is a shock to see Morimura with his very oriental body, taking the role of figures in famous European paintings.'[74] It is mainly due to the 'Western' acceptance of his art, which suggests that he is not really ridiculing European culture, that these people accept his 'cheeky' approach.

Most of the interviewed curators believe that Morimura had not consciously addressed the 'Western' art market when using 'Japanese' aspects in his art. I agree with them, since Morimura's usage of both 'Japanese' and 'Western' elements is part of his artistic language, often carrying critical meanings. It is not a marketing strategy but rather an expression of a serious artistic concern, which I will explore further in the third section of Part 3.

In contrast, Japanese artists of the following generation have used 'Japanese' aspects deliberately in order to respond to an 'Orientalist' demand. The most important example is the above-mentioned Murakami Takashi, who has had great commercial success and gained attention from many art critics and academics in North America and Europe in the last ten years. Murakami has adapted a flat *manga* style in his work; he has presented a visual language that 'Western' viewers already associated with Japan. This also shows that there has been a shift of Japan clichés in 'the West': the 'Fujiyama and Geisha' cliché has been making room for '*manga* and high technology'. Jacqueline Bernd has found a persuasive definition for Murakami's well planned strategy to gain success in the art world by responding to this new cliché: 'neo-japonism'.[75]

Another example for an artist consciously meeting 'Orientalist' demands of the international art market could be Mori Mariko, who studied at the Chelsea College of Art and Design in London and knew the 'rules' of both the Japanese and the 'Western' art system. Kasahara has argued: 'to say it directly, she is a beautiful woman who makes use of a Japanese form of expression which is appreciated in the West.' Indeed, when presenting herself in the video installation *Nirvana* (1997) as a young goddess in a *kimono*, flying between computer-generated alien-figures, Mori responds to general clichés: Japan is not only the 'land of the geisha' but also where 'old tradition meets latest high technology'. The European art world's reaction to Mori's 'high technology' art has been analysed in an essay by Gunhild Borggreen; Borggreen highlights how *Nirvana* was exhibited at the Venice Biennale in 1997 in the Nordic Pavilion instead of in the Japanese equivalent.[76] The other artists of the Pavilion, three Nordic and one American artist, exhibited rather 'hands-on work', contrasting with Mori's high-tech video. In this way, as Borggreen has concluded, cultural clichés of the

74 KUMAGAI (1995): 36.

75 BERNDT (2005): 7; Berndt's essay offers a detailed, critical examination of Murakami's works of art and the way he presents these in the context of *nihonga*, *manga* and 'Japan'.

76 BORGGREEN (2003b): 89.

Nordic were underscored by its juxtaposition with Mori's work.[77] This example again emphasises how the 'Western' art system tends to represent Japanese art through establishing a distinction between 'Us' ('the West') and 'Other' (Japan).

At the same time, Japanese cultural foundations and galleries have also made use of Orientalism. Sawaragi has criticised this harshly:

> Japan, as a state, determinedly and eagerly appropriates an Orientalist image. By pretending the artists who satisfy Orientalism are a part of her heritage and by exporting their works "back" to the West to fulfil a demand, this country tries to give contemporary Japanese art "international relevance"...[78]

Sawaragi might be correct in criticising the art scene for using clichés as a marketing strategy and presenting a simplistic image of Japan to 'the West'. However, the use of national clichés is a complicated issue: Who defines what a cliché is? When is the use of clichés part of an artistic language and when is it simply a marketing strategy?

Nanjô has found the right words when explaining the problems that Japanese artists face in an international market. The text was written in 1989 but still seems relevant today:

> The problem is one of position: where does an artist place himself in relation to the complex issues of localism, internationalism, modernism and tradition? When a Japanese artist intends to create an original work of art, he is frequently in danger of falling into the trap of an exotic Japonisme for which *ukiyoe* [woodblock prints] were once praised in Europe. On the other hand, if he were to produce work similar to Western contemporary art, he would run the risk of being regarded as an imitator... The question is, how can an artist present an international and universal work of art, without losing his own cultural and national identity?[79]

There are no answers or solutions to the problems that Nanjô addresses. They rather raise more questions: Where are the lines between 'localism' and 'internationalism' in art today? Is it possible to juxtapose 'modernism' and 'tradition'? What is 'originality'? How can such thing as a 'cultural and national identity' be defined in our globalised world?

---

77 IBID (2003): 89.

78 SAWARAGI (1992): 388.

79 As cited in WILKES TUCKER and FRISS-HANSEN and RYÛICHI (eds.) (2003): 264.

8. Photography in Japan

The Japanese term for photography, '*shashin*' is composed of the characters *sha*, meaning 'to reproduce' or 'to copy', and *shin*, meaning 'truth'. In the latter half of the 18th century, the artists Shiba Kôkan and Satake Shôzan used the word to describe the realism of 'Western' art; however, in the late 1860s it became associated with photography.[80] The characters illustrate how early Japanese photographers viewed photography as the process of 'making a copy' of a 'true' subject.

Photography was introduced to Japan in the late 1850s; as one of the first Japanese professional photographers, Ueno Hikoma opened a photo atelier in Nagasaki in 1862. One year later, Felice Beato, a photojournalist, and Charles Wirgman, correspondent of the *Illustrated London News*, opened a photo atelier in Yokohama. Although Beato took a great number of journalistic photographs, it was his introduction of studio photography to Japan that made him influential for Japanese photography, especially in the Meiji period. During this time, photographers created a vast number of studio photographs of models staging scenes of a 'traditional' life.[81] The photographs, which were mainly produced for and popular among 'Western' tourists, were often taken with backdrops of 'typically Japanese' landscapes, such as Mount Fuji.[82] The production and export of these souvenir pictures mainly took place in Yokohama and Nagasaki. Thus, this early commercial photography is referred to as 'Yokohama *shashin*' and 'École de Yokohama'.[83]

With the introduction of the dry plate process in the 1880s, photography was simplified and no longer the exclusive preserve of professional practitioners. In 1889, William K. Burton, a Scottish engineer and professor at the University of Tokyo, and Ogawa Kazumasa, photographer and publisher, were two of the founding members of the amateur club Nihon Shashinkai (Japan Photographic Society). The club proclaimed that photography should not only be used for practical purposes but also as an art medium.[84] Amateur photogra-

---

80 IIZAWA (1994): 39–40.

81 I put the term 'tradition' in quotation marks in order to highlight its complexity; a 'tradition' is often, at least partly, 'invented'. The concept of the 'invention of tradition' was introduced by the British historians Eric Hobsbawm and Terence Ranger: 'traditions' are influenced by socio-political interests and thus do not represent authentic, accurate history. In many cases, they are deliberately constructed to serve an ideological purpose, e.g. fostering national identity and unity. In the field of Japanese studies, the 'invention of tradition' has been explored, for instance, in VLASTOS, Stephen (1998): *Mirror or Modernity: Invented Traditions of Modern Day Japan*. Berkeley, Los Angeles and London: University of California Press.

82 DELANK and MARCH (2002): 11.

83 IBID: 8–9.

84 The Japan Photographic Society which was founded in 1889 ceased to exist after the end of the 19th century due to its main sponsor's bankruptcy. In 1924, another photographer's club with the same name was founded. This club has continued until today and has about 200

phy was also promoted by photography magazines, which often served as instruction manuals. In 1894, Konishi Honten (later renamed Konica Corporation), a distributor of photographic equipment, established the magazine *Shashin geppô*. Two years later, the company Asanuma Shoten began to publish the magazine *Shashin shinpô*. However, it was not until the introduction of the Eastman Kodak vest-pocket compact camera in the middle of the Taishô era (1912–1925), that photography became more accessible to everyone. When the compact camera was launched in the Japanese market, it was relatively low-priced which allowed 'middle-class people' to afford it.[85]

There are numerous amateur photography clubs and organisations in Japan. The Nihon Shashin Kyôkai (Photographic Society of Japan, PSJ), founded in 1952, is an independent amateur and professional photography club. It contains approximately 1560 members.[86] Like most of the clubs, the PSJ promotes a great variety of photographic activities, such as competitions, exhibitions and the publication of periodicals. The Nihon Shashinka Kyôkai (Japan Professional Photographers' Society), with more than 1800 members, could be viewed as a more 'elite' society for professional photographers. The society's activities include the promotion of the copyright system for photographs, photography exhibitions, international exchange, and the publication of periodicals.[87] The Zennihon Shashin Renmei (All-Japan Association of Photographic Societies, AJAPS), which was founded in 1926, is supported by the Asahi Newspaper Company. The AJAPS consists of about 18.000 members and sponsors photography competitions, such as the All-Japan Photographic Contest, the Japanese Nature Context, and the International Photographic Salon of Japan.[88]

Together with such photography organisations and amateur clubs, various camera companies, galleries and numerous magazines form a huge 'photography network' in Japan. For example, the magazine *Asahi Camera*, which was founded in 1926 by the Asahi Newspaper Company, is the voice of the AJAPS. Furthermore, it is the oldest Japanese photography and camera magazine to be published. On 300 to 400 glossy pages, the magazine contains photographs by professionals as well as amateurs, equipment reviews, exhibition reviews and schedules. It has a monthly circulation of 62.500 copies.[89] After World War II, the photographer Kimura Ihei was a key staff member of the magazine; the magazine's *Kimura Ihei Award* has become one of the most prestigious photography awards in Japan. Another popular monthly magazine is *Nippon*

---

members. For more information on the Japan Photographic Society which still exists today see: JAPAN PHOTOGRAPHIC SOCIETY (2009): unnumbered.

85 RYÛICHI (1999): 23–24.

86 THE PHOTOGRAPHIC SOCIETY OF JAPAN (2009): unnumbered.

87 THE JAPAN PROFESSIONAL PHOTOGRAPHER'S SOCIETY (2009): unnumbered.

88 THE ALL-JAPAN ASSOCIATION OF PHOTOGRAPHIC SOCIETIES (2009): unnumbered.

89 JMPA (2009): unnumbered.

Camera, founded in 1951 by the photography critics Tanaka Masao and Ikegami Yûichi. It features photographs by established or promising photographers, and presents articles about various topics relating to photography, such as equipment reviews, book reviews, photographic techniques, and a monthly photography contest.

A vast number of photography galleries can be found in Tokyo, mainly on the Ginza or in Shinjuku. Most galleries, such as the Fuji Salon, Canon Salon, or Pentax Salon, are supported by camera and film companies. In short-term exhibitions, the galleries feature individual photographers as well as the winners of amateur competitions. The Zeit-Foto Salon, managed by Ishihara Etsurô, is one of the few independent photography galleries which work like a European art gallery: the photographs, like the paintings that the gallery represents, are sold as 'works of art',[90] the gallery presents itself on art fairs and cooperates with art museums, and, most importantly, it is not sponsored by any camera company. In other words, it deliberately presents itself in an 'art context'.

Photography has developed into a web of camera companies, magazines, photography galleries and amateur clubs, promoting various photographic activities. Not only is photography an important business in Japan, it also is a system based on a great number of amateur photographers and camera fans. Henceforth, this thesis will reference this system as the 'photography world', in contrast to the 'art world'.

9. Photography Education

Although modern art education in Japan began in 1876, training in photography did not start until the establishment of a photography course at the Tokyo School of Fine Arts in 1915. The course was terminated after twelve years, producing only thirty-six graduates. The reason given was that 'photography and print departments belong in a craft school which is neither a purely fine arts school nor a purely industrial arts school'.[91]

In 1923, the company Konishi founded the Konishi Shashin Senmon Gakkô (Konishi Professional School of Photography), which became independent and was renamed Tôkyô Shashin Senmon Gakkô (Tokyo Professional School of Photography) in 1926.[92] Today, the school's name is Tôkyô Kôgei Daigaku

90 For instance, this is evident in the way the Zeit-Foto Salon presents itself on its homepage: it is described as 'the very first gallery that deals with photographs as art pieces in Japan'. ZEIT-FOTO SALON (2010): unnumbered.

91 YAMAMOTO (1987): 16–17.

92 KÔGEI TOKYO POLYTECHNIC UNIVERSITY (2009): unnumbered.

(Tokyo Polytechnic University) and it has remained one of the most popular schools for photography, animation and media arts in Japan. Other schools offering photography courses include the Nihon Shashin Gakuen (Japan Photographic Academy) and the Tôkyô Sôgô Shashin Senmon Gakkô (Tokyo College of Photography). The curriculum mostly focuses on techniques; photography is not studied from an artistic perspective but rather from a practical and industrial viewpoint. The only university with a renowned tradition in photographic education is the Nihon Daigaku (Nihon University), producing numerous famous photographers, such as Dômon Ken. As mentioned in 4., it was only in recent years that photography was introduced to other Japanese art academies. Most Japanese artists who worked with the photographic medium in the 1990s, such as Morimura Yasumasa or Yanagi Miwa, did not have a photographic education but started as students of other genres.

Only two of the artists this thesis is concerned with, did not study at art academies: Yamanaka Manabu studied at the Ôsaka Shiritsu Kôgei Kôtô Gakkô (Osaka City Kogei School), which has a design and new media focus, and Izima Kaoru was a student at the Tôkyô Sôgô Shashin Senmon Gakkô (Tokyo College of Photography). After graduation, Yamanaka worked as an assistant for a fashion photographer. Izima stopped attending college after a short time and also began working as a photographer's assistant. Not only are both Yamanaka and Izima rather seen as '*shashinka*' ('photographers') than 'artists', but also they view themselves as 'photographers'. In Japan, their work has only been exhibited within the 'photography world'.

Yamamoto Kazuhiro has pointed out persuasively that there is a connection between the photographic education system and the difficulty that many Japanese people have in viewing photography as art: 'this [education] situation in Japan obstructed direct exchanges between art and photography, and this is probably the reason for the lack of students who view photography from a generally artistic viewpoint.'[93]

Although there are a vast number of photo books in Japan, there are few publications on photography, photographic art, or photography theory, which meet an academic standard.[94] Similarly, there are many popular photography magazines which have a high printing quality but few academic articles.[95] This again emphasises that photography has be treated rather as a technique than an art genre.

---

93 YAMAMOTO (1987): 16.

94 Exceptions include TOKYO METROPOLITAN MUSEUM OF PHOTOGRAPHY (1995); KASAHARA (2002); ÔSHIMA (2004); FUKAGAWA (2007).

95 The magazine *Shashin sochi,* edited by the critic Ôshima Hiroshi, was an exception. It was a journal of photography criticism written from an art theory perspective with each issue being devoted to a special topic. However, the magazine was only published thrice yearly between 1980 and 1986.

10. 'Photography' and 'Photographic Art'

Ever since its invention, there has been a tension in photography between 'applied art' and 'higher art', providing fuel for debates and raising questions as to whether photography is truly 'art'. To add a new chapter to these controversies is beyond the scope of this thesis. Rather, I would like to examine the problematic relationship of 'photographic art' with 'photography' in Japan.

There have always been photographers who have argued that photography could be art: for example Nakayama Iwata explained in an essay in 1928 that it is wrong to think of painting or sculpture as a higher art form than photography; 'of course there are photographs that could be called "pure art".'[96] Yasui Chûji argued in 1942 that 'for the *art* (my italics) of photography, temporal and spatial choice plays an important role.'[97]

However, not every 'photograph' is viewed as an 'artwork', likewise not every 'photographer' is an 'artist'. In my interviews, Isshiki Yoshiko along with Kokatsu Reiko and other curators have clearly differentiated between 'photographers' on the one hand and 'artists using photography as a medium' on the other. Isshiki and Kokatsu have agreed that Araki Nobuyoshi is close to the art world but still a 'photographer', whereas Morimura Yasumasa, Yanagi Miwa and Mori Mariko are 'artists using photography'. Although such categorisations are often subjective, they lead to important questions on the differences between 'photography' and 'art photography' in Japan.

The division is inextricably intertwined with the context in which the works are presented. 'Photography' and 'art photography' are two separate systems, yet use the same medium. Depending on the context, photographs are placed in one of the categories, further codifying their terms of reference and status. As Kasahara has stressed, the differences between works of 'contemporary art' and 'contemporary photography' are 'nothing more than secondary factors such as: the artist's major in university; ... in what department within a museum the works are exhibited; or whether the works are presented and sold in galleries specializing in photography or in ... contemporary art.'[98] As the quotation makes clear, the differences are often independent of the works themselves. This might be one reason why there are still debates as to the lines between 'photography', 'art' and 'commercial photography'. Iida Shihoko has emphasised how the debate continues today:

> ... a debate continues concerning the line between "contemporary art", "contemporary photography" and "commercial photography"; or more specifically, the division between "photography as contemporary art,"

[96] As cited in SPIELMANN (1985): 244.
[97] As cited in SPIELMANN (1985): 246.
[98] KASAHARA (2001): iv.

> "photography that aims to be an art that is independent of 'contemporary art'," and "photography that doesn't aim to be art". ... the criteria for these categories aren't based on artistic worth or the value of the method of expression or concept. Rather, they are based on the "medium (what kind and which book, magazine, or exhibition)" used to introduce a work to a public that is adroitly isolated within Japan. ... this debate... is rooted in the difficulty of making value judgments due to the fact that anyone can express themselves in the medium, and narrow-minded criticism that focuses solely on judgments within the world of photography yet reveals the desire of a significant number of people to classify photography as "art."[99]

A quotation by Ishiuchi Miyako corroborates this, highlighting the frictions between 'photography' and 'art' in Japan:

> There are so many camera magazines and so many amateur photographers. For them it seems hard to acknowledge photography as art. And there is a tradition that the art world does not like to acknowledge photography as art either ... It seems that there is a real hostility between art and photography ... There is a real discrimination against the term "photographer"...

Iida's description of the criticism by the 'photography world' as 'narrow-minded' and Ishiuchi's use of the terms 'hostility' and 'discrimination' suggest that the debate between the 'photography world' and the 'art world' is often not a critical one; it is not based on the images but rather on a heated up, political discussion. As previously mentioned, there is a strong photography network in Japan, linked to the camera and film industry, and based on a large number of amateur photographers. This power of the Japanese photography industry also becomes clear in Yamamoto Kazuhiro's observations at the Photokina Trade Fair and the Art Fair in Cologne in 1990. Yamamoto's quotation not only reflects his frustration with the contemporary art system in Japan but also illustrates the dominance of the Japanese photography industry and its presence in an international market:

> At the Fotokina, the floors were overflowing with Japanese businessmen all dressed alike in their rat-coloured uniforms. But, no one Japanese was to be seen at the Art Fair ... with the exception of the participating artists. Such examples are too numerous to be mentioned, but they all derive from the same irresponsibility of the Japanese system, which structurally continues to treat coldly all related to the arts, and Contemporary Art in particular ... It can surely be said that talented young artists are appearing one after another ... But does the present environment in our country provide the circumstances under which their works can be displayed and

[99] IIDA (2008): 37.

> viewed in a manner befitting their true value. The answer to this question must … be a pessimistic one.[100]

What are the reasons for this strong separation of the 'photography world' and the 'art world' in Japan? The answer seems to be connected to the different paths which art and photography have historically followed. Firstly, photographic education and art education have mostly been divided. Secondly, 'Straight Photography'[101] and Realism have played an influential role in the history of photography in Japan. Another quotation by Yamamoto highlights how German Photography has influenced artists in Japan and how Straight Photography has become associated with photography in general:

> Photojournalism, based on the straight photograph, had come upon the scene in Germany by 1920, and there was a growing trend for photographers (in Japan) to publish their work in the printed mass media ... Two successive world wars further strengthened the character of photography as a medium for transmitting information, and the straight photography became the major form of photographic expression. … the straight photography which developed from the 'real photo' and found its application in photojournalism became the major form of photography as a mass media society took shape.[102]

The photographer Dômon Ken, who became a jury member for the monthly photography contest of the magazine *Asahi Camera* in 1950, was one of the initiators of the Realism movement in Japan. This movement strongly reflected the desire of amateur photographers to 'confront the severe realities of the post-war period, as well as their distrust of the closed, salonlike character of the pre-war photography world'.[103] In 1952, Kimura Ihei also joined the jury. Based on the great number of camera magazines, such as the *Asahi Camera*, the Realism movement became extremely popular. Both Dômon, who is known for his documentary photographs of the survivors of the atomic bombing in Hiroshima, and Kimura, known for his photographs of post-war life in Japan, criticised Art Photography. Perhaps it is symbolic that Dômon and Kimura have become two of the most renowned Japanese photographers; it reflects how 'photography' is associated with photographs of the Realism movement and is almost synonymous with 'Straight Photography'.

Another point to consider is the lack of a tradition in Japan of using photography as a medium in the 'art world' compared to, for example, Ger-

---

100 YAMAMOTO (1990): unnumbered.

101 The term 'Straight Photography' refers to photography with an emphasis upon direct documentary.

102 YAMAMOTO (1987): 17.

103 WILKES TUCKER and FRIIS-HANSEN and RYÛICHI (2003): 211–212.

many or the USA. Yamamoto has argued that the trend for using photography in the art world started later than in 'the West', where photography was already established as an art medium by the end of World War II. In Japan, it was only in the 1970s that photography was applied to art, namely in the context of Photorealism and Conceptual Art. However, 'because of the insubstantial foundation for interaction between art and photography in Japan',[104] the use of photography in art has been separate from the history of photography.

Overall, 'art photography' and 'photography' have followed different paths and existed in different systems, which only started to overlap in the 1990s, as the following section will show.

11. Contemporary Japanese Photographic Art

11.1 Contemporary Japanese Photographic Art and the Japanese Art System

Since the 1970s and 1980s, the photographic medium has increasingly become popular among Japanese artists. Not only is this linked to the general increase of new media usage in art but it is connected also to practical reasons connected to the Japanese environment. One point to consider is the deficiency of space, especially in Tokyo. In my interview, Isshiki Yoshiko pointed out that photographic art usually does not require much space in the creative process, whereas for paintings or sculptures larger studios are needed. Furthermore, good cameras are low-priced and easy to obtain in Japan. Yanagi has always taken photographs of her crafts and installations; Mori Mariko worked as a photo model before creating artistic photographs. As such, many artists were somewhat familiar with photography even before using it as an art medium.

Since the 1980s, photographs by 'Western' artists, such as Jeff Wall, Cindy Sherman or Andreas Gursky, have been accepted as artworks and exhibited alongside paintings in art museums. As Thomas Pfister pointed out in 1999, the boundaries between 'art photography' (done by photographers) and 'art with photography' (done by artists) have become blurred or disappeared entirely.[105] However, in Japan, it was only in the 1990s that the strengthening and professionalisation of the infrastructure for the production, distribution, and exhibition of photographic art began.

In 1967, the Pentax Camera Museum in Mashikomachi was founded, featuring cameras and photographic equipment. In 1983, a Dômon Ken museum was established in his birthplace, Sakata. However, no public art museum

---

104 YAMAMOTO (1987): 17.
105 PFISTER (1999): 22.

had a photography collection. Kasahara has stated in my interview: 'in Japan, there was no art market for photography, and there were no art galleries and no museums. Hence, it was natural for photographers to publish photo books and to use photography magazines.'

In the late 1980s, the situation changed, as an infrastructure for photographic art began to develop. Yamamoto Kazuhiro wrote in 1987: 'in the 80's … art-oriented photography has begun to give off a new light. As the environment surrounding photography begins to show faint but definite signs of life, and communication between the fields of art and photography is starting to grow.'[106] This 'environment surrounding photography' included international exhibitions at Japanese art museums, which introduced a variety of photographic practices and issues to the Japanese public. Furthermore, national, municipal and private museums founded photography collections. In 1988, the Kawasaki City Museum initiated a photography collection. One year later, there followed the Yokohama Museum of Art, and in 1995, the Tokyo Metropolitan Museum of Photography inaugurated its permanent building in Ebisu (Tokyo). The National Museum of Modern Art had had plans to include modern photographic art in its permanent collection since the 1950s, but only started doing so in the 1990s.

As photography became more recognised by art museums, the interaction between Japanese and 'Western' museums increased. Fukagawa Masafumi has stressed that the contact with 'the West' had an impact on the Japanese art world: 'Japanese museums and galleries now started to pay attention to photographers popular in the West, such as Araki and Moriyama'.

Photographic art started to become acknowledged in Japan; as Kasahara wrote in 2001, 'the recognition of photography as art' was 'finally starting to take root.'[107] Ishiuchi Miyako is a good example for a 'photographer', who gradually became recognised in both the Japanese and 'Western' art scene. Photography awards[108] as well as the publication of Ishiuchi's series in photography magazines, such as *Nippon Camera* and *Asahi Camera*,[109] and her numerous volumes of photographs illustrate how Ishiuchi has been active in the 'photography world'. In addition, her work has been displayed in photography galleries, such as the Nikon Salon and the Zeit-Foto Salon.[110]

---

106 YAMAMOTO (1987): 17.

107 KASAHARA (2001): iii–iv.

108 Ishiuchi was awarded various photography prizes, such as the *Kimura Ihei Award* in 1979, the *Higashikawa Award* in 1999, and the *Shashin no Kai Award* in both 1999 and 2003.

109 For a list of magazines which have featured Ishiuchi's work see ISHIUCHI and MEGURO ART MUSEUM (2008): 392–396.

110 The Nikon Salon exhibited *Yokosuka Story* in 1977, *APARTMENT* in 1978 and 1979, and *Endless Night* in 1980. The Zeit-Foto Salon exhibited *Chromosome XY* in 1995, *1·9·4·7* in 1997, *SCARS* in 1999, and *Hiroshima Is* in 2008.

However, since the mid-nineties, Ishiuchi's work has also increasingly been displayed in the 'art world'. She participated in many group exhibitions in the 'Western' art system.[111] In 2005, the series *Mother's* was exhibited at the Japanese Pavilion of the 51st Biennale of Venice.[112] Ishiuchi's prominence is also evident in her work being featured in solo exhibitions and in the collection of art museums.[113] Furthermore, in the 1990s, Ishiuchi's work gained attention and criticism in the 'art world'.[114]

The awarding of the *Kimura Ihei Award* reflects how this new recognition of photography in the 'art world' influenced the 'photography world'. The photography award has been given annually to Japanese photographers since 1975. In 1993, Morimura Yasumasa was nominated. This led to a debate among the jury as to whether his art could be considered 'photography' or not. Morimura said in my interview: 'in the end, I did not win the award because too many jury members argued that my work was fine art and not photography. And the *Kimura Ihei Award* was supposed to be a photography award.' As such, the jury decided to differentiate between 'photography' and 'photographic art': Morimura's art was considered inappropriate for the award.

However, a number of young women, the *gâri fotogurafâ* ('girly photographer'), including Hiromix, Ninagawa Mika and Nagashima Yurie, emerged to widespread public and critical attention at the end of the 1990s. All three mentioned were awarded with the *Kimura Ihei Award* in 2001. In 2003, Sawada Tomoko received the award for her photographic 'self-portraits' in various costumes. Fukagawa has emphasised the symbolic meaning of this: 'Sawada Tomoko getting the *Kimura Ihei Award* was a big thing. Only those who release the shutter used to be viewed as photographers. They represented the award. But that concept broke down.'[115] In 2006, Takano Ryûdai received the award for his *In My Room* series of male nude photographs.

---

111 These include *Japanese Art After 1945* at the Guggenheim Museum in 1994, *The Desire and the Void. Contemporary Japanese Photography* at the Kunsthalle Wien in 1997, and *The History of Japanese Photography* at the Museum of Fine Arts in Houston in 2003.

112 It was the first time after almost thirty years that a photographer represented Japan in a solo show at the Venice Biennale. Shinoyama Kishin's works had been exhibited in a solo show in 1976.

113 For example, she had a solo exhibition at the National Museum of Modern Art Tokyo and at the National Film Centre Tokyo in 1999. In 2006 the *Mother's* series was shown at the Tokyo Metropolitan Museum of Photography. Other examples are the *Hiroshima* series at the Hiroshima Museum of Contemporary Art, and a large retrospective entitled *Hiroshima/Yokosuka* at the Meguro Museum of Art in Tokyo in 2008. Ishiuchi's work is included in the collection of the Museum of Modern Art in New York, the Yokohama Museum of Art, the Kunsthaus Zürich etc.

114 For a list of articles and a complete bibliography consult ISHIUCHI, Miyako and MEGURO ART MUSEUM (2008): 392–411.

115 Fukagawa has emphasised this aspect in my interview and in FUKAGAWA (2007): 272.

Nanjô has emphasised that this change of the award led to debates among photographers: 'there is a strong photographic tradition isolated from the art world. Hence, there are a great number of amateur and professional photographers who wanted to get the *Kimura Ihei Award*. In other words, there is a large group of people who wonder why Gursky or Morimura's works are viewed as good.' The artistic concept of photographs has gradually become more important for the *Kimura Ihei* jury than the photojournalistic aspect.

The increasing number of artists using photography, and the increasing number of art museums featuring photography have weakened the Japanese 'photography world'. Furthermore, as Morimura has pointed out, digitalisation has also had an impact: 'the base of the Japanese photography world consisted of mostly male amateur photographers, who were in love with cameras, lenses etc. But, because everybody in the era of digital photography can easily take photographs, the base of the photography world has been weakened.'

In summary, the relationship of the 'art world' with the 'photography world' has changed since the early 1990s. An increasing number of artists have used the photographic medium, and photographic art has become gradually institutionalised. Rather than regarding magazines or books as the ultimate genre for the presentation of photographic works, the number of photographers who are producing photographs as prints for the art market has increased greatly. As recent winners of the *Kimura Ihei Award* show, the boundaries between 'photography' and 'art photography' have become blurred and the influence of the 'photography world' is fading.

However, despite these advances, the environment surrounding contemporary photography in Japan in the 1990s was rather chaotic and still difficult for artists. Kasahara has written:

> Recognition of the sale of photographs as being akin to that of paintings and sculptures has not yet taken root, and not only individual collectors, but also organizational collections are few in number. And even the amassing of collections by public museums … are suffering from financial deficiencies in their budgets for collecting since the bursting of the economic bubble – which is a tragic state of affairs. To be sure, the number of photographic exhibitions at museums is increasing, but they are undertaken with a background of far lower budgets than those used for exhibitions of paintings, and even at museums that have photographic sections, whose curators systematically collect works, the number of exhibitions presented is still rather small.[116]

Although the Japanese market for photographic art greatly developed in the 1990s, it remained in a state that could not be compared with the established

116 KASAHARA (2001): x–xi.

markets of the USA and Europe. Moreover, as my analysis of Japanese art critique has shown, the market developments have not led to a higher quality of art discourse: there is few critical commentary on art works; exhibition reviews are rather superficial. The same applies to photography critique: although there are a vast number of volumes of photographs in Japan, there are few publications on photography which meet an academic standard.[117]

11.2 Contemporary Japanese Photographic Art and the 'Western' Art System

Since the late 1980s, art photography has increasingly been exhibited within the 'Western' art system. Jeff Wall and other artists have helped for the medium to become an autonomous art form; their large photographs are not only sold for high prices but have also been displayed in art museums. Considering this new presence of photographs in art museums, it is perhaps not surprising that Japanese photography also has become more popular. However, there are various other circumstances that should be taken into account when examining Japanese photography within the 'Western' art system.

As previously mentioned, the number of Japanese artists operating with the photographic medium, as well as the number of Japanese photographers making use of the art market, has increased. While photographic art gradually has become institutionalised, Japan reached out for greater international interaction, with global and domestic repercussions. Japanese curators, such as Nanjô Fumio or Fukagawa Masafumi, cooperated with American and European curators in exhibitions of Japanese photographic art.[118]

Photographic artworks can be easily shipped overseas. The digital progress has made it even more simple; photographs can be sent on a disk and easily presented worldwide. In addition, Nanjô has stated in a lecture on photography in Japan that one of the reasons for sending photographic art to the Singapore Biennale in 2008 was its low price.[119] The practicality and low price of photographic art certainly are important 'external factors' for its international market presence.

---

117 Exceptions include TOKYO METROPOLITAN MUSEUM OF PHOTOGRAPHY (1995); KASAHARA (2002); ÔSHIMA (2004); FUKAGAWA (2007).

118 Nanjô cooperated with American curators for the exhibitions *Against Nature* (1988) at the Grey Art Gallery in New York and for the exhibition *A Cabinet of Signs. Contemporary Art from Post-Modern Japan* (1991) at the Tate Liverpool; Fukagawa worked together with Swiss curators for the photo exhibition *In die Felsen bohren sich Zikadenstimmen. Zeitgenössische japanische Photographie* (1993) at the Kunsthaus Zürich.

119 NANJÔ, Fumio, lecture on photography: *Shashin nit tsuite* (On Photography), 25. 11. 2008 at the Institute of Interregional Philosophy of Waseda University.

Furthermore, the popularity of Japanese photographic art might be connected to a phenomenon that Susanne Boecker has described by using the metaphor of the 'green card' (see 7.3). Only those artists whose work is 'Western' enough for the 'Western' art system but at the same time associated with 'typical' characteristics of their country of origin posses a 'green card'.[120] On the one hand, photography is accepted as an art medium in 'the West' while also being associated with Japan and its photography industry. On the other hand, a quotation by Miwa Yanagi reflects the perspective of Japanese artists:

> Photography is more neutral (than *nihonga* or *yôga*) because it is new … and if we look at *purikura*[121] or other strange photography customs, it somewhat seems as though photography fits in our society… Painting and sculpture are connected to such a long history, if you exhibit paintings in the European art world, people always compare you to some European artist or school and then they sometimes add some exoticism to it. When you do photography that happens less.

Yanagi's statement not only shows that photography in Japan is generally viewed as a medium that suits contemporary Japanese society, it also highlights how photography is considered a more neutral art medium than *nihonga* or *yôga* since it is less associated with 'Western' or 'Japanese' history. Thus, it can be easier for Japanese artists to present photographs than paintings on a 'Western' market.

At the same time, paradoxically, photography has been used as a rather 'non-neutral' medium when representing 'exotic' images of Japan. As Claudia Delank has pointed out, after the opening of Japan, photography was used as a means to react to the 'Japan fashion' in 'the West' in a commercially successful way.[122] Photographs of 'ancient Japan' were produced for a 'Western' audience: European photographers, such as Felice Beato and Raimund von Stillfried, as well as Japanese followers, such as Kusakabe Kinbei, staged 'typically Japanese' scenes in their studios, such as tea ceremonies, dances and even the suicide ritual *seppuku*. These souvenir photographs were bought by tourists and exported in albums to Europe and America. Photography in the Meiji era was used as a medium to create a romantic stereotype of Japan, in order to meet 'exotistic' expectations.

The first photographer to become commercially successful in the 'West' in the 1980s was Araki Nobuyoshi, whose work could be seen as reminiscent of

---

120 BOECKER (2004): 193.

121 *Purikura* (from the English 'print club') are photographs taken in photo sticker booths. After taking photographs, users can digitally alter and decorate them on small screens inside or next to the booths and finally print them out as small stickers. *Purikura* stickers have been popular in Japan since the middle of the 1990s, especially among young women.

122 DELANK and MARCH (2002): 20.

Japanese photography in the Meiji period. Araki's best-known photographs, which have especially become known through volumes of photographs published by Taschen Verlag, include images of Japanese women as 'exotic erotic objects'.[123] The women, often bonded or/and wearing a *kimono*, lie vulnerably exposed on the floor or hang on the wall. The photographs confirm a general stereotype of Japanese eroticism in 'the West': simply put, Japanese women are obedient Geishas. I will return to this cliché in more detail in the third section of Part 3. Araki's popularity in 'the West' is controversial insofar as it is linked to an exotistic projection of Japan as the 'Other', which makes the interpretation for 'Western' viewers easy. A detailed examination of 'Western' interpretations of Araki's photographs and the role that Taschen played in his career, as well as critical analyses of Araki's photographs would be relevant topics for further research.

Araki also is an example of an artist who plays upon the line between 'photography' and 'art photography'. For instance, his series *Sentimental Journey* (1971) ironically questions the status quo of photography: the snap shot series presents private snap shots of his honeymoon, however, at the same time, some of them appear to be metaphors for marriage in general. For instance, a photograph of his wife sleeping in a canoe can be interpreted as an intimate snap shot as well as a metaphor of marriage as a shared voyage to death: both his wife's sleep and the canoe's voyage on the sea can be viewed as symbols of a transition between life and death. This image is a good example of how Araki's photographs of the *Sentimental Journey* series are often more complex as they might seem at first sight. In the afore-mentioned lecture, Nanjô has put emphasis on the way Araki began his career with constructed photographs before shifting focus to snap shots. According to Nanjô, Araki's position is somewhere 'in-between': he is not part of the 'photography environment' but also not part of the 'art environment'. However, there is most likely no Japanese photographer whose work is better known in 'the West'.

'Photography' and 'art' have followed separate paths in Japan, and it was only in the 1990s that they started to overlap. Iida has stressed that the criteria of whether images are viewed as 'photography' or 'art' both within the 'photography' and the 'art system' are 'domestic, sensible and hard to understand from a 'Western' viewpoint'. Hence, some photographers who are not

---

123 Araki has had exhibitions in various galleries, such as the Galerie Kamel Mennour in Paris, the gallery Lau in Los Angeles and the Jablonka Galerie in Cologne, as well as in museums, such as the Museum of Modern Art Frankfurt and the Stedelik Museum voor Actuele Kunst in Gent. However, his popularity in 'the West' is largely based on publications by the publisher Taschen Verlag, including *Works of Nobuyoshi Araki: Sentimental Travelogue v. 7* (1996), *Works of Nobuyoshi Araki: Private Diary 1980–1995* (1996), *Tokyo Comedy: Nobuyoshi Araki* (1997), *Polaroids* (1998), *Araki. Tokyo Lucky Hole* (2005), *Subway Love* (2006) or *Dirty Pretty Things* (2007).

presented as artists in Japan, for example Yamanaka Manabu and Izima Kaoru, are exhibited in Europe and North America as 'artists'; their photographs are treated as 'artworks'. In other words, the Japanese differentiation between 'photographic artworks' and 'photographs' loses its relevance as soon as the works are presented in the 'Western' art system.

On the one hand, this leads to controversial phenomena such as Araki's fame, which might be based on a 'Western' and 'exotistic' view of Japan, or, as Fukagawa put it, on a 'misunderstanding' (see 7.3).

On the other hand, this is a chance for talented Japanese photographers to have a career: support for photographic art in Japan in the 1990s was meagre; thus, many photographers were employed in commercial photography to make a living (see 7.1). However, in 'the West', they could present their photographs within the art system. Yamanaka and Izima are good examples of this. In my interviews with curators, Yamanaka was either not known or referred to as a 'photographer',[124] while Izima was known as working commercially in Fashion Photography.[125] Izima has stated: 'Japanese photography critics and art critics have not commented on my work yet. They either ignore me on purpose or they don't know me.'[126] In contrast, 'Western' art museums and galleries have exhibited both Yamanaka's and Izima's works. As such, the 'Western' art system offers opportunities for photographers to present their work independent of sometimes narrow-minded categorisations by the Japanese 'photography world' or 'art world'.

12. Conclusions

Although the 1990s in Japan are often referred to as the 'Lost Ten Years', with regards to the 'art' and 'photography world' at least, they could rather be viewed as a time of change, advancements and internationalisation. A great number of new museums and galleries featuring contemporary art were estab-

124 Kasahara argued that Yamanaka belonged to 'another category' that she did not know enough about; Iida did not know his work; Isshiki explained that Yamanaka was not part of the 'mainstream'. Fukagawa, Kokatsu and Kitamura refused to comment on his work. Only Nanjô was well familiar with Yamanaka's work.

125 Iida, Kitamura, and Kasahara pointed out that Izima is not recognised as an artist but as a 'cameraman' or 'commercial photographer'. Isshiki stated that Izima is 'locally famous in Germany' but not in Japan, whereas Nanjô and Kokatsu both refused to comment on Izima's work, stating they did not know it well enough. Fukagawa was the only person who found Izima 'interesting since his work is somewhere in-between fashion photography and art.' In an interview with the American film director Chad Fahs, the editor and creative director Goto Shigeo emphasised that he did not expect Izima's photographs to be evaluated as contemporary art (GOTO, Shigeo, 09. 08. 2008, at the GIP gallery in Tokyo).

126 IZIMA, Kaoru, conversation with the author, 12. 11. 2008 in Izima's studio in Tokyo. All subsequent quotations by Izima are from this interview, unless otherwise stated in the footnote.

lished, and collaborative exhibitions of contemporary art between 'Western' and Japanese museums increased.

However, it was only during that period that the museums' infrastructure started to develop and it was still difficult for Japanese artists to have a career in Japan. Furthermore, the market for contemporary art has remained small, censorship is still an issue, there are few government subsidies, and criticism of art and photography lacks in depth.

Since the early 1990s, there has been a re-examination of Japanese art history: as examined in 5., academic publications have focussed on domestic developments in Japan as well as the terminological and institutional foundations of the discipline of art history in the Meiji era. In addition, gender studies developed in the 1990s; however, they had to fight harsh criticism and have thus remained a minor field in Japanese art history. The notion of 'art' was introduced to Japan as a 'Western' concept in the Meiji era. Furthermore, since the Meiji era, public education emphasised 'Western' music and art, resulting in a Japanese insecurity towards 'Western' culture. Hence, the opinion of 'the West' still played an important role in the 1990s Japanese art system – an art system which was just beginning to appreciate its own contemporary art.

When presenting their works in the 'Western' art market, Japanese artists face various difficulties: How can they avoid exoticism, Japonism and yet present 'Japanese' artworks? Moreover, who should decide which works are interpreted as 'art' in an international, yet 'Western' art system?

After photography was introduced into Japan, it developed into a powerful business, and led to the formation of a web of camera companies, photography galleries, magazines, clubs and technical photography schools. Photography and art have followed different paths, which only started to converge in the 1990s when Japanese photographic art increasingly became acknowledged in both Japan and overseas. It has been difficult and precarious to find criteria within photographic images to clearly differentiate between 'photography' and 'art photography'. This distinction is rather influenced by the medium and the context that the works are presented in. However, the Japanese differentiation between 'photographic artworks' and 'photographs' loses its relevance when the works are displayed within the 'Western' art market. In view of Japanese 'photographers', such as Yamanaka Manabu and Izima Kaoru, this provides opportunities to present their works as 'art'. Whether their 'works of art' are convincing or not remains to be seen in the following chapters, which will describe and interpret the images.

Recent winners of the *Kimura Ihei Award* show how the boundaries between 'photography' and 'art photography' have become blurred, as the power of the 'photography world' is decreasing. Only time will tell how this may affect Japanese photographic art.

Part 2:
Case Studies: Ten Photographic Artworks of the 1990s

1. Morimura Yasumasa's *Portrait (Futago)* and *Red Marilyn*

1.1 The Work of Morimura Yasumasa (∗1951 in Osaka, lives and works in Osaka)

Morimura graduated from the Faculty of Fine Arts at the Kyôto Shiritsu Geijutsu Daigaku (Kyoto City University of Art) in 1978. Two years later, he became an assistant at the university and worked for Ernest Sato, a former photojournalist of *Life Magazine*. Morimura's early photographs are reminiscent of Sato's or Moholy-Nagy's still lifes: the black and white photographs somewhat 'abstract' objects, such as a fork and a light bulb, often by emphasizing light and shadow or creating sharp contour lines.[1] Morimura made a living through teaching as a supply teacher at art academies until the end of the 1980s.

Morimura's earliest photographic 'self-portrait', *Portrait (Van Gogh)* (1985), is his first artwork to feature a 'Western' painting. After making a coat out of fabric and a pipe out of clay, Morimura applied thick dabs of colours to both. He applied make up to his face to make it appear as though it were painted with thick brushstrokes, positioned himself in front of a painted background and let an assistant take the photograph. In this way, he created a photograph which is reminiscent of Vincent Van Gogh's painting *Self-portrait with Bandaged Ear* (1889).

Portrait (Futago) (Twins) (1988–1990) references Édouard Manet's painting *Olympia* (1863) and presents Morimura not only as the cocotte Olympia but also as a Black servant. Both *Portrait (Van Gogh)* and *Portrait (Futago)* are analogue photographs. At the end of the 1980s, however, Morimura also began to use digital techniques, often in order to impersonate multiple figures within one image.

Morimura first attracted international attention at the 1988 Venice Biennale, which was directed by Giovanni Carandente. Since then, his art has been shown in several group and solo exhibitions in galleries and art museums worldwide.[2] Most of Morimura's works have remained photographs which

---

1 Examples of Morimura's early photographs are mostly untitled and inaccurately dated to the early 1980s.

2 Group exhibitions with Morimura's work include *Post Human* in 1992/1993, *Japanese Art After 1945: Scream Against the Sky* at the Guggenheim Museum in New York in 1994, *The History of Japanese Photography* at the Museum of Fine Arts in Houston in 2003 etc. Morimura has had various solo exhibitions, for example *Daughter of Art History* at the Sagacho Exhibit Space in Tokyo and the Nicola Jacobs Gallery in London in 1989, *Rembrandt Room* at the Hara Art Museum in Tokyo in 1993, *Beauty Unto Sickness* at the Yokohama Museum

feature himself impersonating figures of art history, popular culture or politics. For instance, the exhibition *Self-portrait as Actress* in 1996 presented photographs in which Morimura 'masqueraded' as movie stars, such as Marilyn Monroe or Brigitte Bardot. In 2001, *An Inner Dialogue with Frida Kahlo* featured digitally edited photographs of Morimura as Frida Kahlo. In 2007, Morimura finished the series *Requiem for the XX Century*, in which he impersonates influential males of the 20th century, including Albert Einstein and Che Guevara.

Morimura's body of artwork also includes artist books, performances, videos and installations. In terms of subject matter, he has concentrated on questions of identity with regard to gender, nationality and ethnicity, as well as on the appropriation of famous images. Furthermore, he has published numerous articles, combining anecdotes with social issues and art commentary.[3] The intertwined relation of originality and imitation is consistently addressed in his articles; Morimura has stated that imitation is the starting point of his work but in the end there is always a new original picture.[4] My analysis of *Portrait (Futago)* and *Red Marilyn* will explore if Morimura's artworks corroborate his statement.

The following paragraphs are concerned with the series *Daughter of Art History* and *Self-Portrait as Actress* and provide a detailed examination of two artworks: *Portrait (Futago)* is an example of Morimura's adaptations of 'icons' of art history and *Red Marilyn* represents his artworks featuring 'icons' of popular culture.[5] However, before focussing on the two images, the concepts 'portrait' and 'self-portrait' in Morimura's art will be analysed briefly.

---

of Art in 1996, *Yasumasa Morimura, Actor/Actress* at the Contemporary Arts Museum in Houston in 1997, *Self-portrait as Art History* at the Tokyo Museum of Contemporary Art in 1998, *Self-Portraits: An Inner Dialogue with Frida Kahlo* at the Luhring Augustine gallery in New York and the Galerie Thaddaeus Ropac in Paris in 2001, *A Story of M's Self-Portraits* at the Kawasaki City Museum in 2002, *Los Nuevor Caprichos* at the Shugoarts gallery in Tokyo, the Luhring Augustine gallery in New York in 2005, *Seasons of Passion / A Requiem: Chapter One* at the Shugoarts gallery in Tokyo in 2006, *Yasumasa Morimura – Requiem for the XX Century. Twilight of the Turbulent Gods* at the Fondazione Bevilacqua La Masa in Venice in 2007, *Yasumasa Morimura: Seasons of Passion / A Requiem: Mishima* at the Art Gallery of New South Wales in Sydney in 2008, *A Requiem: Art on Top of the Battlefield* at the Tokyo Metropolitan Museum of Photography in 2010.

3 MORIMURA (1998); MORIMURA (2000); MORIMURA (2001a); MORIMURA (2001c).

4 MORIMURA (2000): 80.

5 I use the term 'icon' in this thesis in a rather colloquial sense: an 'icon' is a generally well-known image or a person whose image in the media has made him or her an object of attention and devotion.

1.2 Morimura's 'Portraits' and 'Self-Portraits'

The term 'portrait' usually defines the image of a human being, be it a sculpture, painting or photograph, which represents his or her looks and/or his or her 'personality'. As such, the likeness of the portrait to the 'person' seems to be the most basic and relevant condition of this genre.

Morimura's photographs can be viewed as 'portraits' for three reasons. These reasons are based on different levels of argumentation, namely on visual likeness, the artist's self-consciousness and the concept of a 'person' or 'personality'.

Firstly, the photographs are 'portraits' in a general sense: they (re)present human beings. Furthermore, looking at the artworks closely, it becomes obvious that Morimura never fully 'disguises' himself as somebody else: as evident in *Portrait (Futago)* and *Red Marilyn*, he includes details which differ from the appropriated image and which reference his own background. For instance, in *Portrait (Futago)*, he inserts a *manekineko* (beckoning cat), a typically Japanese object, into his photographic 'imitation' of Manet's *Olympia*. In *Red Marilyn*, he shows himself with fake female breasts which are attached to a transparent brassiere; the obvious fakeness of the breasts highlights his maleness. In other words, Morimura as a Japanese male artist remains present in the photographs. As such, the works represent Morimura 'himself' to a certain extent.

Secondly, a quotation by Morimura emphasises that he views his different artistic 'masquerades' as parts of 'himself': 'I continue to create self-portraits, in order to find various sides of myself'.[6] As this statement shows, Morimura suggests to the viewer that a clear differentiation between his appropriation of an existing image and his individual 'self' is impossible; rather, they are inextricably intertwined. However, Morimura's statements about his 'self' and his 'self-consciousness' are topics which I do not want to examine further in this study; rather, I would like to explore critically how the concept of the 'self-portrait' is present in his photographs. This brings me to the third and most important reason.

The concept of a 'person' and his or her recognisability in an image is rather complex, especially in a postmodern context. From a postmodernist perspective, the notion of a 'person' is generally not viewed as static and autonomous but rather as influenced by various social factors; like the human 'body' a 'person' is subject to constant change.[7] Gottfried Boehm has argued

6 MORIMURA (2001a): 205; FRITSCH (2008): 78–82.

7 This is evident, for instance, in Michel Foucault's analyses. Foucault deals with the 'person' as a subject which is constantly entering into new social and political relations, e.g. see *The Birth of the Clinic* (1963) or *Discipline and Punish* (1975).

that the portrait can be defined by its intention to visualise something of a person's inside, a 'personal core'.[8] This argument is connected to an emphasis on distinctive individuality; however, if a 'person' in our postmodern times is understood as something flexible, the idea that a 'portrait' or 'self-portrait' must show a human being in a distinctive, 'individual' manner, is obsolete. Moreover, if 'personality' only exists within a certain time, culture and society and is thus always influenced by socio-historical structures, the differentiation between a person's 'core' and 'social role', between one's 'real look' and the 'disguise' as 'somebody else' is obsolete. As such, the titles 'portrait' and 'self-portrait' for Morimura's works appear as 'postmodern puns': if postmodern notions of the 'self' and 'person' are understood as flexible, Morimura can present himself in multiple and ever-changing ways and nevertheless entitle them as 'self-portraits'. In consequence, a photograph of Morimura wearing a wig and make-up, 'masquerading' as the French painting figure Olympia may as much be a 'portrait' of him and his 'personality' as a photograph of the 'artist' without make up. If the notions of a 'person', 'individuality' and 'self' are all in flux, one's 'portrait' and 'self-portrait' may be as well.

The relationship of the term 'masquerade' with 'person' and 'personality' reflects this 'postmodern', flexible concept on an etymological level: the 'person' and thus also the concept of a 'personality' derive from the Latin word 'persona', which might be borrowed from the Etruscan 'phersu' and originally meant 'character in a mask'. As such, the term 'person' is linked to a 'mask'. The history of the 'personality' with 'mask' is a complex one and surely beyond the scope of his thesis; however, I would like to highlight that the etymological link between 'person' and 'mask' corroborates my argument: there is no such thing as a distinctive and static 'individuality'. Consequently, it is not possible to clearly differentiate between a 'real portrait' which presents one's 'individual core' on the one side and an image in which somebody 'wears a mask' on the other. Keeping this etymological relationship of a 'personality' with a 'mask' and the complexity of the concept of a postmodern 'individuality' in mind, I put quotation marks around the term 'masquerade' when using it in the context of Morimura's art.

1.3 The *Daughter of Art History* Series

The *Daughter of Art History* series, which began in 1985 with the artwork *Portrait (Van Gogh)*, has continued until today. It is a series of photographs in which Morimura impersonates well-known 'Western' and Japanese paintings'

---

8 BOEHM (1986): 25.

subjects as well as objects. The referenced artworks include masterpieces by Goya, Rembrandt, Leonardo da Vinci, Édouard Manet and Itô Jakuchu.

Portrait (Van Gogh) and *Portrait (Futago)* are typical of the series *Daughter of Art History*: Morimura exhibits them in huge golden frames like traditional 'Western' paintings, their size proportions differ from the 'original' artworks and they are enlarged. With a size of 166 x 366 cm Morimura's *Portrait (Futago)* is larger than Manet's *Olympia* (130.5 x 190 cm). *Portrait (Van Gogh)* (120 x 100 cm) is almost twice as large as the artwork it references. By blowing up the size, Morimura creates a visual paradox. On the one hand, the images look powerful and reminiscent of the grand tradition of European paintings, suggesting the grandiose and the epic; as such, the photographic medium seems to challenge the tradition of the painting. On the other hand, the large size establishes parallels with billboard posters and art posters which have been replicated many times.

1.4 *Portrait (Futago)* (Twins) (1988–1990) (Colour photograph) (Fig. 1)

1.4.1 Description and Formal Analysis

There are two versions of *Portrait (Futago)* (Twins): the first, 'small-sized' version (94.5 x 133.7 cm) is from 1988 and has an edition of five; the large-sized version (266 x 366 cm) was created in 1990 and has an edition of three. When presented in a museum, the large version is used; the photograph is exhibited in a thick golden frame.

Portrait (Futago) first appeared in the ON gallery, a small gallery in Osaka. The huge photograph was in a thin silver frame and could be viewed immediately upon entering the exhibition room. It grabbed the viewer's attention as it was hung in isolation and covered almost the entire wall. On the right wall, *Portrait (Shonen 1, 2, 3)* (Young Boy 1, 2, 3) was exhibited, also in thin silver frames and almost covering the entire wall. Both works reference paintings by Manet, which are said to be based on the model Victorine Meurent and which are now located in the Musée d' Orsay in Paris.

Portrait (Futago) is Morimura's earliest photograph in which he impersonates two figures. On the left side of the artwork he presents himself as a naked slender young person with a curly ashblond wig, wearing golden jewellery, a red flower in his hair and pink high-heeled mules. He lies outstretched on a bed, leans his back on cushions and looks directly into the camera. His buttocks and legs lie on white cloth, decorated with embroideries of golden cranes and silver flowers. With his left hand he is concealing his genitals and with the right hand he is holding a piece of the cloth. His right shoe appears to have fallen on the bed and lies next to a ceramic black-golden cat that has her left paw upraised as if waving. As his left leg is lying over the right one, Morimura's bare foot is hidden by the shoe. On the right side, Morimura appears as a Black female servant in a huge pink dress, holding an extravagant bouquet of flowers in her hand.

When looking at the photograph closely, it becomes obvious that it reflects different 'reality levels'. The background, splendidly decorated in dark colours, is painted. In the left upper corner of this painted background, there is a dark-green curtain hanging over some kind of a dividing wall. The dividing wall is decorated with red and golden rhombic ornaments and a golden border. The right side is designed in dark-turquoise tones with several gold leaf ornaments. This background contrasts with the 'real' bed, cushions and other props in the foreground. In addition, it contrasts with the 'real' artist impersonating both the person on the bed and the servant in the background. In other words, the image shows a 'real' human being and interior in front of a painted, 'non-real' background. Morimura explains the process he employed in making the artwork:

> I prepared a backdrop ... For the servant on the right-hand side, I painted a body, leaving a hole for the head ... I applied makeup to my entire body, reclined nude on the divan, and took the first photograph. Then I applied the face makeup for the servant, stuck my head through the hole, and took the second photograph. Afterward, I pieced together the two photographs to create a final single image.[9]

Comparable to a theatre performance, Morimura arranged a scene with a painted backdrop, props, costumes and himself as an 'actor' in two roles. However, *Portrait (Futago)* is a silent, motionless photograph. As such, the final artwork could be described as a montage of two photographic 'mise-en-scènes' (staged scenes, literally: 'to put in the scene'), or moreover, 'tableaux vivants' ('living pictures').[10] Photographic tableaux vivants were popular in the 19th and early 20th century, sometimes including nude scenes. The nude motif in tableaux vivants provides a parallel to the subject matter of *Portrait (Futago)* – I will return to this in 2.2 of Part 3.

Portrait (Futago) is more than a disparate conglomerate of props, costumes and a painted background since it combines the different 'reality levels' in a harmonious way. The fact that Morimura put his head through a hole in the painted background is not visible in the photograph if one does not know it. The curved dark-green curtain merges into the painted background. In addition,

---

9 MORIMURA (2003a): 123.

10 A tableau vivant could be defined as a 'bodily re-enactment of or a reference to an artwork'; FOLIE and GLASMAIER (2002): 9.

the composition of the image suggests no division between the 'real' foreground and the painted background. Moreover, the golden boarder of the dividing wall in the painting ends as a vertical line in Morimura's pubic area and thus connects the back- and foreground on a compositional level.

There are many more elements to take into account when analysing the composition of this final image. Firstly, a repetition of triangle shapes is noticeable: at the top on the left of the photograph, the upper contour of the big white cushion contrasts with the dark background and seems to continue in the curved outline of Morimura's blond hair, peaking out at the top of his head. From there the line goes down again as Morimura's light upper arm contrasts intensely with the dark background. The combination of these diagonals and the horizontal line of the bed form a triangle. On the right side of the picture, the contours of the upper part of the servant's body together with the horizontal line of the upper part of the bed form a second triangle. Those two triangles resting on the horizontal base of the bed suggest stability. A third and reverse triangle can be visualised by combining the outline of the naked man's left arm with the line of the servant's right arm. The two diagonals meet in a spot where the golden border of the dividing wall ends as a vertical line. In this way, the arms, the vertical line of the wall and the outline of Morimura's left leg all lead to his hidden sex, which thereby becomes the centre of focus.

The photographic image is arranged in many circular lines and round forms: for example, various round elements on the painted dividing wall, Morimura's curly hair, the flowers, the floral embroideries and the contours of the cat. The round forms not only evoke a sense of motion but also provide a counterpoint to the stability evoked by the triangular forms.

The colours are pure and intense; the golden and silver embroideries, many details such as coloured finger nails, red lips, golden jewellery on Morimura's neck, ears and hand, as well as red, pink and white flowers, the servant's pink dress and the ornaments in the background create a vibrant impression. The white cushions, the light base of the embroidered cloth, Morimura's blond curls and his light skin form a light composition, which contrasts with the dark colours of the background.

The contrast of lights and darks suggests a horizontal division of the image, which is interesting in regard to the subject matter. The servant's light pink dress and the white flowers in the bouquet seem to follow the lightness of the bed and the naked skin. At the same time, the servant's skin as well as her 'reddish-brown' headpiece blend into the darkness of the background. In this way the colours show segregation: the naked subject looks directly at the viewer, taking on the role of the main photographic object. In contrast, the Black maid only slightly steps out of the dark to present the bouquet of flowers. She is looking in the direction of the person on the bed, who does not pay her any attention. Even though the light colour of her dress can be interpreted as part of the foreground, the colour of her skin causes her to fade into the background.

I will return to many of these visual elements in the third chapter since they carry important meaning for the analysis of national identity and gender. The following section will compare *Portrait (Futago)* with the referenced *Olympia* in order to examine which elements Morimura copies and which ones he changes.

1.4.2 Morimura's Photograph *Portrait (Futago)* and Manet's Painting *Olympia*

Morimura's *Portrait (Futago)* is an appropriation of Manet's painting *Olympia*. Like in *Olympia*, a naked slender young person lies outstreched on a bed, leaning the back on cushions and looking directly into the camera. Similar to the main character of Manet's painting, Olympia, Morimura conceals his genitals with his left hand. In the right background, Morimura appears in the disguise of a black woman in a pink dress, holding a bouquet of flowers in her hand. The setting, the postures of the 'two' people and the naked person's unflinching look at the viewer make the reference to *Olympia* obvious. However, there are several differences to Manet's image.

The golden earrings, the necklace and the bracelet of the figure on the bed in *Portrait (Futago)* are references to the jewellery that Olympia wears; however, the hair and flower appear to be different (fig. 2, 3 and 4). In contrast to Olympia's dark auburn hair, which is tied up, Morimura wears a short curly blond wig. The bloom in his hair differs to Olympia's salmon-pink flower as it consists of two vibrant red petals with a waxy structure; the form and the structure of the flaps look like anthuriums. Regarding the piece of the ornate cloth in Morimura's right hand, one sees a long square-cut sleeve and recognises the cloth as a *kimono*. The white base of the *kimono* is embroidered with several golden cranes and silver flowers. The black cat in Manet's painting is staring at the viewer and standing on the bed, back arched and holding up her tail while wagging it (fig. 6). When Manet painted *Olympia* the black cat was associated with witchcraft and, as Alan Krell has pointed out, with 'promiscuous and potentially dangerous sexuality.[11] Furthermore, the term could 'designate a "cocotte", one of the many euphemisms for a registered prostitute'.[12] However, the cat in Morimura's version is a ceramic black-golden cat sitting and raising her left paw (fig. 5). This *manekineko* (beckoning cat) is a popular sign of good luck and can be seen in the entrances of shops and restaurants.

11 KRELL (1996): 59.
12 IBID: 59.

These differences show clearly that Morimura did not blindly copy Manet's work but rather changed several details, 'japonising' the painting. In addition to differences in content of the presented scene, the use of colours and forms in *Portrait (Futago)* must also be taken into account: the colours are brighter, much more saturated and vivid than the mixed colours in Manet's painting and there are more pink, red, gold and silver tones. Many floral and ornamental details are assembled in the decor as well as on the *kimono* adding a decorative quality to the artwork. In so doing Morimura certainly exceeds Manet's work in terms of opulence and splendour. Furthermore, as stated in 1.3, *Portrait (Futago)* is larger than Olympia. Taking this visual language into account, *Portrait (Futago)* exceeds an aesthetic, which could be viewed as 'kitsch'. It is reminiscent of large posters of folk culture rather than 'high art'. However, at the same time, its 'in your face' approach also expresses confidence. The 'folk culture' aspect as well as the confident expression of the photograph are related to the content of *Portrait (Futago)*; I will explore and interpret this in the third section of Part 3.

1.4.3 *Portrait (Futago)* as a *Mitate-e* and Appropriation Art

Morimura's use of the painting *Olympia* as means to create *Portrait (Futago)* could be linked to the Japanese tradition of *mitate-e* ('looking and comparing pictures' or 'analogue pictures'). Likening one thing to another, *mitate* is a metaphorical intellectual game in both poetry and visual art. In *mitate-e*, which is a complex genre in woodblock prints, historical events, classical paintings or works of literature are referenced in order to illustrate or comment on contemporary figures and events.[13] As Timothy Clark has pointed out, *mitate-e* require 'sophisticated reading'; they contain codes which 'can only be unlocked through familiarity with related ... pictures both ancient and modern'.[14] In other words, a *mitate-e* is grounded in a shared familiarity with a certain motif or image; without the viewer's knowledge of the referenced element(s), the image does not reveal its full range of meanings.

Morimura's choice of the famous artwork *Olympia*, which many viewers of *Portrait (Futago)* should be familiar with, and his linkage of past elements to the present are reminiscent of a *mitate-e*. Only a connoisseur of Manet's *Olympia* and the contemporary context of Morimura' photographic take on it can

13 For a detailed analysis of *mitate-e* see CLARK (1997) and the catalogue of the exhibition *Juxtaposition (Mitate) and Slumming (Yatsushi) in Early Modern Japanese Culture*, which was curated by Joshua Mostow in Vancouver in 2010.

14 CLARK (1997): 21

appreciate the complexity of *Portrait (Futago)*. Hence, I agree with Robert Singer's argument that Morimura's self-portraits 'strongly suggest the mitate'.[15]

Fukuda Miran is another artist who has used *mitate* as an artistic technique in the 1980s and 1990s. Using painting, collage, lenticular plastics and computer techniques, Fukuda blurs the distinction between photography and painting. In photographs of famous artworks, such as Leonardo da Vinci's *The Last Supper* (1997), she questions the relationship between paintings and photographic reproductions. This method contrasts with Morimura's to a great extent: it does not include the artist in the images and Fukuda does not construct or stage scenes but takes photographs of existing images. However, her approach can be compared to Morimura's insofar as both artists question the relationship between 'Western' art and a Japanese audience. Thus, it is not surprising that their art has been exhibited together several times.[16]

Both Morimura's and Fukuda's work can also be viewed in connection to 'Appropriation Art'. Although there are artists, including Andy Warhol, Roy Lichtenstein or Elaine Sturtevant,[17] who borrowed and copied existing images already in the 1960s, it was only in the 1980s that the term 'Appropriation Art' came into use. Sherrie Levine quoted entire artworks in her own work, for example by photographing photographs of Walker Evans. Other artists playing with questions of originality and working with photographic appropriation include Cindy Sherman and Jeff Wall.

Morimura referencing a painting through an extremely large photograph in a golden frame highlights and perhaps even parodies the new status of photography as 'art'. Since the 1980s and 1990s photographs, for instance by Wall and Sherman, have increasingly been exhibited in art museums and galleries, a privilege previously only afforded to paintings. The most obvious parallel between Wall, Sherman and Morimura is the adaptation of art historical motifs as well as popular images, be they explicit references to existing images, such as Morimura's *Daughter of Art History* series, or implicit references to images of film culture, such as Sherman's *Film Still* series.

However, there are two relevant characteristics of Morimura's approach which contrast to Wall's and Sherman's. First, Morimura includes painted objects and backgrounds in some of his photographs: for instance, the dividing wall in the background of *Portrait (Futago)* is painted, whereas the bed and Morimura are 'real'. The painted background not only references the appropriated image *Olympia* being a painting, but also creates an aesthetic impression

15 SINGER (1994): 31.

16 For example, at the exhibition *Homage to Spanish Still Life by Yasumasa Morimura and Fukuda Miran* at the Nagoya City Art Museum in 1992.

17 While Andy Warhol and Roy Lichtenstein mostly appropriated images of popular culture, Elaine Sturtevant copied works by artists including Robert Rauschenberg, Jasper Johns and Warhol, using their original techniques, such as screen printing.

which differs from the 'real' elements. The soft ornaments and the intermingling colours of the background exude the aesthetic of painting while the sharp contour lines of the objects and of Morimura in the foreground appear 'photographic'. As such, the photographic medium is not used as an alternative to painting but rather as an extension – Morimura combines painting and photography in order to create a specific aesthetic impression.

Second, Morimura distances himself from the images that he represents by making his 'masquerade' obvious through various details; as the interpretations in the third chapter will show, his 'Japanicity' as well as his 'masculinity' remain present in the artwork. As such, another culture and gender are brought into the appropriated 'Western' images of women.

The photographic medium as a means to appropriate paintings and its connection to questions about originality in a world flooded by an image plethora are interesting issues. However, a detailed comparison of Morimura's work and other Appropriation Artists would require a separate study.

Portrait (Futago) is a complex work of art portraying body issues as strongly linked to traditions in art history and socio-cultural history. Part 3 will return to *Portrait (Futago)* by raising questions on Morimura's as well as Olympia's naked body in an art historical context (2.2), by analysing Morimura's body as a screen of 'national identity' in a 'postcolonial' context (3.) and by exploring gender concepts (5.4).

1.5 The *Self-portrait as Actress* Series

The *Self-portrait as Actress* series was presented in Morimura's solo exhibition *The Sickness unto Beauty – Self-portrait as Actress*[18] in the Yokohama Museum of Art in 1996. The exhibition displayed forty-eight large-sized colour

18 The title *The Sickness unto Beauty* refers to Sören Kierkegaard's book *The Sickness unto Death*. Kierkegaard's 'sickness' does not describe a physical illness but rather a sense of despair; 'death' is a spiritual end. To find one's true self, one must not only be conscious of one's own self but also of having been created by God. Referencing Kierkegaard's title, which again is a quotation from the Bible (John 11.4: Jesus says: 'This sickness is not unto death' before he raises Lazarus from the dead), Morimura suggests a new way of dealing with human existence. Replacing 'death' with 'beauty', he not only decontextualises the citation from its Christian background, but also makes beauty the central focus of the series. While in Kierkegaard's writing despair leads to death, in Morimura's exhibition it leads to beauty. Beautiful looks appear to be not only the result of Morimura's sickness but also its remedy, as the photographs are titled '*self*-portraits'. As such, Morimura adapts Kierkegaard's definition of the self from a conscious level to something visible. In light of this philosophical background, the exhibition title can be interpreted as a reference to the artist, who is 'sick' of looking like a Japanese man but finally finds his 'self' when he 'masquerades' as beautiful Hollywood actresses.

photographs of Morimura 'masquerading' as twenty different actresses in movie classics, eight small-sized black and white photographs of him impersonating starlets in portraits, and a film.

Some of the colour photographs are detailed compositions referencing key scenes of famous films, such as the end of *Bonnie and Clyde* (1967) (*Self-portrait as Actress/After Faye Dunaway*) (fig. 7). However, Morimura always changes details or adapts the scene into his own Japanese background, for example by transposing Jodie Foster's character of the young prostitute Iris in *Taxi Driver* to an unexpected setting in Osaka. The complex photographic production process, in which Morimura was supported by assistants, make-up artists and costume directors, is itself reminiscent of that of Hollywood films.[19] Other photographs are stark close-ups of Morimura against a monochrome background dressed in the costumes of famous film characters.

Morimura determined the way the artworks were exhibited in four rooms. While the first room contained large photographs of Morimura as 'Western' actresses, the second room presented viewers with three even larger photographs of him as Japanese actresses.

The third room was dedicated to Marilyn Monroe: *White Marilyn* (230 x 300 cm) was to be found at the end of the room, *Black Marilyn* (220 x 167 cm) against the left wall and *Red Marilyn* (220 x 167 cm) against the right (fig. 8). The photographs were attached to black metal scaffolding about half a metre in front of the walls. The only light came from small lights installed above the photographs, which intermittently flashed up every few seconds, only to fade once again to complete darkness. Torn wallpaper clung to the walls, hung from the scaffolding and laid scattered on the floor. Around the corner, an old-fashioned ticket booth was installed alongside a neon 'cinema' sign. This part of the room was lit by dim antiquarian lamps on the walls, which served to create the atmosphere of an old and deserted cinema foyer. The three images are alike in means of their luscious colourfulness, large size and poster-aesthetic. With regard to issues of gender, however, they are different: while *White Marilyn* depicts the artist's mimesis as a 'woman', *Black Marilyn* and *Red Marilyn* expose a more complex gender identity. I will return to the complex gender identity represented in *Red Marilyn* in Part 3.

The photographs in the first two exhibition rooms evoke nostalgic feelings in the viewer of film classics, whereas the third room has a more disconcerting effect: the artworks are attached to scaffolding in 'shabby' surroundings, which contrasts with the 'kitschy' poster-aesthetic of the photographs. The dim illumination punctured by the flashing lights causes the photographic objects to

---

19 This became obvious when the author examined Morimura's creation of an artwork in his studio in Osaka, 12. 12. 2008. In addition, this can be seen in a documentary: KISHIMOTO (1996).

twinkle like 'stars' in the darkness. This flashing of the lights and the 'shabby' setting with the torn wallpaper could be interpreted as symbols of impermanence: a Hollywood star may shine bright, however, it is just a question of time until the celebrity is forgotten, with pieces of his or her posters laying scattered on the floor. As such, the exhibition serves not only as a reference to the classical Hollywood film and its reception, but also as a critical visualisation of celebrity fame. While the first rooms mirror the dream world of films, the third room is a testament to the filmstar's mortality.

The following section will focus on one of the Marilyn Monroe images, *Red Marilyn*. After analysing Morimura's posture and the artwork's aesthetic impression, I will compare the image with the referenced photograph *Red Velvet, Pose 1*. Following this, Morimura's embodiment of Marilyn Monroe, representing the concept of a Hollywood 'star', will be of interest.

1.6 *Self-portrait (Actress) / Red Marilyn* (1996) (Colour Photograph in Red Frame) (Fig. 9)

1.6.1 Description and Formal Analysis

Red Marilyn first appeared in a Japanese popular magazine before it was shown to the art world; the men's magazine *Panja*, which featured men's products, actresses and cars, published one of Morimura's actress-impersonations monthly, starting in August 1994. The feature was entitled *Descent of Actresses*. The photograph of Morimura as Marilyn was the first image of that special feature.

When exhibited in a gallery or museum, the artwork is displayed in two different sizes: the small-sized version (120 x 95 cm) has an edition of five, the large-sized version (220 x 167 cm) has an edition of three.

Red Marilyn's first appearance in a museum was in the large-sized version and as part of the afore-mentioned solo exhibition *The Sickness unto Beauty – Self-portrait as Actress* in the Yokohama Museum of Art in 1996.

In the photograph, Morimura is posing on a dark-red cloth, completely naked apart from a dark-blond curly wig and fake breasts, attached to a transparent brassiere. He is turning his head towards the sky, his red lips opened alluringly while he averts his long-lashed, lowered eyes away from the viewer. As regards his posture, it is noticeable that his right arm and knees are turned forward to the light source outside of the photograph, while the left upper arm is bent backwards, thus hiding the left half of his face and showing the viewer his hairless arm pit. Morimura stretches his right arm, grasping the fabric with his right hand. The legs are drawn close together so that his genitals cannot be seen. On the one hand, Morimura opens his body for the viewer's gaze by bending his arm behind his head and stretching his right away from his body; on the other, he closes his legs and hides half of his face. This alternation between revealing and disguising the body suggests a salacious dynamic to the work.

The naked figure is shown from a frontal perspective and the photographic gaze comes from above. However, the photograph is attached to scaffolding and the spectator has to look up to see the work. Consequently, there is a contrast to be made between the superior photographic viewpoint and the spectator's inferior position.

As regards the composition, the naked body and the cloth both occupy approximately half of the image. Morimura positions himself in the middle of the composition and is surrounded by the cloth, which virtually flows out of the photographic borders. By moving in different directions, the figure dynamically dominates the whole image. While there are some straight verticals in the upper part of the fabric, curved pleats dominate the lower part. Looking at the body, curvaceous forms, such as the lips, ornamental curls, large breasts, the curved bottom and round toes, dominate the work; these may be associated with 'the feminine' and create a dynamic impression. In addition, a vivid red dominates the artwork: the red of the cloth, the lips, nails and toenails, all in the same tone, as well as the red frame. Morimura's light skin and his shining dark blond hair contrast sharply with the red. Juxtaposed against the red fabric and dark blond hair, the almost white body becomes the focus of attention.

The theatrical light not only makes the skin appear smooth but also produces sharp contrasts: In contrast to the brightly illuminated parts of Morimura's body there are shadows on the fabric behind Morimura's back and under his stomach, fake breasts, bottom and knees. The strong contrast of light and dark emphasises the rips and the muscles of the stomach and buttocks.

Morimura's twisted posture, altering between revealing and disguising his body, together with his elaborate make-up and the theatrical light, highlight that he intentionally and seductively poses in front of the camera. As such, *Red Marilyn* evokes a strong sense of artificiality and stagedness.

1.6.2 *Red Marilyn* and *Red Velvet, Pose #1*

Red Marilyn references the pin-up photograph *Pose #1*, which is part of the series *Red Velvet Photos* (1949) featuring the model Norma Jean Baker (fig. 10). The photographer Tom Kelley took twenty-four photographs of the twenty-two-year old woman, who was at that time not yet successful as an actress. In 1951 the photographs were published in a calendar, and two years later *Playboy* printed *Red Velvet, Pose #1* as a centrefold in its first edition. Thus, it could be assumed that Morimura selected *Red Marilyn* as the first photograph in *Panja's* special feature to make a reference to the photograph in the very first issue of *Playboy*.

The background of the photo shooting cannot be reconstructed. It is obvious, however, that the image was originally a pin-up photograph of an unknown model. It was not until Marilyn Monroe became an international film star, that *Red Velvet, Pose #1* developed into a symbol of her sexual charisma.

Comparing *Red Marilyn* with the pin-up, it is striking that Morimura adopts its composition, the model's pose and even small details, such as the red polished nails and toenails. Thomas Miessgang has described these similarities as 'stunning Trompe-l'œil-effects'.[20] However, there are many elements in the photograph, which serve to show that *Red Marilyn* is not a copy: Morimura's wig is not as curly and voluminous as Marilyn's hair, his skin is lighter and his mouth is less open than hers so his teeth can not be seen. There is a stronger contrast of dark and light in *Red Marilyn*, which causes harsh shadows on Morimura's skin as well as strong body outlines, whereas the contours of Marilyn's body are much softer. Pleats on Morimura's bra and its lighter colour illustrate the border between Morimura's skin and the breasts-dummy.

The wig, with its shining synthetic fibre, the fake breasts, the loud colours and theatrical light all lead to an aesthetic which exceeds *Pose #1* in terms of artificiality. As such, *Red Marilyn* emphasises the referenced photograph as being part of the Hollywood 'dream factory' featuring its most famous icon, 'Marilyn'.

1.6.3 'Marilyn': the Film Icon and Hollywood Star

The popular film icon 'Marilyn' could be defined as containing both the actress as a product of the film industry, and the 'real' person, with whom one can identify on a human level. Constantly alternating between artifice and human, 'Marilyn' offers a multifaceted surface upon which different interpretations can be projected. Understanding both Norma Jean Baker and Marilyn Monroe has become an unattainable objective; the two are products of discourse and collective dreams described in the media, art and any written studies that use her as a topic.

Stressing artificiality in *Red Marilyn*, Morimura makes a reference to 'Marilyn' being a mix of filmic and biographical identity, a product, image, myth. He assumes the guise of one of the most famous film icons and yet reveals it as little but a 'masquerade'. In addition, Morimura references a photo-

[20] MIESSGANG (2006): 125.

graph from the series *Red Velvet Photos* and entitles it as *Red Marilyn*, in spite of the fact that the model's name at that time was not yet 'Marilyn'. As such, a shift of time and reality is manifested in the artwork, stressing the artificiality of 'Marilyn' even more.

A 'star' is always a mystical being and linked to the spectator's dreams of a better world. Thus, the way Morimura displays the photographs of himself as 'Marilyn' on scaffolding above the spectator seems altogether more plausible; the contrast of the spectator's perspective looking upwards and the photographer's viewpoint looking downwards is closely associated with the idea of 'Marilyn' being a product of consumption. While the film industry has the power to decide on 'Marilyn' from above, the viewer's perspective is from below, where she can only be adored as a 'star' in the 'Hollywood-sky'.

The dark side of being a film star is emphasised in the exhibition room by the flashing lights and the torn wallpaper; the dark and shabby surroundings can be interpreted as a manifestation of transience. Marilyn's stardom is highlighted by the flashing lights only to fade into darkness soon after.

In light of these considerations, *Red Marilyn* draws attention to 'Marilyn' from two perspectives. First, she is a most popular, yet mortal film icon, artificially created by the dream factory Hollywood and the media. Second, she is recognised as a 'star' and consumed by a large audience on a global scale.

1.6.3 *Red Marilyn* in its Contemporary Art Photography Context

In the context of art in the 1990s, a comparison of *Red Marilyn* with Zoe Leonard's large-sized cibachrome photograph *Pin-up #1 (Jennifer Miller does Marilyn Monroe)* (1995) is of particular note, as Leonard also references *Red Velvet, Pose #1* (fig. 11).

Both artworks are similar in using a large-sized colour photograph as their medium. However, in contrast to *Red Marilyn*, *Pin-up #1* does not show the artist, Zoe Leonard, but another person; thus, it is not a 'self-portrait'. In addition, both works have in common that they play with gender categories. Similar to Morimura's twisted posture in *Red Marilyn*, the pose of Jennifer Miller is associated with the effeminate. Yet, her body does not suit the codes of pin-up-models: her 'beefy' body is hairy, she has a beard and she grins unashamedly into the camera. As such, *Pin-up #1* is a provocative parody, reminiscent of Judith Butler's call to destroy the confines of gender by way of exaggeration. Leonard's work seems to condemn the aesthetic of the photograph that it is based on. In contrast, *Red Marilyn* rather adopts its colourful and glossy qualities. It draws attention to the artificiality of the icon 'Marilyn' and yet, at the same time, also reflects the popular power of the Hollywood aesthetic and perhaps also Morimura's own fascination with it.

The two artist's similar and yet contrasting views on 'Marilyn' would be an interesting topic of further analysis; however, this is beyond the scope of my study.

Part 3 will return to *Red Marilyn* by examining Morimura's nakedness and his posture in an art historical context (2.2). Furthermore, 5.4 of the third chapter will raise questions on the gender which is/are represented in the image.

2. Yamanaka Manabu's *Arakan #1* and *Gyahtei #17*

2.1 The Work of Yamanaka Manabu (∗1959 in Hyogo, lives and works in Tokyo)

After graduating from Ôsaka Shiritsu Kôgei Kôtô Gakkô (Osaka City Kogei Highschool), Yamanaka worked as a fashion photographer's assistant in Osaka. He then moved to Tokyo and started to shoot photographs for advertisements. While making a living through these jobs, he has created his photographic series.

In his first series, *Arakan* (1983–1988), Yamanaka took photographs of homeless people living on the streets of Japan. The following, *Fujohkan* (1988–1991), depicts a range of animal cadavers. In *Gyahtei* (1993–1998), Yamanaka portrayed naked women aged between ninety and one hundred. In *Dohshi* (1998–1999), Yamanaka developed the theme of poverty by showing soiled naked children, living in refugee camps in the Philippines. The latest series, *Jyoudo* (2001–2002) is concerned with deformed human bodies. All series consist of large-sized analogue photographs in black and white; Yamanaka has stated that he prefers 'orthodox photography'.

The series' titles, such as *Arakan* (the 'worthy one'), *Gyahtei* ('going beyond') and *Dohshi* ('purity'), are terms which are not used in everyday Japanese but are reserved for Buddhist terminology. In exhibitions, the photographs are presented with these Buddhist titles and short Buddhist comments.

Since his first solo exhibition of the *Arakan* series at the Yûrakuchô Asahi Gallery in Tokyo in 1989, Yamanaka's work has been displayed in 'Western' galleries and art museums.[21] In 2001, the Museum Morsbroich (Germany) fea-

21 For example, Yamanaka's work was featured at the Fruitmarket Gallery in Edinburgh in 1994, at the Waschhaus Potsdam in 2000 and the Wood Street Gallery in Pittsburgh in 2001. Starting in 1997, Yamanaka has consistently exhibited his work at the Stefan Stux Gallery in New York. He has participated in numerous group exhibitions in art museums, such as *The*

tured his photographs in a solo exhibition titled *Menschenbilder* (Human Images). This title seems appropriate for Yamanaka's work in general since most of his photographs show humans. The full-body portraits focus on 'social outcasts', such as the homeless or the aged; they are individually positioned in front of a neutral background of either white or grey.

The photographic process mostly involves spending a large amount of time with the photographic subjects before they allow Yamanaka to take a photograph; Yamanaka has explained that it takes several years to complete a series. Hence, the final photograph could be seen as the result of a lengthy approaching process between the photographer and his motif.

The following paragraphs are concerned with two series. The *Arakan* series deals with homeless people who are likened to Buddhist disciples. The *Gyahtei* series is concerned with the bodies of old women who appear to be captured just before their death.

2.2 The *Arakan* Series

The *Arakan* series consists of sixteen black and white analogue photographs, taken between the years 1983 and 1988. The larger-than-life full-body portraits show unkempt homeless individuals in Japan. All photographs have an edition of six.

Apart from *Arakan #14*, all artworks feature a man. With regard to the production process, Yamanaka has explained in my interview that he went to urban areas where homeless people search for food in the early morning before the refuse collection service takes away the garbage. He had to spend a large amount of time with the homeless people until they let him take one or two photographs. The photographs were taken in various areas in Tokyo, including the Ginza and Shinjuku, and in Osaka, such as Tennôji, Umeda and Namba. However, the individuals are all positioned in front of neutral walls which could be anywhere. Hence, the images do not provide any information about the urban surrounding. The artworks are numbered; no information about the homeless people's names, age or their family background is given.

The vertical size of the photographs and the fact that they are mounted on wooden panels is reminiscent of traditional Japanese Buddhist paintings; I will return to this, as well as to the title *Arakan* in the sixth section of Part 3. The following section will examine *Arakan #1* in further detail.

Desire and the Void. Art and Photography in Japan in the Kunsthalle Vienna in 1997, *In Visible Light: Photography and Classification in Art* at the Oxford Museum of Modern Art in 1997, *The Time of Our Lives* at the Museum of Contemporary Art in New York in 1999, and *Skin Talk* at the Musée de la Civilisation in Québec in 2003.

2.3 *Arakan #1* (1983–1989)
(Gelatin Silver Print on Wooden Panel) (180 x 90cm) (Edition of six) (Fig. 12)

2.3.1 Description and Formal Analysis

Arakan #1 is a full-body portrait of a slim middle-aged man, standing barefoot in front of a white wall. Over a soiled shirt and tattered shorts, he is wearing a large, dirty blanket on his shoulders, reaching down to the ground. His shorts are torn at the front so that parts of his pubic area are slightly visible. His dark hair is matted to 'dread locks', hanging down to his stomach. His mouth is mostly concealed by his long, grey beard. The photograph is sharply focused so that every small detail, such as the hair on the man's legs, can be seen clearly.

By positioning the man in the vertical middle and leaving no space at the top or bottom of the photograph, Yamanaka emphasises him as the main (and only) photographic subject. Light shines on the man's face, highlighting the contrast between his face and dark hair as well as his garments. The darkness of the clothes, splattered with dirt, also contrasts sharply with the lightness of the wall; the man's figure can be differentiated from the background by sharp contour lines. Together with the horizontal base of the ground, the body contours form a soft triangle, suggesting stability and creating a harmonic composition. Furthermore, Yamanaka's photographic gaze on the man comes from a slightly inferior position; as a result, the homeless man exudes a dignified and elevated impression.

The subject stands with his legs apart and his left leg is positioned slightly in front of the right. Clasping his hands in front of his stomach, he seems not to know what to do with them. He is bending forward a little and tilting his head to his right side. The clasping of his hands and the posture of his head make him appear somewhat insecure. Looking directly and intensely at the photographic lens, however, he seems not only aware of himself being photographed but also self-conscious and confident enough to return the viewer's gaze. He is knitting his brows, creating a thoughtful and earnest expression on his wrinkled and yet well-proportioned face. He seems aware of his soiled clothes and his exposed pubic area, but more indifferent than ashamed.

The man is wearing his own clothes and is photographed as a homeless man in a Japanese city. However, he is positioned in front of a neutral background and staring intensely into the camera lens. Hence, the photograph displays a melange of documentary street photography and artificial portrait photography, which is typical of Yamanaka's series in general.

The black and white aesthetic creates a tranquil and artificial, rather than realistic or shocking atmosphere. In Susan Sontag's words, the black and white makes the image 'more tactful, more decorous ... less voyeuristic ... or crudely lifelike than in colour'.[22] This aesthetic and the presentation of the man in front of a neutral background evoke a sense of universality. There are no details giving information about the man's identity, his geographical background or the time when the photograph was taken.

Light illuminates the man's face, emphasising its symmetrical features and earnest, wise expression. It seems as if the man's hard life has been recorded into every wrinkle of his face and every tear and stain on his clothes. His long blanket, beard, wrinkled face and earnest intense look evoke a timeless sense of sageness.

In light of these considerations, *Arakan #1* does not focus on a homeless individual but rather presents the viewer with a sage-like man who appears to have gained 'wisdom' by experiencing a hard life.

2.3.2 *Arakan #1* in its Contemporary Art Photography Context

The melange of documentary street photography and artificial portrait photography in *Arakan #1*, as well as the motif of a homeless person in a large city, is comparable to Andres Serrano's photographic series *The Nomads* (1990). This series consists of half-body portraits of the homeless in New York, taken in an improvised studio in the subway. Like Yamanaka, Serrano elevates the social status of his subjects by showing them in large-sized photographs with artificially bright illumination, posing them almost 'majestically'. However, the colour photographs were taken inside, they feature mostly Black men and, as the title as well as the subway studio suggest, the photographed objects are viewed as 'nomads' rather than sages.

Luc Delahaye's series *Portraits/1* (1996) is also comparable to the *Arakan* series. The series consists of ten large-sized black and white portraits of homeless people in Paris. In contrast to Yamanaka, Delahaye randomly asked homeless people to have their photograph taken alone in a photo booth. Consequently, Delahaye was absent when the photograph was taken – he included a moment of coincidence in the artistic production process. The automatic gaze of the photo booth lens differs to Yamanaka's human gaze in the *Arakan* series. Firstly, the photo booth's close-up perspective, which is associated with passport photographs, contrasts with Yamanaka's more distant viewpoint. Secondly, the anonymous relationship of the homeless Parisians with an automatic lens inside of a booth contrasts with the relationship of Yamanaka and the people who let him finally take a photograph after a lengthy approaching process.

---

22 SONTAG (1979): 28.

A more detailed comparison of Yamanaka's series in Tokyo/Osaka with Serrano's series in New York and Delahaye's series in Paris is, unfortunately, beyond the scope of this thesis.

6.1 in Part 3 will return to *Arakan #1*, examining the motif of a sage-like homeless man in relation to the artwork's title in a Buddhist context.

2.4 The *Gyahtei* Series

The *Gyahtei* series consists of seventeen black and white analogue photographs of naked women of startlingly old age, taken between the years 1993 and 1998. All of the life-sized full-body portraits have an edition of six. Yamanaka took a large number of photographs of both old women and men; however, he chose only seventeen photographs of women for the final series.

The women, who are between ninety and one hundred years old, are positioned in the centre of a continuous white background. All but one photograph show the subject standing frontally. The exception is a low shot of an almost bald woman lying on her right side. Although the photographs are taken at the women's homes, they do not include any visual or textual clues about these. The title does not contain the women's names or any personal information; all photographs are merely numbered.

With regard to the photographic production process, Yamanaka spent time with the photographic objects by working as a volunteer nurse for the elderly. He has explained this as follows: 'two or three times a week I went to old people's homes and took care of their needs. I bathed them, fed them, read to them, and took them to the toilet.' It was only after developing an intimate relationship with the old people and their families, that Yamanaka took the photographs. When the old women/men were at home without their families, Yamanaka would tell an assistant to come over and prepare a 'studio' with a white paper background. Yamanaka would first bathe the woman/man and then tell her/him that the photographs were necessary for their medical records. He would then ask her/him to stand in front of the white paper and take a few photographs. In this way, the old people did not know that their photographs were taken for artistic purpose and that their bodies would be used as objects of large-sized artworks.

Without a doubt, Yamanaka's act appears condemnable from a moral perspective; the existence of the *Gyahtei* photographs is based on deceit and their exhibition violates the privacy rights of the old women. Especially when considering Japan's tradition of respecting the elderly, which I will return to in 2.3 of Part 3, Yamanaka's behaviour appears impudent: He treats the women's bodies as aesthetic objects without asking the women for their permission. Furthermore, Yamanaka would have had to obtain the approval of each photographed person to avoid an infringement of privacy under the Japanese privacy laws. However, if Yamanaka had told them that their photographs would be exhibited in public, they would most probably not have participated. The old women's ignorance and the long relationship with their nurse Yamanaka have helped to create a specific atmosphere in the photographs, as I will examine in the following section. In addition, Yamanaka has stressed in my interview that he 'genuinely and wholeheartedly cared' for the women and that the photographs are the 'outcome of his love' for them. In other words, he never intended to violate the women's privacy rights. This does not excuse Yamanaka's lie, however, it does explain his actions.

2.5 *Gyahtei #17* (1995)
(Gelatin Silver Print on Wooden Panel) (182 x 92 cm) (edition of six) (Fig. 13)

2.5.1 Description and Formal Analysis

Gyahtei #17 is a full-body 'portrait' of a thin old woman, standing naked in front of a blank, white background. She is positioned in the horizontal middle of the photograph, and there is almost no space at the top and bottom.

Similar to *Arakan #1*, the black and white aesthetic, the positioning of the woman in front of a neutral background and, additionally, her nakedness convey a sense of timelessness. There are no details defining the woman as an individual person; the viewer does not know her name, family background, or past.

The woman's white hair seems to be bound together in a knot at the back, however some strands have escaped, flying in the air. Her unsymmetrical and haggard face is full of wrinkles, under her eyes there are tear sacs, and next to her nose there is a spot, which could either be dirt or a big mole. As her breasts are hanging, the stomach is covered with wrinkles and layers of skin, hanging down and hiding her belly button. The pubic area appears to be hairless, its skin is sagging and hanging.

The woman is pressing her lips together as if she is concentrating on the photograph being taken. Slightly crouching, she is standing with her knees close together, her shoulders hanging down and her big toes bent. Her hands are softly holding on to her slim thighs and it seems as if she does not know where to put them. This posture makes her look fragile, shy and ashamed of her nakedness. Her eyes are asymmetrical with drooping eyelids creating a tired expression on her face. However, looking at the photographic lens, she seems to trust the photographer and is aware and confident enough to return the viewer's gaze.

Raking artificial light illuminates her face and breasts, emphasising the uneven body terrain, covered with an almost infinite number of very fine wrinkles. This light, the blank background, the black and white and the large size of the photograph highlight the woman's skin and body as the main motif of the artwork. Moreover, this aesthetic conveys a sense of stylisation: although the woman is naked and exposed, the photographic lens does not focus on her nakedness in a voyeuristic way, but rather studies every detail of her old body's wrinkle-pattern. Hence, I agree with Anna Hammond, who has compared the women's skin in the *Gyahtei* series with paintings from the past; the skin is 'as draped as the fabric in a Byzantine painting'.[23] In other words, the women's wrinkled skin is viewed from an aesthetic, almost abstract viewpoint.

Nevertheless, the viewer is directly confronted with the woman's gaze and her life-sized naked body. Michael Amy has described the viewer's reaction as 'empathy, both for these fragile subjects and, ultimately, for ourselves'.[24] The photographs show how 'age obliterates', and Yamanaka challenges the viewer with it in a 'grim, startling and unsentimental way'.[25] I would agree with Amy in that the viewer is confronted with age in a rather 'unsentimental way' – the woman's anonymity, the neutral background and the artificial lightening result in an aesthetic which focuses solely the aged body. The women's bodies are 'unsentimentally' reminiscent of the viewers' own destiny of ageing and dying. The haggard woman in *Gyahtei #17* literally embodies the decay of life; like a withered fruit almost all the elasticity and juice from her body is gone.

2.5.2 *Gyahtei #17* in its Contemporary Art Photography Context

Andres Serrano's large-sized photograph *The Model* (1994) features a naked old woman, smoking a cigarette. Comparing and contrasting the two seemingly alike images *Gyahtei #17* and *The Model* (1994) reveals important differences.

Gyahtei #17 and *The Model* both show an old naked woman in a large sized photograph; the aged female body is the main focus of both images. However, there are three main differences between the two works. Firstly, the women present themselves differently: The old woman in *Gyahtei #17* appears, as described in the previous section, fragile and shy, timidly looking back at the viewer. In contrast, the woman in *The Model* does not look at the viewer but

---

23 HAMMOND (2001): unnumbered.
24 AMY (2000): unnumbered.
25 IBID: unnumbered.

poses deliberately as if she were lost in thought. Holding a cigarette in her left hand and leaning on a walking stick with her right, she appears aware of her posture; as the title states, she is a model. Her self-conscious pose and calm facial expression suggest that she is at ease with her nakedness. In short, *Gyahtei #17* exhibits an old woman in order to present the aesthetic of her body, whereas *The Model* features an old woman's self-exposure.

Secondly, the two images show the female body in different contexts. Simply put, the black and white photograph *Gyahtei #17* merely focuses on the naked female body; the background is white, the viewer does not know anything about the woman. As the title corroborates, Yamanaka uses the woman as a Buddhist symbol of ageing and dying – I will explain this in 2.3 of Part 3. In contrast, Serrano deconstructs the tradition of the female nude in Western visual culture, by presenting an *old* woman as 'the model'. Furthermore, he includes a blurred background, in which a naked young woman appears to be lying on a bed. The colour photograph presents a situation: the people's nakedness, the bed and the cigarette all become parts of a narration, stereotypically either suggesting a 'shooting' with 'models' posing for photographs, or sexual intercourse between the two women. At first sight, both the self-confident, naked pose and the sexual association contrast with the main subject's old body. However, the photograph then reveals how these contrasts are socially constructed: female attractiveness and sexuality have generally been equated with youth, especially in popular media images. Serrano uses the old woman to attack the cliché of the young female model and the intertwined tradition of the nude in 'Western' visual culture, which I will explore in 2.1 of Part 3.

Thirdly, the difference of the two referenced contexts, namely Buddhist culture and the 'Western' tradition of the nude, results in contrasting symbols: The fragile, old body in *Gyahtei #17* personifies decay and death, whereas the old body in *The Model*, strong enough to strike a pose, represents sexuality and thus life.

There have been photographic series focussing on old people shortly before their death, such as Richard Avedon's portraits of his father, *Jacob Israel Avedon* (1973), or Enari Tsuneo's series *One Hundred Year Old People* (1980). Like Yamanaka's *Gyahtei* series, both feature old wrinkled faces in black and white. However, in contrast to the *Gyahtei* series, these are portrait series and do not show naked bodies.

Ishiuchi Miyako's series *Mother's* (2005) includes large-size photographs of her old mother's body. The focus on wrinkled skin in black and white results in a comparable 'stylised' aesthetic. However, unlike the *Gyahtei* series, the photographs are close-ups and never show the complete body.

In conclusion, there is no photographic series of naked aged women in 'Western' or Japanese art history similar to the *Gyahtei* series. In my interview,

Nanjô Fumio has emphasised that he considers the series as art historically relevant and would have liked to send it to the Singapore Biennial to represent Japan in 2008. However, due to censorship in both Japan and Singapore, he changed his mind (see Part 1).

Part 3 will return to the old female body in *Gyahtei #17* by comparing and contrasting its nakedness with images of 'Western' and Japanese art history. In the religious context of the sixth section of Part 3, the series' title *Gyahtei* and its Buddhist meaning will also be analysed further.

3. Mori Mariko's *Tea Ceremony III* and *Pure Land*

3.1 The Work of Mori Mariko (∗1967 in Tokyo, lives and works in New York and Tokyo)

Mori worked as a fashion model and designer before graduating from the Bunka Fukusô Gakuin (Bunka Fashion College) in Tokyo in 1988. In the same year she moved to London, to first attend the Byam Shaw School of Art and then the Chelsea College of Art and Design. Since embarking on a Study Program at the Whitney Museum of American Art from 1992 to 1993, Mori has lived and worked mostly in New York.

In the mid-nineties, Mori attracted attention in the art world with large-format colour photographs featuring herself. In these, she appears in different fantastic costumes, including a cyborg costume in *Subway* (1994) and that of a computer game heroine in *Warrior* (1994). The 'surreal' scenarios are mostly set in central districts of Tokyo, such as Akihabara or Shinjuku. There is no interaction between Mori and the other people in the scene. Mori appears as if she were from another world and time. In Norman Bryson's words, she seems like a 'creature from the [contemporary] image-stream suddenly manifesting in the real world'.[26]

Mori's photograph *Pure Land* (1996–1998) and its video counterpart *Nirvana* (1997) reflect a shift in her work towards more spiritual themes. In using traditional symbols of Buddhism, Shintoism, and East Asian mythology in a colourful pop style, she has cast herself as goddesses, shamans and futuristic priests.

Mori's body of artwork also consists of 3D-videos, drawings, glass sculptures and installations with fibre-optic devices. Her colossal installations in-

[26] BRYSON (1998): 77.

clude the interactive *Dream Temple* (1999), which was produced with the support of Sony Corporation, computer specialists and sound technicians.[27]

Since the early 1990s, Mori has not only participated in group exhibitions[28] but has also had solo exhibitions in galleries and museums worldwide.[29] She was awarded with *Special Mentions* at the Venice Biennale in 1997. Mori's work can be found in various private and public collections.[30]

Her 1990s photographs with their colourful style and figures which appear to have derived from the world of popular culture, could be deemed as being connected to a Pop Art tradition; art critics have repeatedly compared Mori's work to Pop Art.[31] Indeed, similar to Andy Warhol's art, some of Mori's photographs adopt popular culture on a superficial level, however, when closely scrutinised, they can be interpreted as critical. Norman Bryson has written that Mori's photographs can be perceived as socio-critical.[32] I agree with Bryson: as I will argue in 5.1 of Part 3, Mori offers a critique of the female images that she embodies and their social contexts through means of exaggeration and contrast.

A differentiation between Mori's early photographs of herself as a fantastic character in Tokyo and her later photographs as religious figures in a 'poppy'

---

27 Mori's installations have enormous production values and might be debatable in their dependence on cutting edge technology. As the artist Dave Beech warned, some of the high tech works could possibly 'comprise an enviable trade show stand...[but] it can be difficult to see the art when the technology is as impressive as this.' BEECH (1998): 35.

28 Group exhibitions featuring Mori's work include *Guys and Dolls* at the Postmasters Gallery in New York in 1995, *Cities On the Move* at the Wiener Secession in Vienna in 1996, *The Desire and Void* at the Kunsthalle Vienna in 1997, *Span* at the Shanghai Museum in 1998, *Apocalypse: Beauty and Horror in Contemporary Art* at the Royal Academy of Arts in London in 2000, *Au-delà du Spectacle* at the Centre Georges Pompidou in Paris in 2000 and 2001, *My Reality* at the Brooklyn Museum of Art in New York in 2001, *Monument to Now* at the DESTE Foundation for Contemporary Art in Athens in 2004, and the Venice Biennale in 2005.

29 Mori's solo exhibitions include *Close-up* at the Project Room in New York in 1993, *MADE IN JAPAN* at the Shiseido Gallery in Tokyo in 1995, *Mirage* at the Galerie Emmanuel Perrotin in Paris in 1996, *Play with Me* at the Dallas Museum of Art in 1997 and *Mariko Mori* at the Museum of Contemporary Art in Chicago in 1998. In the exhibition *Esoteric Cosmos* in 1999, the Kunstmuseum Wolfsburg presented Mori's photographs, videos, and the *Body Capsule* that Mori used for performances. The *Dream Temple* was presented at the Prada Foundation in Milan in 1999 and at the Rooseum Center for Contemporary Art in Malmo in 2000. In 2002 the Museum of Contemporary Art in Tokyo dedicated the solo exhibition *Pure Land* to Mori's works. In 2003, her exhibition *Wave UFO* was shown in the Kunsthaus Bregenz (Austria) and the Public Art Fund in New York.

30 Mori's works is featured in the collection of the Museum of Contemporary Art in Chicago, the Shiseido Co. Ltd in Tokyo and the French National Collection of Contemporary Art etc.

31 MOLON (1999): 20; KING (1998): 33; BLAIR (1996): 132; Mori herself stresses that Warhol had a great influence on her work: 'we're all children of Andy Warhol' as cited by KING (1998): 34.

32 BRYSON (1998): 80.

spiritual atmosphere should be noted. The following paragraphs are concerned with one photograph of each phase. *Tea Ceremony III* (1994) is an example of Mori's early photographs, and *Pure Land* (1996–1998) represents her later photographs referring to spirituality and religion.

3.2 The *Tea Ceremony* Series (1994–1996)

The *Tea Ceremony* series consists of three large-sized colour photographs; they have never been exhibited together. All photographs are unframed and mounted on wood and aluminium. They are presented behind glass. In *Tea Ceremony I* Mori stands next to four businessmen who sit around a table in an office. In both *Tea Ceremony II* and *Tea Ceremony III* she is outside, in the city of Tokyo. Her clothes and the tray with teacups are similar in all works.

As Mori has stated, *Tea Ceremony II* and *III* were based on a 'guerrilla-like performance' with Mori serving tea to random strangers on the street.[33] However, the following section will focus on *Tea Ceremony III* as an individual artwork – the performative background will only be considered when it is relevant for the photograph's aesthetic impression.

3.3 *Tea Ceremony III* (1994)
(Cibachrome Print) (122 x 153 x 6 cm)
(Edition of four and one artist's print) (Fig. 15)

3.3.1 Description and Formal Analysis

Tea Ceremony III features Mori serving tea in front of a modern glass building in an urban environment. She is standing in the right foreground with a small tray in her left hand and a teacup in her right. Mori wears a white blouse, a blue vest, and a blue short skirt; under these clothes, she wears a shiny silver costume which tightly wraps her body like a second skin. This costume also includes a skin-tight cap on which two outward protruding ears are attached. In the right background, there is another grey building on which a sign is attached saying Tôkyô Môdo Gakuen (Tokyo Fashion School). On the left hand side, two middle-aged men in grey suits are walking to the left, as if leaving the scene. Although they are close to Mori, they do not seem to notice her and face the opposite direction. It seems that they have just passed her by. Behind Mori, there is another young woman who also does not look at her, and walks in the

[33] MORI, Mariko, e-mail conversation with the author, 14. 09. 2009. All subsequent quotes by Mori in this chapter are from this interview, unless otherwise stated in the footnote.

same direction as the men. In the background two other men and a woman are walking into the opposite direction as Mori, turning their backs on the camera.

With regard to the composition, there is a striking dynamic to the left. The contours of the glass building, the direction which the men are headed towards, the woman behind Mori, and Mori's gaze to the left, all emphasise a motion to the left-hand side of the photograph. The six men and women together form a line leading to the left side of the photograph. Mori positions herself in the right foreground, outside this dynamic which moves left.

The colours convey the major role of Mori in the scene. In comparison to the dull colours of the pedestrian's clothes, Mori's blouse shines in a snow-white tone. This contrasts with the dark luscious blue of the vest and the skirt. The strong red of her lips and fingernails also stand out against the light hues of the white blouse, the silver costume and the white teacup. Mori's skin is pale while the faces and hands of the men as well as of the woman behind Mori are darker and more yellow. Thus, the difference between Mori and the other people in the scene could also be reflected in their skin colours. In addition, the contours of the pedestrians, especially of the two men in the foreground, are blurred while Mori's body sharply stands out of the surroundings. This contrast might lead to the assumption that Mori digitally inserted herself into the photograph. However, Mori has stated that the photograph is not digitally altered but based on a real performance. Nevertheless, the disparity of the photographic sharpness highlights the tea-serving woman as the main photographic object. Altogether, the contrasting vivid colours and sharpness make her eye-catching.

Mori's body language and her gaze suggest that she is focussing on some point outside of the photographed scene. Her head is slightly bent to her left and the upper part of her body is bent forward. She smiles and appears to be addressing someone outside the photograph by offering tea. Mori's legs are rigidly parallel; her bearing gives the impression that she is keeping her body stiff and taking the tea offering seriously. The combination of her slight bending, smile, and stretched legs results in a pose that expresses respect, courtesy, and subordination towards the person she offers the tea to.

3.3.2 Tea Ceremony or Tea Serving?

The tea ceremony in Japan has had a longstanding tradition. The custom of tea drinking was introduced to Japan in the 9th century; however, it was in the 12th century that a new form of powdered green tea and the ritualised style of its preparation were brought to Japan, developing into the art of the tea ceremony. Since the 16th century, especially under the influence of the monk Sen no Rikyû (1522–1591), tea drinking has spread to all levels of society. In the 20th century, tea ceremony has become a popular hobby amongst Japanese women; there are tea clubs at high schools, colleges, universities, as well as local chapters of established tea schools.

At its most basic, a tea ceremony involves the calm preparation and serving of a bowl of green tea to one or more guests, performing prescribed rituals. In each school, there are several variations of the method of preparing and drinking the tea, the types and forms of utensils, as well as the type of tea used. The host of a tea ceremony usually wears a *kimono* and guests are also expected to wear a *kimono* or formal wear. An explanation of tea supplies and the various styles of tea ceremonies is beyond the scope of this thesis, however, it is essential to reiterate that tea ceremony in Japan is an art form, consisting of strictly defined rules and rituals.

Tea Ceremony III does not show a traditional tea ceremony but a young woman who is serving tea. Gijs van Tuyl has written in an exhibition catalogue that in *Tea Ceremony III*, the ancient ritual of the Japanese tea ceremony encounters the ultramodern business world.[34] Karin Higa has described 'Moris's tea ceremony' as unusual since the 'participants' are not in a 'traditional *tatami* room with *tokonoma* and Japanese art' but 'casually stroll by'.[35] However, I would like to consider the fact that without the title, the viewer would not be able to establish any connection to the rituals involved in a 'tea ceremony': Mori is standing and serving tea from teacups; she looks more like a waitress than a tea master. While tea ceremonies are rituals which are at least one or two hours long, the people in the photograph seem to be in a hurry, ignoring Mori's offer.

The act of tea serving is not the same as a tea ceremony. For this reason, the title *Tea Ceremony* could suggest that Mori is playing with the 'Western' viewer's expectations and clichés. The photograph does not possess a Japanese title, addressing an international (mainly 'Western') public. As part of Zen culture, the Japanese tradition of the tea ceremony is known to 'the West'. Although tea serving in Japan is not associated with a traditional tea ceremony, 'Western' viewers could link it to ceremonies or even see them as one of the same. As such, the artwork's title *Tea Ceremony* ironically illustrates a 'Western' cliché of Japan.

Moreover, Mori's respectful pose could be linked to regulatory norms for women in the Japanese business sector. Women working in Japanese companies are subjected to behavioural norms: they have to observe certain codes of conduct in certain situations, for example when serving tea or coffee. This regulation of manners, which is comparable to the stringent rules in tea ceremonies, could possibly be another reason as to why Mori titles her photograph

34 VAN TUYL (1997): 11.
35 HIGA (1996): 7.

'*Tea Ceremony*'. This idea will be examined further in the context of 'social codes' in the fourth section of Part 3, while the fifth section will view Mori's appearance and pose from a gender perspective.

3.4 *Pure Land* (1996–1998)
(Glass with photo interlayer) (305 x 610 x 2.2 cm)
(Edition of three and one artist's print) (Fig. 16)

Pure Land is the photographic counterpart of the 3D Video Installation *Nirvana* (1997); Mori is wearing the same costume and the surrounding is also similar. In the video, she appears to be flying around in a cosmic landscape, surrounded by little musicians who are computer-generated. She is humming and whispering echoed rhymes as if meditating. The video was exhibited at the Nordic Pavilion of the Venice Biennale, which awarded Mori with *Special Mentions*. Only a group of twenty people was permitted to view the seven minutes video at a time. Also, 3D glasses were required. At the end of the video, a fan came on and blew cool, scented air into the audience's faces. The 3D presentation and the air at the end of the screening, reflect the entertaining aspect of Mori's work. The reduction of the group emphasises the artwork's somewhat meditative character, which is also a relevant characteristic of *Pure Land.*

3.4.1 Description and Formal Analysis

In *Pure Land*, Mori is 'flying' between six computer-generated figures over a huge lotus blossom and a light pink lake with small islands. The little figures play different musical instruments, and sit on blue bubble-clouds, which seem to be floating in the air. They all have big round heads with big eyes and sharp ears, small bodies and are reminiscent of little aliens in a Japanese cartoon or computer game. In the far background the viewer sees a digitally created desert-like landscape. On the right hand side of the background there is an object which resembles a futuristic temple or spacecraft but cannot be identified at first sight.

Mori wears a pink *kimono* and a golden headdress decorated with ornaments. Her hair is tied up around her head as if it were part of her headdress. A shawl, attached to her *kimono*, is fluttering over her head, forming a circle around the upper part of her body. Mori faces the viewer with a half smile. As her light blue eyes do not have pupils, her gaze is empty. In her left hand she holds a small transparent gem, whereas her right hand is in a religious-style pose; a circle is made with the forefinger and the thumb while the other three fingers point upward.

The viewer's attention is immediately drawn to Mori in the centre with the musicians evenly placed on both other sides. On either side, a musician is present in the far background, facing her and floating in mid-air. Two more musicians, on either side, are situated in the middle of the photograph, and the pair nearest to the viewer is moving away from her. This composition creates a sense of harmony.

With the wide size of the photograph (six metres), the line of the ground in the far distance, and the islands, horizontal lines dominate, which suggest a sense of tranquillity. However, the circle formed by Mori's shawl, her body, the musicians, the bubble-clouds, and the lotus blossom balance these horizontal lines, emphasising the harmony of the whole scene. The circular lines and organic forms also convey a sense of motion. This is intensified by the swing of Mori's *kimono* and her shawl; she seems to be floating in air. The two musicians in the foreground are both blurred, which makes them appear as if they are moving quickly towards us.

The large island in the foreground is cropped at the bottom of the photograph, and seems to continue outside the camera's field of view. Hence the viewer gets the feeling of standing inside the scene with Mori flying slightly above him.

The dominant colour of the photograph is a light shade of pink. Not only Mori's robe and shawl, but also the landscape is bathed in pink tones. The musicians are pastel-coloured, blending into the scene. The lotus bloom and the object in the right far distance are both designed in mainly pink and orange colours. The sky and water smoothly illuminate the scenario with the water under Mori being the most luminous part of the photograph. The use of gentle gradations, the light and the soft pastel-colours unify Mori, the musicians, and the landscape.

The round and organic forms (such as Mori's body, the little musicians, bubble-clouds, lotus flower, and islands) convey a sense of naturalness. However, Mori's light blue eyes without pupils and the alien-musicians' eyes without an iris appear 'unreal'; the pink landscape, Mori's dress, and the computer-generated figures suggest a sense of otherworldliness. Even though Mori looks more 'real' in the photograph than the objects and the landscape created on the computer, she blends into the scene. Her pink dress mirrors the colours of her surroundings and her vacant gaze makes her appear as far from our world as the alien-like musicians.

The sense of otherworldliness is linked to the title *Pure Land*. Its meaning, the artwork's complex iconography and the relationship of its cartoon-like aesthetic with its motifs will all be analysed in 6.2 of the third chapter, when focussing on the 'body' in relation to religion.

4. Ishiuchi Miyako's *SCAR 1983 illness* and *Chromosome XY s. o.*

4.1 The Work of Ishiuchi Miyako (∗1947, born in Nittamachi,[36] lives and works in Tokyo)

Ishiuchi began studying design at the Tama Bijutsu Daigaku (Tama Art University) in 1966. She soon changed to the weaving class and eventually, after four years, stopped going to university.

Ishiuchi had regularly attended photography exhibitions and in 1977, this influenced her to start photography. The 30-year-old woman borrowed a friend's photographic equipment and revisited Yokosuka, where she had grown up, taking photographs with a handheld camera. The town was a major U.S. Navy base, thus it was influenced by the presence of American soldiers. Ishiuchi mainly took photographs of places where this American presence was prominent, such as the harbour with US battleships and the red light district. In the same year, she exhibited the images in the *Yokosuka Story* series.

According to Ishiuchi, she had never thought of becoming a professional photographer and held an office job until 1995. In the 1980s and 1990s she was offered commercial photography jobs, for example with the fashion label Comme des Garçons in 1993. 'Commercial photography didn't suit me,' she explained in my interview, 'I even thought about completely quitting photography'. As a result, there is a gap in Ishiuchi's artistic career in the 1980s. The next photographic series, *1·9·4·7* (1989), features close-up photographs of hands and feet of women who were born in 1947.

At the end of the 1990s, Kasahara Michiko suggested that Ishiuchi's oeuvre could be divided into two major phases; the first consisting of *Yokosuka Story* (1977), *APARTMENT* (1978), and *Endless Night* (1981) and the second being her photographs of the human form, starting with the series *1·9·4·7* (1989).[37] The series *Mother's* (2005) and *Hiroshima* (2008), which were created after Kasahara's statement and which focus on the possessions of the deceased, suggest that a third phase has started.

The first phase features old building 'surfaces', jerry-built apartments and rooms of former nightclubs. The black and white pictures were taken with a handheld camera and shot with 35mm film. The subjects, such as a former brothel (*Endless Night*), reflect sensitive post-war issues. Ishiuchi's later vol-

---

[36] The district Nitta became part of the city of Ota in 2005.

[37] KASAHARA (1999): 307–308.

umes of photographs titled *Yokosuka Again (1980–1990)* and *Endless Night 2001* feature more recent works that could be seen as a reconsideration of the work of this 'first phase'.

After *1·9·4·7*, Ishiuchi photographed the body of the female poet Ito Hiromi, assorting the images in a series titled *Hands, Feet, Flesh, and Body: Hiromi 1955* (1995). *1906 to the skin* (1994) again focuses on a body, namely of the male Butoh dancer Ono Kazuo.[38] The following series *Chromosome XY* (1995) are portraits of men and close-up photographs of their physique; *SCARS* (1992–ungoing) features different people's scars. In this way, the second phase focuses on the human body, revealing skin textures in extreme detail. Again, all photographs are in black and white.

The series *Mother's* (2005) combines elements of the first and second phase. It consists of large black and white as well as colour photographs of Ishiuchi's deceased mother's possessions, such as her underwear, shoes and lipsticks. Like the buildings and apartment interiors in the first phase, the objects are no longer used. As such, the images evoke a sense of transience. At the same time, the series includes close-up photographs of Ishiuchi's old mother's body, which are comparable to the works of the second phase.

Ishiuchi's latest series, *Hiroshima* (2008), is similar to the *Mother's* series insofar as it features colour photographs of relics of clothing, shoes and other personal possessions which remain from the atomic explosion. Although the photographed items are on display at the Hiroshima Peace Museum, Ishiuchi's photographs do not indicate this in any way; some of the clothing were photographed on light boxes and appear to float in a timeless space.[39]

On the whole it appears that the human body was a relevant motif in Ishiuchi's work especially in the second phase – in the 1990s. The following paragraph is concerned with the series *Chromosome XY* and *SCARS*. Needless to say, this thesis focuses on Japanese photographs of humans in the 1990s; hence, Ishiuchi's work during her first phase, as well as the series *Mother's* or *Hiroshima* will not be examined.

---

[38] Butoh (*butô*) is a dance and performance art which originated after World War II under Hijikata Tatsumi and Ono Kazuo. The genre is hard to define since there are almost as many styles as there are performers. It typically involves unconventional and highly stylised movements, borrowing elements of both 'Western' and Japanese traditional dance forms. It often includes taboo topics and is mostly performed in white body make-up.

[39] For a list of galleries and museums which have featured Ishiuchi's work see footnotes 110, 111 and 113 in Part 1.

4.2 The *Chromosome XY* Series

Seventy-nine black and white photographs from the *Chromosome XY* series were published in the photo book *Sawaru Chromosome XY* (To Touch Chromosome XY) in 1995.[40] Close-up photographs of male bodies are interspersed with facial portraits. Under each portrait the model's name is given, whereas the close-up photographs are merely presented with their initials and a number.

In the *Chromosome XY* exhibition at the Zeit-Foto Salon in 1995 and at the Third Gallery Aya in 1996, eighteen of these close-up photographs were displayed. The large-sized photographs were exhibited in thin dark-grey frames, whereas the smaller ones were exhibited in silver frames with a passepartout. Ishiuchi claimed that she did not wish to exhibit the portraits then.

Most of the series' subjects are Ishiuchi's friends and some are fellow photographers, such as Fukase Masahisa. However, in contrast to the photography book, the prints in the exhibitions are numbered and presented without any names or initials so that the identities of the men are not clear.

4.3 *Chromosome XY s. o.* (1995) (Gelatin Silver Print) (Fig. 17)

4.3.1 Description and Formal Analysis

Chromosome XY s. o. exists in two sizes: 105 x 73 cm (edition of eight) and 50.8 x 61 cm (edition of fifteen). It was not featured in the volume of photographs of 1995 and was not exhibited in the *Chromosome XY* exhibitions. However, it was part of other exhibitions, such as *The Desire and the Void. Contemporary Japanese Photography* in the Kunsthalle Wien in 1997. It is presented in a thin black frame.

The photograph depicts a slim and almost hairless chest and stomach of a man. The smooth skin does not show any wrinkles; the man must be in his twenties or thirties. He is holding his left arm close to his body, while very slightly turning his left side backwards; the right arm cannot be seen in the photograph.

The middle line of the chest is located in the middle of the photographic composition, dividing the image into a lighter and a darker side: whereas the left side of the body is dark, the right side is illuminated with the man's left arm shining white. Light and dark are not strongly contrasting but merging into each other, evoking soft shadows on the 'torso', gently highlighting the slender body's muscles. The contour lines of the body are also not sharp but quietly

40 ISHIUCHI (1995).

merge into the background. The nipples and the oval navel seem to be arranged symmetrically on the body; if they were linked by lines, they would form an inverted triangle. The symmetry implies harmony with the triangle form adding to the lightness of the composition. The close-up perspective, the harmonious composition and the soft contours create an impression of gentle intimacy; the viewer looks tenderly at the slender body of a stranger.

With regard to the photographic viewpoint, the body is photographed face-on, not from any angle. This results in a 'neutral' and 'respectful' gaze insofar as the camera is not 'looking up' or 'looking down' on the naked body's owner. The image shows a male chest, stomach and one arm; the other parts of the body are missing. However, the photographic composition does not seem like an incomplete body image, but rather is a self-contained artwork.

4.3.2 *Chromosome XY s. o.* as a Self-Contained 'Torso' or the Manifestation of *Ma*

The formal analysis made clear that although the photograph only shows parts of the body, it is a self-contained image. As such, *Chromosome XY s. o.* could be seen as somewhat reminiscent of sculptures in 'Western' art history, such as Michelangelo's non-finito or Auguste Rodin's torsi. Like *Chromosome XY s. o.* they can be viewed as body images which 'continue' in the viewer's mind but at the same time exist as autonomous artworks. For example Rodin's famous *Walking Man* (1877–1878) should not be seen as a fragment missing the head and its arms but rather as a self-sufficient artwork. In both Ishiuchi's close-up photographs of the *Chromosome XY* series and Rodin's torso sculptures, body parts can be interpreted as forms existing for their own sake.

In addition, it is a Japanese tradition to show a detail vaguely rather than presenting the whole clearly, leaving the full picture to the viewer's imagination. This concept of the 'in-between' can be linked to the notion of *ma*, which is best described as a consciousness of space or a consciousness of temporal intervals. *Ma* can be found in various contexts of Japanese everyday life and culture, for example in music, architecture or fine art.[41] In music, the term '*ma*' is best translated as a temporal 'in-between' or a 'pause' between sounds; in visual culture, it is a spatial interval, or a 'gap' between forms, for instance the empty spaces in a house or a painting. However, it is not only something that is created by compositional elements but also by the imagination of the audience who experiences these: listening to a piece of music or looking at a work of fine art, the audience experiences how sound and non-sound, or form and non-form

41 For more information on *ma*, see Ingrid Fritsch's essay on the 'in-between' in Japanese culture; FRITSCH (2000).

create an interval. In this sense, the aesthetic of *Chromosome XY s. o.* can be explained as a manifestation of *ma* – created by both the space between the body's details, such as the nipples and the navel, and the space between the pictured details of the body and its totality which can only be imagined by the viewer.

The third chapter will return to *Chromosome XY s. o.*, examining it from two different viewpoints: 2.4 will analyse the naked body and the above mentioned idea of a self-contained body image, whereas 5.3 will interpret its 'masculinity'.

4.4 The *SCARS* Series

The *SCARS* series consists of large black and white close-up images of various scars on different people's bodies. It shows heterogeneity of skin; some skin is wrinkled and old, some is smooth and young. There are both male and female bodies, however, the sex is often unclear, as is the location of the scar on the body.

Twelve images from the series were presented at the Zeit-Foto Salon in 1999. The large images were presented in a dark-grey thin frame, the small ones were in a thin silver frame. Following this, parts of the series were exhibited in group exhibitions as well as in retrospectives featuring Ishiuchi's different series. At the *Kyoto Art Festival* in 1999 and the *History of Japanese Photography* exhibition in 2003, the artworks were presented with titles referring to the date of the event which caused the scar, the year they were photographed, and their general cause, such as an accident or an illness. In other exhibitions, including the *SCARS* exhibition at the Zeit-Foto Salon and the *Time Textured in Monochrome* retrospective at the Tokyo Museum of Modern Art in 1999, the photographs were merely numbered. In 2005, the *SCARS* series was published in a book.[42]

4.5 *SCAR 1983 illness* or *SCARS #36* (1994)
(Gelatin Silver Print) (108 x 74 cm) (edition of ten) (Fig. 18)

4.5.1 Description and Formal Analysis

SCAR 1983 illness exists in three sizes: 150 x 100cm (edition of five), 108 x 74cm (edition of ten) and 28,8 x 42cm (edition of ten). The photograph shows a huge scar on the side of a buttock going down to the thigh; the dusky character

42 ISHIUCHI (2005).

of the close-up makes it difficult to identify clearly its location on the body. The buttock is cropped at the left side so that only about one third of it appears in the photograph, and the thigh is cropped at the bottom so that the leg is not seen. The scar seems to begin at the top left of the photograph and goes down the thigh, continuing outside of the image.

With regard to the forms, the photograph is strongly dominated by curves; not only the contour lines of the bottom and the thigh are curved but also the scar itself. Being in the middle of the image and having a curved shape, the scar takes up a large part of the whole composition. Hence, it is given a special importance and becomes the main focus of the photograph.

From the right side, light is shining on the body so that the lower front part of the thigh on the right is almost completely white, whereas the lower back part is in darkness. The upper part of the scar is dark and has a sharp outline, contrasting with the blurring lightness of its lower part. Even though the strong light evokes black and white contrasts, the soft shadows on the skin, its pores and small wrinkles appear in a grey tone, creating an impression of faintness.

The structure of the skin with its wrinkles and uneven parts seems typical of the skin of a middle-aged adult; however the age or sex of the person who bears the scar and the illness that caused the scar are not clear. Thus, the scar as such is the main focus of the image; the individual person and the circumstances are not important.

On the one hand, the scar as a long curve, continuing outside of the photographic border, is a striking line on the soft skin. On the other hand, the curved form suggests a natural motion in the composition. The scar seems to change constantly from being an interruption in the structure of unblemished skin to a part of the skin pattern itself.

In conclusion, Ishiuchi presents the scar not only as a disruption of the body but also as part of a harmonious composition; skin is used as a surface for a pattern consisting of pores, shadows and a vibrant curve. The overall mood of the image is rather quiet. The viewer is not shocked by the huge scar but looks at it as if it were a dynamic line in an abstract work of art.

4.5.2 Scars, Time and Memory

After a wound has healed, it leaves a scar. The scar continues to alter as new collagen is formed. It might fade, however, there will always be some visible evidence of the injury as hair follicles and sweat glands do not grow back. Scars are, in Christopher Y. Lew's words, 'physical remnants of past events in a person's life.'[43]

---

43 LEW (2005): 54.

Moreover, scars are marks of an accident, illness, surgery or other forms of usually painful crises. Matsuda Rie has emphasised this aspect of pain in the *SCARS* series: 'even after the wound has healed, the pain occasionally recurs. Each time the pain comes back, the person suffering from the scar is reminded of the major incident that caused it.'[44] Despite the argument that this might be true biologically, *SCAR 1983 illness* is composed harmoniously. Gentle light and blurred contours create a calm instead of a sorrowful impression. The scar seems like an inevitable part of a present body, just as memories are inevitable parts of our present. As such, the aspect of pain does not dominate the atmosphere of the image.

Margarett Loke has found a paradox in the *SCARS* series: 'scars – signs of the body's fragility – are paradoxically transformed into marks of endurance and strength.'[45] However, is not this 'paradox' of 'fragility' and 'strength' the main characteristic of scars in general? Scars are always evocative of wounds on the one hand and healing on the other. Scars symbolise pain, disorder and human fragility. At the same time, they result from a biological healing process: the body's *repairing* of a wound. This 'paradoxical' characteristic of scars is well reflected in the aesthetic of *SCAR illness 1983*: On the one hand, the long curved scar is a striking line on the soft skin. On the other hand, the curved form suggests a natural motion in the composition and blends into the pattern of healthy skin. Like memories of a crisis in the past, the scar seems to change constantly from a dissoluting factor to a natural and accepted element in our present life. Hence, as Angela Schneider has written, each scar becomes a Memento Mori but is also reminiscent of the body's overcoming of a threatening event.[46] On the one hand, scars are reminiscent of our ephemerality, on the other hand, they symbolise a triumph over frightening incidents and hence represent life.

The photographs of the 'first phase' of Ishiuchi's œuvre depict scenes on the street or inside buildings, the works of the 'second phase' focus on the human body, and the 'third phase' has concentrated on personal belongings. However, one topic has been consistently relevant in Ishiuchi's work – the phenomenon of time, intertwined with our memory. Ishiuchi's photographs show surfaces, be they of houses, objects or people, representing the effects of time on a universal level. Unlike Ishiuchi's other series, the *SCARS* series focuses on scars; however, it seems like an extension of the main idea embodied in the other series, namely to show the influence of time on anything and any-

---

44 MATSUDA (1999): 100.
45 LOKE (2000).
46 SCHNEIDER (2006): 246.

body. Thus, I agree with Sandra S. Phillip, who has argued that the *SCARS* series could be seen as Ishiuchi's 'consummate work.'[47]

In Part 3, I will return to the time and memory aspect, interpreting the relationship of the motif scar and the photographic medium as a tautology (7.1).

5. Yanagi Miwa's *Elevator Girls 3F*

5.1 The Work of Yanagi Miwa (∗1967 in Kobe, lives and works in Kyoto)

In 1990 Yanagi graduated from the crafts department of the Kyôto Shiritsu Geijutsu Daigaku (Kyoto City University of Arts), where she had been making *kimono* and traditional crafts before shifting focus to fibre installations. Her interest in photography began when photographing her installations.

While making a living through various jobs, Yanagi became interested in the motif of 'elevator girls', young women who operate elevators in Japanese department stores. Before dealing with this topic photographically, Yanagi presented a 'performance' entitled *White Casket* in the year 1993; in the small rental gallery Space Niji in Kyoto, two uniformed models sat in front of an artificial yet real looking elevator door. In front of them, there was a stand with an album with portrait photographs of them, reminiscent of those in *tsurigaki* (matchmaking albums). The models were smiling all the time and neither one was allowed to speak nor move. Hence, Yanagi might be right when stating that *White Casket* was not exactly a 'performance' but more a 'live sculpture'.[48] The next work, *Expo Bunnies* (1994), featured fourteen young women who acted as tour guides at the exhibition *Art Now* in the Hyogo Prefectural Museum of Art. The tour guides, who presented the other art objects of the exhibition, not only had to wear the same uniform but also to speak in the same manner. Following this, Yanagi created a range of digitally altered photographs featuring women as elevator girls. This *Elevator Girls* series (1994–1999) will be discussed later in this chapter.

The following series, *My Grandmothers* (1999–ongoing) consists of photographs depicting young women as they imagined themselves half a century later. The title might be misleading since most of them do not imagine themselves having grandchildren. Yanagi gathered most of the women at her previous art exhibitions and on the Internet, interviewing them about their future visions. With theatrical make-up, costumes and digital manipulation, Yanagi

47 PHILLIPS (2005): 132.
48 As cited in GONZALEZ-FOERSTER, OBRIST and YANAGI (2003): 44.

then transformed the young women into the aged characters they described. There is little trace of families; the women look independent and assertive, for example riding on a motorbike on the Golden Gate Bridge or hugging a female lover after a house party.

Concerning the technique, the large-sized photographs of the *Elevator Girls* and *My Grandmothers* series consist of image compositions generated from photographic registrations of real people with a digital camera, as well as from digitally edited and created components.

The next series, *Fairy Tales* (2004), features black and white photographs referring to various folk tales recorded by the Grimm Brothers and Hans Christian Andersen, as well as to Gabriel Garcia Marquez' short story *The Incredible and Sad Tale of Innocent Erendira and Her Heartless Grandmother* (1972) and to Abe Kôbô's novel *Suna No Onna* (The Woman in the Dunes) (1962). Contrary to the fairy tales, the young girls break away from their passive role: in *Sleeping Beauty* a little girl self-confidently fights against a witch as if to defend herself against a hundred year sleep (fig. 19). Children impersonate not only the girls but also the old women in the photographs. As witches, the girls wear wrinkled silicon masks, their young bodies contrasting with their old faces. For this reason, the viewer is confronted with hybrid identities: the face is that of an 'evil' old woman, the body is that of an 'innocent' young girl. The series ironically comments on fairytale stereotypes of old evil women, who are juxtaposed with innocent girls. Both female clichés are led ad absurdum.

Yanagi has not only created photographic series but also video installations, such as *Kagome Kagome* (1998),[49] featuring young women who transform from nurses in white uniforms into elevator girls and airhostesses. In the video installation *Granddaughters* (2004), old women from various countries sit in front of the camera like television presenters and talk in their own languages about their grandmothers.

Common to all of Yanagi's series is their focus on female subjects. The *Elevator Girls* explores Japanese society's expectations of young women, as I will examine in 5.1 of Part 3. The *My Grandmothers* series deals with women's ageing and future dreams, and the *Fairy Tales* series empowers young female characters of 'Western' fairy tales by depicting them as self-confident, active heroines.

Yanagi made her debut in the 'Western' art world in 1996, when Morimura Yasumasa introduced the *Elevator Girls* series to Peter Weiermair, who was the curator of the exhibition *Prospect '96* at the Schirn Kunsthalle and the Frank-

[49] Although '*kagome*' literally means the mesh of a cage, the repetition '*kagome kagome*' refers to a children's game. One child who is chosen as the demon is blindfolded while the others join hands, chant and walk in circles around him. When the song stops, the demon has to guess who stands behind him.

furter Kunstverein. Since then, Yanagi has participated in international art events and group exhibitions.[50] In the last ten years she also had solo exhibitions in galleries and museums worldwide.[51]

The following paragraphs are concerned with the *Elevator Girls* and one example of the series. The *Grandmothers* and the *Fairy Tales* series will not be analysed since they were not created in the 1990s.

5.2 The *Elevator Girls* Series (1994–1999)

The *Elevator Girls* series consists of twenty-two artworks. The photographs are characterised by their expansive, panoramic format. Face-mounted onto acrylic, giving them a shiny surface, they are presented in darkened spaces with dramatic spotlighting.

Not every individual photograph is titled *Elevator Girls*; rather, they have various titles, such as *Aquajenne in Paradise* (1996) and *Eternal City* (1998). However, after finishing the series, Yanagi titled the entire series *Elevator Girls*. When the works are exhibited in Japan, they are mostly presented as *Annaijô no heya*, which literally means 'the attendant's rooms' or 'the attendants' room'.[52] The term *annaijô* is composed of the characters '*annai*', which could be translated as 'to explain' or 'to show somebody around', and '*jô*', which means 'young lady' or 'miss'.

There are three major differences between the titles *Elevator Girls* and *Annaijô no heya.* Firstly, the latter includes the term *heya* ('room'). By using 'room' as its subject and 'attendants' or 'attendant's' as a pronoun, the title fo-

50 Art events featuring Yanagi include the Taipei Biennial in 1998, the Melbourne International Biennial in 1999, the Yokohama Triennial and the Lyon Biennial in 2001, and the Venice Biennale in 2009. In addition, her work was featured in group exhibitions, such as *The Desire and the Void. Japanese Contemporary Photography* at the Kunsthalle Vienna in 1997, *The History of Japanese Photography* at the Museum of Fine Arts in Houston in 2003 and *Der Kontrakt des Fotografen* [The Photographer's Contract] in the Museum Morsbroich in Leverkusen in 2006.

51 Galleries which have featured Yanagi's work in solo exhibitions are for example the Galerie Almine Rech in Paris in 2000 and 2003, the Shiseido Gallery in Tokyo in 2002, and the Gallery Wohnmaschine in Berlin in 2003 and 2005. The Guggenheim Museum in Berlin featured her work in *Miwa Yanagi – Sammlung Deutsche Bank* in 2004. In the same year, the Marugame Genichiro-Inokuma Museum of Contemporary Art in Kagawa showed her work in an exhibition entitled *Darkness of Girlhood & Lightness of Aging*. The Hara Museum of Contemporary Art in Tokyo presented Yanagi's photographs in the exhibition *The Incredible Tale of the Innocent Old Lady and the Heartless Young Girl* and the Ohara Museum of Art in Okayama had an exhibition with Yanagi's art entitled *Madame Comet* in 2005. The Chelsea Art Museum in New York had an exhibition entitled *Miwa Yanagi* in 2007, as did the Museum of Fine Arts in Houston in 2008.

52 In Japanese it is not clear if the noun is used in the singular or plural form.

cuses on the setting rather than the people. Secondly, the term '*annaijô*' is used in a wider sense than '*erebêtâ gâru*' (elevator girl) and has different connotations. *Annaijô* is a broad term and used for any woman who works in a public institution providing information for customers. When working in department stores, an *annaijô* is referred to as a *depâtomento gâru* (department girl). However, in contrast to *depâtomento gâru*, the term *annaijô* includes the woman's explanatory role; her job of 'showing' something to the customer is denoted in her profession. Thirdly, the Japanese title does not indicate whether it refers to one or many attendants, since singular and plural use the same grammatical form.

The main reason why the English title does not use 'attendant' as an equivalent of *annaijô* might be the fact that the English term can be applied to both men and women. In contrast, the *jô* of *annaijô* would have to be translated as 'miss'. Instead of using a correct yet awkward English translation of *annaijô*, such as 'female attendant', Yanagi chose a title which indirectly also highlights the young age of the women working as department store attendants ('girls').

The photographic series does not only show women inside of elevators but also in various other places inside department stores; the title *Department Girls* would thus have been more accurate. However, *Elevator Girls* is perhaps a more 'catchy' title since neither the profession nor the term exists in Europe or America. In this way, *Elevator Girls* not only focuses on the young female subjects of the photographic series but also catches the 'Western' audience's attention by sounding like an English neologism. A 'Western' viewer might be surprised by the term and wonder what 'elevator girls' are.

5.3 *Elevator Girls 3F* (1998)
(C-Print, Diasec) (Fig. 20)

5.3.1 Description and Formal Analysis

Elevator Girls 3F exists in two different sizes: the large version, 180 x 213 cm, is an edition of five, the small version, 90 x 106.6 cm, is an edition of fifteen. They are presented in a thin black frame.

The photograph shows nine young women standing and sitting on the floor around the back half of an octagonal glass hole. The shiny hole in the brown ground is divided into descending shelves, on which various white women's shoes are aligned.

The women all wear the same uniform: a navy blue short dress and round hat, a white bow tie, white gloves and white shoes. They all have pale-white skin and wear the same bright-pink lipstick. In the background, there are two doors with strongly reflecting oval windows, through which we see light purple flowers on the floor. The doors and the wall between them are painted in a light green-turquoise colour. As a result, the image is dominated by a stark contrast of blue and white in the middle and by a pastel-coloured green-turquoise tone in the background. The outlines of all the photographic objects are crisp and the whole image seems sharp and clear.

Regarding the perspective, two dark pillars and blue shining glass at the front constitute a little less than a quarter of the image on each side. The viewer gets the feeling of standing in front of an elevator, the doors of which are opening or closing in that very moment, so that he can just glimpse the inside. The viewer is in a position where he looks down at the women, who are all slightly smiling and looking into the hole, either not seeing or deliberately ignoring the viewer.

The octagonal hole in exactly the middle of the image is eye-catching and its form is repeated by the contour lines of the ground; the whole elevator seems to be an octagon. There are five girls to the left of the hole's back and four on the right. They do not have any mutual eye contact as they all stare at the hole. One woman on the left side is sitting on the border of the octagon with her legs dangling into the hole, while one on the right side is putting a shoe into the hole as if to replace it on a shelf. This almost equal arrangement of the women evokes a harmonious composition, highlighting the staged character of the scene. In addition, the women's concentration on the hole instead of looking at each other creates a sense of self-containment.

The viewer's perspective and the fact that the women do not return his gaze evoke a barrier between the viewer and the women; they live in a different world. As Rachel Kent put it, there is no visible entry or exit point in all of the *Elevator Girls* photographs; 'they are self-contained environments...'[53] This aspect of an artificial closed environment is emphasised by the many reflective elements in the image. To begin with, the windows of the two doors in the background return bright light as neon lights behind the doors shine through. Furthermore, there are small lamps inserted into the ground shining into the room. The glass octagon in the middle with white shoes also contributes to the lightness of the scene. The white skin and the white parts of the uniform seem to reflect this light. Finally, the parts of the door that can be seen in the front include shiny turquoise-green glass elements. This use of shiny surfaces and bright light evokes a sense of technicality as well as a feeling of otherworldliness. The intense colours of the uniform emphasise this and contrast with the flowers behind the windows in the background. It seems unnatural that there

53 KENT (2002): 51.

are flowers growing behind these windows, hence they do not function as an organic element in the scene but, quite contrarily, underline its artificiality.

The octagonal hole in the middle with its white shoes and the fact that there are young women sitting around it seem artificial. The sharp outlines of the photographic objects, the reflections and the bright colour all seem unreal; the photograph does not conceal the use of computer graphics. As such, the scenario's content as well as its aesthetic create an image showing a strangely 'futuristic' world. Why is there a hole with shelves in the middle of an elevator floor and why are there women all dressed alike gathered around it, staring at the shoes? Why are they fascinated by these white shoes, if not mesmerised by them? Yanagi creates an unreal, 'science-fiction-like' scene, raising many questions that cannot be answered logically. In the third chapter I will analyse this 'dream-like' aesthetic further.

5.3.2 *Elevator Girls 3F* in its Contemporary Art Photography Context

The large size of the *Elevator Girls* photographs, the way that they are face-mounted on acrylic and their presentation in darkened spaces with dramatic spotlighting are comparable to photographs by Jeff Wall. However, Yanagi's works strongly contrast with Wall's in their focus on Japanese women in a fantastic surrounding.

Regarding the motif of numerous young women's uniformity, the women's blank facial expression and their self-containment, *Elevator Girls 3F* is comparable to photographs of Vanessa Beecroft's performances. Since 1993, Beecroft's performances have featured numerous women wearing similar clothes and wigs and looking alike (for instance *vb12* in 1995, *vb16* in 1997 or *vb36* in 1998). In addition, there are performances of men in similar uniforms (for instance *vb39* in 1999 or *vb42* in 2000). The models mostly do not talk, move or interact with the audience. However, Beecroft's *performances* are considered as artworks, whereas the photographs are primarily taken for documentary purpose. A further comparison of the *Elevator Girls* images with Beecroft's performances seems interesting but rather irrelevant in this study, since it seeks to focus on Japanese photography instead of inter-media analyses of performance and photography.

Part 3 will return to *Elevator Girls 3F*, examining the women's uniformity and their role in Japanese department stores. It will also analyse the photographic subjects with regard to their representation of Japanese 'feminine ideals', comparing and contrasting them with Mori in *Tea Ceremony III*.

6. Izima Kaoru's *Otsuka Nene Wears Tuzigahana*

6.1 The Work of Izima Kaoru (∗1954 in Kyoto, lives and works in Tokyo)

Up until the 1970s, Izima studied at the Tôkyô Sôgô Shashin Senmon Gakkô (Tokyo College of Photography). After working as a photographer's assistant, he travelled America, taking photographs which he exhibited at the Ginza Nikon Salon in Tokyo in 1977. According to Izima, the photographs of this first exhibition, titled *It's a Beautiful Day,* do not exist anymore.

During his twenties and thirties, Izima's income depended on fashion and commercial photography, film and TV work. He has claimed in my interview to have never anticipated being able to make a living from his photographic art.

In the early 1990s, Izima's photographs were dominated by the topic of unconventional human 'beauty'. The series *New Beauty I,* published in 1993, is a collection of 450 black and white portraits of the actress Karen Kirishima with various stockings over her head and face. The stockings make Kirishima's face almost unrecognisable; in some images her face appears 'squashed', in others it is elaborately bonded, reminiscent of the art of bondage. In other words, her face would generally not be considered 'beautiful' but rather deformed. The aesthetic of the photographed face suggests a strong sense of artificiality: Izima uses the human head and face like clay, freely (de)forming and shaping them into a sculpture. Hence, the images suggest that the notion of human 'beauty' is something which is not defined by the model but rather by the photographer, creating his own image of the photographed person. Moreover, 'beauty' is always defined by society, 'bonding' humans. In some images, the way that Kirishima wears the stockings is reminiscent of a bank rubber, in others she sticks her tongue out at the viewer; this also suggests the importance of irony and humour in Izima's work. The follow up, *New Beauty II – Colored Beauty* (1995), consists of images of vibrantly 'coloured' models. The works demonstrate 'beauty' independent of skin colour, displaying inhumane colours, such as 'rose pink', 'lilac' or 'mahagony'. With artificial colour applied on their faces and in some instances their bodies, the models irrespectively appear 'beautiful'. The pun 'coloured' corroborates the pertinence of humour in Izima's work. Similarly, the increasingly eased interpretation of Article 175 of the Penal Code allowing the depiction of pubic hair (see Part 1) inspired Izima to produce the series *Hairmode* (1994) juxtaposing the display of pubic hair next to the coverage of other body parts.

In 1994, Izima started to edit the quarterly magazine *zyappu*.[54] The magazine looks like a glossy fashion magazine with photo captions displaying the brand and price of each piece of clothing. It was, however, a forum to publish unconventional fashion photographs, not only for Izima, but also for other photographers.[55] Unconventional insofar as the photographs often differ from mainstream fashion images: they show models laughing, screaming, or appearing larger than the average model.

The name 'zyappu' (formerly spelled 'jap') is derived from an American derogatory term for Japanese people that originated during World War II. In 1997 the following definition began to appear on the content page of every *zyappu* issue:

> zyappu [jap] n. 1. a disparaging word for Japanese. 2. the name of a fashion magazine in Japan which was first published in 1994. 3. Japanese who have a free and independent spirit.

This definition shows the transformation of a word with a negative connotation into the positive expression 'independent spirit'. The magazine functions as a medium for this transformation, changing a formerly derogatory term into one with an artistic uplifting meaning. From 1997 the articles in *zyappu* were written in *rômaji* (Romanised Japanese letters), which is unusual in Japan and awkward to read. The use of *rômaji* is not only reminiscent of the USA's attempt after World War II to simplify the Japanese writing system, but it also emphasises the magazine's unconventional artistic style and its international yet Japanese appeal.

Izima started to have exhibitions in Japan in the early 1990s.[56] In 1999, he had his first exhibition overseas when the gallery Büro für Fotos[57] in Cologne saw his *Landscapes With a Corpse* series (hereafter, *Landscapes* series) featured in the small German art magazine *PlantSüden* and decided to display it in the art event *Tokyo Shock*. Since then, Izima's photographs have been displayed

---

54 After 21 issues the publication was discontinued due to the publisher Korinsha's bankruptcy in 1999.

55 Izima also published some of his photos under the alias Arizona Goro.

56 For example Izima's work was shown in the Hankyu Department Store in Osaka in 1990, in the gallery Verita in Tokyo in 1993 and at the Solaria Plaza Zephyr in Fukuoka in 1995.

57 The gallery Büro für Fotos changed its name in 2007 when the gallerists Kudlek and van der Grinten combined their business; today it is the Kudlek Van der Grinten gallery.

in galleries worldwide, increasingly attracting high bids on the art market.[58] In the last few years they were also shown in European art museums.[59]

The following paragraphs will introduce the *Landscapes with a Corpse* series to then focus on its sequence *Otsuka Nene Wears Tuzigahana* (1999) by providing a detailed description and a formal analysis.

6.2 The *Landscapes with a Corpse* Series (1993–ongoing)

The *Landscapes* series presents elaborately staged 'death' scenes, professionally shot at various locations in Japan and overseas, featuring (mostly female and Japanese) TV stars, actresses and models.[60] The series consists of fifty sequences,[61] which are composed of three to five photographs, taken from different angles and distances. The title of each sequence names the model as well as the luxury designer label she is wearing.[62]

The colourful images are taken at various locations, such as a private kitchen, public men's room or Mount Fuji. Izima invents the 'death' scenes in cooperation with the models, who pose in fashion pieces and settings of their choice; they tell Izima about their own death fantasy. A team of stylists, make-up artists and assistants supports Izima before and during the shooting.

The range of 'deaths' is striking: for instance, Natsuki Mari is lying on a truckload of red tomatoes that have been dumped on the ground (fig. 21), and Koike Eiko is lying in a large colourful *pachinko* arcade over numerous silver *pachinko* balls, which have spilled onto the floor; [63] she must have died from

---

58 Izima's work has been featured in the Emmanuel Perrotin gallery in Paris, the Andreas Binder gallery in Munich, the Kudlek Van der Grinten gallery in Cologne, and the Von Lintel gallery in New York. For further information on prices see DLK COLLECTION (2009): unnumbered.

59 Izima's work was shown in various group exhibitions, such as *Six feet Under* (Kunstmuseum Bern) in 2006, *On/Off* (Royal Academy of Arts in London) in 2008, *Der Kontrakt des Fotografen* [The Photographer's Contract] (Museum Schloss Morsbroich in Leverkusen) in 2008, and *Garten Eden* (Garden of Eden) (Kunsthalle Emden) in 2008.

60 Out of the fifty models, only two are male. From here on, all reference to models shall refer to the female models if not otherwise stated. Thus, the female pronoun 'she' will be used instead of 'she or he'.

61 The series now officially consists of fifty sequences, however, if one also includes the ones which have never been exhibited, there are more.

62 Most models are *tarento* (from the English 'talent'), who are famous in Japan as TV stars, actresses and models, such as Koike Eiko, Natsuki Mari or Hasegawa Kyoko. However, there are also 'Western' models, such as Helen Noguerra, Barbara Rudnik and Erin O'Connor. The clothes are designed by well-known luxurary labels such as Chanel, Gucci, Louis Vuitton, and Vivienne Westwood.

63 *Pachinko* is a popular form of gambling with machines that could be described as a cross between pinball and video slot machines. If one wins the silver balls, they can be exchanged

the shock of unexpectedly winning (fig. 22). The viewer is not only surprised but often also amused by the creative and extremely unusual way in which the 'death' is staged. Hence, Ôshima Hiroshi and Tim Griffin have presented compelling views when finding a 'feeling of humor' in the series, and calling it 'strangely humorous'.[64] The sequence with Natsuki Mari is a good example: The contrast between the shiny red tomatoes and the 'dead' woman results in a shock moment as well as amusement about the absurdity of the 'death'. Food is indeed a life-necessity; it seems ironic that a young woman lies 'dead' amongst fresh, ripe, tantalising tomatoes. By means of irony and contrast in both the visual form and the content of the images, a feeling of black humour is evoked. This way of presenting 'death' will be examined further in its Japanese context in 6.3 of Part 3.

In some works, such as *Akikawa Risa Wears Chanel*, bloody scenarios or the model's facial expression make it obvious that she is 'dead' (fig. 23). Akikawa has been pushed so forcefully, her body has penetrated the sofa; her legs remain behind the back of the sofa while her upper body has pushed through. A pair of scissors remains stabbed in her chest. Blood is all over her chest, white bra and white Chanel camisole; her eyes are wide open. In other sequences, such as *Otsuka Nene Wears Tuzigahana*, the model's recumbent pose and her closed eyes could initially also be interpreted as signs of sleep. There is no blood and no weapon to illustrate she 'died'. I will return to this visual ambiguity between death and sleep later in this chapter.

Before the *Landscapes* series was exhibited in galleries, Izima had published the photographs as a regular feature in the magazine *zyappu*. The sequences are numbered and individually published on four pages in each magazine; short fictional articles in Japanese and English accompany the photographs. These articles describe the imaginary cause of death in a tabloid newspaper style, often quoting 'investigating police officers' or 'witnesses'. At the end of each article the 'dead' person's clothing label is mentioned. As such, the genre of tabloid articles is mixed with the genre of Fashion Photography.

It is difficult to categorise the *Landscapes* photographs in *zyappu*: Should they be considered 'fashion photography' or 'art', or are they perhaps both? On the one hand it could be argued that the photographs were created as fashion photographs in a magazine. The use of models and actresses, the extensive composition of the photographs and the designer clothes corroborate this argument. On the other hand, the images have never advertised clothes and never been created on the behalf of a fashion label for commercial purpose. In addition, by depicting 'death scenes' the photographs do not point to a fashion la-

for goods that are available in the arcade's gift shop, which again can later be exchanged for cash at another shop nearby.

64 Ôshima (2000): 52; Griffin (2001): 32.

bel's corporate image. Maybe it is this ambiguity between commercial 'fashion photography' and 'art' which is the source of the fascination with the *Landscapes* series, especially as a feature within *zyappu*. The viewer does not know if the photographs are meant to advertise or not.

However, a differentiation has to be made between the *Landscapes* images when they were published in *zyappu* and the same photographs exhibited as 'art'. The magazine photographs are accompanied by texts influencing the viewer's interpretation. In addition, the aesthetic of the images as magazine photographs printed on paper, often intermingled with the article letters, differs to the same images when presented as C-prints mounted on acrylic. In large size and without the textual parts, the composition of the image as a whole as well as small details are much clearer. In addition, the presentation in large size and behind glass adds to the artificial and sensational impression of the colourful and elaborately staged images.

This thesis will not cover the analysis of the photographs as a feature in *zyappu* but focus on the photographs as 'art'. One sequence should be considered as one artwork. However, as Izima has regretfully stated, the photographs have also been sold separately.

6.3 *Otsuka Nene Wears Tuzigahana* (1999) (C-Colour print) (Fig. 24–27)

6.3.1 Description and Formal Analysis

The sequence *Otsuka Nene Wears Tuzigahana* was first published in *zyappu* in 1999.[65] The artwork consists of four photographs: *Otsuka Nene Wears Tuzigahana #211* (100 x 127cm), *Otsuka Nene Wears Tuzigahana #212* (100 x 127cm), *Otsuka Nene Wears Tuzigahana #213* (100 x 127cm), and *Otsuka Nene Wears Tuzigahana #214* (100 x 79cm). There is a 'museum's edition' of five art works and a 'gallery edition' of ten. The sizes of the 'museum's edition' are the above mentioned; the photographs are not framed but mounted on

65 It was published together with an article written in *rômaji*. The article describes how the 54-year old postman Saito Ryôhei found the dead body of the thirty-year old actress in an old house in Shiroi-machi in Inba-gun (Chiba) on April the 12th at 2:30pm. The police detected the peelings of two tangerines on the table and therefore assumed that there may have been a second person in the room when Otsuka Nene died. However, since they found traces of sleeping pills in her body, the possibility of suicide could not be excluded. The *kimono* that she was wearing was a very special reconstruction of a *kimono* of the Azuchi Momoyama Period, made by members of the Japanese Community of *kimono*s over the course of three years. The *kimono* had been stolen from the office of the Community. The police suspected that Otsuka Nene's death was somehow related to the stealing of the *kimono*. According to the *Kimono* Community such a *kimono* cannot be made again and it was therefore literally priceless. IZIMA (1999): 18–21.

acryl and behind glass. For the 'gallery edition' all photographs are 35.5 x 43 cm, they are mounted on acryl and presented in wooden frames.

Each of the four photographs is taken from a different angle and distance. *Otsuka Nene Wears Tuzigahana #211* depicts a traditional Japanese house with *shôji* paper sliding doors. Most of the doors are open so the viewer cannot only see the outside but also the inside of the house. In the middle of the photograph there is a room with a *tatami* straw flooring and a *kotatsu* table covered with a blanket reaching down to the floor.[66] On the left side of the room, Otsuka Nene is lying on the floor. A wooden post obstructs the front view so that the viewer does not see the young actress at first sight. The sliding door behind her is open and lets bright light into the room.

The vantage point of the photograph is striking; the viewer feels as if he had just entered the main door of the house and is standing in the entrance. On the right side there is a step, which leads to the inner part of the house. In other words, the observer's position is 'in between' the outside and the inside of the house. On the floor of the entrance, there is a pair of Japanese *zôri* sandals, emphasising this 'in-between' position since one has to remove one's shoes before entering a house in Japan.

In *Otsuka Nene Wears Tuzigahana #212* the viewer has the impression that he is standing inside the room and is looking down on the woman, lying in front of him. The *kotatsu* is cropped at the left side and at the bottom of the photograph. The fact that the open door on the left side and the open door behind her are also cropped, emphasises that the photo shows a detailed view of the scenario.

The woman is wearing a *kimono* with an unusual cord-belt. Her arms lie stretched out on the floor, her left knee is bent to the left side. Her eyes are closed and her head lies close to the opened door. All together, the pose suggests that she does not have any control over the different parts of her body and it seems that she fell down on her back. The unnatural bearing of her left knee and the posture of her arms suggest that she is not sleeping but that she fell down and is 'dead'. On the table there are several tangerines, a teacup and sweet wrappings. To the side where she would have been sitting before falling back, there are two tangerine peelings. In the background, parts of the outside space are visible. The sun is shining on the ground and catching a wooden bed frame and a shelf, which seem to have been left on the left side.

#213 is taken from an angle behind the young woman's head, outside the room. It is a close-up photograph of her, again taken from above. Now her face and long black hair, which she is partly lying on, can be seen. Her eyes and mouth are softly closed.

---

[66] A *kotatsu* is a low table frame covered by a heavy blanket, upon which a table-top sits. It is used in winter, and there is a heat source underneath the table or built into the table itself.

The *kimono* is decorated with a red and white chequerboard pattern and a light flower print. On the left sleeve the viewer sees another pattern with leaf-like ornaments in white on a yellow base, on the right sleeve the same pattern is repeated on an olive green base. The *kimono* almost looks like patchwork; it is unusual and distinguishable.

#214 is the only vertical photograph of the series. The vantage point is again relevant; the viewer is standing outside the room on an *engawa* access balcony. On the left side of the photograph the pushed back sliding door can be seen. It covers the lower part of the woman's body so it is possible to see only her head, shoulders and right arm. On the right side of the photograph, the rail of the door and the wooden floor of the *engawa* indicate the outside of the house. The viewer once again feels as though he is between the interior and the exterior of the house. He looks at Otsuka Nene, whose lips seem softly closed, almost forming a slight smile. As described earlier, her eyes are closed. Altogether, the facial expression indicates relaxation rather than suffering.

The colours in the photographs are predominantly subdued and quiet. The warm colour of the straw flooring and the wood of the sliding doors give a natural feel to the house and its atmosphere. Only the red and white pattern of the *kimono* catches the eye. In the first two photographs there is a sharp contrast of illuminated and dark parts; apart from the light of the neon lamps, the entrance to the house and the brown wood are thrown into darkness. Contrary, sunlight is shining through the open door behind the woman's head, illuminating the part of the room where she is lying. In *#211* there is also a contrast between the cold and unnaturally blue neon light and the warm natural sunlight shining on the woman. In *#212* the light shines less on the body; the room is dark and contrasts with the courtyard, where rays of light shine on the ground. In both *#213* and *#214* there is less contrast of light and dark; sun shines on the woman and gently illuminates her face. The warm sunlight seems comforting and evokes a sunny day. It could be interpreted as a reference to some kind of holy light, or to a beautiful place after death. As such, the use of warm light close to the woman could be a hint at the way death is considered a release.

The four photographs are all harmoniously composed. The sliding doors, the floor with partitions, and the wooden beams suggest a sense of technicality and stability. The circular contours of the body, which lies in a diagonal angle to the other lines, suggest motion and highlight the body as the most important subject.

Altogether, the colours, the sunlight and the composition of the photographs result in an artwork which evokes a peaceful atmosphere. 'Death' is not presented as horrible or shocking but rather as quiet and natural.

In *#211*, *#212* and *#214* Izima uses perspectives that show both the exterior and interior. The architecture of the house is traditional; the access balcony and the entrance, where the sandals are lying, symbolise an area 'in-between' the outside and the inside of a house. Unlike in European houses, rooms in traditional Japanese houses are not fixed and borders can be repositioned all the time by opening and closing sliding doors.[67] On the one hand, the opened space conveys a sense of vulnerability: if Otsuka Nene was murdered with the doors open as in the photographs, the murderer could have seen her from outside and had easy access to the inside of the house. On the other hand, the flowing transition between the outside and inside conveys a sense of freedom; since there are no fixed borders, rooms can be newly defined all the time. This inconsistency could refer to the transition between life and death; maybe Otsuka Nene was not murdered but decided to go to another place by committing suicide? *Otsuka Nene Wears Tuzigahana* does not give answers to how the model 'died' but rather addresses the viewer's imagination. This brings me to the question why it could be assumed that Otsuka Nene is 'dead' in the first place. The following section will answer this question.

6.3.2 Why Otsuka Nene is not 'Asleep' but 'Dead'

In *#211* only the upper body of Otsuka Nene can be seen: a post obstructs the front view so that the viewer does not even see her at first sight. Bright light shines into the room; she may have fallen asleep when resting in the sun. In *#214*, it is noticeable that her eyes are closed and that her facial muscles seem relaxed, the mouth indicates a slight smile. Neither her facial expression nor the colour of her skin makes her look 'dead'. Viewing *#211* or *#214* individually, one does not know if she is 'dead' or sleeping.

However, the artwork is composed of the four photographs together. Hence, there are two reasons why it is clear that Otsuka Nene is 'dead'. The first reason is linked to the position of the young woman: The bearing of her left knee to the side and the posture of her arms away from the body in *#212* and *#213* seem unnatural as a sleeping posture. It looks rather as though she fell down when sitting at the *kotatsu* table. Secondly, the variety of angles and distances in the photographs is reminiscent of crime scene photographs, suggesting that the photographer was investigating the scene.

Regarding Izima's œuvre, it is striking that Izima published a volume of photographs titled *Nemuru Matsuyuki Yasuko* (Matsuyuki Yasuko Sleeping) with images of the actress Matsuyuki Yasuko sleeping on the floor.[68] The book is part of a series of *Sleeping Actresses*. Izima has explained that the

---

67 On the relationship between the inside and the outside of Japanese houses and the area of the 'in-between' see SHIMADA (1994): 126–128.

68 IZIMA (2003).

photographs were never meant to be exhibited in galleries but rather published in books. However, he could not find a publisher except for the Matsuyuki sequence. The model's vulnerable position is juxtaposed with the viewer's curious (and perhaps voyeuristic) gaze; this is a similarity of the *Sleeping Actresses* and the *Landscapes* series. However, the model's posture changes in the *Sleeping* photographs; for example, Matsuyuki unconsciously moves her head (fig. 28). This could be contrasted with Otsuka Nene's static pose.

Sharing a recumbent posture and the state of wakelessness, death and sleep are analogous. In the English language the expression 'endless sleep' is used as a euphemism for 'death', and sleep has been used as a metaphor of death in Christian religion and 'Western' culture.[69] In the Japanese language there also exists the word *eibô*, which literally means 'endless sleep', denoting death. However, the analogy of sleep and death is not as common in Japanese as in European culture. Rather, death is described by referring to seasons or scenes in nature, for example in *haiku* poems.

In summary, individual photographs of the *Landscapes* series play with the ambiguity between death and sleep; it is not evident in every image that the models are 'dead'. However, as in *Otsuka Nene Wears Tuzigahana*, each sequence includes at least one photograph which makes it more or less clear that the model is a 'corpse' (as the series' title also states). Besides, the sequential form with the different distances and angles suggests that the photographer is investigating the cause of 'death'. In contrast to photographs from Izima's *Sleeping* series it is remarkable that the model never changes her pose. As such, it is clear that she is 'dead' although her 'death' may seem as peaceful as an 'endless sleep'.

6.3.3 *Otsuka Nene Wears Tuzigahana* as a Narration

Both the content of each photograph and the sequential structure of the artwork suggest a narration. Firstly, details, such as the tangerine peelings or the open sliding doors, offer possible interpretations as to how Otsuka Nene 'died'. Secondly, the sequential form evokes a feeling of walking around the scene: in *#211* the viewer feels as if he were about to enter the house; in *#212* he has ar-

69 The best-known Christian example is a Bible passage in which Jesus tells his disciples about Lazarus' death: 'our friend Lazarus has fallen asleep, but I am going there to awaken him.' (Johannes 11: 11–14). An example in literature could be Hamlet pondering his existence in his monologue *To be or not to be* in the third act of Shakespeare's *Hamlet*. To Hamlet, death like sleep is a chance to escape from the unmerciful world he is living in ('... and by a sleep to say we end The heart-ache and the thousand natural shocks That flesh is heir to'). However, death also is an unknown place which he is afraid of ('to sleep, perchance to dream, aye there's the rub; For in that sleep of death what dreams may come').

rived inside; in *#213* he has walked around the 'dead' body and is standing next to it; in *#214* he has walked out through the sliding door.

The *Landscapes* series in Japanese was originally titled *Shitai no aru fûkei* (Landscapes with a Corpse) but in the fourth volume of photographs Izima changed it to *Saigo ni mita fûkei* (The Last Viewed Landscape). In my interview, Izima has pointed out that the photographic sequence could be viewed through the eyes of the model: 'the viewer gradually retreats from the corpse until the scene is far away. This is the perspective of the dead person's soul'.

However, a viewer usually looks at the sequence hanging on a gallery or museum wall from left to right. In addition, the photographs are numbered with the most distant photograph coming first. Hence, Izima's suggestion to view the photographs from the 'perspective of the dead person's soul' is neither evident in the images nor in the way these are presented. As described above, the usual way of looking at the sequences is from the perspective of someone discovering the 'death'. I agree with Peter Weiermair's interpretation that the viewer 'becomes a detective'.[70] This 'detective' viewpoint references the genre of Crime Photo-graphy; the photographs seem as if they served the purpose of presenting evidence to solve crimes.

6.3.4 Crime Photography

Izima has claimed in my interview that he was 'inspired by American police photos, since photographs taken by the Japanese police never get published'. *Otsuka Nene Wears Tuzigahana* corroborates the influence of crime scene photographs: *#211* is taken from far away as if to record the surroundings, *#212* shows the corpse and a detailed view of the inside, *#213* and *#214* are close-ups of the body from different perspectives. Apart from *#211* all photographs show the corpse from above. This bird's eye perspective is typical of police photographs of corpses.[71]

The photographic medium has traditionally been seen as a medium of neutral documentation; since its invention it has been used for scientific investigation and evidence gathering. Photographs have generally been viewed as confirmations of truth; however, from the very beginning, they have often been staged or altered.[72] The progress of digitalisation since the 1990s has made the

---

70 WEIERMAIR (2008): 6.

71 This can be seen in various police photographs, e.g. PHILLIPS (1997): 91, 94, 105, 109.

72 The history of photography has always been intertwined with manipulation; in the late 19th century dead family members were inserted into family pictures, death scenes were staged, and corpses were photographed to look as if they were alive. In addition, airbrushing was invented in the late 19th century already; for instance, Stalin had frequently airbrushed his enemies out of photographs.

manipulation of photographic images even easier and more common. Izima's *Landscapes* photographs are taken from different angles as if to investigate a crime scene. At the same time, they are too perfectly composed to be real and do not conceal the fact that they are staged. Furthermore, the images are digitally altered; for example the colours are enhanced and details are changed. The 'documentation' of staged, digitally altered 'death' scenes can be interpreted as an ironic reflection on photography and people's belief in it as a medium of 'truth'.

Crime Photography in general has been emancipated from its function of preserving evidence and has been moved into an aesthetic field.[73] In the 1990s, books on historical crime photographs were published, such as Luc Sante's *Evidence* (1992) and Joel-Peter Witkin's *Harms Way: Lust & Madness, Murder & Mayhem* (1994), both dealing with photographs not as objective documents but rather as images. In 1997 the exhibition *Police Pictures: The Photograph as Evidence* in the Grey Art Gallery in New York revealed the aesthetic qualities of mug shots and crime scene photographs.

As Luc Sante has written, police photographs may 'inspire horror, as well as pity, and maybe morbid fascination and dull voyeurism.'[74] He has explained our fascination with a certain intimacy: 'this is an excruciatingly intimate sight, and perhaps it is the burden of this intimacy that makes the corpses in these pictures seem more real than the living cops or spectators who can be peripherally glimpsed.'[75] These voyeuristic elements and a sense of 'invasion of privacy' also seem relevant in *Otsuka Nene Wears Tuzigahana*. Firstly, the viewer enters a private house. Entering the house or the apartment of a woman in Japan is a rather intimate act. Secondly, he looks down on a woman, who is lying 'dead' on the floor; she is in a vulnerable position. Yet, the scene is 'fake'; the model is *acting* as a 'corpse'. Unlike photos of real corpses, the *Landscapes* series is ambiguous – the photos pretend to reveal, yet what emerges is perfectly staged.

6.3.5 *Otsuka Nene Wears Tuzigahana* in its Contemporary Art Photography Context

The use of Crime Photography as inspiration is not new in the art world; already surrealist artists of the 1920s used crime scene photographs as artistic material. In addition, Marcel Duchamp and Andy Warhol have created works

---

[73] REGENER (2000): 38.
[74] SANTE (1992): xi.
[75] SANTE: 63.

referencing mug shots as well as death or disaster images. I will return to Warhol's work in 7.2 of Part 3.

More contemporary photographs featuring elements of crime and death are Janet Fries' photographs of homicide scenes in 1970s San Francisco or Andres Serrano's series *The Morgue* consisting of close-up images of corpses in the 1990s. However, these photographs are not staged and contrast aesthetically with Izima's series.

When analysing *Otsuka Nene Wears Tuzigahana* in its Japanese context, the comparison with Araki Nobuyoshi's photographs seems unavoidable. There are various photographs by Araki, such as in his series *Tokyo: A City Heading for Death* (1990), which are similar to Izima's series insofar as women are presented as being completely at the viewer's mercy. Often they are bonded, naked and lie, exposed and vulnerable, on the floor. Another example is Araki's photograph *Untitled* (2004/2006), which shows a young woman in a *kimono* from a bird's eyes perspective (fig. 29). She is lying on a bed and her *kimono* has been opened, exposing her pubic area. A small dinosaur toy seems to approach to the woman's genitals. Like Araki's photograph, the images of *Otsuka Nene Wears Tuzigahana* are predominantly taken from above; the viewer's gaze on the model seems dominant. As previously explained, the cord belt around Otsuka Nene's *kimono* is unusual. It could either be interpreted as somehow connected to her 'death' or as a playful reference to Araki's famous photographs of bonded women.

However, *Otsuka Nene Wears Tuzigahana* and the other *Landscapes* images differ from Araki's photographs of women in various aspects. For instance, Izima's photographs do not show as much naked skin as Araki's: contrary to the above-mentioned work by Araki, Otsuka Nene's *kimono* covers her body completely.

Moreover, I agree with Charlotte Cotton, who has pointed out that Izima's *Landscape* photographs 'combine a seductive photographic style with a *narrative* [my italics] told from a sexualized point of view.'[76] As previously mentioned, a narration is evident in both form and content of *Otsuka Nene Wears Tuzigahana*. This narrative quality cannot be found in Araki's works.

Morimura Yasumasa's *Self-portraits as Actress* series (1996) includes a photograph referencing the dramatic death scene at the very end of the film *Bonnie and Clyde* (1967) (fig. 7). *After Faye Dunaway* depicts Morimura in the role of Bonnie, who is lying on a pile of car tyres; the bearing of her legs and arms away from the body suggest that she does not have control over her muscles; Bonnie is 'dead'. Shiny red 'blood' dramatically contrasts with her white dress. Bonnie is photographed from a bird's eye view, which makes her look

[76] COTTON (2004): 69.

more vulnerable. Elaborate make up, long eyelashes, red lips and a blond wig make Morimura look like a 'film star'. The large-sized photograph is comparable to Izima's *Landscapes* images in several ways: in its colourful and dramatic aesthetic, in its obvious stagedness, and by featuring a 'female' lying on her back representing a convergence of 'beautiful femininity' and 'death'. However, contrary to the *Landscapes* series, Morimura's work features the artist himself masquerading as the 'Western' film character Bonnie. Hence, it raises questions about film, gender and national identity.

In an international art context, the *Landscapes* series could be compared and contrasted with works by Cindy Sherman. Hasegawa has found similarities between Izima's photographs and Sherman's *Untitled #153* (1985), which shows the artist as a 'corpse' lying in a field with her eyes wide open (fig. 30).[77] The photograph is part of a photographic series, which is often referred to as the *Fairy Tales/Disasters*. Like most photographs of the *Landscapes* series, *Untitled #153* is taken from above. Similarly, the artwork's artificial blue lighting, and Sherman' s light-blue hair and face create a stylised, artificial atmosphere; the viewer knows that the woman is not a real corpse. However, the uneven structure of Sherman's skin, its light-blue colour and the dirt on her face and clothes make her look deformed. It seems as if her body has started to decay. As such, Sherman creates a morbid atmosphere which contrasts with the fashion aesthetic of the *Landscapes* series. In addition, contrary to Izima's series, the untitled photograph is not presented as a sequence; the narrative aspect is not as relevant.

As a series, the *Landscapes* photographs could be compared to Annika von Hausswolff's *Back to Nature* (1992–1993) and Yann Toma's *Crimes sur Commande* (Crimes On Command) (1998–2005). Hausswolff's series consists of large photographs in which young female 'corpses' are strewn across Nordic landscapes. Like Izima, the Swedish photographer stages crime scenes with female objects in landscapes and could therefore be seen as his Nordic counterpart. However, Hausswolff's photographs are not concerned with fashion and the women are mostly more or less undressed. In addition, the images are not as colourful and extensively staged. Hausswolff's gaze on the women, together with the series' title, seem rather like a critique against the tradition of regarding woman as nature opposed to men as culture. In *Back to Nature* the 'female' is ironically and brutally reunited with 'her element' nature.

In *Crimes sur Commande*, a series of large-format photographs, Toma also stages fictitious murder scenes as imagined by his models. Like Izima, he often uses a bird's eye perspective and plays with the 'documentation' of staged scenes, critically reflecting the photographic medium as a means to provide evi-

---

77 HASEGAWA (2008): 16.

dence. The photographs' aesthetic differs to that of Izima's series since the photographs are in black and white and the 'dead' objects are often male. Contrary to the *Landscapes* series, each photograph is considered as an artwork; there are no sequences.

According to Izima, he did not know Hausswolff's and Toma's works. However, as this section made clear, the motif of a staged 'death' was not as unusual in 1990s photographic artworks as it might seem. A more detailed comparison of the *Landscapes* series and Araki's, Sherman's, and mostly, Hausswolff's or Toma's photographs would be an interesting topic of future study.

Otsuka Nene Wears Tuzigahana not only references Crime Photography but many more cultural topoi and genre. For instance, the presentation of a 'beautiful' and yet 'dead' woman could be linked to art historical traditions, such as the motif 'Death and the Maiden'. I will analyse this from a gender perspective in 5.2 of Part 3. Furthermore, the artificial 'death' aesthetic could be linked to a specifically 'Japanese' cultural and religious background, which will be explored in 6.3. Following this, 7.2 will analyse the *Landscapes* series in its 1990s Fashion Photography as well as media imagery context. The ephemeral character of the photographic medium, i.e. a topic of Roland Barthes' discourse on photography, will also be of interest.

Part 3:
The Body as a Screen: Readings of the Analysed Artworks

The first chapter has explained the complex Japanese 'art' and 'photography' contexts the artists of this thesis are situated in. It has become obvious that the backgrounds of, for example, Morimura Yasumasa's work and Izima Kaoru's, differ to a great degree. In other words, the artworks this thesis is concerned with include images which are, in Japan, categorised as 'art' as well as images which are viewed as 'photography'. Moreover, the descriptions and formal analysis in the second chapter have shown great differences regarding the ten photographs' form and content. For instance, Yamanaka's and Ishiuchi's analogue photographs in black and white contrast strongly with Yanagi's and Izima's digitally altered colour images. The *Gyahtei* series is concerned with naked old women, who do not even know that their photograph is being taken for art purposes, whereas, in contrast, Mori and Morimura both 'masquerade' and pose for photographs. As such, this thesis includes black and white analogue photographs as well as digital colour images; it includes images with a more 'authentic' approach, as well as more 'fictitious' staged ones; it includes stylised close-up images of naked skin as well as narrative photographic sequences with detailed settings and elaborately chosen garments; it includes photographs in which the artist is 'behind' the camera as well as photographs in which he is in front of the camera.

However, all works present the viewer with a human body, which can be interpreted as a 'screen' for art historical and socio-political issues, including problems of 'national' identity, gender and religion. The following section will define the term 'body' and introduce body theories relevant for this study, before explaining the concept of viewing 'the body as a screen'.

1. Body Theories and Definition of 'the Body as a Screen'

With regard to human beings and animals in general, a 'body' denotes the physical structure of an individual. It covers the entire organism, which usually consists of a head, neck, torso, two arms and two legs, and numerous internal organ groups such as a central nervous system. However, as the sociologist Bryan Turner has stated, the term is somewhat ambiguous: 'the body is a material organism, but also a metaphor; it is the trunk apart from head and limbs, but also the person (as in "anybody" and "somebody").'[1] As such, 'body' is a rather complex term: it refers not only to physical material, be it with or with-

1 TURNER (1984): 7–8.

out the head and limbs, but is also associated with 'personhood' – a concept which is tied to socio-historical structures and interpreted differently in various academic fields, including law, medicine and philosophy.

In the 1980s and 1990s, a shift in philosophical subjects, such as sociology, cultural studies and visual studies, led towards a new research focus on the 'body'. This could be described as the 'body turn', contrasting, for instance, with the former focus on language (linguistic turn). It has become a generally accepted assumption that far from being immutable, 'body' as well as 'person' should better be described as the results of social, political and cultural pressures. Both the way we look at a 'body' and the way we show it is determined by historical and socio-cultural factors. Michel Foucault contributed the most to the spread of this argument; however, it was also other members of poststructuralist and gender movements, who gave actuality to the human body.

This has resulted in a veritable explosion of interest, evident in the growth of sociological,[2] historical and socio-cultural publications,[3] as well as conferences and graduate schools concerned specifically with the body.[4]

Before explaining 'the body as a screen' in this thesis, some relevant concepts of (postmodern) body theories will be summarised briefly. Norbert Elias' interdisciplinary work *Über den Prozess der Zivilisation* (The Civilising Process), first published in 1939, could be interpreted as an early precursor to the Foucauldian concept of the human body as being inseparably bound to society's power structures and discourses. Elias has stated that any individual ac-

---

2 FEATHERSTONE, Mike and Bryan S. TURNER (1991): *The Body: Social Process and Cultural Theory*. London: Sage; SHILLING, C. (1993): *The Body and Social Theory*. London: Sage; SYNNOTT, Anthony (1993): *The Body Social: Symbolism, Self and Society*. London: Routledge; FALK, Pasi (1994): *The Consuming Body*. London: Sage; TURNER, Bryan S. (1996): *The Body & Society*. London: Sage.

3 German publications in historical and socio-cultural studies include VAN DÜLMEN, Richard (ed.) (1996): *Körper-Geschichten. Studien zur historischen Kulturforschung* [Body-Stories. Studies on Historical Culture Research]. Frankfurt am Main: Fischer Taschenbuch; LIST, Elisabeth and Ernst FIALA (eds.) (1997): *Leib, Maschine, Bild, Körperdiskurse der Moderne und Postmoderne* [Body, Machine, Image. Body Discourses of the Modern and Postmodern Era]. Wien: Passagen; SARASIN, Philipp (2001): *Reizbare Maschinen – Eine Geschichte des Körpers 1765–1914* [Irritable Machines: A History of the Body 1765–1914]. Frankfurt am Main: Suhrkamp: Francke; BARKHAUS, Annette and Anne FLEIG (eds.) (2002): *Grenzverläufe. Der Körper als Schnitt-Stelle* [Border Lines. The Body as an Interface]. München: Fink.

4 Graduate schools in Germany include *Körper Macht Geschichte. Geschichte Macht Körper* [Body Power History History Power Body] at the University of Bielefeld in the late 1990s and *Körper-Inszenierungen* [Body staging] (1997–2006), combining theatre studies, art history as well as philosophy at the Freie Universität Berlin. The conferences include *Was steckt hinter dem Body turn?* [What is the Body Turn?] at the Katholische Akademie Bayern in 2004, *Für Dein Alter siehst Du gut aus!* [Considering Your Age You Look Good!] at the Gießen University in 2008 or *KörperWissen – Erkenntnis zwischen Eros und Ekel* [Body Knowledge – Awareness Between Eros and Disgust] in 2009 in Tübingen.

tion is related to a certain historical and social context which is always in flux. Human beings are 'variable' and can be 'modelled' during the process of civilization.[5] Consequently, there is no external position of certainty and no universal understanding beyond history and society.

In *Discipline and Punish*, Foucault further develops this idea by analysing a set of operations and procedures which manipulate and control the human body in society. Referencing Georg Rusche and Otto Kirchheimer's *Punishment and Social Structures* (1939), Foucault agrees with the authors' proposition that in our societies, the 'systems of punishment are to be situated in a "political economy" of the body'.[6] He explains that even when the punishment is not violent, 'it is always the body that is at issue – the body and its forces, their utility and their docility, their distribution and their submission.'[7] As such, the body is 'directly involved in a political field; power relations have an immediate hold upon it; they invest it, mark it, train it, torture it, force it to carry out tasks, to perform ceremonies, to emit signs.'[8]

'Discipline' in Foucault's sense refers to processes of surveillance, classification, labelling, analysis and correction. 'Disciplinary technologies' are dispersed in everyday practices through social institutions, including schools, prisons and hospitals, and aim to create a 'docile body that may be subjected, used, transformed and improved'.[9] Thus, as he has summarised in the introduction of *The History of Sexuality*, the body is an outcome of the social power play: 'power reaches into the very grain of individuals, touches their bodies and inserts itself into their actions and attitudes, their discourses, learning processes and everyday lives'.[10] The boundaries between socio-cultural norms influencing the 'body' and people's internalisation of these are fragile. Foucault's perspective on the 'body' as being constituted by social power relations brought a conceptual shift of broad significance to social sciences, including gender studies.

Both feminist and queer studies have challenged conventional or traditional understandings of the relationship between anatomy and social roles. There is no such thing as a neutral representation of gender and sex. Representations are not innocent; they rather carry an irredeemable cultural history of sexual relationships. Although Judith Butler was not the first to assert the social construction of gender,[11] her work *Gender Trouble* (1990) has achieved a

5 Elias (1969b): 377.
6 Foucault (1991): 25.
7 Ibid: 25.
8 Ibid: 25.
9 Ibid: 136.
10 Foucault (1978): 39.
11 Consider texts by Simone de Beauveoir, Michel Foucault, Jacques Lacan and Monique Wittig.

representative status among these theories, illustrating how gender is constantly reproduced through discursive and performative action. In *Bodies that Matter* (1997), Butler has further developed this argument, explaining that even sexual difference is not only a 'function of material differences which are not in some way both marked and formed by discursive practices... The category of "sex" is, from the start, normative; it is what Foucault has called a "regulatory ideal".'[12] Furthermore, it is a process 'whereby regulatory norms materialize "sex" and achieve this materialization through a forcible reiteration of those norms.'[13] In other words, for Butler, both 'gender' and 'sex' should not be understood as static descriptions of what one is but rather as norms which define a body within the domain of cultural intelligibility; social regulatory norms constantly materialise and reiterate 'sex' and 'gender'.

In addition, Butler has argued that the 'body' could be described as a dynamic interaction between matter and mind: 'the very contours of the body are sites which vacillate between the psychic and the material. Bodily contours and morphology are not merely implicated in an irreducible tension between the psychic and the material but are that tension.'[14] This not only corroborates the assumption mentioned earlier that the 'body' is more than physical material, but it also suggests that its contours are constantly in flux and indeterminate. The concern with the interplay of texts, images and physicality which posits a 'body' in process, never fixed or solid, but always multiple and fluid is one that resonates also in the work of Elizabeth Grosz. As Grosz has written in *Volatile Bodies,* 'the stability of the unified body image, even in the so-called normal subject, is always precarious. It cannot be simply taken for granted as an accomplished fact, for it must be continually renewed.'[15] As a consequence, she has re-examined traditional distinctions, such as 'mind' vs. 'body' and 'inside' vs. 'outside', for instance by exploring 'how the subject's exterior is psychically constructed; and conversely, how the processes of social inscription of the body's surface construct a psychical interior.'[16]

In summary, poststructuralists and feminist theories have questioned historical and cultural 'givens' of the 'natural body' and its supposed 'immutability', positing instead a textual and performative corporeality. However, while the 'body' can never be reduced to a physical object, neither it can be constructed as a purely discursive entity. Moreover, the material and the discursive are mutually determining. Following Foucault, I view the 'body' as a surface for social inscriptions and codes, produced and developed through vari-

---

12 BUTLER (1993): 21.
13 IBID: 22.
14 IBID: 66.
15 GROSZ (1994): 43–44.
16 GROSZ (1995): 381.

ous regimes of discipline and training. Although the female body may be Butler's and Grosz' primary point of interest, their analysis is relevant for this thesis in their focus on the normative character of human bodies and their marginalisation by various factors, such as gender and race. As such, I view the 'body' as a 'political arena'[17] or a 'screen' reflecting contemporary socio-cultural views.

In the following sections, it is the photographic bodily representation, rather than the human body itself, which will be of interest. The title of this thesis includes the word 'body' in its singular form. However, this does not mean that I understand it as a universal unchangeably fixed category. Rather, I am concerned with multiple fluid 'bodies', marked by an infinite array of differences, such as sex, gender, skin colour, social class, and age.

In viewing some of the artworks analysed in the second chapter, such as Mori Mariko's *Pure Land*, one might declare them to be a product of the artist's imagination, a depiction of a dream world. Nonetheless, it must also be admitted that even the most absurd image will, in part, represent a 'real' world, including the artist's own recollections and aspirations. Consequently, the artworks will undoubtedly reflect, in one way or another, the general value system of the society from which they were born, and more particularly its views on bodily ideals, 'national' identity, social behaviour, gender and religion.

The term 'screen' is used in this thesis for 'projections' on three different levels. In the following interpretations, the photographs reveal 'texts' which are inscribed on the human body by Japanese society. At the same time, the artists inscribe their own ideas and critical messages onto 'body images'. Moreover, due to my subjective viewpoint as an art historian with a specific German and Japanese background, I also project my own thoughts on the artworks. As such, the term 'screen' should be understood as a flexible 'umbrella term' which covers inscriptions on the 'body' by society, by the referenced artists and by myself.

In the interest of making the following sections more accessible to the reader, I have grouped them under seven major headings: The Naked Body, The Body and 'National' Identity, The Body and 'Social Codes', The Gendered Body, the Religious Body and, the Body and Photographic Discourses. Each of these sections will interpret one or more artworks which were analysed in Part 2, focussing on different body issues in a socio-cultural context. Some artworks will be examined in more than one section since they can be looked at from different viewpoints. The overlaps and flows between the diverse topics should be apparent, and in many cases, a particular sub-chapter might just as easily have appeared in several other sections. Just as the 'body' is understood as a

[17] HUBER (1996): 7–16.

multiple and fluid concept, the following headings should be viewed as offering one possible reading amongst many others. Thus, despite being presented here as separate categories for methodological reasons, the areas of debate are often interlinked and cannot be clearly demarcated from each other.

2. The Naked Body

The artworks described in the second chapter include photographs of more or less naked bodies: *Portrait (Futago)*, *Red Marilyn*, *Gyahtei #17*, *Chromosome XY*, and *SCAR 1983 illness*. This section will contextualise and interpret nakedness in these works. First, when could an unclothed body be defined as 'naked' and when is it 'nude'? Following this, the unclothed human body as a motif in European and Japanese art history will be analysed briefly. When and how did Japanese art adopt the 'Western' notion of the 'nude'? 2.2 will then relate this European as well as Japanese art historical background to Morimura's *Portrait (Futago)* and, to a lesser extent, to *Red Marilyn*. Following this, 2.3 will focus on the aged female body in *Gyahtei #17*, viewing it also in both a European and a Japanese art historical context. 2.4 is concerned with *Chromosome XY s. o.* and *SCAR 1983 illness*, comparing their presentation of nakedness with torso and landscape images.

2.1 'Naked' or 'Nude'? The Body in Art History

2.1.1 Typical Characteristics of the 'Nude'

When referring to the human body, the term 'naked' generally describes a body without clothing or any other covering. In contrast, the 'nude' body is a rather complex concept defining a specific art genre.

Firstly, the 'nude' is strongly connected to the viewer's gaze: a 'nude' image is always made for a spectator. Referring to Kenneth Clark's *The Nude*, John Berger has stated persuasively in his *Ways of Seeing* that 'a naked body has to be *seen* as an *object* [my italics] in order to become a nude.'[18] Berger's use of the word 'object' suggests the second characteristic of the 'nude', which is intertwined with the first: a 'nude' body is not 'natural' but rather artistically idealised as an object. It is dependent on contemporary taste and designed in order to flatter the viewer. Clark has described this idealisation as a 're-formation' from natural 'nakedness' through conventions and poses to the 'nude',

---

18 BERGER (1972): 54.

defining it as a 'balanced, prosperous and confident' body.[19] Thirdly, the 'nude' often covers parts of the body. As Elisabeth Bronfen has put it, a nude appears to be depicting a moment of exposure, however, it then reveals a gesture of disguise.[20] Bronfen has explained her argument by referring to images by Lucas Cranach the Elder, in which Venus 'veils' her pubic area with a small transparent cloth. However, this aspect of exposing and yet disguising seems relevant for many traditional 'nude' paintings as well as for popular pin-up photographs, be they with or without a cloth. For instance, in *Red Marilyn*, Morimura opens his body for the viewer's gaze by bending his arm behind his head and stretching his right away from his body, yet, he closes his legs and hides half of his face. This exposing and yet, at the same time, disguising pose clearly references the body language prominent in pin-up photographs.

Agreeing with Elisabeth Bronfen, I am aware of the difficulty in differentiating clearly between 'naked' and 'nude' bodies; body images are never unambiguous but rather allow more than one interpretation depending on the viewer's perspective.[21] Or, to put it in Lynda Nead's words, perhaps 'there can be no naked "other" to the nude, for the body is always already in representation'.[22] However, as the aforementioned quotations by Berger, Clark and Bronfen show, there are typical characteristics of the 'nude' body in art history. Thus, for methodological reasons, I will, for now, differentiate between more neutral representations of the 'naked' body and the idealised, sensual 'nude'.

2.1.2 The Nude in European Art History

The history of the nude body in European art is as old as art itself;[23] it cannot be explored in this thesis in detail. Instead, the specific role of the female nude since Renaissance art should be examined briefly.

Leonardo da Vinci used the male body as a representative of the perfect human being, Michelangelo illustrated his specific art concepts through the male body: an idealism based first on nature and later on rather artificial artistry (manierism).[24] However, it was mostly the female body which was painted by numerous artists to illustrate their skills. For example, Rubens or Titian

19 Clark (1972): 1.
20 Bronfen (2003): 1.
21 Ibid: 6.
22 Nead (1992): 16.
23 The small yet voluptuous figurine Venus of Willendorf (c. 24,000–22,000 BCE) is believed to be one of the oldest sculptures of a female nude. She was discovered in the Austrian village Willendorf in 1908.
24 Bonnet (1997): 71.

'showed off' repeatedly with their naturalistic paintings of women's naked skin, trying to find its perfect incarnadine. The art critic Ludovico Dolce praised Titian's painting *Venus and Adonis* (1553–1559) as showing Venus' 'flesh' in such a 'real' and 'sensual' way that every viewer's blood would start to pulsate through his veins.[25] In other words, painting became somewhat synonymous with the image of the woman: the beauty of painting as well as its ability to present 'reality' illusionistically was represented through an illusionistically 'real' and 'beautiful' woman. Being painted mostly by men for men, it is not surprising that the female nude has been juxtaposed with her male spectator by numerous artists in their works[26] as well as by writers in analytical texts.[27] Silvia Eiblmayr has highlighted the role of Venus, who has literally 'embodied' the concept of 'art': she was associated with the idea of an 'artistic ideal'.[28] Not only Venus, but also many other Christian, mythological and historical figures, including Bathseba and Susanna, Aphrodite, Diana, Leda (with the swan), the Three Graces, numerous nymphs, and Odalisque were presented alluringly as naked young women in paintings. In addition, there are allegories, such as Vanity and Truth, which have been symbolised by a female nude.

In the 19th and early 20th century, various photographers, including Julian Mandel, Edward Weston and Alfred Cleney Johnston, started to take photographs of semi-nude and nude young women, posing them amid drapery, veils, flowers and Oriental braziers. A great number of early nude photographs reference mythological themes and art historical motifs.[29] In early 20th century London, nude tableaux vivants became a form of live show entertainment, for instance at the Windmill Theatre; it was legal to be nude on stage as long as one was not moving. In Berlin, Olga Desmond posed nude imitating classical Roman sculptures, such as Venus. All these examples considered, the female nude has been prominent in paintings as well as photographs and even tableaux vivants on stage. The nude woman has represented her (male) creator's painting skills as well as contemporary ideals of beauty – often in the disguise of religion, mythology and allegory.

---

[25] As cited in ROSKILL (1968): 212–214.

[26] This is obvious, for instance, in Albrecht Dürer's print *Artist Drawing a Nude* (1538).

[27] For instance, BERGER (1972), CLARK (1972) and FOUCAULT (1978).

[28] EIBLMAYR (1993): 69.

[29] Gaudenzio Marconi's photographic album *Nudes and Angels* (1870s), František Drtikol's *Salome* (1923) etc.

2.1.3 How the 'Nude' Became 'Naked' in European Art History

In painting, the notion of the ideal female nude was broken by Gustave Courbet's 'realistic' paintings of rural women who had been considered unworthy of being art objects. Furthermore, Éduard Manet shocked the contemporary academic art world by replacing the Venus or Odalisque image with a 'real' prostitute in his famous work *Olympia*. In addition, Manet depicted her with strong contour lines; a naturalistic impression of her body and flesh tint does not appear to be relevant to him. Anne-Marie Bonnet has described Courbet's and Manet's approaches as 'manifests of modern painting' and has highlighted how both artists used the female body provocatively in order to illustrate their art concepts: 'the nude became naked'.[30] In other words, the 'natural', naked body of Olympia symbolises Manet's 'realistic' painting concept, in contrast to the aestheticised nude in paintings of Venus, for instance by Titian.

In summary so far, the female nude as an alluring ideal of femininity has had a long history in Europe and is closely intertwined with the medium of painting. Later, it also became popular in (staged) photographs and tableaux vivants on stage. The nude was questioned in paintings of the modern era when the concept of 'reality' and thus also natural 'nakedness' were considered more important than idealisation. These art historical backgrounds will be relevant later in this chapter, for instance when analysing Morimura's *Portrait (Futago)*.

2.1.4 The 'Naked' Body in Japanese Art History

The female 'nude' in 'Western' art history can be contrasted with female 'nakedness' in Japanese art history. The appearance of any unclothed figure had been rare in Japanese artworks before 'Western' influences. The few depictions of naked bodies or body parts could be categorised into three main types of images.

The first group of images shows naked bodies in rather natural and non-sexual situations. These depictions could be connected to a Japanese tradition of seeing and yet ignoring nakedness depending on its context. Numerous authors have examined this, linking it to the custom of public and partly mixed bathing.[31] For instance, the German doctor C. H. Stratz and the ethnologist Hans Peter Duerr have argued that the Japanese may be at ease with public mixed bathing because they notice nakedness only when it is considered inappropri-

---

30 BONNET (1997): 72.

31 For more information on bathing and nudity in daily Meiji Japan life see LINHART (2007).

ate.[32] Consequently, nakedness is not noticed in the bath, as it is considered appropriate rather than immoral or erotic.

The scientist and traveller Emil Selenka has described Japanese people during public mixed bathing in the Meiji era as acting 'innocently' like 'Adam and Eve before the fall from grace'.[33] In addition, some people had private bathtubs in front of their houses and 'bathed where everyone walking past could see'.[34] Duerr has used Erving Goffman's term of 'civil inattention' to explain this behaviour: although one sees others' naked bodies and is somewhat ashamed of it, one is able to be at ease simply by not paying attention.[35] Shimada Shingo has corroborated this argument, stating that a relaxed handling of nakedness is possible as long as certain rules define it as a matter of course; these rules are literally inscribed onto the bodies of people who are naked in public baths almost every day.[36]

Consequently, one way of depicting naked women (and men) in Japanese art is to show everyday-life bathing scenes, which naturally legitimated nakedness or even, made it necessary.[37] For instance, a woodblock prints triptych from the series *Imayô nenjû gyôji* (Modern Annual Events) (mid – late 19th century) by Ochiai Yoshiiku depicts the women's section of a public bath (fig. 31). Some of the women are still dressed, some are in the process of undressing and some are naked, washing themselves. On the left side, there is a group of women who are engaged in an argument; perhaps they are fighting over a washing trough. One woman is grabbing another woman; a third woman has fallen down on the floor. In the background on the right, a figure who could be the bath attendant is watching the scene and laughing. This image exemplifies how nakedness is not considered 'erotic' and is not even the focus of the work. Rather, Yoshiiku presents us with an everyday-life scene, highlighting the lively atmosphere in the bath in a humorous way. The individual bodies and their anatomy do not appear to be important – depicted in motion and as a group, they rather form a dynamic composition. The same can be said about a comic *manga* by Kawanabe Kyôsai depicting the Seven Lucky Gods (*shichifukujin*) taking a bath (1881) (fig. 32).[38] The gods' bodies are imbued with caricature and stylisation: for instance, Hotei has his fat body scrubbed by

32 STRATZ (1925): 112–113, 128–129; DUERR (1992): 120–121.

33 SELENKA (1925): 206.

34 LINHART (2007): 159.

35 DUERR (1991): 121.

36 SHIMADA (1994): 201–202.

37 For example, works by Utagawa Toyokuni, Utagawa Yoshiiku, Kitagawa Utamaro, Torii Kiyonaga and Katsushika Hokusai. For detailed information see STRATZ (1925): 169–194.

38 Later, Kawanabe Kyôsai created a similar image in ink, colour, gold and silver on paper (1884–1886), probably juxtaposing it with an image of *Hidari Jingorô and the Kyoto Doll* as a pair. For more information see CLARK (1993): 56–57.

two struggling young boys, Benzaiten tips uninhibitedly a bucket of water over her head, and Bishamon sits inside the bath tub, causing it to overflow. The image is unusual in depicting all of the gods naked, however, it typically shows them in a situation in which it appears appropriate to be naked. As such, Japanese art history includes 'natural' and often humorous depictions of naked humans as well as gods, which legitimate their nakedness with daily situations, especially bathing.[39] Such 'naked' bodies contrast to 'nude' bodies as things of beauty.

The second group of Japanese naked body images are rather rare pictures which examine the human body from a somewhat scientific viewpoint. Maruyama Ôkyo's work *Jinbutsu seisha sôhon* (Complete Folio of True Figure Studies) (1770) (fig. 33) is an example of this group, featuring full-scale paintings of naked men and women of different ages, as well as detailed close-up images of genitalia.[40] Next to the images, there are annotations defining the bodies' sex and ages. Although the pictures are stylised and linear, the range of figures with the accompanying annotations suggests that Maruyama was doing some sort of a survey; as John Teramoto has argued persuasively, this should be viewed 'along the lines of eighteenth century encyclopaedic interests.'[41] It is most likely that Maruyama was acquainted with anatomical illustrations in both imported 'Western' texts and native Japanese works.[42] Perhaps, as Teramoto has suggested, Maruyama even looked at actual models.[43] The *Jinbutsu seisha sôhon* consists of three hand scrolls, two of which must be viewed side by side since the figures are depicted across both scrolls with the seam between them as a longitudinal axis. This peculiar format together with the large size of the figures and their unusual nakedness suggest that Maruyama wanted to deal with the human body in a new way – he viewed it from an aesthetic perspective and yet, with scientific interest.

As a third group, there are 'erotic' images which show unclothed women and men in *shunga* woodblock prints (literally 'spring pictures', woodblock prints with sexual content) or *bijin-e* (literally 'images of beauties'), which both became popular in the late 17th century. However, in the Japanese culture before the Meiji era, it was the veiled body rather than the naked which was regarded as beautiful or desirable; nudity in general was not considered erotic.[44] This is probably linked to the rather relaxed handling of nakedness in daily life,

---

39 Other examples of images depicting (semi-) nakedness in a natural context could be pictures of women diving for abalones (*awabi*), for instance by Kitagawa Utamaro.

40 For a detailed explanation see TERAMOTO (2000): 193–215.

41 IBID (2000): 197.

42 IBID (2000): 205.

43 IBID (2000): 193.

44 For more information see NOMURA (1990) and SCREECH (2009): 117–128.

for instance in the context of bathing, and can be corroborated by detailed descriptions of clothing in literature as well as a focus on it in visual art.

For instance, Murasaki Shikibu's *Genji monogatari* (around 1021) contains numerous descriptions of the main protagonist Genji as well as various women, focussing on their garments and the way that their figures appear wrapped in a *kimono*.[45] In his famous essay on Japanese aesthetics, *In'ei raisan* (In Praise of Shadows) (1933), novelist Tanizaki Junichirô goes as far as comparing Japanese women's bodies to a stick: 'they [the women] remind me of stick dolls, for in fact they are nothing more than poles upon which to hang clothes. As with the dolls their substance is made up of layer upon layer of clothing...'[46] Tanizaki's quotation well expresses that the notion of *kimono* dressing is a form of *creating* a new bodily shape rather than enhancing existing ones. Furthermore, as Ofra Goldstein-Gidoni has highlighted, 'the female body is "corrected" by pads and belts before putting on a *kimono*'.[47] This 'correction' could be contrasted with that through corsets in Victorian times since it hides female curves instead of enhancing them. When the main protagonist of Natsume Sôseki famous novel *Wagahai wa neko de aru* (I Am a Cat) (1905), the tomcat, visits a public bath, he states that the history of men is a history of clothing; 'when you see a human being without clothing, you do not get the feeling of seeing a human – you get the impression of unexpectedly meeting a monster.'[48] The humorous likening of naked humans to 'monsters' again emphasises how Japanese culture traditionally did not consider nakedness as beautiful.

Due to this cultural focus on the clothed body, it is not surprising that numerous protagonists in *shunga* are half-clothed during sexual intercourse – their bodies are decoratively wrapped in *kimono* solely with their large genitals exposed.[49] Various woodblock prints by Utagawa Kunisada, Keisai Eisen or Kitagawa Utamaro depict sexual intercourse in all sorts of positions and a great variety of participants. Although showing different people and sexual actions, the images mostly focus on the patterned *kimono* and genitals – the protagonist's figures and naked skin do not appear to be important. Timon Screech has highlighted that Japanese ideals of eroticism in art derive from clothed bodies rather than naked ones, especially in *shunga*: the images show 'figures clothed because that was considered the best way to make available a palpable, but

---

45 BENL (1966): 79, 98, 105, 207, 216, 236, 594.

46 TANIZAKI (1977): 29.

47 GOLDSTEIN-GIDONI (1999): 361; for more information on the body in *kimono* see DALBY (1993) or HENDRY (1993).

48 NATSUME (1996): 322.

49 For more information on the depiction of genitals as well as the role of *kimono* and naked skin in *shunga*, see LINHART (1999): 125–128 and SCREECH (2009): 117–128.

restrained, eroticism … the clothes themselves carry sexual weight'.[50] Screech has persuasively juxtaposed the focus on clothing and genitals in *shunga* with the 'Western' nude:

> 'The Western genre of the nude downplays the genitals. With so much erotic power inherent in the secondary sexual characteristics, it could afford to. Genitals, in a sense, are not really needed… *Shunga*, however, take the reverse path and, in the absence of secondary sexual characteristics, necessarily rely on genitals to hold the viewer.'[51]

The genre of *bijin-e* or *bijin-zu* (literally 'image of a beauty') is more similar to European nude images since the artworks focus on (mostly female) 'beauty'. For instance, there are woodblock prints of *yuagari-bijin* (the 'beauty/beauties after the bath'), which depict one or more young women just after taking a bath. However, most *bijin-e* images, including *yuagari-bijin-e* by Kitagawa Utamaro or Chôkosai Eisho, do not show completely unclothed bodies but rather reveal body parts, such as the neck or the breasts. As such, 'the artists [of *bijin-e*] showed a much greater interest in clothes and accessories than in corporeality,'[52] the bodies were again considered more beautiful when (at least partly) veiled in clothes.

An exception is Kitagawa Utamaro's painting *Nyûyoku bijin-zu* (Bathing Beauty Image) (around 1799), which depicts a completely naked woman who is about to enter a bathtub. The viewer sees her from behind; the fact that she does not notice the viewer's gaze results in a sensual, almost voyeuristic tension. However, the woman's 'incorrect' anatomy and the strong contours create a sense of artificiality and a graphic style which are a strong contrast to the aesthetic of naturalistic European paintings. Although depicting her naked, Utamaro does not focus on corporeality. Rather, he presents us with a purely aesthetic image in a linear perspective.

In light of these considerations, the group of 'erotic' images, whether they are 'in your face' scenes of sexual intercourse in *shunga* or depictions of beautiful women in *bijin-e*, never focus on the naked body in a naturalistic way. The images either present the body wrapped in *kimono*, exposing enormous genitals, or they present its naked form in a graphic and almost abstract way. Japanese art never had the function of presenting the viewer with a likeness of the 'real' naked body. Rather, it presents the body as an aesthetic, stylised form; some body parts are only hinted at, as they are considered aesthetically not relevant.

---

50 Screech (2009): 114–115.
51 Ibid: 112.
52 Berndt (2008): 316.

In summary, contrary to European art history, there are few artworks in Japan before the Meiji era which depict naked human bodies. If humans are completely unclothed, such as in images of bathing or in Maruyama's *Jinbutsu seisha sôhon*, they are predominantly viewed as un-erotic objects. The human body was rather considered beautiful and desirable in clothing. Thus, *shunga* and *bijin-e* mostly depict their protagonists veiled in *kimono*, exposing only parts of their bodies. *Bijin-e* come closest to the 'Western' concept of the female 'nude' since they present women as alluring and ideal art objects. However, even if the women are completely naked their linear bodies can hardly be compared to the corporeality presented in European oil paintings.

All these things considered, the specific forms of nakedness in Japanese artworks could be explained with social factors, such as the handling of nakedness in public baths or the sensual associations of bodies in *kimono*, as well as with art media and technique factors, such as the linear perspective and graphic style used in Japanese paintings and woodblock prints. Consequently, the motif of naked women in Japanese art history strongly differs from the 'Western' female nude. I agree with Jacqeline Berndt, who has stated that '... all those bodies [in *shunga*, *bijin-e* etc.] had in common that they were naked, not that they were nudes.'[53]

2.1.5 How the 'Naked' Became 'Nude' in Japanese Art History

The previous sections have contrasted the female 'nude' as a 'beautiful' object and a symbol of skilful painting in 'Western' art history, with female 'nakedness' in Japanese art history. However, Japan's contact with 'the West' precipitated an alteration of its view on nakedness in society as well as on naked body images.

In 1871, the government gave an ordinance to all heads of Tokyo households that 'they were responsible to ensure that all people had to be dressed,' and nudity in public soon became prohibited (Article 22).[54] Japan sought to become a 'modern' and 'civilized' country; the goal was, as Sepp Linhart has written, to present the 'Western' powers with 'an image void of sex and nakedness'.[55] In addition, soon after Manet created *Olympia* in the late 1860s, the 'Western' concept of 'art', painting techniques and art history were introduced to Japan (see Part 1). Consequently, as part of the canon of 'Western' art, the concept of the 'nude' was also implanted. Anne-Marie Bonnet has described Manet's approach in *Olympia* as a 'manifest of modern painting', highlighting

53 BERNDT (2008): 316.
54 LINHART (2007): 169.
55 IBID: 169.

how he used the female body provocatively in order to illustrate his 'realistic' art concept: 'the nude became naked.'[56] However, it could be argued that in Japan, at the same time, the 'naked became nude'.

When Japanese artists started to adopt the 'Western' genre of the nude, they did so by painting predominantly Caucasian women in oil colours – the medium, the motif and the motif's body were all similarly foreign. For instance, Kuroda Seiki's *Chôshô* (Morning Toilet) (1893), which he painted during his stay in Paris and which is said to be the very first full-nude painting in Japan,[57] depicts a French model. She looks into a mirror and is viewed from behind. Kuroda's triptych *Chi Kan Jô* (Wisdom, Impression, Sentiment) (1897) (fig. 34) is probably the first nude painting that deploys a Japanese model and was painted as well as exhibited in Japan. However, the woman's face as well as body proportions with rather long legs and large breasts appear Caucasian. This is perhaps connected to Kuroda's ten-year stay in France, however, it also emphasises how the genre of the nude was associated with Caucasian women. According to the critic Kimura Shôhachi, Japanese women at the time were inappropriate for nude paintings, due to their 'short stocky legs, their cat's backs and huge heads.'[58] Kimura's quotation reflects how Japan's modernisation, forced upon Japan by 'Western' powers, resulted in a Japanese complex towards 'the West' and consequently also Caucasian bodies. Caucasian body proportions appeared more suitable for nude paintings than the Japanese and more desirable in general. Jacqueline Berndt has concluded persuasively: the 'nude' in modern Japan was a symbol of 'cultural modernity'; consequently, 'Western' bodily forms were favoured.[59] I will return to this aspect in 3.1.

Another reason for painting women with Caucasian body proportions is linked to dealing with nakedness differently depending on its social context. As aforementioned, nakedness in public baths appeared 'appropriate' and was dealt with in a relaxed way. However, depicting a naked woman posing for an image was new to the Japanese and appeared rather 'inappropriate'. Thus, it must have been easier for Japanese artists to paint Caucasian bodies: the bodies of 'the Other' were less bound to Japanese traditions and could be more easily used to break social conventions.[60]

---

56 Bonnet (1997): 72.

57 The painting does not exist anymore since it was destroyed when Tokyo was bombarded in June 1945.

58 As cited in Berndt (2008): 326.

59 Ibid: 311.

60 This aspect is still relevant today. In Japanese TV, images of naked Japanese women appear on late-night television or advertisement for sex trade. However, when it comes to advertisement for mainstream products, mostly White people are shown breaking the conventional rules of Japanese society – as 'outsiders' they are freer to do things that Japanese people would usually not do. Thus, it is not surprising that nude representations of (mostly Caucasian) foreigners are more common in advertisements for mainstream products and

Posing nude was new to Japanese women. Thus, their facial expressions and their pose in early photographs often reflect their insecurity. Iizawa Kôtaro has compared early nude photographs with later ones of the photography book *Meiji ratai shashinchô* (Nude Photographs of the Meiji era) (1970). In the early photographs of the Meiji era, both the photographers, who did not know how to make the women look attractively 'nude', and the girls appear to be ashamed.[61] The women are 'naked' rather than 'nude'. Similarly, Kuroda's painting *Chôshô* was quite different from traditional European nude paintings since it justifies the model's nakedness not by references to religion, mythology or Orientalism, but by the 'allegedly "natural" setting' of a woman's boudoir'.[62] As Berndt has argued, the situation's rather 'natural' and spontaneous impression is due to the 'absence of plain posing'.[63] All these things considered, early Japanese nude photographs as well as paintings appear less idealised and more 'natural' than most of their 'Western' counterparts. It could be argued that the bodies of early Japanese nude images are in a state between being 'naked' and 'nude'.

When 'Western' and early Japanese nude images were shown to the Japanese public in the late 19th century, they attracted attention. At first, it was not appreciated, but considered inappropriate. Returning to some of my arguments mentioned earlier in this section, this is not surprising. Firstly, it has been explained that *kimono* create new bodily forms rather than enhance existing ones. For instance, female *kimono* create lines rather than highlight curves – unlike in 'Western' clothing, the curves of the female breasts, the buttocks and the legs are strongly reduced. Thus, both Western women's clothing as well as Caucasian bodies in paintings must have appeared unusual to Japanese people. In Natsume Sôseki's novel *Wagahai wa neko de aru* (I Am A Cat), cited earlier in this section, there is a passage which reflects this well. While looking at humans in a public bath, the tomcat reflects upon 'Western' clothing.[64] He ridicules the way that dresses unveil the body: 'these ladies unveil their décolleté, shoulders and arms and call the result evening gown. What an impudent behaviour!'[65]

Secondly, due to a plain and rather graphic style in ink paintings and woodblock prints, Japanese art history had not known corporeality in a 'Western' sense. The way that oil paintings rendered Caucasian nude bodies naturalistically must have appeared exotic to Japanese people. This is reflected in a fa-

---

businesses where 'naked depictions of Japanese would be considered inappropriate.' CREIGHTON (1995): 137.

61 IIZAWA (1992): 28–30.

62 BERNDT (2008): 313.

63 IBID (2008): 313.

64 NATSUME (1996): 318–322.

65 IBID (1996): 321.

mous scandal caused by the display of Kuroda's *Chôshô* at the 4th National Industrial Fair in Kyoto in 1895. Georges Bigot's caricature *La femme nue de M. Kuroda* (1895) depicts the astonished audience: people in front of Kuroda's painting stare at the body with their faces reflecting surprise. One girl even covers her eyes as if she were ashamed of seeing the image, while at the same time holding up her kimono and exposing her own legs. New censorship laws prohibited 'real-looking' depictions of naked bodies in a public context. Nude paintings and sculptures were either partly covered-up with a loincloth (as had happened with Kuroda's *Chôshô* when the Tennô visited the exhibition in Kyoto) or they were secretly shown in extra rooms of the exhibition venue where only adult men from the better circles were allowed admission with special permission.[66]

In the 20th century, the bodies in Japanese 'nude' paintings and photographs became increasingly idealised. Iizawa has contrasted the nude photographs of the Taishô and Shôwa era with the afore-mentioned Meiji era images: the women are now professional models who are used to 'be seen', knowing how to show their bodies alluringly.[67] Furthermore, the bodies in nude paintings now look recognisably 'Japanese'; for instance, the models in Yorozu Tetsugorô's nude paintings have obvious East-Asian proportions. Besides, the nude body crossed over into the traditionalist *nihonga* genre; for instance, Hashiguchi Goyo created numerous woodblock prints of Japanese nudes. Similarly, commercial posters increasingly included partly unclothed women, advertising mostly for alcohol and cigarettes. An example is the Sapporo beer poster of 1908, depicting a young woman, probably the famous dancer Sadayakko, standing next to an extremely large bottle (fig. 35).[68] She is veiled in a completely transparent cloth as if she were trying to represent the aforementioned typically nude characteristic of exposing and yet disguising.

Such images show clearly how the formerly 'naked' body had become 'nude'. In other words, Japanese imagery had adopted a rather 'Western' gaze on the naked human body. Thus, I agree with Norman Bryson's argument that the woman was a 'medium of intramale exchange' in the process of Japan's assimilation to 'the West'.[69] The process of social and cultural assimilation to

66 BERNDT (2008): 320.

67 IIZAWA (1992): 33; for instance Nojima Yasuzô produced numerous nude photographs in the Taishô era, which look rather 'professional' with self-confident models.

68 Other examples include an advertisement poster for *Tengu tobacco* (1900), depicting a nude woman in front of a mirror, and a photographic poster for *Akadama Port Wine* (1922) with a smiling nude woman, whose breasts and lower part of the body are covered in darkness. For further information on these images and Japanese advertisement with beautiful women (*bijin*) in general, see YAMAMOTO and TSUGANESAWA (1992): 286–303.

69 BRYSON (2003): 98.

'the West' was figured 'through a female iconography,'[70] the traditionally 'naked' woman gradually became a modern 'nude'.

2.2 A Double-Parody of the Female Nude or the Return of the Male Object in Visual Art: Thoughts on *Portrait (Futago)*

In 'Western' art history, Manet's *Olympia* reflects a turning point from the idealised 'nude' to a more 'naked' body. At the same time, it was created shortly before Japanese artists started to adopt the 'Western' notion of the female 'nude'. Thus, Morimura's appropriation of *Olympia* within a Japanese context could be interpreted as a reference to both European and Japanese art history.

2.2.1 A Double-Parody of the Female Nude

Regarding European art history, *Portrait (Futago)* could be interpreted as a 'double-parody'; this is due to the appropriated *Olympia* itself being something of a 'parody'. There are two main reasons. Firstly, *Portrait (Futago)* could be defined as a 'double-parody' as regards the artwork's medium. Morimura has photographed a tableau vivant consisting of studio props, a painted background and himself in two roles. He was able to insert himself twice into the image by means of a photographic collage. As such, he has appropriated Manet's painting *Olympia* by using a different artistic technique. Similarly, the way Manet depicted the figure Olympia can be seen as ushering in a new era of artistic technique, i.e. an era of painting in which there was no longer an emphasis on naturalism. As mentioned in 2.1, the female nude in European art since Renaissance times had been inextricably intertwined with the medium of oil painting, illusionistically presenting corporeality. Manet, however, painted Olympia provocatively with strong linear contours, suggesting an almost flat, unnaturalistic and Japonistic aesthetic; I will return to the influence of Japonism in 3.1. In conclusion, the photographic collage *Portrait (Futago)* not only references the rather realistic and partly linear painting *Olympia* but also earlier, more naturalistic paintings of, for instance, Venus. In extremely large size and a golden frame, the photographic collage parodies the high status of the genre oil painting and its naturalistic aesthetic. Moreover, by taking a photograph of a tableau vivant, Morimura also indirectly points at photographs and tableaux vivants with female nudes, which were prominent in the 19th and early 20th century.

---

70 IBID (2003): 117.

Secondly, *Portrait (Futago)* is a 'double-parody' considering the motif of the figure on the bed. Morimura adopted Olympia into his Japanese context, using his own Japanese male body as well as a *kimono* and *manekineko* (beckoning cat). Similarly, Manet had implanted the mythological image of Venus and Odalisque into the context of contemporary Parisian prostitution and projected it provocatively onto the 'real' body of Olympia. This realism exposed the mystique of the nude as a theatrical sham. Consequently, the main figure on the bed in *Portrait (Futago)* does not only reference the cocotte Olympia in Manet's painting but indirectly also nude women, especially Venus and Odalisque, in earlier European artworks. In other words, Morimura not only references a famous modern image of a French woman of the late 19th century but also a Roman goddess and a Turkish chambermaid – he parodies a long tradition of showing female nudes in European paintings.

Manet shocked the academic art scene as he depicted a prostitute who is looking unflinchingly at the viewer and demanding his attention as if he were a potential client. Through the way she returns the viewer's gaze with an unrepentant stare, suggesting self-confidence in her sexual display, Manet has somewhat empowered the female nude and allowed her to be more than a passive object of voyeurism; instead of merely occupying the position of a nude to be consumed, she assumes a role of agency. By reclining nude on the bed *himself*, Morimura goes one step further than Manet: he brings 'masculinity' to the image, providing an ironic critique of conventional gender relations in 'Western' art history. Although Olympia is a 'real' woman, instead of an idealised goddess, she still is a woman, reinforcing the dichotomy of the male viewer and the artist Manet on the one side, and she as the female object on the other. As Kasahara has pointed out persuasively, Morimura has inverted the roles of 'looking' and 'being looked at' by firstly using a male body instead of a female and secondly by using his own. As such, he not only questions the heterosexual power relation of the male 'customer' with the cocotte Olympia, but also leads the relationship of the male painter to his female model ad absurdum.[71] This argument similarly applies to *Red Marilyn*. The photograph challenges gender categories in film culture and pin-up images by parodying the male viewer's gaze as well as the male photographer's gaze towards the nude actress: Morimura is both the creator of the photographic image and its alluring 'sex object'.

2.2.2 The Return of the Male Object in Visual Art

In light of Japanese art history, *Portrait (Futago)* not only references Japan's adoption of the 'Western' notion of the female nude but also highlights its

[71] KASAHARA (2002): 95–96.

influence on Japanese views on the male body. As argued earlier in this section, the introduction of Western painting in the Meiji period led to a new understanding of nakedness in Japanese art – the 'naked' became 'nude.' This development in art and popular imagery is intertwined with a change in the Japanese viewpoint on gender relations. Simply put, it established the 'Western' dichotomy of the 'male gaze' versus the beautiful 'female body'.

Watanabe Tsuneo and Iwata Jun'ichi have offered an interesting viewpoint, arguing that there could be a profound relationship between the Japanese implementation of the female nude and the development of a social 'taboo on homosexuality'.[72] Male-male eroticism had been prominent both sexually as well as aesthetically in pre-modern Japan. Male youthful beauty, personified by the *wakashû* ('young man') as an erotic object for both women and men, had been a relevant topic in literature as well as visual art especially between the 16th and 18th century.[73] However, due to 'Western' influence in the Meiji era, male-male eroticism became repressed socially as well as culturally; it was no longer celebrated in literature, theatre, and art but rather discouraged as an 'evil custom' of the past. At the same time, the 'Western' concept of the female nude influenced Japanese visual culture, including *yôga*, *nihonga* and commercial posters. As evident in the aforementioned Sapporo beer poster (1908), Japanese imagery adopted a 'Westernized' gaze on the female body.

Watanabe and Iwata have argued that the decline of male-male eroticism was 'strictly parallel to beauty being taken over by women.'[74] The conclusion that beauty was 'taken over by women' might be too generalised as there are contexts in which male beauty and eroticism play an important role, e.g. in *kabuki* theatre or *manga*. However, I would agree that the 'Western' binary of the 'male gaze' and 'the female body' has repressed the beauty of the male body in the everyday imagery of the 20th century.

Firstly, women are much more present as beautiful objects in popular imagery than men. Today, Japanese cities are full of images of women: for instance, erotica magazines are visibly placed in 24hour shops and men look at images of nude women in sports magazines on the subway.[75] Kasahara Michiko's explanation of her *Love's Body – Rethinking Naked and Nude in Photography* exhibition[76] includes the following passage:

> It [the exhibition] will attempt to free itself from the *traditional form of bodily expression "the nude,"* [my italics] to restore the body and sexual-

[72] WATANABE and IWATA (1987): 12.

[73] For a detailed analysis of male-male sexuality and eroticism in Japan see PFLUGFELDER (1999) or MOSTOW (2003).

[74] WATANABE and IWATA (1987): 13.

[75] KASAHARA (1998b): 10–11.

[76] The exhibition was shown in the Tokyo Metropolitan Museum of Photography in 1998.

> ity that has never been expressed in the genre of the nude, while looking at the new possibilities and meaning of bodily representation.[77] [sic]

This statement shows that Kasahara seeks to present 'alternative' forms of nakedness as the 'Western' concept of the 'nude' is now viewed as a 'traditional form'. Kasahara does not mention that the concept of the 'nude' had no tradition in Japan before the Meiji era; the female nude body has become completely embedded in Japanese culture.

Secondly, in everyday life, the Japanese male is less associated with a beautiful body than the female. This is, for instance, evident in the difference of male and female clothing: similar to 'Western' business environments, Japanese business men generally wear a dark suit which masks the bodily forms underneath, whereas women wear blouses and skirts which show their bodies more. The stereotypical image of 'the Japanese man' is rather 'asexual': he has to be a good company worker, a responsible citizen and a representative of his family. As Laura Miller has explained, Japanese men and women have evaluated men 'primarily on the basis of character, social standing, earning capacity, lineage and other social criteria'.[78] This started to change in the 1990s, as I will argue in 5.3. However, until then, attractive physicality was excluded from the stereotypical 'Japanese man' of the 20th century; rather, he was associated with his work and social responsibility.

Taking these considerations into account, it could be argued that by reclining nude on the bed with his slender body fitting well into the image, Morimura reanimates a motif of Japanese culture which started to fade shortly after Manet painted *Olympia*: the alluring aesthetic of the male body.

In summary, in light of the complex art historical background, *Portrait (Futago)* as a *photograph* of Morimura's naked *male* body seems like an ironic reference to the high status of the genre of oil painting and the tradition of presenting the female body for the male gaze. As such, *Portrait (Futago)* references clearly European art history. At the same time, by inserting his discernibly Japanese body as well as Japanese props into the image, Morimura references a traditional Japanese aesthetic of the male body which was marginalised by the female nude. By looking at the viewer self-confidently, Morimura highlights the sensuality of his body, as if he wanted to claim back the tradition of the *wakashû* ('young man'). In doing so, he presents the viewer with a body which appears neither 'nude' nor 'naked' and neither 'female' nor 'male' but rather 'mixed' or 'hybrid'.[79]

---

77 KASAHARA (1998a): 185.

78 MILLER (2006): 37.

79 I use the term 'hybrid' not as part of a 'postcolonial' discourse but in a broader and more colloquial sense: it stands for a blend of multiple genders, sexes, nationalities and identities.

The notion of the *wakashû* and Morimura's 'hybrid' nakedness are inextricably intertwined with gender issues which I did not explore in this section: if Morimura's gender in *Portrait (Futago)* and *Red Marilyn* had to be defined, what would it be? This question will be examined in the gender section in 5.4. Furthermore, the Black servant in *Portrait (Futago)* plays an important role, especially considering the artwork's political context. I will return to this in 3.1.

2.3 The Aged Female Body: Thoughts on *Gyahtei #17*

2.3.1 Old Bodies in 20th Century Imagery

Our attitudes towards ageing have gone through profound changes during the 20th century; it has become normal for the majority of the 'first world' population to live to one's seventies or beyond. Partly in consequence, partly due to the low birth rate, old people currently account for a higher proportion of the population than ever before. In Japan, more than 21% of the population were over 65 years old in 2007;[80] Japanese society is getting ever older. At the same time, the media vigorously promotes youth by advertising images of young fit bodies whereas the old and weak are excluded. Old people are almost invisible; it seems as if society has become incapable of contemplating their bodies with serenity. Taking this into consideration, Yamanaka's *Gyahtei* series appears as a 'wake up call' highlighting the existence of startlingly old people and, more particularly, drawing attention to the aesthetic of their naked bodies.

2.3.2 The Naked Aged Female in Art History

The *Gyahtei* series features solely women. Although Yamanaka has stated that he did not bear any art historical motifs in mind when creating the series, its focus on old female bodies could firstly be related to a tradition in 'Western' art history. In various drawings, paintings and sculptures, especially of medieval times, the naked female body has been used to illustrate decay and transience; the curves are gone, the skin has become wrinkled, the faces are gaunt. For example, in the painting *Die Drei Lebensalter des Weibes und der Tod* (The Three Ages of the Woman and Death) (around 1510) (fig. 37), Hans Baldung Grien juxtaposes the body of a young woman with that of a child, an old woman and a skeleton. The body of the old woman, whose wrinkled skin and breasts are hanging, contrasts with the young woman's curvy body and smooth

80 HANDELSBLATT (2007): unnumbered.

skin.[81] Her old body is a symbol for the momentariness of the young woman's beauty and fertility.

There are few depictions of unclothed bodies in Japanese art history (see 2.1) and moreover, even fewer depictions of naked old women. These few depictions could be categorised into three main groups of images. The first group shows naked old women in everyday situations, such as in a public bath. Ochiai Yoshiiku's woodprint from the series *Imayô nenjû gyôji* (Modern Annual Events) (mid – late 19th century) (fig. 31), mentioned in 2.1, is an example of such an image. Among the many women, there is one woman, whose skin is darker and wrinkled and whose face is gaunt. In contrast to the other women, her hair is grey and patchy. A young woman is sitting next to this old woman and appears to wash her back. The artwork depicts an ordinary setting in which the old woman is used as one realistic element among others. In other words, neither her individuality nor her naked body are of particular relevance. Rather, the image seeks to convey the typically lively atmosphere of a public bath. Similar to the other people in the picture, the aged woman is a detail within a vivacious composition. Yoshiiku presents us with a variety of naked bodies which could be seen when going to the women's section of a public bath – bodies of young women, old women and children.

Another example of this category could be two sketches by Katsushika Hokusai on a scrapbook page depicting an old naked woman with a trough washing herself (fig. 36). The linear style of the drawings realised in few strokes conveys a graphical and almost caricature-like impression. The drawings convince through their accentuation of the old female body's most characteristic features, such as the hump and wrinkled skin, studying the way the body appears during the custom of washing oneself. The woman's face with her closed eyes expresses concentration on the activity and yet, it conveys a sense of relaxation as her scrawny back is scrubbed by a child.

The second group of images depicting naked old women are pictures which consider the body from an almost 'scientific' viewpoint. As afore mentioned, Maruyama Ôkyo's *Jinbutsu seisha sôhon* (Complete Folio of True Figure Studies) (1770) is a rare example of this group. It features paintings of naked men and women of different ages as well as close-up pictures of body parts, such as legs, mouths and genitalia. As John Teramoto has pointed out, the large-scale full-body image of an old woman (fig. 33) reflects Maruyama's careful observation; one can be persuaded easily that he was looking at a model.[82]

81 Other examples include the wooden sculptures *Garstige Alte* (Sour Old Woman) (1500) (Städtische Galerie Liebighaus, Museum alter Plastik. Frankfurt am Main), *Nackte Alte* (Naked Old Woman) (1530/40) (Städtische Galerie Liebighaus), *Alte Frau, sitzend* (Old Woman, Sitting) (1520–1525) (Victoria and Albert Museum, London), and the oil painting *Die Sieben Lebensalter* (The Seven Ages) (1544) by Hans Baldung Grien.

82 TERAMOTO (2000): 193.

Here, the old woman's naked body is used as an element of a comparative survey which could be linked to the encyclopaedic interests of 18th century Japan. However, similar to the images of the first group, the use of linear perspective and the limited number of brushstrokes create a rather graphic style.

Japan has had a long tradition of respecting the elderly. This is mainly connected to the filial piety and ancestral worship of Confucianism, which had been integrated into Buddhism when Buddhism was entrenched as a religion in China. It was also maintained in Japanese Buddhist and Shintô beliefs, which were intertwined in pre-modern times. In post-war Japan, the respect for the elderly is evident, for instance, in the 15th of September having been a public holiday titled the 'day for respecting the elderly' (*keirô no hi*) since 1966. Furthermore, compared to other industrial nations, there are few nursing homes. It is still not common and generally considered irresponsible to place one's parents into a nursing home.

However, at the same time, Japan has also had a tradition of marginalising and demonising old women. One example is the mythological motif of the *obasuteyama* (literally 'mountain where old women are abandoned') (since the 13th century). This motif of abandoning old people who were a burden on their families and leaving them in a desolate mountain to die is, for instance, described in Fukazawa Shichirô's novel *Narayama bushi-kô* (The Ballad of Narayama) (1956). In addition, there was a trend in the late Edo and early Meiji era to depict old women as evil in literary works as well as in theatre plays and popular images. Susanne Formanek has analysed this motif and its social context in her extensive work *Die böse Alte* (The Evil Old Woman) (2005). Agreeing with Hirota Masaki and Dorothea Gasztner, Formanek has explained this negative cliché of old women with the misogynistic teachings of Buddhism refusing women from gaining enlightenment as well as with the subordinated role of women in Confucianism, which became popular again in the Edo period.[83] Returning to my categorisations of the naked aged woman as a motif in Japanese art history, the third category could consist of book illustrations and woodblock prints depicting these evil women. It is striking that they are mostly half-naked, exposing their breasts (fig. 38, 39 and 40). Similar to European medieval artworks which juxtapose old women with girls, the *ijiwaru baba* ('nasty old woman') or *onibaba* ('evil old woman') is often depicted next to a young woman (fig. 38 and 39). However, in contrast to European works, including the aforementioned work by Baldung, the young women are never nude but wear a *kimono*. It is not their eroticism and fertility which is most relevant, it is rather their beauty and their 'normal' appearance. The young women are juxtaposed with the old women who are depicted half-naked in or-

[83] FORMANEK (2005): 18.

der to enhance their animalistic expression. Their bodies are withered and wrinkled and yet, they seem powerful, strong and hungry. Their exposed breasts along with their unkempt hair symbolise wild behaviour.

Gyahtei #17 cannot be categorised into one of these groups. The woman is neither shown naturally in an everyday bathing scene nor as a wild evil being. It could be argued that photographing her naked body in front of a neutral background with sharp focus and in large scale is most comparable to Maruyama Ôkyo's approach in the image of the old woman in *Jinbutsu seisha sôhon.* Both works study the woman's naked body almost scientifically and yet view it from an aesthetic perspective. At the same time, considering the mass of nude images in Japan as well as worldwide today, *Gyahtei #17* could be interpreted as a reminder of youthful beauty's momentariness. As such, it is somewhat comparable to European works, such as the aforementioned painting by Baldung. As a counterpart to the girl's body, the old woman's body becomes a symbol of transience. However, given the fact that the *Gyahtei* series consists of seventeen photographs which all feature full-body images of startlingly old women on their own, the work is unique in both a Japanese and 'Western' art historical context.

2.3.3 The 'Beauty of Decay'

In the photographic production process between 1993 and 1997, Yamanaka took a large number of photographs of both old women and men. However, he chose only images of women for the final series, stating in my interview that 'there were more women than men who were that old.' Indeed, according to a survey conducted by the Japanese Prime Minister's department in 1998, there were 1,9 times more women aged over 75 years than men and even 2,4 times more women over 85 years.[84] The older the population, the higher its female percentage.

Moreover, as Yamanaka has explained, women's bodies have a higher proportion of fat; 'when they get old, they have more hanging skin creating individual wrinkles'. This quotation underlines how Yamanaka was not interested in old people from a sociological or documentary viewpoint. He rather chose those whose bodies were most appropriate for his series aesthetically. The old women visualise best how young and fertile bodies shrink when getting older. Their skin has become extremely wrinkled as life increasingly vanishes – they personify age and decay. The series' aesthetic viewpoint is also obvious when considering the fact that the photographs do not provide any personal information. It is not the individuals but rather the ageing of their bodies which

[84] LINHART (2000): 76.

seems to be the artworks' main motif. The way that all women are equally presented in large-sized, sharp, black and white photographs as well as the way they are positioned in front of white backgrounds forces the viewer compare and contrast the different bodies. The seriality puts emphasis on the similarities in human ageing and dying.

As mentioned in Part 2, the woman in *Gyahtei #17* was tended by Yamanaka as a voluntary nurse twice or thrice a week. This relationship is relevant for the artwork's atmosphere, since the woman trusts the photographer. Yamanaka has taken care of her needs for months, bathed her and thus seen her naked many times before. She looks shy and ashamed of her nakedness, however, she has enough confidence to directly look at the photographic lens. Together with the photograph's stylised aesthetic, the woman's direct gaze at the viewer saves her from becoming an object of pity; although her frail and old body seems to announce her impending death, the image does not convey a pessimistic impression. This rather unsentimental presentation of the aged body is perhaps linked to the fact that old age in Japanese culture has not only been viewed negatively as biological decline. Rather, ageing has also been regarded positively as an opportunity of getting closer to another Buddhist realm and gradually moving towards nirvana. Moreover, the photograph's aesthetic focus on the woman's wrinkle pattern and skin drapery makes her radiate a subtle beauty. This beauty could be described as a 'beauty of decay'. I will return to this 'beauty' in 6.3 when analysing *Gyahtei #17* in its cultural context influenced by Buddhism.

Returning to the differentiation between the 'naked' and the 'nude' body at the very beginning of this section, it could be questioned which category *Gyahtei #17* belongs to. It does not need mentioning that the old woman is not presented alluringly like an 'erotic' 'nude'. However, she is not 'neutrally naked' either. Rather, Yamanaka presents us with a stylised picture of an aged naked body looking at it from an investigative and aesthetic viewpoint. As an aesthetic object made for a spectator, the woman even meets John Berger and Kenneth Clark's definition of the 'nude' as a naked body which is 'seen'[85] and 're-formed' into an image.[86] It could be concluded that the photograph resists any categorisation.

By featuring startlingly old women and focussing on their bodies' aesthetic, Yamanaka highlights naked forms which are invisible in mainstream media images. However, considering future prospects, these are at least as representative of the contemporary and, moreover, future society of Japan (and other industrial nations) as young fit bodies. In addition, ageing is a necessary process leading to the end of all life. Yamanaka's study of old female bodily aes-

85 BERGER (1972): 54.
86 CLARK (1972): 1.

thetic could be interpreted as a reminder that every new wrinkle can not only be seen as a sign of decay but also as a natural and even 'beautiful' step leading to another unknown world. Although it is problematic how Yamanaka took the photographs, the *Gyahtei* series applies a counterforce against the mass of youthful nude images that the media as well as the art world presents us with every day.

2.4 The Naked Body as a 'Torso' or 'Landscape': Thoughts on *Chromosome XY s. o.* and *SCAR 1983 illness*

2.4.1 Stylised Images of Naked Body Parts

Both *Chromosome XY s. o.* and *SCAR 1983 illness* provide a contrast to the images analysed in the previous sections insofar as they are fragmentary close-up images rather than full-body pictures. The skin fills out the whole photograph; as described in 4.3 and 4.5 of Part 2, pores, pigments and bodily details create an aesthetic composition in black and white.

How could the body in *Chromosome XY s. o.* and *SCAR 1983 illness* be defined – as 'nude' or rather 'naked'? Similar to *Gyahtei #17*, it could be argued that both images are 'nudes' insofar as the body is presented deliberately as an aesthetic object for a spectator; illumination and composition transform the body into an image. However, with the head missing, the aesthetic impression of *Chromosome XY s. o.* is comparable to that of a torso, for instance by August Rodin; Ishiuchi presents us with a bodily fragment and yet, also, a self-sufficient body image. This notion of being a detail and yet a self-contained picture seems more relevant for the photograph's impression than any alluring tension evident in nude images. *SCAR 1983 illness* differs from conventional nudes in that the use of the close-up perspective causes the viewer to focus on naked skin rather than bodily contours. It is not the body which becomes 're-formed' as Clark's definition of the 'nude'.[87] Rather, it is the body's *surface* which becomes 're-formed' – a landscape of skin with its unique contours, dips and swells. It does not have to be mentioned that the typical characteristic of numerous nude images – the exposing and yet disguising pose – is also absent in Ishiuchi's work. Clark's description of the 'nude' as a 'balanced, prosperous and confident' body,[88] does not apply to *Chromosome XY s. o.* and *SCAR 1983 illness* at all.

Moreover, *SCAR 1983 illness* seems almost 'abstract' since the focus on the body's surface shows its details as parts of an aesthetic composition which

[87] BERGER, (1972): 54.
[88] CLARK (1972): 1.

seems to be independent from the bodily figure as a whole. In addition, there are no attributes which define the person in *Chromosome XY s. o.* and *SCAR 1983 illness*. In the former, it is suggested to the viewer that the body is male, and in the latter he knows that its scar is related to an illness. However, other personal information about the individual depicted is not given. This enhances the photographic focus on the naked body from a purely aesthetic, almost 'abstract' viewpoint.

Taking all these arguments into consideration, it could be concluded that *Chromosome XY s. o.* and *SCAR 1983 illness* are, although aestheticised through the bright illumination and composition as 'nudes', rather 'stylised', and almost 'abstract' images of 'naked' body parts.

2.4.2 *SCAR 1983 illness* as an Abstract Landscape

The slightly blurred close-up perspective in *SCAR 1983 illness* creates an impression which could even be compared to an 'abstract landscape'. A 'landscape' defines an expanse of scenery in nature which is interpreted as a self-contained picture, although it always continues outside the image that one can see in one view. *SCAR 1983 illness* does not depict a natural environment with trees, plants or other elements of nature; however, it shows skin patterns as an autonomous scenery and is, as such, comparable to artworks of landscapes or abstract paintings.

The aspect of being a detail of the whole and yet, at the same time, a self-contained composition is interesting when considering the artwork in its Japanese context; it could be linked to the Daoist and Buddhist concept of there being microcosms corresponding to a macrocosm. The human body has been viewed as a microcosm in correspondence with the macrocosm of heaven and earth since antiquity in China. This is evident, for instance, in the canonical classic of Chinese medicine, *Huangdi neijing* (Inner Canon of the Yellow Emperor).[89] Chinese speaking intellectuals brought this idea of likening the human body to a microcosm to Japan. For instance, the Zen monk Takuan writes in his book *Isetsu* (Medical Discourses) (late 16th–early 17th century):

> Man is a microcosm (*shô-tenchi*) within the macrocosm (*tenchi*). In other words, man is a small macrocosm. … Although man's body is small, its character is no different than the macrocosm. … The reason why the head of man is round is because heaven is round. The reason why man has four limbs is because the earth is square, and has four sides.[90]

---

89 SHIRASUGUI (2000): 45.
90 As cited in IBID: 45.

Takuan's quotation shows how he views the human body in relation to the macrocosm. Consequently, bodily form, for instance the roundness of the head, is defined naturally; following the rules of the macrocosm, every bodily part has its meaning. Moreover, as Zen Buddhism considers every grain of sand to possess the same value as the whole cosmos, every pore of human skin too possesses the same value.

In light of all these considerations, the naked body in *SCAR 1983 illness* could be interpreted as a reminder of the human body being a small and yet precious cosmos. Presenting it aesthetically like a 'landscape', Ishiuchi indirectly draws a parallel between the surface of the human body and the earth with its mountainous as well as hollow forms. Be it with or without a religious context, it could be argued that the body is presented from a viewpoint which is more similar to that of the art genre of landscape images or abstract painting than of nudes. Moreover, *SCAR 1983 illness* elevates those parts of the human body which are usually forgotten or even concealed, including scars and pores, to precious art motifs.

2.5 Conclusions

The alluringly 'nude' female body, which has had a long history in European art, can be contrasted with rather 'naked' bodies in Japanese images before the Meiji era. This art historical context is relevant when considering the motif of the naked body in the artworks this thesis is concerned with. Appropriating Manet's *Olympia*, *Portrait (Futago)* ironically references the tradition of the European female nude as well as its adoption in Japan. However, *Portrait (Futago)* as well as *Red Marilyn* include a discernibly male Japanese body. In this way, Morimura not only challenges the 'Western' concept of the female nude in art and popular pin-up imagery but also combines it with the Japanese tradition of male beauty. On the one hand, he parodies a 'Western' art genre and its gender-relations, on the other hand, he makes use of it in order to bring back a male body aesthetic which has been somewhat repressed in Japanese imagery since modern times: around the same time that the female 'nude' became 'naked' in Manet's *Olympia*, the female 'naked' in Japan started to become 'nude', repressing the beauty of the male body. Morimura presents us with his unclothed body which appears 'hybrid' – even more hybrid than Olympia's, which itself is a mixture of the mythological figures Venus and Odalisque and a Parisian cocotte of the 19th century. Morimura's bodily 'hybridity' is linked to gender issues as well as a complex political background which will be analysed in 3.1 and 5.4.

Gyahtei #17 is comparable to medieval European works by, for example, Hans Baldung Grien, in presenting an aged female body as a symbol of transience. Although it is not juxtaposed with a nude young woman, the old body could be seen as a counterpart to the flood of nude images presented worldwide. At the same time, considering Japanese art history, *Gyahtei #17* shares an aesthetic viewpoint on the aged naked body with Maruyama Ôkyo's painting of an old naked woman in *Jinbutsu seisha sôhon.* Both women are presented in front of a neutral background and in a large-sized image. However, Yamanaka Manabu's aestheticised presentation of the body with bright artificial lighting, a neutral background, and in black and white transforms the woman into an even more 'beautiful' art object; age is viewed as something 'beautiful'. The notion of a 'beauty of decay', which describes the work's impression well, will be explored further in 6.3.

Chromosome XY s. o. and *SCAR 1983 illness* also focus on the body from an aesthetic viewpoint. However, they contrast with the aforementioned works in being close-up images: while the aesthetic of *Chromosome XY s. o.* could be compared to that of a torso, *SCAR 1983 illness* is even more similar to an abstract landscape. Like a landscape, it presents us with a self-contained composition of organic forms, which, nevertheless, continue outside the artwork's frame. This aspect could be linked indirectly to the Buddhist likening of microcosms, such as a Zen garden or the human body, to the world as a macrocosm. Be it in a Buddhist context or not, *SCAR 1983 illness* elevates scars, i.e. body parts which are usually not focussed on in artworks, to precious motifs of art.

What all these artworks have in common is that they do not present naked bodies alluringly as in 'conventional' nude images which I have described in 2.1. Instead, they either reference cleverly the 'Western' tradition of the 'nude', for instance *Portrait (Futago)* and *Red Marilyn*, or they present 'naked' bodies non-alluringly but nevertheless in an aesthetic way, such as in the *Gyahtei* series and in Ishiuchi Miyako's close-up images. They all stand in contrast to images of erotic 'nude' bodies on the one side or neutrally 'naked' bodies on the other. Perhaps, they illustrate the need for new terms to define the different shades that lie between 'nude' and 'naked'.

3. The Body and 'National' Identity

After having focussed on *Portrait (Futago)* with regard to questions on the female nude and the naked body in European as well as Japanese art history in 2.2, the following section will analyse the artwork from another viewpoint: it will relate the image to the colonial background of the 1860s when Manet painted *Olympia.* In addition, it will offer different readings of *Portrait*

(Futago) and *Red Marilyn*, examining how the relationship between 'Japan' and 'the West' is mirrored in the artworks.

The term 'national' identity in the chapter's title should be understood as a methodological construct; I use it as an umbrella term for a set of political, cultural and social features which could characterise 'Japan' and distinguish it from other nations. At the same time, the term refers to the individual's sense of belonging to 'Japan'. As my quotation marks around 'Japan', 'Japanese' and 'national' show, these distinguishing features are not only based on real facts but also on an imagined historical, cultural or ethnic commonality. As such, I draw upon Benedict Anderson's definition of the nation as an 'imagined community', arguing that 'the members of even the smallest nation will never know most of their fellow-members, meet them, or even hear of them, yet in the minds of each lives the image of their communion'.[91]

3.1 The 'Japanese' Body and 'National' Identity: Thoughts on *Portrait (Futago)* and *Red Marilyn*

3.1.1 French Colonial History

Having analysed Morimura in the role of Olympia in 2.2, I would now like to begin this section by looking at him in the disguise of the Black servant, who draws attention to the French colonial history reflected in Manet's painting *Olympia*. Even the 'new art historians' did not consider this aspect when they analysed *Olympia* in the 1980s. As Norman Bryson has criticised, they 'forgot' the servant:

> That neither the 'class' nor the 'gender' interpretation by the new art historians had recognised this […] indicated something rather disturbing: that even the most socially progressive, enlightened Western viewers still could not see race clearly. What were those cultural historians thinking about? How could they have forgotten that the Paris of 1865 was the capital of a vast – and expanding – colonial empire?[92]

Since the invasion of Algeria in 1830, the Second French Colonial Empire had been expanding. Not only had Algeria been conquered by the middle of the 1840s, France had also established a protectorate over Cambodia by 1863. It was also in the 1860s that Napoleon III gained control over Cochinchina. After the Franco-Prussian War between 1870 and 1871 and the founding of the Third Republic in the same year, France acquired further colonial possessions, such

---

91 ANDERSON (1991): 5.
92 BRYSON (1995): 75.

as Tonkin and Annam in Vietnam. Furthermore, several African leaders were forced to sign treaties which gave France the mandate to annex large tracts of the Western Sudan. The French gradually established control over African territories, including Mauritania, Senegal, French Sudan (present day Mali), French Guinea (present day Guinea), the Ivory Coast, Upper Volta (present day Burkina Faso), Dahomey (present day Benin) and Niger. At the beginning of the 20th century, these eight colonies were united in a federation named 'Afrique Occidentale Française' (AOF). Colonialism was also evident within France; in the late 18th century, African slaves were an important economic element in European trade, especially in Great Britain and France.

In this context, the servant in *Olympia* reflects brutal colonialism and underscores the consistent manner in which Blacks were subordinated. In addition, viewers of the painting in Manet's time might have seen the servant's skin as an element which emphasises the moral 'dirtiness' of the prostitute. Some contemporary critics also viewed Olympia's rather brown contour lines and her hands as 'dirty'.[93] This shows how skin colour was associated with moral attributes: while whiteness symbolised purity, darker colours were associated with immorality. French society of Manet's time categorised both prostitutes and Blacks as 'low class' and 'immoral'.

The history of European colonialism at the end of the 19th century can also be connected to the photographic medium of *Portrait (Futago):* photographs recorded and defined those who were colonised, while at the same time reassured the European photographers and viewers of their own superiority.[94] Europe was viewed as a norm, upon which all other cultures were judged. As Liz Wells has pointed out, 'the sense of "Otherness" and exoticism was not only captured "in the field" but was also exploited by photographers working in commercial enterprises'; this is evident in studio photography and postcard culture, for example in Algeria.[95] French photographers constructed exotic images which suited their own colonial fantasies and those of their European consumers.

Returning to *Portrait (Futago)*, Morimura as the Black woman wears a light-pink, 'Western' dress, like the servant in *Olympia*. This emphasises the adoption of 'Western' culture by the colonised, or in Homi Bhabha's words, the dress is part of the 'colonial mimicry'. Bhabha defines 'colonial mimicry' as

---

93 For instance, Louis de Laincel stated in 1865 that Olympia's contour lines were dirty ('crasse qui enduit leurs contours') and her hands were soiled ('aux mains sales'); as cited in CLARK (1978): 142.

94 See also PROCHASKA (1991), EDWARDS (1992) or BATE (1993).

95 WELLS (2007): 223; In the *Colonial Harem* (1987), Malek Alloula discusses images of Algerian women taken by French studio photographers in Algeria. She highlights how colonial power was represented through gendered relations with the White, male photographer abusing the 'non-White', female subject; ALLOULA (1986).

the 'desire for a reformed, recognizable Other'.[96] However, 'colonial mimicry' is ambivalent; 'in order to be effective, mimicry must continually produce its … *difference* [my italics].'[97] Although the Black servant in *Olympia* is wearing a 'Western' dress, her skin colour makes it obvious that she is not Caucasian. Her Blackness is emphasised even more as it contrasts with the light colour of the dress and its 'Western' design. As such, mimicry is a camouflage destined to fail; it is 'the sign of the inappropriate … a recalcitrance which coheres the dominant strategic function of colonial power' and which 'intensifies surveillance'.[98] However, Morimura's ethnic position as a 'Yellow' artist is clearly different from that of a 'White' or a 'Black' person in France. This enables him to highlight the political background of Manet's *Olympia* from a viewpoint other than that of a European or an African artist. On the one hand, he impersonates not only a White but also a Black person, he represents the colonist and the colonised simultaneously. His impersonation of both figures is stressed in the title *Futago* ('twins') stating that the two are related. On the other hand, the term 'twins' emphasises that the White cocotte and the Black servant were both subordinated in the society of Manet's time.

In conclusion so far, *Portrait (Futago)* highlights the colonial context of Manet's time in different ways: firstly, within the staged scene, it is relevant that Morimura not only disguises himself as Olympia but also as the Black servant. His dark make-up contrasts with the light-pink 'Western' dress, revealing it as 'colonial mimicry'. Secondly, the photographic medium is reminiscent of images of the colonised in anthropological photographs as well as staged studio photographs, for instance in Algeria. Thirdly, the word *Futago* in the title highlights the subordinated position of both Olympia and the Black servant.

The complex socio-historical and political context of *Olympia* may be a reason why Victoria Schmidt-Linsenhoff has argued that Morimura does 'not define his *Japanicity*' but analyses 'the gender coded significants of ethnicity in *European* masterpieces [my italics]'.[99] Fukagawa Masafumi has stressed that the most important concept of *Portrait (Futago)* is Morimura's use of his body as a source of irritation in order to reveal traditional (European) views; 'Morimura as an Asian man disguises himself as a prostitute in order to reveal the one-sided, dominant masculine gaze on naked women as well as the discrimination with which 'the West' used to view Black women.'[100] Although I have stated that *Portrait (Futago)* draws attention to the French colonial context of the modern era, I do not agree with Schmidt-Linsenhoff or Fukagawa in

---

96 Bhabha (1994): 122.
97 Ibid: 122.
98 Ibid: 122–123.
99 Schmidt-Linsenhoff (2005): 20.
100 Fukagawa (2007): 283.

excluding Morimura's 'Japanese' background from the artwork's meaning. As I have described in Part 2, 'Japanicity' is present in the artwork as a Japanese artist lies on a *kimono*, next to a Japanese *manekineko*. In light of his Japanese heritage, Morimura transposes the power-relations of France and its African colonies reflected in *Olympia* to draw attention to the history of his own country.

3.1.2 The Historical Background of Japan

In order to understand this profound political and socio-cultural history, the *kimono* and cat as well as Morimura's gaze in *Portrait (Futago)* should be analysed in further detail. In pre-modern times, certain types of *kimono* were reserved for certain classes of people; colour, length, and breadth of sleeves indicated 'information about the age and social or martial status of the wearer.'[101] The cranes and the gold and silver brocades on white ground indicate that the *kimono* in *Portrait (Futago)* is a bridal one. In Japan, the crane (*tsuru*) is considered a national treasure, appearing in folklore, art and literature as a symbol of peace and longevity. As monogamous birds, cranes also symbolise loyalty and long relationships. Therefore, it is not surprising that Norman Bryson and Ruth Wright-Jasinowski have interpreted the *kimono* as a traditional bridal *kimono* (*iro-uchikake*).[102] Morimura himself has emphasised that the flower decoration on the *kimono* (*hanamishô*) is a 'popular Japanese folklore' element.

The cat in *Portrait (Futago)* is a *manekineko*, a 'beckoning cat' (fig. 41).[103] The upraising of her left paw means 'come in' as she is inviting customers. *Manekineko* come in all sorts of colours, however, they are most commonly white with black and orange patches or gold. The different colours are associated with different attributes: black *manekineko* are believed to ward off misfortune by fighting against the evil powers of the black cat.[104] In contrast to Manet's work, the cat is not used as an obvious symbol of promiscuity. However, considering the history of the *manekineko*, she can be seen as a sexual talisman. Replicas of male genitals were often displayed as objects of luck and worship in geisha houses in the Edo period. However, under the influence of Christianity in the Meiji period a new law was enacted, which prohibited the making, selling and displaying of anything resembling genitalia. As a conse-

101 HENDRY (1993): 78.

102 BRYSON (1995): 75; WRIGHT-JASINOWSKI (2001): 307.

103 The *manekineko* which is used in *Portrait (Futago)* is an artwork itself and was part of an exhibition at the gallery View in Osaka in the 1980s. Similar white *manekineko* were handed to different artists, who painted and styled them individually for the exhibition.

104 ARAKAWA and BANDO (2001): 16.

quence, they were soon replaced by the *manekineko*.[105] As Inoue Shôichi has emphasised, *manekineko* were originally only used in geisha houses and pubs in red-light districts.[106] He has corroborated this argument by citing Arisawa Yôtarô, who did research on toys in the Tokyo area in 1935: 'it does not have to be mentioned that the majority of people who had a *manekineko* belonged to brothels …'[107] Inoue has also cited a section of Tokuda Shûsei's literary work *Tabi no soko* (The sole of *tabi*-socks)[108] (1913) since it shows clearly how the *manekineko* used to be associated with prostitution. By describing a *manekineko* on a cupboard, Tokuda implicitly defines the place that his main protagonist is visiting as a brothel.[109] The *manekineko* appeared inside geisha houses and on signs attached to the houses before it became popular as a general sign of good luck (fig. 42).

The 'sexual' history of the *manekineko* is not well known in contemporary Japan. However, like the opulently decorated bridal *kimono*, the *manekineko* is generally seen as part of Japanese folklore. In addition, it represents widespread folk superstition rather than elite religion. This seems relevant as it can be seen in connection to Olympia being a prostitute and thus part of the 'low class' rather than 'high society'. As such, Morimura uses the 'low class' element of *Olympia* in a Japanese context.

Bryson has pointed out persuasively how the combination of the bridal *kimono* and the *manekineko* spell out a great stereotype of Japan: 'geisha, the figuration of Japan-as-woman, and as the predestined object of the West's colonial depredations'.[110] I would add that Morimura's returning of the viewer's gaze on his naked body can also be seen in the context of geisha photographs, which were popular at the end of the 19th century. As Doris Croissant has explained, 'female sitters in Japan avoided looking straight into the camera, whereas courtesans established eye contact as a sign of seduction'.[111] The direct gaze into the camera was viewed as immoral and associated with women working in the entertainment industry.

To understand Bryson's statement about the geisha as a symbol of 'colonial depredations', historical facts have to be taken into account. Japan has never been a 'Western' colony but in the 1860s, when Manet completed his scandalous painting and 'Western' powers were expanding their colonies, Japan was

---

105 Manekineko Club (no year).
106 Inoue (1998): 194.
107 As cited in Inoue (1998): 194.
108 *Tabi* are ankle-high socks with a split for the big toe. Both men and women wear them with thronged footwear, such as *zori* or *geta*.
109 Inoue (1998): 195.
110 Bryson (1995): 75.
111 Croissant (2008): 290.

forced to open its borders.[112] The Shogun signed trade treaties, establishing diplomatic relations between Japan and 'Western' countries. These unequal treaties, having been forced on Japan through gunboat diplomacy, not only gave 'Western' nations unequivocal control of import tariffs but also secured the right of extraterritoriality to all their nationals.

The opening up of Japan and the contact with 'the West' precipitated an alteration in Japanese society. The Shogun resigned, the Tennô was restored to power and the Meiji Restoration (1868) initiated many reforms. As Iida Yumiko has written, the restoration embodied the mixed intentions of 'establishing a strong, modern state in order to secure national autonomy, and a democratic nation in order to liberate society from the feudalistic socio-political system.'[113] Numerous 'Western' institutions were adopted, including a Prussian style government as outlined in the Meiji Constitution. The 'Western' influences went far beyond political and social reforms. For instance, as Timon Screech has pointed out, the 'Western' scientific gaze changed Japanese imagery and Japan's view of the world: already in the late Edo period, the encounter with 'the West' 'provoked a change in Japan that particularly related to systems of visual awareness – indeed, to a reassessment of the entire faculty of sight.'[114]

As Japan aspired to be on equal footing with 'the West' politically, culturally and socially, individuals were urged to embrace change and set their minds to emulating 'the West' for the sake of national prosperity and power. Japanese elites, including figures such as Fukuzawa Yûkichi, undertook rhetorical campaigns to convince the populace to adapt 'Western' ideas.[115] The common slogans of the early Meiji era attest to an enthusiastic will to embrace a 'Western' style modernisation: *bunmei kaika* ('civilization and enlightenment') and *wakon yôsai* ('Japanese spirit and Western learning'). Japanese people eagerly embraced European philosophy, literature, art, fashion and popular culture, combining it with 'traditional' elements.

---

112 The borders of Japan had been closed for approximately 250 years: During the early part of the 17th century, the Tokugawa Shogunate had suspected that European traders and Christian missionaries were forerunners of a military conquest by European powers. As a consequence, it had enacted a foreign relations policy under which neither foreigner nor Japanese could enter or leave the country with the exception of Dutch and Chinese merchants on the island of Dejima in Nagasaki. This era of *sakoku* (literally 'lock up of the country') ended in 1853 with the arrival of Commodore Matthew Perry of the U.S. Navy, who requested Japan open to trade with 'the West'.

113 IIDA (2002): 12.

114 SCREECH (1996): 1.

115 For instance in the work *Bunmei-ron no Gairyaku* (Introduction to the Theory of Civilization) of 1875, Fukuzawa portrays how history has developed from 'barbarism to civilization', concluding that the 'Western' imperial model was not only inevitable but also desirable for the Japanese; IIDA (2002): 12.

Various photographs taken in the Meiji era present an aesthetic which is somewhat comparable to *Portrait (Futago)*: For example in 1872, Uchida Kuichi took a photograph of Iwakura Tomomi, the Prime Minister elect, who poses in a Samurai dress and hairstyle, yet holding a 'Western' style hat in his hand and wearing 'Western' shoes (fig. 43). He sits on a chair, surrounded by four other Japanese statesmen all wearing suits. As in Morimura's photograph, 'Western' clothing and interior design is mixed freely with 'traditional' Japanese elements. In this context of the early Meiji era's mix of 'Japanese' and 'Western' aesthetics, I would like to return to a detail, which has not been considered in the literature on *Portrait (Futago)* yet. Why does Morimura choose to wear a blond wig while Olympia's hair is brown?

The blond curly hair is an important detail as it is a typical Caucasian sign and contrasts strongly with the Black skin colour of the maid in the background. At the same time, it contrasts with Morimura's Asian facial features and, although not visible in the photograph, his naturally black hair. In Japan blond hair is considered typically 'Western' – exotic and desirable, as natural blondes are still a rarity. Furthermore, blond hair has been a feature of female attractiveness in Europe and America; 'feminine icons' like Marilyn Monroe coloured their hair in light blond tones. Hence, the blond wig might not only represent 'the West' but also the influence of 'Western' female beauty ideals on Japanese women. As Laura Spielvogel has explained, the tension between 'tradition' and 'Western modernisation' affected the style of Meiji era geishas:

> Fair skin, jet black hair, and small lips and eyes continued to be part of the beauty ideal, recalling the standard of femininity set by the imperial court of the Heian period. But at the same time … the traditional Japanese coiffure was altered to incorporate Western trends. The bun was lowered and reduced in size to imitate a Western look, and permed curls added softness at the nape of the neck.[116]

This incorporation of 'Western' aesthetic ideals is also reflected in Norman Bryson's description of the Meiji era woman as a 'medium of intramale exchange' in the process of Japan's cultural assimilation to 'the West' (see 2.1).[117] Japanese women started to wear bustles and bonnets like European women because both they and their husbands thought that this was what men desired. 'By possessing what Western men desired, they could enter into the orbit of the West through identification'.[118] The process of assimilation to 'the West' was 'figured through a female iconography; the relationship between the

116 SPIELVOGEL (2003): 147.
117 BRYSON (2003): 98.
118 IBID: 98–99.

men who ruled the modern world was visualized across the bodies of women …'[119]

Against this background, the blond wig in *Portrait (Futago)* is reminiscent of images of Japanese wearing 'Western' clothing and imitating 'Western' manners, for example in the club Rokumeikan.[120] The obviously fake hair, contrasting with Morimura's dark eyebrows and eyes, functions as a humorous exaggeration of Japanese women imitating what they perceive to be the 'Western' ideal as they strive to be objects of desire to ('Western') men.

If Caucasian beauty ideals have been incorporated into Japanese culture since the Meiji era, the American occupation after World War II reinforced this by bringing American popular culture to Japan. This is reflected in Morimura's masquerade as Marilyn Monroe in *Red Marilyn.* In the post-war era, American films were extremely popular in Japan. Morimura has pointed out in my interview how actresses like Audrey Hepburn or Marilyn Monroe were viewed as 'princesses from a completely different world' and especially adored by a female audience which dreamt of looking and being like them.

Morimura's white skin, the dark-blond curly wig, the red coloured lips and the large breasts in *Red Marilyn* are attributes which reference Hollywood beauty ideals. Kudô Megumi has examined how Japanese advertising and product imagery, especially of the Taishô (1912–1926) and early Shôwa era (1926–1989), have established a Westernised feminine beauty ideal with white skin, big eyes, long eyelashes and Caucasian facial proportions.[121] She has argued that although white skin also used to be seen as an aristocratic beauty ideal before the modernisation, it gained a new meaning as it turned into a symbol of the 'Western body'.[122] In addition, the colouring of hair in brown and dark-blond tones has become popular amongst Japanese women and, in more recent times, also amongst men. The size of female breasts was rather unimportant in pre-modern Japan as the *kimono* with its many layers retained their size and shape. However, as Laura Miller has explained, the 'homogenization of beauty imaging has led to consideration of the size and shape of the breasts as an important index of female attractiveness'.[123] The Japanese peoples' regard for white skin and large breasts as attractive, illustrates 'the power of media im-

---

119 IBID: 117.

120 The Rokumeikan was a social club in Tokyo, where high-ranking Japanese could mix with Western visitors in an atmosphere comparable to what was imagined by the Japanese to be the social whirl of Paris or London. The British architect Josiah Conder designed the building, which was then completed in 1883. For further information on the Rokumeikan and on the role of women at its balls see BRYSON (2003).

121 KUDÔ (2003).

122 IBID: 63.

123 MILLER (2006): 71.

ages' and 'the influence of American culture' on Japanese beauty ideals.[124] When taking this into consideration, *Red Marilyn* could not only be interpreted as symbolic of a Japanese desire for 'Western' film stars and the dream world they embodied, but also, on a more general level, as of the Japanese absorption of Caucasian body ideals.

The European and American influence on Japan in the Meiji era and after World War II did not only lead to an enthusiastic absorption of 'Western' culture and body ideals. As Iida Yumiko has argued, embracing modernisation in the Meiji era also meant 'accepting a lesser identity in the international political representational scheme as a 'non-Western' other.'[125] Thus, the parameters of the dilemma of Japanese national identity are likened to the fact that 'Japan as a culturally unique space is authorized by, dependent upon, and mediated through the universal gaze of the West'.[126] A sense of 'being marginalized by universal representation cultivates in the Japanese a "nagging urge" for a self-knowledge that can only be obtained by adopting "the view point of the other".'[127] In other words, the adaptation of European and American elements led not only to a fascination for the superior 'West' but also to a national complex by viewing Japan's 'national identity' in relation to 'the West'.

For instance, the novelist Natsume Sôseki criticised the fact that Japan's civilisation was 'externally motivated'.[128] In his famous lecture *The Civilization of Modern-day Japan*, he summarised the feelings of many Japanese in the Meiji era as follows: '... because age-old customs cannot be changed overnight, all we can do is mechanically memorize Western manners – manners which, on us, look ridiculous.'[129] This quotation well expresses the sense of inappropriateness felt by many Japanese as the familiar customs were subordinated to 'Western' imports. Furthermore, his description of 'Western' manners as looking 'ridiculous' on the Japanese, can be connected to Bhabha's 'colonial mimicry' mentioned earlier. Returning to Bhabha's argument that 'colonial mimicry' is a 'sign of the inappropriate,'[130] *Red Marilyn* also seems to reflect the destined 'failure' of the Japanese film audience. Undoubtedly fake breasts and strong muscles serve to denote Morimura's masculinity, and the black eyeliner highlight his Asian eye form. Whereas Norma Jean Baker could become 'Marilyn' by bleaching her hair as well as wearing make-up and figure-enhancing clothes, Morimura is limited by biological and ethnic boundaries. As such,

124 IBID: 98.
125 IIDA (2002): 15.
126 IBID: 15.
127 IBID: 15.
128 NATSUME (1911): 272.
129 IBID: 279.
130 BHABHA (1994): 122.

Red Marilyn strongly reflects the impossibility for Morimura as well as the Japanese film audience to look like the desired Hollywood actresses.

Having focussed on the influence of the Meiji Restoration on Japanese society and the Japanese perspective towards 'the West', I would now like to examine the 'Western' viewpoint and return to Bryson's argument that the lying figure in *Portrait (Futago)* is referring to the geisha as a symbol of 'colonial depredation'. Indeed, Japan has been viewed both as the land of the aggressive samurai or the tender geisha.[131]

Prejudices toward 'Japan,' as well as 'Orientalism' as a doctrine in Edward Said's sense are intertwined with gender: generally, 'the West' is a strong man, 'the East' is a weak woman. In his famous work *Orientalism* (1978), Said has defined 'Orientalism' as 'a style of thought based upon ontological and epistemological distinction made between "the Orient" and (most of the time) "the Occident."'[132] Said has argued that a 'Western' tradition of false images of Asia and the Middle East had served as an implicit justification for Europe and the US' colonial and imperial ambitions. Thus, *Orientalism* deals 'not with a correspondence between Orientalism and Orient, but with the internal consistency of Orientalism and its ideas about the Orient ... despite or beyond any correspondence, or lack thereof, with a "real" Orient.'[133] As these quotations show clearly, Said has viewed 'the Orient' as an image in 'Western' culture which is based on the distinction made between the exotic 'Other' and the normal 'oneself'. The cliché of the geisha and the metaphor of Japan as a geisha should be embedded in this discourse on the non-European 'Other'. This discourse is multi-layered and complex: for instance, the Japanese have helped to construct an Orientalist image. As Francis Jarman has noted, 'part of the blame must be ascribed to the Japanese themselves, who have helped to build up the image of their culture as one that is unique and inaccessible.'[134] This ideology of uniqueness is linked to the rather nationalistic academic discipline of *nihonjinron* ('discourse on the Japanese').

The geisha cliché is the prototypical myth of the Japanese woman as an object of 'Western' desire, especially in the Meiji era. Moreover, the image of the Japanese woman is a 'key element in Western sentimentalisation of Japan'.[135] In various media, such as literature, music, theatre, photography and art, the geisha was tied to an exotic ideal of female submission, servitude, and availability.

---

[131] For instance, *Pays de Mousumés! Pays de Guerre!* by Charles Pettit (1905) and most famously, Ruth Benedict's *The Chrysanthemum and the Sword* (1946) illustrate this rather paradoxical and stereotypical depiction of 'Japanese' culture.

[132] SAID (1978): 2.

[133] IBID: 5.

[134] JARMAN (1998): 120.

[135] IBID: 104.

In the literary field, this is, for instance, reflected in Pierre Loti's novel *Madame Chrysanthème* (1887) and John Luther Long's short story *Madame Butterfly* (1898).[136] It can also be found in operettas and operas, amongst which Sydney Jones' operetta *The Geisha* (1896) and Giaccomo Puccini opera adaptation of Long's story *Madama Butterfly* (1904) are best known.[137] At the end of the 19th century and in the early 20th century, the Kawakami theatre troupe with the geisha-star Sadayakko toured through the USA and Europe. Sadayakko not only became a star in Europe but also reinforced the image of the exotic Japanese woman. The 'Western' audience was fascinated by the Japanese props and *kimono* used in her performances; in France there was even a Sadayacco *kimono* designed, which became a popular item at the Au Mikado in Paris.[138] In his book on Japanese body and beauty ideals, first published in 1902, the German doctor C. H. Stratz pointed out that the *kimono* had become fashionable among women in Europe,[139] dedicating a whole chapter to it.[140] As Douglas Sladen and Norma Lorimer stated in 1904, it was especially the colourful *kimono* of unmarried women, working in the entertainment sector, which fascinated both 'Western' men and women.[141] Against this background, the colourful 'folklore'-like courtesan *kimono* in *Portrait (Futago)* is reminiscent of the 'Western' fascination for *kimono* in the Meiji period.

Sadayakko was often described as 'gracious', 'tender' and 'childlike'; for instance, the Italian newspaper *Corriere Della Sera* praised her as being endowed with 'Oriental charms' and being 'soft' and 'delicate' and 'infantile'.[142] Furthermore, 'the emotion she arouses in us … is the same as that aroused by a little domestic animal.'[143] Such descriptions of infantile grace, smallness and even the likeness to a little pet are not unusual in the literature on Japanese women during that time. For instance, at the beginning of *Madame Chrysanthème*, when the French naval officer Loti approaches the port of Nagasaki, he

---

136 Although *Madame Chrysanthème* and *Madame Butterfly* are the most famous examples of literary work reflecting the geisha cliché, there are many more novels and (fictious) travelogues which were extremely popular, for example Douglas Sladen's *A Japanese Marriage* (1895), Clive Holland's *My Japanese Wife* (1895) and Carlton Dawe's *A Bride of Japan* (1898).

137 The European fascination for the Japanese woman is also reflected in various other operas and operettas, such as Charles Lecocq's opera *Fleur-de-thé* (1868), Camille Saint-Saens' opera *La Princesse Jaune* (1872), Emile Jonas' operetta *La Japonaise* (1874), Gilbert and Sullivan's operetta *The Mikado* (1885), Louis Varney's operetta *La Japonaise* (1888), Gaston Serpette's operetta *Mé-Na-Ka* (1892), André Messager's opera *Madame Chrysanthème* (1893) and Pietro Mascagni's opera *Iris* (1898).

138 Downer (2003): 188.

139 Stratz (1925): 102.

140 Ibid: 99–111.

141 Von Schlabrendorf (1990): 37.

142 As cited in Downer (2003): 187.

143 Ibid: 187.

gets the idea to marry a Japanese woman, whom he imagines as a 'small woman with yellow skin colour, black hair and eyes of a cat'.[144] 'She will not be taller than a little doll. It will happen in a house of paper, nicely in the shadows, in-between green gardens.'[145]

There are mainly two reasons for this emphasis on the 'childlike' look of Japanese women: On the one hand, it is due to a curious fascination for the smallness and the body proportions of Japanese women which are different from Caucasian women. As Eva von Schlabrendorf has pointed out, 'Western' visitors in the 19th century were astonished about how small and petite the Japanese women were – 'rather dolls than humans.'[146] On the other hand, a child or a pet is connotated with a minor position as it has to be educated and nurtured by adults. As such, the likening of the geisha to a child or a 'domestic animal' is a clever yet crude legitimation of the White man's superiority. If Japan is personified by an infantile woman, this then legitimises the West's treatment of Japan in forcefully teaching her how to become a modern adult. This feeling of superiority can be corroborated by a passage in Long's *Madame Butterfly* (1898). When lieutenant Pinkerton's American wife Adelaide meets his Japanese wife Cho-Cho-San ('*chôchô*' literally means 'butterfly'), she indirectly shows how she sees herself as being part of a superior civilisation: she calls Cho-Cho-San a 'lovely ... plaything'.[147] This is juxtaposed with Cho-Cho-San's viewpoint of worshipping the White woman; to her the blond American is 'more beautiful than the Sun-Goddess'.[148]

The geisha cliché was strengthened in the Meiji era through numerous studio photographs of geishas and other women, mostly working in the entertainment sector. Photographers like Felice Beato created a vast number of studio photographs staging scenes of a 'traditionally Japanese' life (see Part 1). The production and export of these souvenir pictures developed into a flourishing business. Examining postcards of Japanese women of the late 19th century, produced by the Detroit Publishing Company, Ellen Handy has pointed out that the subjects were not identified as individuals but rather labelled as beautiful clichés: for instance as 'Miss Pomegranite', 'Queen of the Geisha' or 'A Tokio Bell'.[149] The women are not displayed working but rather posing in portraits or undertaking decorative leisure or household activities; they are shown, in Jarman's words, 'as childlike "butterflies."'[150] This again shows how the Japanese woman was reduced to a pretty and harmless image.

---

144 LOTI (no year): I.
145 IBID: I–II.
146 VON SCHLABRENDORF (1990): 32.
147 LONG (1905): 80.
148 IBID: 82.
149 HANDY (1998): 98.
150 JARMAN (1998): 104.

In Japanese port cities, such as Yokohama and Nagasaki, souvenir pictures of geishas soon became fashionable among tourists and were sold in galleries, for instance in George Bigot's gallery in Yokohama. Furthermore, the 'Western' fascination for the Japanese woman and her garment is mirrored in 'Japonistic' paintings, for example by James McNeill Whistler or Claude Monet.[151] In 1867 Japan took a pavilion at the World's Fair and many Parisian artists and collectors saw Japanese artworks. After Japan opened its ports to trade, shiploads of *kimono*, fans, lacquers, accessories and woodblock prints were exported to France and England. Japanese art had a profound impact on 'Western' art in regard to both subject matter and techniques. Portraits of a 'Western' or 'Asian' female dressed in a *kimono* surrounded by Asian props became popular and the Japanese woodprint-aesthetic such as asymmetrical composition, strong lines, empty spaces and flat colours led to the development of new painting methods.[152]

Manet too was interested in Japanese woodblock prints and inspired by their style. In his art Japonism is, as Jacques Dufwa has summarised, 'primarily to be seen in his decorative and flat configuration. Black ... has the effect of contrasting the colours, just as it does in Japanese prints'.[153] *Olympia* illustrates this well: Not only the Japanese dividing wall in the background but also the style of the painting reflect Manet's interest in Japanese art (fig. 2). There is shadow and plasticity in the bedclothes, the flowers, the curtain and the servant's dress but Olympia's body is painted nearly flat and, with its strong contours, stands out against the dark background.

Dufwa has described the synthesis of volume and flatness in *Olympia* as a 'collision of Oriental and Western stylistic impulses'.[154] This expression is interesting as it could almost be applied to *Portrait (Futago)* as well. The 'collision of Oriental and Western impulses' is translated from a stylistic level in *Olympia* to something new and more tangible in *Portrait (Futago)*. Morimura

---

151 The term 'Japonism' was coined by the French art critic Philippe Burty in 1872 and refers to the Western fascination for Japanese art, which lead to an influence on European artistic movements. For further information on Japonism see DUFWA, Jacques (1981): *Winds from the East: A Study in the Art of Manet, Degas, Monet and Whistler, 1856-86.* Stockholm: Almqvist and Wiksell International; BERGER, Klaus (1992): *Japonisme in Western Painting from Whistler to Matisse.* Cambridge: Cambridge University Press; WICHMANN, Siegfried (1999): *Japonisme: The Japanese Influence on Western Art since 1858.* London: Thames and Hudson.

152 Famous examples of Japonistic painting subjects are e.g. James McNeill Whistler's *The Princess from the Land of Porcelain – Rose and Silver* (1863), Édouard Manet's *La Dame aux Eventails* (1873-74), Claude Monet's *La Japonaise* (1876), Vincent van Gogh's *The courtisan (after Eisen)* (1887) or Pablo Picasso's *Sada Yakko* (1901). Many other works by Edgar Degas, Van Gogh, Whistler, Henri de Toulouse-Lautrec or Aubrey Beardsley show an obvious influence of Japanese aesthetics in their style.

153 DUFWA (1981): 179.

154 IBID: 58.

further develops Manet's approach in *Olympia* by creating a photographic collage of 'Western' and Japanese objects, clothes and symbols. Considering that *Olympia* itself already exhibits the influence of Japonism, Morimura's Japonising interpretation is cleverly connected to the art historical background of Manet's masterpiece.

The Japanese internalisation of 'Western' ideals in the Meiji era, as well as the 'Western' 'Orientalist' fascination for the exotic 'Other' reflected in Japonism, are issues which were still relevant in the late 1980s when Morimura created *Portrait (Futago).* Thus, I would now like to offer another interpretation of the work by considering the socio-political background of the late 1980s and early 1990s.

3.1.3 The Japanese Background of the 1990s

In her book on identity and nationalism in Japan since the post-war era, Iida Yumiko has described the late 1980s and the 1990s as a time in which Japan was seeking a new identity: 'the spectre of an inarticulate, free-floating desire for identity seeking a concrete foundation upon which to fix ideal meaning appears to be intensely present.'[155] She has described this identity-seeking as being influenced by the idea of postmodernism on the one hand and nationalism on the other:

> … identity was characterized by the so-called 'postmodern' cultural attributes of lightness, fragmentation, and stylistic sophistication freed from the burden of representing meaning and content … The other side of these nihilistic and optimistic characterizations of Japanese identity … was constituted by the rise of *nihonjinron*, the discourse of Japanese uniqueness.[156]

In 1990, the cultural anthropologist Aoki Tamotsu explained persuasively that there were mainly two positions among Japanese intellectuals concerned with a 'Japanese identity': On the one hand, there are the supporters of internationalisation who seek to give up on the ideology of a 'unique' Japanese culture. On the other hand, there are those who emphasise the differences between the Japanese culture and other cultures.[157]

In this context, *Portrait (Futago)* seems to represent two basic positions. On the one hand, the artwork is a photographic appropriation of Manet's *Olympia*: the amalgam of signs, styles, and structures culled indiscriminately

---

155 IIDA (2002): 244.
156 IBID: 7–8.
157 AOKI (1990): 145–146.

from 'Western', 'African' and 'Japanese' cultures of the past and present could be described as a typically 'postmodern' approach.[158] The blond wig and the insertion of Japanese elements into the originally French image evoke a feeling of humour and irony – also typically 'postmodern' stylistic elements.[159] On the other hand, the artwork references Japan's historical background of the 1860s and raises questions about the relationship between 'Japan' and 'the West'. Using Japanese 'traditional' clichés, such as the *kimono* and geisha, Morimura highlights not only 'Western' fantasies but also how ideas of a 'unique Japanese culture' have been prevalent in the Japanese discourse on Japan.

By juxtaposing an ironic, parodic style with rather serious, political questions on Japanese identity, *Portrait (Futago)* reflects the two main characteristics of the contemporary discourse on Japan, described by Iida and Aoki. Another quotation by Iida corroborates this interpretation:

> In short, contemporary Japan finds itself locked in the double-bind of late modernity, torn between two contrary 'aesthetic solutions' to its dilemma: the nihilistic and ironic positioning of simulated identities, and the attempted recovery of 'true' identity and meaning by means of an existential leap into the realm of imagination.[160]

Morimura's 'masquerade' as a White prostitute and a Black servant could be described as an 'ironic positioning of simulated identities', whereas his reference to the early Meiji period and 'traditional' Japanese elements represent seeking a 'true' and 'Japanese' identity.

Be it an ironic or a nationalistic approach, be it an approach of internationalisation or keeping 'uniqueness', Japanese 'national identity' has always been considered in its relation to its powerful 'Other', namely 'the West'.[161] Thus, it seems that the discourse on 'Japanicity', at least in the 1980s and 1990s, still reflects a complex regarding 'the West'. This is expressed ei-

---

158 The term 'postmodern' has a long and disputed history and has been defined in different ways; for an analysis of the term, see, for instance, HUTCHEON (1988). I use 'postmodern' here in a colloquial sense, grounded in definitions by Jean-François Lyotard and Douglas Crimp in the late 1970s: postmodernism is mainly characterised by the rejection of the grand metanarratives of modernism; see LYOTARD (1979) and CRIMP (1979). Within visual culture, this has led to an eradication of modern boundaries between high and low forms of art, a disruption of genre conventions with collage, pastiche and fragmentation, and a pluralist play with diverse styles, citations and appropriations. Artists whose work has been described as 'postmodern' include Sherrie Levine and Cindy Sherman; CRIMP (1979): 87.

159 For instance, Linda Hutcheon has emphasised the importance of irony in postmodern culture. HUTCHEON, Linda (1987): *A Poetics of Postmodernism: History, Theory, Fiction*. London and New York: Routledge; HUTCHEON, Linda (1998): *The Canadian Postmodern*. Toronto: Oxford UP; HUTCHEON, Linda (2000): Irony, Nostalgia and the Postmodern: A Dialogue (with Mario Valdés). In: *Poligrafías* 3, 2000): 29–54.

160 IIDA (2002): 258.

161 AOKI (1990): 146; IIDA (2002): 3–4.

ther by an extreme propagation of a unique Japanese culture or by its self-degradation.

With regard to visual media and beauty ideals in Japan in the 1980s and 1990s, Caucasian and Eurasian models were still omnipresent as ideal images in fashion magazines and TV commercials. Many Japanese coloured their hair in brown tones and women underwent eye-lid surgeries.[162] Tawada Yoko has linked such cosmetic surgery to Japan's inferiority complex towards 'the West' especially after Japan's defeat in World War II. In her opinion, the Western-American physiognomy represents 'the winner' and as one wants to be part of this winner aesthetic, one chooses cosmetic surgery.[163] I will return to her argument at the end of this section.

In an analysis of Japanese TV advertisements, Michael Prieler has emphasised that Caucasians are 'signifiers of a world beyond Japan, particularly the West.'[164] They attribute a positive image to a product, which is 'possible because of the general positive perception of White people in Japan'.[165] This contrasts with the depictions of Blacks: there are few Black people who appear on TV and 'typically they tend to be well-known athletes, dancers or musicians'.[166] In the 1980s, there were discussions about racist advertising representations, such as the Black caricature character on the logo of the Japanese drink Calpis. The controversies over the representation of Blacks in commercials and trademark characters occurred around the time of Prime minister Nakasone's famous statement about American minorities.[167] In 1986, Nakasone Yasuhiro remarked on the higher Japanese IQ compared to Americans. When criticised for this, he explained that Americans were not less intelligent but due to there being so many Blacks and Hispanics, America could not compete with Japan. As the images of Blacks in advertisements as well as Nakasone's racist statements show, stereotypes about Black people as well as prejudices towards them have remained a problem.

In addition, stereotypical images of both the 'Occident' and the 'Orient' are still prevalent. A quotation by Edward W. Said from 1978 about Orientalism being reinforced constantly seems relevant even today:

> One aspect of the electronic, postmodern world is that there has been a reinforcement of the stereotypes by which the Orient is viewed. Television, films, and all the media's resources have forced information into

---

162 This surgery creating the 'double-eyelid' (*futae mabuto*), is the most commonly performed cosmetic procedure in Japan. For more information on Western beauty ideals and Japanese cosmetic surgery see FRÜHSTÜCK (1997): 15–19 or KEELAN (2001): 76.

163 TAWADA (1996): 221.

164 PRIELER (2006): 6.

165 IBID: 6.

166 CREIGHTON (1995): 152.

167 IBID: 153.

> more and more standardised moulds … standardisation, and cultural stereotyping have intensified the hold of the nineteenth century academic and imaginative demonology of "the mysterious Orient".[168]

This 'mysterious Orient' can be found, for instance, in literary works. Karina Kleiber, Renate Giaccomuzzi and Sandra Lyne have examined how 'Western' novels since 1945 have made use of stereotypical images of the Japanese 'exotic' woman.[169] A famous novel using the geisha cliché is Arthur Golden's work *Memoirs of a Geisha* (1999), which clearly reinforces Asian women's exoticism instead of providing a realistic description of a geisha's life.[170] The persistence of the geisha cliché is also evident in the book cover of *Memoirs of a Geisha*. Sandra Lyne has analysed this cover as well as those of Wei Hui's *Shanghai Baby*, Lisa Dably's *Geisha* and Lesley Downer's *Geisha: The Secret History of a Vanishing World.*[171] They all have in common that Asian women are presented in 'fetishised fragments, and depicted as frozen in time, severed from modernity';[172] the colours red, white and black are dominant and the women recall the cliché of a geisha. Examining Cees Nootebooms novel *Mokusei* (1982) and Alessandro Barrico's *Seta* (Silk) (1996), Giacomuzzi has concluded that one motif has remained constant: a 'Western' man conquers a Japanese woman in a manner 'similar to colonial capture'.[173] Giacomuzzi's quotation underlines that the dichotomy of the masculine Occident and the female Orient has remained popular. As such, Orientalism persists in popular culture; there is 'a continuing, emerging discourse on the erotic/exotic through cinematic and textual fictions'.[174]

Moreover, the 1980s and 1990s have created new stereotypes. A fascination for Japanese popular culture, echoed in the *manga* and *anime* boom, and the Japanese influence on 'Western' fashion and art led to the coining of the term 'Neo-Japonism'. Photographers and artists, such as Araki Nobuyoshi and Murakami Takashi, have responded to a somewhat 'Orientalist' demand (see Part 1).

As such, *Portrait (Futago)* draws attention to a Japanese complex-fascination for 'the West' as well as to a 'Western' Orientalist viewpoint, which should be understood not only as a reference to history but also to contempo-

---

168 SAID (1978): 26.

169 KLEIBER (1990): 44–53; GIACOMUZZI (2000); LYNE (2002).

170 The geisha who had allowed Golden to interview her responded by emphasising that he insulted her and that the story was ficticious: 'Golden got the organization of the geisha house wrong … He wrote that book on the theme of women selling their bodies. It was not that way at all.' As cited in FOREMAN (2003): 36.

171 LYNE (2002): 1–2.

172 IBID: 2.

173 GIACOMUZZI (2000): 172.

174 JOLLY (1997): 15.

rary problems. However, does the artwork offer any answers to questions on Japanese 'national' identity at the end of the 20th century?

Returning to the aesthetic impression of *Portrait (Futago)*, the work presents a collage of 'Western' and 'Japanese' symbols, which exceeds Manet's work in terms of colourfulness and size. The artist seems self-assured when showing his body. The same can be said about *Red Marilyn*: Morimura poses confidently in a large photograph dominated by a powerful red, showing his naked body in bright light. Morimura's direct gaze into the camera in *Portrait (Futago)* is not only reminiscent of Olympia's self-confident eye contact with the viewer but also seems as if he were demanding acceptance of who he is. His facial expressions as well as the brightness of the large-sized photographs demonstrate that Morimura does not present himself as a victim. His facial expression reflects confidence. Thus, although the artworks highlight the influence of the powerful 'Western Other' on Japan, Morimura distances himself from an inferior position and a complex toward 'the West'.

Japan's embrace of 'Western' fashion and body ideals in the Meiji era, as well as after World War II, have led to a Japanese body consciousness which posits itself through its relation to 'the West', often in a self-degrading manner; however, the late 1980s and 1990s appears to be a time of change. Returning to the influence of EuroAmerican images on Japanese body ideals and cosmetic surgery, Tawada Yoko's explanation that Japanese women seek to be part of the Western-American winner aesthetic and thus choose cosmetic eye shape surgery,[175] is not convincing anymore. Although the ideals of appearance used to be inextricably bound up with EuroAmerican dominance, it seems that they have developed into a specific 'Japanese' aesthetic. They are not directly bound up with an imitation of 'the West' anymore, they are no 'colonial mimicry'. In Laura Miller's words, 'Japanese body and beauty work has moved beyond a brute stage of emulation'.[176] She is right when criticising the foreign 'Ethnocentric' assumption that 'whenever Japanese people appropriate some aspects of EuroAmerican body aesthetics' it must reflect their 'desire to become something other than Japanese.'[177] Moreover, this simple assumption seems to reinforce an Orientalist perspective on Japan as an infantile geisha, imitating the powerful 'West'. For example, as regards the surgery of eye shape and lids, the situation is more complex: firstly, a large proportion of Japanese are born with double-lidded eyes,[178] and secondly, the influence of J-Pop stars with large eyes, such as Hamasaki Ayumi, or *manga* characters is more relevant in Japan than that of American popular culture. As Morimura pointed out in my

---

175 Tawada (1996): 221.
176 Miller (2006): 123.
177 Ibid: 123.
178 Ibid: 116.

interview in 2008, Japanese hair style and make-up are no longer 'Western-style' but rather '*anime* style', emphasising that Japan has gained confidence through its international economic success of game and *anime* culture.

Morimura's 'Japanese' body and 'Japanese' background are obvious in both *Portrait (Futago)* and *Red Marilyn*. As such, Morimura distances himself from the desire of becoming the 'Western Other'. I agree with Shimizu Akiko when stating that Morimura reveals that 'he is not aiming at the complete identification with the object that he embodies there.'[179] The identities presented are rather culturally hybrid and ambiguous: Morimura as a 'Yellow' man disguises as a 'White' woman lying on a *kimono* in juxtaposition against a 'Black' servant, who wears a 'Western' dress. By freely uniting Japanese, African and European elements, a 'trans-cultural' and 'trans-racial' reality is created. As explained before, the *kimono* and the *manekineko* seem to belong to stereotypes of 'Japan', while the blond curly hair and the maid's dress are 'Western' symbols. But do such distinctions work in our postmodern, globalised world? The blond hair and the dress could also be seen as manifestations of 'Western' cultural influence on its (former) colonies and Japan. Similarly, the *kimono* and especially the *manekineko* as a popular kitsch object in numerous shops suggest the presence of Neo-Japonism in 'the West'.

3.2 Conclusions

Morimura's *Portrait (Futago)* highlights critically the socio-political background of Manet's *Olympia*. As Morimura impersonates not only a White but also a Black person, he represents simultaneously the French colonist and the African colonised. Furthermore, by equalising the White cocotte and the Black servant as 'twins', he compares the subordination of prostitutes with that of Black people in Manet's times.

Against Japan's historical background, the artwork also juxtaposes two other viewpoints. The first concerns the Japanese perspective and the influence of 'Western' powers on Japan in the Meiji era. In Hasegawa Yûko's words: 'Morimura tells us about a blind longing for the West: about Japanese acting in Western dramas wearing fair-haired wigs or appearing in oil paintings dressed in Western style.'[180] The Japanese fascination for 'Western' culture and body ideals has been re-enforced by the American Occupation – *Red Marilyn* emphasises the influence of Hollywood icons while showing that their Caucasian looks and their dream lives were out of the reach of the Japanese film audience. This Japanese assimilation of 'Western' ideals often suggests a sense of

[179] SHIMIZU (2008): 65.
[180] HASEGAWA (1997): 18.

inferiority, which is linked to the fact that since the Meiji era, 'Japan' has defined its national identity through the gaze of 'the West'.

The second viewpoint concerns the EuroAmerican 'Orientalist' perspective, namely the romantisation of the 'exotic Other'. The cliché of the geisha not only represents a 'Western' fascination for petite, gracious Japanese women, but also highlights how 'the West' has corroborated its superior position by juxtaposing it with the image of a pretty, yet weak and childlike female.

Furthermore, the influence of Japanese culture on 'Western' art is reflected in the definition of the term 'Japonism' in Manet's time and is evident in his painting *Olympia*. As such, *Portrait (Futago)* offers at least three readings connected to the (art) historical background of Manet's time both in France and Japan.

At the same time, *Portrait (Futago)* draws attention to a Japanese complex-fascination for the 'West' as well as to a 'Western' Orientalist viewpoint in contemporary times. However, the late 1980s and 1990s seem to be a time of change – ideals of appearance, such as large eyes or curly brown hair, have developed into a specific 'Japanese' aesthetic which references *anime* and *manga* rather than 'Western' looks. Morimura's discernible 'Japanese' body as well as, in *Portrait (Futago)*, the 'Japanese' props suggest that Morimura did not aim at the complete identification with the 'Western Other'. The identities presented are rather 'hybrid'. In addition, they are confidently presented in a colourful composition and in large size.

By highlighting the complex political background of *Olympia* and yet at the same time confidently pointing at a culturally hybrid environment, *Portrait (Futago)* seems to recognise contemporary Japan in a rather optimistic way. The incorporation of 'Western' elements into Japanese culture has become part of Japan's cultural heritage, constantly creating a new 'original' culture. This brings me back to Morimura's argument that, in his art, imitation is a starting point for creating a new original work (see 1.1 of Part 2). *Portrait (Futago)* corroborates this statement: through the photographic appropriation of a French painting, Morimura has presented us with a new Japanese photographic original which offers at least as many readings as *Olympia*.

4. The Body and Social Codes

The critical messages behind *Elevator Girls 3F* and *Tea Ceremony III* are inextricably intertwined with the artworks' specifically Japanese social context. In the following sections, I will try to 'decode' and interpret bodily 'codes' used in this Japanese context, particularly in department stores and offices.

Before examining these in the artworks, two umbrella terms will be defined first: 'system' and 'social codes'.

In general, the notion of a 'system' could be defined as a whole which is formed by organised relations between different elements and participants. In sociology, Talcott Parsons and Niklas Luhmann have used the term, both attempting to present a general theory of society and its structures. It does not need mentioning that this thesis will not sociologically apply Luhmann's complex system theory. However, Luhmann's argument that society is a 'system' consisting of numerous 'subsystems', which (re)produce their distinctive identity through various forms of communication,[181] seems useful as a theoretical image and an analytical tool for the following sections. Subsystems in Luhmann's sense, including economic institutions, science, law and the art system, are defined by a boundary between their interior and exterior. In other words, the 'notion of systems' is also a 'notion of distinction' between two sides, namely 'the system on the one side and the environment on the other.'[182]

The differentiation between the systems' insides and outsides could be connected to the idea of 'social codes'. As systems in Luhmann's sense are autopoietically organised, each system's inside works and communicates according to its own 'codes'. In the following sections, I will use the expression 'social codes' as an umbrella term for all kinds of regulations and signals connected to the human body which represent the participant's belonging to a certain social system. Garments, hair-do, make-up, speech, voice tone and body language could all be defined as 'social codes' since they serve as signs of belonging to a certain system while simultaneously differentiating the same individual from other systems; they include and exclude at the same time.

The aspect of social inclusion and, at the same time, exclusion is often linked to standardisation. Ritualised speech, body language and dress standardise individual people's appearance and assign social identity. Various systems, such as prisons, schools, and the military, use uniforms as a form of standardisation. Brian McVeigh has highlighted the ubiquity of uniforms in Japanese society:

> Japan is a uniformed society. There are the *sararîman* ("salary man", i.e. white-collar workers) in their dark-blue suits, white shirts and conservative ties… the OLs ("office ladies", i.e. secretaries) in their prim company uniforms; sharply dressed and hated "elevator girls" whose robotic but delicate gestures and soft voices guide customers on and off department store elevators…[183]

[181] LUHMANN (2002).
[182] LUHMANN (2002): 118.
[183] MCVEIGH (2000): 1.

McVeigh's quotation shows how Japanese society uses uniforms, gestures and voice in order to divide strictly between the different subsystems and their participants. Uniformisation begins in nursery school, continues in high school and stops during university when students are free to wear the clothes and the make-up they like. However, as soon as graduates apply for jobs in the economic sector, they again start to wear 'uniforms', i.e. similar looking business garments. As Karel Van Wolferen has concluded, Japanese society expects people to stick to their social roles, making these roles clear with 'their dress, speech and behavior'.[184]

However, an individual does not belong invariably to only one system at a time. Rather, one changes between different systems and codes, for instance differentiating between the workplace and the family. There are a great number of academic books and articles which have stressed the flexibility of Japanese 'identity' and its dependence on particular contexts.[185] I put the complex term 'identity' in quotation marks, referring to it as the idea of a distinct individuality which, nevertheless, can never be fixed. This flexible 'identity' concept is closely intertwined with the Japanese language, for instance with its many different words for the first and second person singular, depending on the context and one's addressee (*boku*, *ore*, *uchi*, *watashi*, *watakushi*, *ware*; *kimi*, *omae*, *anata*, *ware* etc.). As Dorinne Kondo has written, 'boundaries between self and other are fluid and constantly changing, depending on context and on the social positioning people adopt in particular situations'.[186] Or in Suzuki Takao's words, 'the self is defined in relation to the addressee, only after having assimilated oneself into the addressee's position'.[187] Both quotations underline how different social systems and people define an individual's speech, constantly creating his or her 'identity'. This also applies to body language, clothing and other 'social codes'.

Set against this theoretical background, 4.1 will focus on the appearance and postures of the photographic subjects of *Elevator Girls 3F*, interpreting these in connection to the system of department stores in Japan. Following this, 4.2 will explore the way in which typical 'social codes' of both female and male employees of a Japanese company are presented in *Tea Ceremony III*.

---

[184] VAN WOLFEREN (1990): 333.
[185] SUZUKI (1986), KIMURA (1995), UEDA (1998) etc.
[186] KONDO (1990): 31.
[187] SUZUKI (1986): 156.

4.1 The System of Japanese Department Stores: Thoughts on *Elevator Girls 3F*

This section will first explain briefly the social background of shopping in Japanese department stores in order to give an introduction into the context in which elevator girls work. Following this, the 'social codes' used by elevator girls will be examined within the specific atmosphere of department stores. Lastly, I will interpret *Elevator Girls 3F* as a critical comment on consumerism in Japan.

4.1.1 Elevator Girls in Japanese Department Stores and their 'Social Codes'

Numerous retailer companies, such as Mitsukoshi and Takashimaya, trace back their history to *kimono* and cotton goods shops. In 1904, the Mitsukoshi Company became Japan's first modern department store, simulating 'Western' department stores; Takashimaya opened a store in 1916. Both have maintained an emphasis on clothing, interior decorations and luxurious products, which contributes to a sophisticated atmosphere in the stores. Following this, private railway companies started to build department stores directly linked to their lines' termini in the 1920s. For example, the first Hankyû department store was opened at the Umeda railway station in Osaka in 1929. As Yanagi has explained, some of the *Elevator Girls* photographs include architectural components of the Hankyû department stores in Osaka and Kyoto. However, the backgrounds, such as the elevator in *Elevator Girls 3F*, are digitally altered and combine elements of various department stores worldwide.

Japanese department stores are not only places to shop but also entertainment and cultural centres, comprising educational facilities, theatres or event spaces for art and local produce exhibitions. Okabe Aomi has highlighted the fact that department stores, such as the Hankyû, have always exhibited arts and crafts; they have not only focused on the selling of goods but also on displaying 'beauty' (*bi*).[188] Hasegawa Yôko has emphasised the politeness found in Japanese department stores:

> The exaggerated politeness and service, part and parcel of the decorative and almost ritualistic nature of the elevator girl in Japan, are unimaginable in Europe or the United States. This departmentstore ethos of politeness and service, and expression of middle-class status, combined with the custom of over-wrapping purchases, adds value to the product and has come to symbolize the typically Japanese ritual of shopping.[189]

188 OKABE (2003): 266.
189 HASEGAWA (2002): 132–133.

Both quotations underline that Japanese stores seek to present a world of beauty and politeness to a degree which can hardly be compared to their European counterparts. This is evident in the cashier's artistic wrapping of the sold items before handing them to the customer.[190] In addition, like the wrapping of goods, the presence of elegantly dressed 'department girls' (*depâtomento gâru*, abbreviated as *depaga*) obediently greeting the customer and bowing before him, can be interpreted as a decorative element adding value to the products and the shopping atmosphere. 'Elevator Girls' (*erebêtâ gâru*, abbreviated as *erega*) are 'department girls' who operate the elevators. They all wear the same uniform, speak the same text and use the same stylised gestures. In contrast to the women in *Elevator Girls 3F*, they usually stand inside an elevator on their own, mechanically explaining which items are sold on the different floors. However, the decorative character of elevator girls is more important than their explanatory role. Young and pretty, smiling and speaking with a high-pitched soft voice, they help to create a somewhat dream-like shopping experience, in which the customer is treated respectfully 'like a king'.

The balanced arrangement of the women in *Elevator Girls 3F*, revealing the staged character of the scene, highlights the dream-like atmosphere in department stores. Furthermore, the shiny hole with shoes in the ground, the women's concentration on it, and the computer-generated scenario with the flowers in the background evoke an artificial, science-fiction like atmosphere. Gianni Romano has described the world presented in the *Elevator Girls* images as a 'dreamscape'.[191] This expression reflects how the department store makes the customers feel as if they were in a fantastic world, different from 'real' everyday life.

By depicting nine young women wearing the same uniform and lipstick, *Elevator Girls 3F* highlights the phenomenon of elevator girls looking and acting almost the same. Their standardised appearance is not unusual in Japanese department stores – most employees, be they sales assistants or attendants, have to wear uniforms. This is supposed to add to a 'harmonious' aesthetic impression. Similarly, the black colour of the elevator girl's hair can be linked to the idea of harmony: although many Japanese people dye their hair, numerous companies require their employees to have black hair to maintain 'the harmony of the company'.[192] In addition, the standardised look results in an equalisation of the women; there is no visible hierarchy between them. It is important to remember that, in contrast to the 'Western' concept of individuality, looking

---

190 The highly developed culture of wrapping in Japan has been examined by Joy Hendry; HENDRY (1990) and HENDRY (1993).

191 ROMANO (2000): 60–63.

192 In the mid-nineties, an employee who had dyed his hair brown won a court case against his employer that had fired him because he did not completely dye his hair back to black as ordered by the company. The Japanese company claimed that 'he disrupted the harmony of the company'; MCVEIGH (2000): 112.

and acting like everyone else in Japan is generally not considered unusual. Shops often advertise for their products, such as clothing or make-up, by stating that they are bestsellers and popular among other people.

The standardised appearance of elevator girls makes clear that the women belong to the department store system, differentiating them from the consumers. There is a line between the products, elevator girls and the other subjects belonging to the department store on the one side, and the consumers on the other. Hendry has offered a convincing comparison of the machine-like language of elevator girls with that of tour guides and bus drivers who provide information about locations near the stops they make: 'where a human being is carrying out a mundane and repetitive task like this, they will almost certainly be neatly attired in the company uniform, usually down to a pair of clean, white gloves ..., which provides a last symbolic separation from the public with whom they deal.'[193] As such, the uniforms with white gloves, the speech and the ritualised gestures are all social codes which provide a separation between the inside of a sales or service system, and its outside, namely the customers. Moreover, Hendry has interpreted the elevator girls' use of polite formal sentences, uttered in stilted tones, as well as their uniforms as a form of 'protection': they serve 'to protect the incumbent ... in an occupation potentially open to the possibly unwelcome advances of strangers'.[194]

In light of these considerations, the standardised social codes used by elevator girls aim to add beauty and value to the products, and politeness to the shopping atmosphere. Yet, at the same time, they create a protective barrier between the department store and the customers. *Elevator Girls 3F* emphasises the elevator girls' similar appearance and behaviour by showing nine of them in one image. I will return to the motif of standardisation at the end of this section.

In *Elevator Girls 3F*, it is not only the women's similarity which highlights the barrier between the department store on the one side and the customers on the other. It is also the perspective of the image with the pillars at the front and the many reflective elements, creating a self-contained environment to which the viewer does not have access. Furthermore, the women do not return the viewer's gaze but stare with a somewhat empty expression onto the shoes.

The women's decorative appearance combined with their blank facial expression and almost empty gaze is reminiscent of both mannequins and fashion models. A quotation by Jean Baudrillard on models and their 'beauty' seems insightful:

> Irregularity or ugliness would bring out a meaning again: they are excluded. For beauty here is wholly in abstraction, in emptiness, in ecstatic

193 HENDRY (1993): 87–88.
194 IBID: 87.

> absence and transparency. This disembodiment is ultimately encapsulated in the gaze. These fascinating/fascinated, sunken eyes, this objectless gaze – both oversignification of desire and total absence of desire …[195]

Baudrillard's description of the models and their gazes also applies to the women in *Elevator Girls 3F* and brings me to an important characteristic of the artwork. It has been argued that social codes, such as the similar uniform, the make-up and also the empty facial expression, define the women as elevator girls belonging to the department store system, separating them from the customer side. However, conventional elevator girls *stand* in the elevator, explaining which goods can be found on the different floors. Yanagi breaks this rule by showing the women sitting on the floor. In doing so, she points at the other side of the system – the consumption side.

The women stare at the white shoes with 'fascinating/fascinated sunken eyes'; they are 'ecstatically absent' as if they were mesmerised by the white shoes. They let go of all the regulated body language they have learnt. Their fascination with the shoes reflects the seductive power of the department store; it is not only a 'dream world' which offers beauty and politeness, but also a 'sham world' which seduces and manipulates the customers.

Furthermore, shoes are stereotypically seen as fashion objects that *women* love to possess in great variety and number. Aligned on shiny surfaces in the middle of a group of women, the shoes are a symbol of *female* materialistic pleasure. As such, *Elevator Girls 3F* could be interpreted as a take on the phenomenon of young Japanese women spending a lot of money on fashion items. Since the 1980s, increasing numbers of women do not marry until they are in their thirties or forties. Working while still living with their parents, relieving them of housing, food and utility expenses, the women have a large amount of money for shopping. Yanagi has pointed out how brand industries, such as Prada or Hermès, succeed in Japan due to these women who are often called 'parasite single' (*parasaito shinguru*) in colloquial Japanese.[196] Since the economic boom of the 1980s in Japan, young single women have been recognised as potentially the largest group of consumers; they often have more time to go shopping than men, and spend a lot of money on clothing and luxury goods.

All these things considered, *Elevator Girls 3F* shows the female inside and outside of the department store system, namely the decorative representation of the female figure within the world of consumption as well as the large number

---

195 BAUDRILLARD (1998): 281.

196 WAKASA (2001); According to a statistic of 2004, Japanese people in general have become by far the largest consumer group of American and European designer-brand fashion goods. Their purchases account for 40 percent of this global market. BARDSLEY and HIRAKAWA (2005): 111.

of female consumers who are 'hypnotised' by designer goods. In Japan, both the decorative, harmonious inside of department stores and their consuming outside are mostly female indeed. The leaders of large retailer companies are male, however, the 'beautiful' dream world that they sell seems rather feminine and addresses a female target group. This aspect also applies to other industrialised countries. Celia Lury has highlighted in her study on consumer culture that women are the principle targets of many consumer goods, as well as the objects used in advertisements. Subject and object, 'women are both consumer and consumed, consumers, indeed of themselves'.[197]

4.1.2 *Elevator Girls 3F* as a Socio-Critical Work of Art

Kasahara Michiko has interpreted the *Elevator Girls* series as a critical comment on obsessive consumption: the images 'despair of an oppressive consumer society in which the only values are material objects, physical appearance, and the pursuit of wealth'.[198] I agree that *Elevator Girls 3F* should be viewed as a socio-critical image. However, the way in which Yanagi expresses her critical view is indirect and detracts only subtly from the images' aesthetic. This is linked to the fact that the photograph makes use of the same social codes as the department store and its advertisement. Firstly, the image features pretty, young women in a balanced composition. In their neat uniforms and with elaborate make-up, the women look as 'decorative' as real elevator girls. Secondly, *Elevator Girls 3F* is a large-sized, colourful and glossy image, as 'alluring' as advertisement photographs presented in light boxes. This strategy might be more effective in communicating its critical message than a transparent 'in your face' parody; it seduces the viewer before revealing its criticism. At first, the viewer is allured by the colourful print, presenting a dream world with prettily uniformed women. It is only at second sight when he realises that the image presents an artificial displacement of numerous similar looking women in a small elevator, that he starts thinking about it critically: why do the women stare at shoes instead of communicating with each other? Why are their gazes blank and how could they lose control? The first moment of seduction makes the viewer experience the dangerously seductive power of department stores as well as the comforting aesthetic of standardised female ideals.

Returning to the aspect of standardisation, this is another important message of the photograph. *Elevator Girls 3F* is not only critical of obsessive consumption and materialism; it also highlights standardisation in Japanese society. Standardisation may lead to positive equality and comfort, and yet, also

---

197 LURY (1996): 135.
198 KASAHARA (2007): 100.

to a loss of individuality. Yanagi has explained that she is critical of standardisation in Japanese society, but also comforted by it because she is used to it.[199] The ambiguity between criticism and comfort expressed in Yanagi's quotation is well reflected in the way in which elevator girls are shown as similar, decorative objects in the large-sized, colourful *Elevator Girls* images. Gianni Romano has summed it up nicely when stating that the images 'derive from a socially critical, creative stance' and yet, 'succeed in seducing the viewer, just as we might presume that they seduce the artist herself'.[200]

As a consequence of the economic recession of the 1990s, the number of elevator girls has declined, and most department stores have abolished them completely. Hence, *Elevator Girls 3F* draws attention particularly to the 'Bubble Econonomy' era of the 1980s and early 1990s and its excessive materialism.

4.2 The System of Japanese Offices: Thoughts on *Tea Ceremony III*

The previous section has highlighted distinctions between a system's inside and its outside, for instance the selling inside of the economic system of department stores, and the consuming outside. It has been stated that the inside of a system often uses standardised social codes; both women and men are subjected to dress and behavioural norms. However, there are also major differentiations within a system: for example, in a Japanese office, *sararîman* (literally 'salary man', white-collar workers) use different social codes from *ôeru* (literally 'OL', abbreviation of 'office ladies', secretaries). This subsection will juxtapose the two Japanese employee stereotypes *sararîman* and *ôeru* by analysing the way they are presented in *Tea Ceremony III*. How could their garments be described, how do they look and what does their body language express? Can the artwork be linked to a socio-critical message?

4.2.1 The *Ôeru* vs. the *Sararîman*

Tea Ceremony III shows Mori Mariko serving tea in front of a large glass building on the left side and a grey concrete or stone building on the right (see 3.3 of Part 2). Although there is a sign attached to the grey building defining it as the Tokyo Fashion School, at first sight, the buildings look like typical office buildings. If Mori did not wear a shiny silver cap with two outward protruding ears, and a silver costume under her secretary-like dress, the photograph would appear to be showing a somewhat ordinary scene during lunchtime: a secretary or

---

199 As cited in GONZALEZ-FOERSTER, Hans Ullrich OBRIST and Miwa YANAGI (2003): 47.
200 ROMANO (2000): 63.

waitress offers tea to men in suits who are leaving the office building to have their lunch outside.

The men on the left side wear the typical 'uniform' of a *sararîman*: a dark suit, a white shirt with a 'greyish' tie and black leather shoes. The garments represent their work in the business sector and convey a rather conservative impression. As Joanne B. Eicher and Mary Ellen Roach-Higgins have noted, 'the male white-collar worker's biological presence has been diminished by the shape and volume of his business suit that masks his body contours.'[201] This quotation can be corroborated by the two *sararîmen* – the suits fit the men's bodies rather loosely and mask the bodily forms underneath. In addition, even the highest buttons of the men's shirts are closed; the garments veil the body almost completely. The *sararîmen*'s 'biological presence' as well as any aesthetic or sensual impression of their bodies is strongly restrained.

By comparison, Mori wears a snow-white blouse, a vest in a sumptuous blue colour, and a short blue skirt. The strong red of her lips and fingernails stands out against the light hues of the white blouse and the silver costume underneath. Mori's garments contrast with the men's in their strong colours as well as in their shape. As Eicher and Roach-Higgins have noted, the 'shape and volume (in proportion to body size) of females' business dress reveals body contours more than the dress of males.'[202] Indeed, Mori's vest fits tightly to her upper body, the upper buttons of her blouse are open.

In addition, the short skirt reveals Mori's slim legs, which are emphasised by her shiny silver tights and the high heels. As Laura Spielvogel has examined in her study on beauty ideals and fitness in Japan, legs are an important beauty factor for Japanese women: '… far more important than the size of one's breasts are the shape and slenderness of one's legs. … A beautiful leg line, as it is described in popular magazines and at the beauty salons, is … perfectly aligned from ankle to hip.'[203] Mori's dress emphasises her body proportions more than the men's; the emphasis on her legs can be interpreted as an emphasis on her feminine 'beauty'.

With regard to skin colour, it is eye-catching that the men's skin is darker and more yellow than Mori's pale skin. White skin is a beauty ideal in Japan, thus, Mori's whiter skin could also be interpreted as a 'beautiful' attribute. Furthermore, Mori is a young woman who appears to be in her twenties, whereas the men must be in their forties or fifties.

The contours of the pedestrians, especially of the two men in the foreground, are blurred while Mori's body stands out from the surroundings sharply. This is perhaps connected to the fact that the photograph is based on a

---

201 EICHER and ROACH-HIGGINS (1997): 20.

202 IBID: 20.

203 SPIELVOGEL (2003): 164–165.

performance: the people on the left could be strangers passing by who did not pay attention to the photographer, whereas Mori stood still, waiting for the photograph to be taken. The disparity of the photographic sharpness enforces the contrast between the men and Mori. Firstly, Mori is emphasised again as an aesthetic object: the sharp contours highlight her bodily forms as well as her smiling face. In contrast, the men's bodies and faces are less clear. Secondly, the blurred contours highlight the men's walking movements. In this way, the men's visual appearance seems less important than their movements, whereas Mori is accentuated as a 'beautiful' object, remaining in the same position. This contrast is further emphasised by the composition of the image: the contours of the glass building, the direction which the men are headed towards, the woman behind Mori, and Mori's gaze to the left, all create a dynamic to the left-hand side of the photograph. However, Mori positions herself in the right foreground, outside this dynamic.

Moreover, as I have mentioned in 3.3 of Part 2, Mori's body language and her gaze suggest that she is offering tea to someone outside the photograph. The combination of her slight bending, leg stretching and smiling results in a pose which expresses utmost respect, courtesy, and subordination towards the person that she offers tea to.

All these things considered, *Tea Ceremony III* juxtaposes the two *sararîmen* with Mori by means of visual contrast. In other words, the men and Mori are shown with very different social codes. Mori appears as a 'pretty' woman, wearing colourful garments, which emphasise her 'biological presence'. Her skin is lighter than the men's and she is younger. Standing in a subordinated pose outside of the photographic dynamic to the left, she offers tea to male pedestrians. In contrast, the *sararîmen*'s bodies are masked by their loose business suits; the photograph does not focus on their appearance but rather on their movements, emphasised by blurred contours.

The visual contrast between Mori and the men can be linked to the different status of men and women in the Japanese business sector in the 1990s. While the typical *sararîman*, a 'middle-class, heterosexual, married' middle-aged man, is 'responsible for and representative of Japan',[204] the *ôeru*'s major role is to support him. *'Ôeru'* as an abbreviation for 'office lady' is a term which refers to the majority of women working in a Japanese office. The term reflects a (male) expectation of these women, namely to act gently and elegantly like 'ladies'. In the 1990s, most female employees in the business sector were working as *'ôeru'*, doing secretary work, while also serving tea and coffee to businessmen during their meetings. An 'office lady' would serve drinks in a polite and subordinated way as Mori does in the photograph. Hence, I agree

[204] ROBERSON and SUZUKI (2003): 1.

with Norman Bryson and Carol Eliel, who have both identified Mori's role in *Tea Ceremony III* as that of a *ôeru*; Bryson calls her a 'pixified office lady'[205] and Eliel refers to her as a 'traditional office lady'.[206]

Like Mori, the typical *ôeru* is neatly attired, and often she wears a company uniform. The wearing of company uniforms in an office is associated with *ôeru* since men's 'office-uniforms' are suits. In the 1990s, around 90 percent of *ôeru* in Japanese companies wore a company uniform.[207] McVeigh has argued that there is a connection between the women's uniforms and their low salary:

> As relatively low-salaried secretaries who are expected to work for several years and then quit to become "good wives and wise mothers" (i.e. devote themselves to housework and raising children), "office ladies" are regarded as temporary and supplementary to the permanent and core male workforce. Not surprisingly, then, the uniforms of "office ladies" … evidence the notion that uniformed individuals are those who occupy the lower ranks of an organization (or nationwide economic system) in terms of status and power... [208]

McVeigh's quotation highlights the interrelations of the dress and social rank of *ôeru* in the Japanese work system. As prescribed dress, uniforms in general express the wearer's powerless status; one is not allowed to choose but told by the management what to wear. Mori's dress in *Tea Ceremony III* could either be some company's uniform or a 'typical' *ôeru* outfit. Be it a 'uniform' or not, it represents the *ôeru*'s status in the office: in contrast to *sararîmen*, who are expected to wear restrained suits, the women are expected to look pretty, supporting their male colleagues.

Like the neat 'uniform', Mori's subordinated tea serving can also be seen as one of the many (unofficial) social codes for female employees. They are expected to 'stand still' and offer tea – and they remain in the same inferior position in the company. In contrast, the men's walking movement in *Tea Ceremony III* symbolises the men's activity in the company: they can show their skills and have a career. Furthermore, the businessmen do not appear to notice Mori. This suggests that they are accustomed to women serving them tea; they are not aware of the presence of the *ôeru* even though she is wearing an extremely unusual silver costume under her secretary dress.

In light of these considerations, *Tea Ceremony III* highlights the different social codes used by Mori and the businessmen in order to symbolise critically the gap between women and men in the 1990s Japanese business sector. Although efforts had been made to promote equality, the disparity between men

205 BRYSON (1998): 77.
206 ELIEL (1998): 28.
207 WATANABE (1994): 18.
208 MCVEIGH (2000): 121.

and women's roles, their work responsibilities and their career opportunities was still significant. The number of female employees had increased, but it was still low compared to 'Western' countries. Moreover, more than half of the women in employment only worked part-time.[209] Mae Michiko has emphasised that although discrimination on the grounds of gender was outlawed in 1947, there still is 'structural discrimination' towards women in the workplace.[210] Similarly, Kawai Hayao pointed out in 1997 that although men and women are officially considered equal, traditions do not change that quickly; 'especially within companies the change of the relationship between men and women takes time'.[211] In addition, the German magazine *Japan aktuell* published a report in 1993, which stated that the monthly salary of women in Japan was only 61% of what men earned.[212] This is linked to the 'structural discrimination' towards women; although a great number of women had a university degree, most of them were not handed relevant responsibilities in a company because they would generally leave after getting married, or when having children. Thus, as McVeigh has stated in the aforementioned quotation, women are expected to work only for several years. Although some women resume working in their forties, the long gap from work makes a career difficult and results in most of them being forced to accept part-time jobs with a low salary.

4.2.2 The *Ôeru*'s Masquerade

Returning to *Tea Ceremony III*, it should not be forgotten that Mori does not look like a 'normal' secretary. Mori follows the courteous body language that *ôeru* are supposed to follow, however, she 'breaks' the social code of the uniform: she wears a skin-tight cap with outward protruding ears and a shiny silver costume under her secretary dress. The cap and the costume appear not only in the *Tea Ceremony* series but also in two other photographs, *Love Hotel* (1994) and *Red Light* (1994). In *Love Hotel,* they are combined with a school uniform; Mori sits on a huge round bed in a love hotel,[213] and looks into the camera seductively. In *Red Light*, she stands on a crowded street in Kabukichô, a red light district of Tokyo. She wears a short pink dress over the silver costume. The effect is similar in all photographs: the 'uniform' of a certain social group, be it that of *ôeru*, schoolgirls or prostitutes, is combined with elements of a

---

209 KASAHARA (2008): 141.
210 MAE (2001): 6.
211 KAWAI (1997): 245.
212 CHAPMAN (1993): 17.
213 Love hotels are short-stay hotels operated primarily for the purpose of allowing couples privacy to have sexual intercourse. Rooms are rented out for hours or an overnight stay. Although they are primarily used by couples, they are also used for prostitution.

fantasy costume, which adapt the conventional look into a more humorous and somewhat 'fantasy-like' image. In *Tea Ceremony III*, it almost appears as if Mori were an 'alien' who had come to Tokyo to work as an *ôeru* in a company.

The building in the right background is the Tokyo Fashion School. By using this background, Mori perhaps playfully hints at her own biography, which includes studying design and working as a fashion model. Furthermore, the fashion school symbolises clothing and masquerade. Mori's silver costume with the long ears is not only reminiscent of fantasy characters, but also addresses the phenomenon of *kosupure* (literally 'cosplay' from the English 'costume play'). The term refers to a popular trend which developed in the 1990s, namely masquerading as *manga* or *anime* heroes, characters from video games and fantasy films. Mori's appearance is not based on a specific character; however, her silver costume could be construed as part of a *kosupure* costume. The combination of the typical secretary style and *kosupure* can be interpreted as a humorous and yet critical likening of female employee's uniforms to a 'masquerade'. Like the silver costume, the blouse, skirt and vest of a secretary are also a 'costume'. Both *kosupure* costumes and the neat dress of *ôeru* are inextricably intertwined with the wearer's social status; they define behavioural norms and create identity. *Tea Ceremony III* criticises the *ôeru*'s uniform as a 'costume' which leads to women's subordination in the male-dominated business sector.

The colourful impression of the large-sized artwork, as well as Mori's silver fantasy costume, combined with her smile, create a bright and artificial atmosphere. Hasegawa has described Mori's critical piece as 'optimistic and cheerful', linking it with Pop Art.[214] I agree with Hasegawa: although *Tea Ceremony III* critically addresses the controversial position of women in the Japanese work sector in the 1990s, it nevertheless exudes a loud and cheerful aesthetic, comparable to many works categorised as Pop Art.

4.3 Conclusions

Both *Elevator Girls 3F* and *Tea Ceremony III* are large-sized colourful photographs featuring 'pretty' young women; their socio-critical messages can only be understood when analysing the artworks in their Japanese context, namely within two economic subsystems of Japanese society: department stores and company offices. Yanagi Miwa and Mori Mariko both highlight standardised 'social codes' used in these subsystems by deconstructing some of them. In *Elevator Girls 3F*, elevator girls lose control and let go of their ritualised body language by sitting on the floor and staring at shoes instead of operating the

[214] HASEGAWA (2002): 132.

elevator. In *Tea Ceremony III*, Mori uses ritualised serving gestures, however, she wears a silver cap with elf-like ears and tights under her secretary dress.

Elevator Girls 3F points critically at the seductive 'dreamscape' aesthetic of Japanese department stores and emphasises the use of standardised social codes by their employees, especially elevator girls. At the same time, the photograph shows women as consumers who are fixated on buying brand goods. In this way, both the decorative inside of the department store system, represented by elevator girls, and the consuming outside, represented by the same young women obsessively staring at shoes, are shown as female. Within the department store, this is perhaps connected to the fact that in Japan, culture and beauty are associated with femininity; females are generally preferred for the work of the department attendant. The consumers are also represented by young women, since they are viewed as 'parasites' of Japanese society spending a large amount of money on designer clothing and accessories. As such, the image is concerned critically with the inside of the department store system as well as its outside, and the way in which both sides are interrelated.

In contrast, *Tea Ceremony III* focuses on disparities *within* a system: the work juxtaposes two *sararîmen* with Mori herself dressed as a somewhat 'alien'-like *ôeru*. By courteously offering tea and wearing a neat uniform, she alludes to the subordinated position of female employees in offices. Like in a tea ceremony, women constantly repeat the same rituals, supporting their male colleagues, whereas the men can 'move on', even ignore the women, and have a career. In addition, the silver *kosupure*-like costume exposes Mori's other garments as nothing but a 'masquerade' creating the social identity of *ôeru*. The subordinated pose, the tea serving, the smiling, the uniform and the elaborate make-up are all 'social codes' which define female employees as 'pretty ladies' instead of workforces with important responsibilities.

Elevator Girls 3F and *Tea Ceremony III* are works with a socio-critical message. However, *Elevator Girls 3F* also reflects the seductive power of department stores as well as of standardisation in society in general. This is due to the fact that it makes use of the same visual language as an advertisement: it is a large-sized, colourful, glossy image with 'pretty' women. Similarly, *Tea Ceremony III* is a large, colourful photograph which features a young 'pretty' woman, smiling and offering tea. Both works deconstruct social codes in not a harsh but a rather colourful and humorous way. Okabe Aomi's argument that Mori's work is critical but, nevertheless, possesses an 'entertaining character',[215] applies to both *Tea Ceremony III* and *Elevator Girls 3F*.

---

215 OKABE (2003): 94.

The socio-critical messages of *Elevator Girls 3F* and *Tea Ceremony III* are linked to women's decorative status and limited career opportunities in the Japanese work sector of the 1990s. This aspect will be analysed from a gender perspective in the following section. The elevator girls' standardised appearance and behaviour are intertwined with Japanese ideas of 'perfect femininity'. Furthermore, I will return to Mori's silver costume and relate it to femininity in Japanese *anime* and *kosupure* culture.

5. The 'Gendered' Body

The term 'gender' has traditionally been used to define the grammatical categories of 'masculine', 'feminine' and 'neuter'. However, since the 1980s, cultural studies have also used it as a social category, their definition of 'gender' proceeding from the now well-established assumption that, in contrast to the anatomical differences between the 'sexes', the 'identity' of men and women is constructed culturally and socially. Feminist theories, for instance by Judith Butler, have interpreted both 'gender' and 'sex' not as facts of what an individual is, but rather as regulatory norms which constantly qualify and materialise a body 'within the domain of cultural intelligibility' (see the first section of this chapter).[216]

Gender studies within art history are a relatively new field of research. In 'Western' art history, their inception is often dated to the publication of Linda Nochlin's 1971 essay *Why Have There Been No Great Women Artists*?. In Japanese art history, gender studies gained momentum in the early 1990s, despite being harshly criticised by numerous Japanese art historians as a 'Western' concept and thus not useful in a Japanese context (see Part 1). While I do not agree with the argument that 'gender' per se is not a useful category in a Japanese context, there are methodological problems. The analytical categories of gender studies were first developed within a 'Western' academic context; how can we ensure that while studying gender systems in Japan (or other 'non-Western' cultures), we do not fall into another trap of Eurocentrism? Afsaneh Najmabadi has addressed a similar concern, defining it as a general problem of 'how concepts travel' through both space and time.[217] Using her studies of Iranian culture, Najmabadi has argued that thinking of gender as a binary of man and woman is a modern, 'Western' imperative:

> ... Our contemporary binary of gender translates any fractures of masculinity into effeminization. Nineteenth-century Iranian culture, how-

[216] BUTLER (1993): 21.
[217] NAJMABADI (2006): 18.

> ever, … had other ways of naming a young adolescent male and an adult man desiring to be objects of desire for adult men that were not equated with effeminacy.[218]

This argument could similarly be applied to gender in pre-modern Japan; e.g., I will consider in 5.4 the '*wakashû*' ('young man'). In other words, it is necessary to bear in mind not only ideas of 'gender' and 'sex' but also the social and cultural determinations that define 'gender studies'. The binary of 'female' vs. 'male' is an analytical tool developed in 20th century 'Western' academia and not equally adaptable to an analysis of artworks of all times and places. Thus, as Najmabadi has written, it is necessary to reframe 'the contingency of emergence of gender and sexuality as … a contingency of our own historical making, as our recognition or our production of subject effects'.[219]

In the following sections I will regard 'gender' as a set of constructions determined by time, place and culture, and will consider these contexts instead of being prejudiced by contemporary 'Western' norms, such as a strict binary of 'male' vs. 'female'. I will follow Chino Kaori's stance, by assuming that (Japanese) people are simultaneously 'masculine' and 'feminine', but that 'in the majority of cases, because of social and historical conditions and pressures, self-regulation has confined males to the "masculine" gender and females confined to the "feminine"'.[220]

With this theoretical background, 5.1 will return to the two artworks analysed in the previous section, *Elevator Girls 3F* and *Tea Ceremony III*, and connect these with Japanese ideals of 'feminine women' in the 20th century. Following this, 5.2 will be concerned with the motif of the female corpse in Izima Kaoru's *Otsuka Nene Wears Tuzigahana*, and 5.3 will focus on the male body in Ishiuchi Miyako's *Chromosome XY s. o.*. Finally, 5.4 will return to *Portrait (Futago)* and *Red Marilyn* to explore Morimura Yasumasa's works from a specifically gender viewpoint: how could his 'hybrid' 'gender' in the photographs be defined?

5.1 'Ideal Femininity': Thoughts on *Elevator Girls 3F* and *Tea Ceremony III*

5.1.1 'Ideal Femininity' in Late 20th Century Japan

In the 1980s and 1990s, elevator girls were generally considered attractive by Japanese men, and their job was sought after by Japanese women. They were,

218 IBID: 13.
219 IBID: 18.
220 CHINO (1993): 20.

as Carola Wanke has written, 'exaggerated female stereotypes', and 'artificial copies of *ideal* images of women [my italics]'.[221]

This is, for example, reflected in the portrayal of the elevator girl Hayakawa Nao (Uchiyama Rina) in the first episodes of the TV drama *Motokare* (Ex-boyfriend) (2003) (see 00:07:45 and 00:07:39 of episode 2, 00:06:09 of episode 1, fig. 44). The main character, Kashiwaba Toji, meets Nao while working in the food section of a department store in Osaka and soon starts dating her. She is a young and generous woman, who is considered *kawaii* ('cute', 'lovable') by all the protagonists in the series. She is juxtaposed with Toji's ex-girlfriend Saeki Makoto, who has become a successful account manager in an advertising agency. It could be argued that Nao represents the post-war ideal of a pretty woman who seeks happiness through marriage and children, whereas Makoto represents a new, more powerful ideal. Makoto is ambitious, has a career and, at the end of the drama, also succeeds in her private life – she wins Toji back. Makoto is a 'winner', representative of women who have both a career and a happy private life, whereas Nao, who increasingly loses the sympathy of her boyfriend and the viewer, represents the old ideal of women who support male colleagues and stop working as soon as they get married. However, had the TV series been produced in the 1990s when Yanagi Miwa created the *Elevator Girls* images, it perhaps would have ended differently. In the old ideal, in order for women to be accepted in the work sector and in Japanese society in general, much depended on their youth, outward appearance and the correct 'feminine' behaviour; elevator girls like Nao represented 'ideal femininity'.

Elevator Girls 3F and *Tea Ceremony III* draw attention to Japanese society's expectation of women to embody this 'ideal femininity'. At the same time, the artworks highlight how women constantly reinforce this ideal through what I have previously called 'social codes', i.e. clothing and make-up, gestures, speech and voice tone. However, how could 'ideal femininity' in late 20th century Japan be characterised? The Japanese word for 'femininity', '*onnarashisa*', has been analysed by Kittredge Cherry: '[Japanese] dictionaries define it in terms of being kind, gentle, polite, submissive, and graceful.'[222] In addition, the characteristic of 'weakness' was sometimes included in the definition until feminist scholars protested in the 1980s.[223]

In the following sections, I would like to examine how *Elevator Girls 3F* and *Tea Ceremony III* display 'femininity': are the characteristics 'kind, gentle, polite, submissive and graceful' as well as 'weak' evident in the way the women are represented? Do the artworks also allude to other 'feminine' characteristics? How do they criticise the notion of '*onnarashisa*'?

221 WANKE (2008): 44.
222 CHERRY (1987): 32.
223 IBID: 32.

5.1.2 'Femininity' as 'Decorative' and 'Graceful' Appearance

One important characteristic of office ladies and elevator girls is their 'decorativeness' (see 4.). Mori in *Tea Ceremony III* is a slim young woman who wears make-up and is dressed neatly, highlighting her legs in shiny tights and high heels. Jeannie Lo has described how she experienced favouritism in Japanese companies towards attractive women who bring 'beauty' into the office;[224] Mori's make-up and her garments, disregarding the *kosupure* part of her outfit represent her as a 'beautiful' *ôeru*. Moreover, her slight smile and the respectful pose appear 'graceful'.

In *Elevator Girls 3F*, the 'decorative' aspect is emphasised through the balanced composition of nine women. The slim and neatly uniformed young women are 'decorative' as individuals and as members of a group. Hasegawa has compared the women's similar appearance to 'dolls' and 'living sculptures', whose 'physical presence' is 'weaker even than that of clothed mannequins'.[225] Indeed, the digitally altered image creates an artificial atmosphere which reduces the women's 'physical presence'; their 'decorativeness' makes them resemble mannequins.

It could be concluded that *Tea Ceremony III* and *Elevator Girls 3F* portray female subjects as 'decorative'; the images allude to the importance of outward appearance for women in the work sector. This could be connected to the inclusion of 'graceful' in Cherry's definition of '*onnarashisa*', 'gracefulness' defining 'beautiful' appearance and an elegant way of bearing one's body. In other words, the women's 'decorative' and 'graceful' appearance represents a relevant attribute of Japanese 'femininity'.

5.1.3 'Femininity' as 'Kind, Gentle, Polite' and 'Submissive' Behaviour

Office ladies and elevator girls are expected to be 'kind, gentle, polite' and 'submissive'. Mori's body language in *Tea Ceremony III* expresses utmost politeness towards the person she is offering tea to. Furthermore, her slight bending suggests submissiveness. Similarly, elevator girls bow to customers when the customers enter or exit the elevators. In the aforementioned series *Motokare*, all elevator girls also open the door of the department store when it opens in the morning. They stand in a line, walk to the doors lock step, open them and welcome the first customers by bowing and saying '*irasshaimase*' ('welcome in') (00:06:08 of episode 1, right film still, fig. 44).

---

224 Lo (1990).

225 Hasegawa (2002): 130–131.

Jugaku Akiko has examined the relationship of 'femininity' with Japanese written as well as spoken language.[226] Her book reveals high intonation and nasal voice,[227] a voice as 'quiet as a mosquito',[228] and specific women's language[229] as characteristics which are appreciated as 'feminine' in Japan. Although the formal language *keigo* is used by both sexes in order to show respect, it is associated with 'feminine' characteristics, such as 'tenderness, loveliness, something precious, softness, obedience and discretion'.[230] Thus, it is not surprising that elevator girls as 'feminine ideals' generally speak quietly with a high nasal voice, using polite *keigo*.

However, this polite, submissive speech and body language are only indirectly present in *Elevator Girls 3F*; the women sit on the floor and stare at shoes. In other words, they do not only break out of the social codes that elevator girls as department store employees are supposed to follow, but they also break out of the behaviour rules they are supposed to follow as Japanese women. They seem more egoistic than polite; they are hypnotised by shoes instead of submissively welcoming the viewer.

In conclusion, Mori adopts the 'femininity' characteristics mentioned by Cherry and the expectations of an office lady: she appears as a 'kind, gentle, polite' and 'submissive' woman, offering tea in a respectful pose. In contrast, Yanagi shows the photographic subjects in *Elevator Girls 3F* as women who are supposed to follow these 'feminine' traits but who are driven by consumerism instead.

5.1.4 *Kawaii* as a New 'Feminine Ideal'

Most women in offices and department stores in the 1980s and 1990s only worked for a few years. This was due to them quitting when they got married or, at the latest, when they had children. In case of elevator girls, they also quit because of the physical and emotional demands of standing in an elevator all day. Furthermore, the stereotype of elevator girls and office ladies is of a woman in her twenties; especially elevator girls are expected to look and act young and 'fresh'. The characteristics 'young' and 'fresh' can be connected to the concept of *kawaii*, which has become another important trait of Japanese 'femininity' since the 1990s. Linguistically, '*kawaii*' is related to '*kawaisô*' ('pitiful', 'touching') and '*kawaigaru*' ('to make a pet of', 'take loving care

226 JUGAKU (1990).
227 IBID: 13–15.
228 IBID: 15–17.
229 IBID: 65–71.
230 IBID: 93–94.

of').[231] The term has been popular in colloquial Japanese since the late 1980s and would be translated best as 'cute', 'lovable' or 'sweet'.

In order to understand Japanese society's expectation of women to be *kawaii*, the broader context of *kawaii* will be explained briefly. 'Cute' things have become a distinctive feature of Japanese products – *kawaii* sells. Not only are there commodities with 'cute' characters à la Hello Kitty, fashion items with frills and ribbons, and 'cute' stationery, but *kawaii* has also been extended to play a role in various companies' marketing; for example, the Asahi Bank has used the characters Miffy and Hello Kitty on credit cards. Furthermore, the *kawaii* trend has influenced girls' and women's behaviour; for instance, they have adopted a round childish script (*marumoji*), and infantile (body) language, such as talking of themselves in the third person, speaking with a squeaky voice, or pouting. As Sharon Kinsella has argued, the *kawaii* trend has entailed the fashioning of oneself into a 'cute' object by deliberately acting childlike:

> Being cute meant behaving childlike – which involved an act of self-mutation, posing with pigeon toes, pulling wide-eyed innocent expressions, dieting, acting stupid, and essentially denying the existence of the wealth of insights, feelings, and humor that maturity brings with it. In cute culture, young people become popular according to their apparent weakness, dependence and inability, rather than because of their strengths and capabilities.[232]

How could 'apparent weakness' become a 'popular' trait and why do young women seek to appear 'infantile'?

Firstly, as Cherry's analysis of '*onnarashisa*' has shown, 'weakness' has been seen as a 'feminine' trait. Women think that by acting childlike, they appear more attractive to men.

Secondly, Kinsella has argued that acting *kawaii* can be viewed as a way to stay free of social responsibilities: 'by acting childish, Japanese youth try to avoid the conservatives' moral demand that they exercise self-discipline and responsibility and tolerate severe conditions while working hard in order to repay their obligation to society'.[233] In other words, *kawaii* can be interpreted as a reaction against social pressure. Similarly, Brian McVeigh has defined *kawaii* as a form of 'resistance' against 'the dominant "male" productivist ideology of standardization, order, control, rationality and impersonality.'[234] In comparison, Iida Yumiko has disagreed with these arguments, stating that the act of rejecting maturity is 'not so much of a conscious political protest, as it is

231 McVeigh (2000): 145.
232 Kinsella (1995): 237.
233 Ibid: 251.
234 McVeigh (2000): 16.

an inability to be otherwise'.[235] She has argued that *kawaii* culture is linked to a 'voluntary disciplining aspect', which is reflected in the popularity of fashion magazines and entertainment guides, such as *J.J.*, *Popeye*, *City Road* and *Pia*. These offer detailed 'guidance': 'what to buy, where to go, what to display, what to read, who is suitable as a friend, how to impress your dates, and so on'.[236] In addition, numerous magazines 'guide' consumers how to look perfectly *kawaii*; they impose body images onto women's minds by giving advice on how to construct the size, shape and posture of one's body through fashion, diet, fitness and cosmetic surgery. As the body is, to say it in Foucauldian terms, an outcome of social power play (see 1.), a woman who consumes 'cute' goods and reads the aforementioned magazines internalises the wish to engineer herself according to an image of 'cuteness'. The perfect female body in contemporary Japan has been described by Laura Spielvogel as an ideal which 'plays up bone-thin skinniness, wide-eyed innocence, cuteness, and youth;'[237] it is an embodiment of *kawaii*.

Taking these arguments into account, the *kawaii* culture of the 1990s appears to be rather complex; one has to differentiate between *kawaii* as a characteristic of Japanese popular culture on the one hand and *kawaii* as a feminine ideal on the other. Considering the ideal of the hard working *shakaijin* ('society-person'), *kawaii* in popular culture can be interpreted as a form of resistance against the social pressure of acting responsibly, working and living for Japanese society. However, considering the fact that many Japanese women have internalised *kawaii*, it strengthens the conventional 'feminine' concept of submissiveness, gentleness and weakness. *Kawaii* can be equated with an infantile appearance as well as behaviour. I am critical of this insofar as it reinforces women's discrimination – comparable to children, women as *kawaii* objects pose little intellectual or social threat to the patriarchal status quo. McVeigh has concluded persuasively: 'cuteness is used to symbolize, reinforce and communicate norms which privileges males over females and is the ideal sentiment for strengthening lines of authority.'[238]

Yanagi has criticised how Japanese women accept their subordination: 'Japanese women think they have to be lovable and are always concerned with how much they are valued by people around them and how much they are loved by them.' This quotation not only stresses how Japan's expectation of women to be 'lovable' pressurises women, but it also shows how they constantly consider the opinion of other people.

---

235 IIDA (2002): 181.
236 IBID: 181.
237 SPIELVOGEL (2003): 7.
238 MCVEIGH (2000): 144.

Returning to *Tea Ceremony III* and *Elevator Girls 3F*, both photographs reference the contemporary *kawaii* ideal by featuring young, slim and 'pretty' women. In *Elevator Girls 3F*, the women are photographed from a high angle, sitting decoratively on the floor. In this way, their 'weakness' and subordination to the (male) viewer is also expressed through the way they are positioned. At the same time, the fact that nine similar looking women sit together and stare at shoes alludes to the pressure that women apply amongst themselves. As mentioned in 4., since the 1990s, 'parasite' women have spent a large amount of money on designer goods, including shoes. I agree with Krestina Skirl, who has read the presentation of numerous similar women in the *Elevator Girls* series as a 'critical comment on the homogenising image of femininity and ideals of feminine beauty'.[239] Firstly, this homogenisation is due to women trying to conform to similar male expectations. Secondly, they all copy the same body images presented in magazines such as *Pia* and consume similar, 'cute' goods. Against this background, the female subjects in *Elevator Girls 3F* draw attention to homogenising 'femininity' images not only in the work sector but also in private life.

5.1.5 *Kawaii* Women in Popular Culture

Tea Ceremony III also highlights *kawaii* as a prominent aesthetic in *anime*, *manga* and Japanese popular culture. Mori's shiny silver costume with the cap complemented with alien- or elf-like ears,[240] references some kind of a 'cute' fantasy character with superhuman powers in *manga* or *anime*. Many stories include female alien, half-alien and humanoid characters,[241] or women with exceptional powers. These heroines combine *kawaii* appearance and behaviour with strength. For instance, the girls in *Sailor Moon* are drawn with childlike features, such as huge eyes, small noses and small mouths, and they wear school uniforms with short skirts, revealing their long, slim legs. Yet, the series also includes situations in which they are shown in actively powerful stances: the girls can change into fantasy warriors fighting against evil. As such, *Sailor Moon* echoes a trend in 1990s *manga*: heroines have increasingly been shown

239 SKIRL (2007b): 3.

240 'Elf-like' in this context does not refer to the image of elves in Germanic or Norwegian mythology. Rather, it refers to the 'elf' as a standardised character found in modern fantasy games and role-play, which is influenced by fantasy novels such as *The Hobbit* (1937) and *Lord of the Rings* (1954) by J. R. R. Tolkien. Fantasy elves are wiser than humans with sharper senses and a stronger mental capacity. Hallmarks of elves are their long and outward pointed ears.

241 For instance, Mizuho Kazami in the *anime Onegai Teacher* (Please, Teacher), Nagato Yuki in *Suzumiya Haruhi no yûutsu* (The Melancholy of Haruhi Suzumiya) and Ryôko in *Tenchi muyo* (No Need For Tenchi).

as 'powerful, independent and often extraordinarily violent fighters,'[242] possessing some sort of superhuman powers or being linked with science fiction technology. However, Sharalyn Orbaugh has found two problems. Firstly, the girls are presented 'with a choice between libidinal activity or power and autonomy. There is no scenario by which a woman can have both'.[243]

Secondly, the majority are 'cyborgs, androids, or aliens' instead of human females; 'their strong and talented bodies are not for maximizing their own pleasure or satisfaction but for serving the purposes of the state or their (always male) creator, or both'.[244] In other words, numerous female characters may demonstrate power, however, their power is not for their own (sexual) satisfaction, and it is enabled and circumscribed by patriarchal control. Therefore, it does not elevate the women to equal or higher social positions than men. Rather, they remain objects of male hegemony. In addition, their predominantly 'sexy' bodies with slim vests, long legs, and big breasts, as well as their 'cute' features reflect male fantasies.

The enormous popularity of *kawaii* women in Japanese popular culture can be linked to a 'complex' of Japanese men after the country's defeat in World War II. As Hasegawa Yûko has written, the defeat led to a 'sense of despair and loss of confidence amongst the Japanese, particularly the male population'.[245] As Hasegawa has argued, this male identity crisis resulted in the establishment of imbalanced gender relations within Japanese society; instead of a mature male seeking a mature female, 'the dependent Japanese male, needing protection, seeks a mother figure as well as a girl whose sexuality is yet to emerge and who responds passively to his overtures'.[246] This argument can be corroborated by the depiction of women in *manga* and *anime*, especially in pornography. In her study of women in pornographic *manga*, Eva Bachmayer has found that the women are 'doll-like' and shown in 'offering-poses'.[247] They are less independent than the men they are juxtaposed with; they are submissive and often not only their looks are childlike but also their body language. For instance, they have a finger inside or next to their mouth.[248]

---

242 NAPIER (1998): 104.

243 ORBAUGH (2003): 226.

244 IBID: 227.

245 HASEGAWA (2002): 128; As Chino Kaori has pointed out, this complex goes back far in Japanese history: the Japanese man of the Heian era already was haunted by the fear of a Chinese powerful 'masculinity' outside of Japan and 'hence could not help but doubt his own masculinity.' The 'anxiety and ambivalence of Japanese men's gender, the deep psychological wound that had its foundation in opposition to the "masculinity" of Kara, that is, the "great foreign country," was first inflicted in the Heian period'; CHINO (1993): 27.

246 IBID: 128.

247 BACHMAYER (1990): 210.

248 IBID: 211–212.

Moreover, they appear both infantile and voluptuous at once – they simultaneously represent a mother and Lolita image. Sexualised *manga* with young girls, mostly combined with violent, pornographic imagery, are called *rorikon manga* ('*rorikon*' derives from 'Lolita-complex' referring to men attracted to young girls). The popularity of *rorikon manga* could be explained not only with reference to men's 'inferiority complex' but perhaps also with their awareness of the increasing social influence of young women, leading to a reactive desire to view them infantised and subordinated.

In summary, 1990s *manga* and *anime* women may have extraordinary power; however, they communicate a *kawaii* trend, which reinforces women's subordination, meeting the expectations of men with an 'inferiority complex'. Mori's costume references these *kawaii* fantasy women, alluding to unequal gender relations in Japanese popular culture; her tea offering not only draws attention to women's low career opportunities in the work sector, but it also critiques women's subordinated position in popular imagery.

Moreover, Mori's costume could also be interpreted as a female character's *kosupure* (literally 'cosplay' from the English 'costume play') (see 4.). *Kosupure* has become popular among young people since the 1990s; the districts Harajuku and Akihabara in Tokyo are well-known *kosupure* gathering places. The term '*otaku*' defines passionate *anime* and *manga* fans that possibly engage in *kosupure*;[249] it is often used as a derogatory expression, describing mostly young males who are socially inept, obsessively indulging in computer games, *manga* and *anime* at home.[250] By offering tea in a *kosupure*-like costume, Mori is particularly reminiscent of waitresses in a *kosupure* café. These cafés, which developed in Akihabara in the 1990s, have a significant presence in *otaku* culture. Maid cafés are the best-known *kosupure* cafés; the waitresses wear 'cute' maid-like dresses, while subserviently serving the (mostly male) customers as though they were their maids. If requested, they even feed customers. Against this background, Mori's submissive tea offering also draws attention to women adopting the look of *manga* and *anime* characters to entertain men in *kosupure* cafés.

---

249 Literally '*otaku*' means 'you' when addressing somebody in a polite way referring to the addressee's home; however, as a noun in colloquial Japanese it could be translated as 'geek' or 'maniac'.

250 The negative connotations of the term were enforced by the Miyazaki Tsutomu incident in 1988 and 1989 which gained high media attention: the *otaku* Miyazaki, who was obsessed with comics of *kawaii* girls, kidnapped, raped and murdered several pre-teenage girls. However, since the early 21st century, *otaku* culture has become more popular, Murakami Takashi's artworks reflecting *manga* and *anime* culture and TV dramas, such as *Densha otoko* (Train Man) (2005) presenting *otaku* as 'anti-heroes'.

5.1.6 *Elevator Girls 3F* and *Tea Ceremony III* as Images of Feminist Critique

Up until this point, I have examined Japanese ideals of 'femininity' and how these are reflected in *Elevator Girls 3F* and *Tea Ceremony III*. However, how do Yanagi and Mori criticise these 'femininity' ideals and could the artworks be categorised as 'feminist'?

A typical strategy to draw attention to gender relations is the 'parodical masquerade' with 'masquerade' referring to the adoption of a certain (gender) identity by wearing some kind of a costume. A 'parody' in general is a humorous, absurd, and often ironic imitation, created to mock or critically comment on something. The comic effect is mostly due to its exaggeration of typical attributes. With regard to gender studies, Judith Butler has argued that a 'parody', for instance the practise of 'drag', can demonstrate playfully that all gender is scripted, rehearsed, and performed.[251]

Krestina Skirl has interpreted Yanagi's approach in the *Elevator Girls* series as a 'feminine masquerade', linking this to a strategy used by feminist artists.[252] Similarly, Carola Wanke has argued that the synthetic cuteness of the elevator girls is a 'masquerade'.[253] I agree that 'feminine masquerade' is a relevant strategy in the series: by wearing a uniform and pink lipstick the women become 'elevator girls' and allegories of Japanese 'femininity'. Similarly, Mori's combination of a secretary outfit with a silver *kosupure* costume in *Tea Ceremony III* highlights playfully how garments engineer 'feminine' identity. In addition, Mori is her own subject; this is reminiscent of numerous feminist artists who have tried to criticise stereotypical images of women by taking photographs of themselves.[254] However, 'feminine masquerade' is a precarious strategy: while trying to break out of conventional female representations, women at the same time show themselves (or other women) as photographic objects. In other words, they place themselves (or other women) within the very same position of patriarchal orders that they seek to deconstruct. Thus, as Silvia Eiblmayr has pointed out, it is difficult for women to criticise female images in visual artworks: 'the woman must make her image status visible first, i.e. she has to set up herself as an "image", yet, at the same time, she needs to include a moment of reflection [within the artwork].'[255] How do Mori and Yanagi include a moment of reflection in their photographs?

---

251 BUTLER (1990): 174–180; 186–190.
252 SKIRL (2007a): 51.
253 WANKE (2008): 44.
254 For example, Ono Yoko, Valie Export, Carolee Schneemann or Cindy Sherman.
255 EIBLMAYR (1993): 198.

Tea Ceremony III appears 'cheerful' at first sight: it is a large, colourful photograph which features a young 'pretty' woman, smiling and offering tea. However, the surprising combination of two stereotypes, namely the *ôeru* and the *kawaii* fantasy woman, reflects Mori's criticism. Both the secretary in a Japanese office and the *manga* woman (or the waitress who dresses up as her in a café) follow male expectations and dream images of women. Mixing these two, Mori inserts a moment of 'parodical exaggeration' into the artwork, critically comparing and mocking two 'feminine' clichés at the same time. Furthermore, the strong visual contrast between Mori and the pedestrians creates the impression that there is a gap between the world of the businessmen and that of the woman. Firstly, this points symbolically at the gap between women and men in Japanese companies regarding their career opportunities. Secondly, it stresses the artificiality of women in *manga* and *anime*. As Cohen put it, Mori as a 'Manga cutie conjures an image of unreal sexuality; non-organic, fluidless, bloodless …'[256] The aspect of 'unreal sexuality' can be linked to the aforementioned *manga* and *anime* women who represent male dream images combined with supernatural powers. The (male) viewer projects his (sexual) fantasies on female heroes which real women could never fulfil.

With regard to *Elevator Girls 3F*, I would point out that the photographic subjects are as young and 'decorative' as real elevator girls in department stores. Thus, at first sight, the photograph does not appear to be a 'feminist parody': rather than 'deconstructing' the seductive aesthetic of elevator girls, it instead emphasises it. It makes use of the same visual language as an advertisement for department stores: it is a large-sized, colourful, glossy image with 'beautiful' women. However, there are two moments of 'reflection'. Firstly, there are nine girls in one elevator, having the exact same skin colour and wearing the same pink lipstick. In this way, Yanagi parodies their similar appearance by means of exaggeration. Secondly, the women stare at similar shoes as if mesmerised by them. Again, Yanagi uses an element of exaggeration to criticise the women's obsession with fashion ideals.

Returning to the question of whether the artworks could be described as 'feminist': if 'feminist' criticism includes any kind of (artistic) statement which draws attention to social, political or economical discrimination and biases against women, both artworks can surely be described as 'feminist'. *Tea Ceremony III* and *Elevator Girls 3F* use the motif of 'feminine masquerade' to highlight stereotypical expectations and images of women in 1990s Japan. Moreover, the artists criticise 'feminine ideals'; although in a rather decorative and subtly humorous way, they nevertheless express their critical viewpoints by means of 'parody' and 'deconstruction'.

---

256 COHEN (1997): 94.

5.2 The 'Beautiful Female Corpse': Thoughts on *Otsuka Nene Wears Tuzigahana*

5.2.1 The 'Beautiful Woman' and 'Death'

The *Landscapes* models are young and predominantly female, have symmetric features and slim figures, wear luxury fashion and are well-known, at least in Japan, as actresses, pop stars and models. In short, they represent women who are considered 'beautiful' in contemporary Japan. Furthermore, most sequences feature only one woman; the viewer is 'alone' with the female model.[257]

This isolated situation creates a feeling of intimacy and a somewhat 'erotic' tension. In *Otsuka Nene Wears Tuzigahana*, this aspect of intimacy is emphasised by the viewer 'entering' the private house in which Otsuka Nene lies. In Japan there is a strict division of the public outside (*soto*) and the private inside (*uchi*); entering a private house or apartment, especially of a woman, is a more intimate act than in 'Western' culture. In addition, some of the images include sexual allusions: for instance, Hosokawa Fumie lies partly veiled by a white sheet, naked in a bed in *Hosokawa Fumie Wears Tiffany* (1995) and Helena Noguerra wears a black collar and lingerie with suspenders in *Helena Noguerra Wears Vivienne Westwood* (2001). The cherry blossoms in *Nagasaku Hiromi Wears Louis Vuitton* (1999) can be interpreted as a 'feminine' attribute; it has often been used in Japanese aesthetics to symbolise sexualized women, for instance in *shunga* woodblock prints.[258] However, the models all pose as if they were dead. In this way, the *Landscapes* images show a 'beautiful woman' in an 'intimate' situation with sexual undertones and yet, in the most passive state possible. In other words, the woman is a sexually attractive and 'beautiful' 'corpse'.

At first sight, a 'sexually attractive woman' and 'death' seem like an antithesis. In general, the 'female' is linked to life, birth and nourishment, instead of death; if a woman dies, she can no longer be 'sexual' and endangers procreation. However, as Edgar Allan Poe has stated famously: 'the death of a beautiful woman is, unquestionably, the most poetical topic in the world.'[259] In other words, the coupling of the notion of 'death' and 'beautiful femininity' offers Poe the highest degree of poetics. This conjunction of the 'beautiful woman' and 'death' will be the topic of the following section. Not only in Poe's work but in 'Western' culture in general, the 'death of a woman' and the

---

[257] Exceptions are: *Hirota Reona Wears Katsura Yumi* (1995), which features a young 'dead' broom lying next to Hirota as a 'dead' bride; *Six Girls Wear X-Girl* (2000) with six girls lying on the beach, and *Kato Ai and Nakashima Mika Wear Vivienne Westwood* (2004) with two women who lie next to each other in midst of cables in a white room.

[258] SCREECH (2009): 149, 153.

[259] POE (1946): 19.

'female corpse' have been popular motifs. In German art criticism, the *Landscapes* series have often been interpreted as being reminiscent of the art historical motif 'Death and the Maiden'.[260] I will first introduce this motif briefly to then compare and contrast it with the *Landscapes* series. Following this, I will examine how 'femininity' and 'death' are equated in *Otsuka Nene Wears Tuzigahana*. How is the 'beautiful female corpse' presented? Do the images go beyond a reiteration of the stereotypical gender relation of the 'active male gaze' vs. the 'passive female image'?

5.2.2 'Death and the Maiden' and the 'Female Corpse'

The motif 'Death and the Maiden' originated from dance-of-death-cycles in Germany, and has occurred in numerous prints, drawings, and paintings since around 1500. Famous examples are works by Nikolaus Manuel Deutsch, Hans Sebald Beham and Hans Baldung Grien.[261] The images show the encounter of young women, who are considered attractive according to contemporary taste, with a figure, often a skeleton representing their deaths. This is frequently of sexual nature and the (often naked) women's reactions range from repulsion to seductive acceptance. Various artworks of the 19th and 20th century, for example by Edvard Munch, Egon Schiele and Joseph Beuys, reflect artists' enduring fascination with this theme.[262]

In Japan, there is traditionally no such juxtaposition of a death-figure and a girl. However, there are ink paintings, for instance by Kawanabe Kyôsai, which were most probably influenced by the 'Western' motif. In a hanging scroll of 1871, titled by Erwin von Baelz as *Schöne von einem Skelett verfolgt* (Beauty Chased By a Skeleton), a skeleton chases a geisha running in high *geta* shoes in moon-light (fig. 45). It appears as if the skeleton has just grabbed hold of her left *kimono* sleeve. As Doris Croissant and Wakabayashi Misako have pointed out, the depiction of a yet 'undecided moment', which leaves it to the viewer's

---

260 This reference is made by: KUNSTFORUM (2001a): 211; SIEDENBERG (2001): 3; BOECKER, (2001a): 39 ; BOECKER (2001b): 214.

261 For example the paintings *Der Tod und das Mädchen* (Death and the Maiden) (1517) by Nikolaus Manuel Deutsch, *Der Tod und das Mädchen* (Death and the Maiden) (1517) by Hans Baldung Grien and the copper engravings *Der Tod und das stehende Weib* (Death and the Standing Broad) (1547) or *Der Tod und das schlafende Weib* (Death and the sleeping Broad) (1548) by Hans Sebald Beham.

262 The oil painting and engraving *Das Mädchen und der Tod* (The Girl and Death) by Edvard Munch (1893 and 1894), the painting *Der Tod und das Mädchen* (Death and the Maiden) (1915) by Egon Schiele, the drawing *Der Tod und das Mädchen* (Death and the Girl) by Joseph Beuys (1957) etc.

imagination if the girl will be caught or not, brings in a new dramatic element into the 'Death and the Maiden' topos.[263]

In all these 'Death and the Maiden' images, a lively young woman is juxtaposed with a personification of 'death' trying to 'get' her. In other words, the 'female' is equated with 'youth' and 'beauty' and contrasted with an 'ugly', skeleton-like allegory of 'death'. Although the *Landscapes* series' themes 'death' and 'beautiful woman' are comparable to the traditional 'Death and the Maiden' motif, the photographs nevertheless differ strongly in the way in which they show the woman's 'death'. Firstly, they do not include any personification of 'death', and secondly, they do not provide an antithesis of 'female' and 'death' but rather a convergence: a 'beautiful female corpse'. Therefore, I would argue that the *Landscapes* series could be compared with depictions of a 'female corpse', which became popular especially in the 19th century.

For example, the drowning of Ophelia in Shakespeare's *Hamlet* has been adopted in various literary works and paintings. Many writers have used the gaps around the character Ophelia in Shakespeare's text to imagine her beauty, mental disorder and death.[264] In fine art, the most famous depiction of Ophelia's death might be the Pre-Raphaelite John Everette Millais' painting *Ophelia* (1851–1852), which shows her corpse in a lake with plants and flowers.[265] In addition, Eugene Delacroix dedicated a lithograph in 1843 and an oil painting in 1853 to Ophelia's drowning. In both works, Ophelia's closed eyes, the trance-like facial expression and her loose dress, partly revealing her breasts and exposing her curvy figure, create a 'sensual' atmosphere. In contrast to Millais, Delacroix dramatically portrays the moment of Ophelia's death – although her body is sinking into the water she is still holding on to a branch.

In recent years there have been staged photographs which reference Ophelia's death, for example Victor Burgin's *The Bridge I* and *The Bridge II* (1984), Tom Hunter's appropriation of Millais' work *The Way Home* (2000) and Gregory Crewdson's *Untitled (Ophelia)* (2001). In addition, the Ophelia image was appropriated in a video clip for Nick Cave's musical ballad *Where the Wild Roses Grow* (1995), directed by the American photographer and director Rocky Shenck. The duet, which was sung by Nick Cave and Kylie Minogue,

---

263 CROISSANT and WAKABAYASHI-OH (1991): 189.

264 For example Arthur Rimbaud's *Ophélie* (1870), *Ophelia I* by Georg Heyms (1910) or *Schöne Jugend* [Beautiful Youth] (1913) by Gottfried Benn, just to mention some poetic adoptions of Ophelia.

265 For a detailed analysis of Ophelia as a motif in art history consult KINDLER (2004) and BAYER (2009); other examples of depictions of 'female corpses' include William Holman Hunt's drawing *The Lady of Shalott* (1850), Paul Delaroche's oil painting *La Jeune Martyre* [The Young Martyr] (1855), H. P. Robinson's photograph The *Lady of Shalott* (1863), Gabriel von Max' oil painting *Der Anatom* [The Anatomist] (1869) and Arthur Hughes' oil painting *The Lady of Shalott* (1872/1873).

is about a young woman and the male singer's admiration for her. However, in the end, he takes her to a river and kills her, stating that 'all beauty must die'. In the video, numerous scenes show Minogue wearing a white dress and red lipstick, floating like a 'beautiful corpse' in water.

In Japanese art history, images of corpses are linked with Buddhist devotional exercise. Since the fifth century, there have been Buddhist texts describing the decay of a corpse in nine stages (*kusôkan*). This decay has also been visualised with the image of a young woman's corpse in *kusôzu* ('images of the nine stages of a decaying corpse'). These docile 'Buddhist Memento Mori' confront the viewer with a visual narration on the decomposition of the woman. In contrast to the aforementioned images of Ophelia and the *Landscapes* photographs, *kusôzu* juxtapose the 'beauty' and sexual attractiveness of a woman in the first of the nine images with her body's decomposition in the latter – sexuality and death are interpreted as opposing elements. The visualisation of a female body's decay should help the viewer to overcome his sexual desires. I will return to *kusôzu* in 6.3.

5.2.3 The Cultural Analogy of 'Death' and 'Femininity'

To return to the *Landscapes* series and the aforementioned Ophelia images: how do they represent 'death' and to what extent do they represent an analogy of 'beautiful femininity' and 'death'? All the Ophelia images show a young woman either at the moment of death or shortly after. She is shown before her body becomes stiff (rigor mortis) and starts to decay: her 'beauty' has not yet begun to disappear. In this way, 'death' is 'gently' visible in the images: it is either an invisible force that Ophelia dramatically fights against, such as in the depictions by Delacroix, or it is the reason behind her inanimate posture. It could even be argued that this inanimate posture emphasises the woman's 'beauty'. With regard to *Otsuka Nene Wears Tuzigahana*, it has been stated that the actress's relaxed facial expression, the warm colours, the sunlight and the harmonious photographic composition result in a work which evokes a peaceful atmosphere (see 6.3 in Part 2). Her 'death' is not presented as something horrible but as a quiet 'beautiful' scene. Otsuka Nene's 'beauty' is emphasised by her lifeless pose making her appear almost like a sculpture. She appears as an 'artwork' within an 'artwork'. As Elisabeth Bronfen has argued, one reason for the cultural analogy of 'beautiful femininity' and 'death' is the equation of 'femininity' with 'image':

> The beauty of Woman and the beauty of the image both give the illusion of intactness and unity, cover the insupportable signs of lack, deficiency, transiency ... Beauty, however, always also includes death's inscription,

> because it requires the translation (be it in fantasy or in reality) of an imperfect, animate body, into a perfect, inanimate image, a dead 'figure'...[266]

The quotation corroborates the argument that 'death' translates Otsuka Nene into an even more 'beautiful' 'female image'. If 'death' enhances the 'beauty' of the 'female' by transforming her into an inanimate art image, 'death' could then be compared to an 'artist': Izima and 'death' together create perfect 'female' images.

These 'female' images are ultimately *passive* and could be juxtaposed with the artist's and the viewer's *active* gaze, which is 'male', both in Izima's series and in the previously mentioned Ophelia images. Similarly, for Poe, the speaker best suited for the 'most poetical topic' should be a 'bereaved lover'.[267] That is to say, the surviving speaker is 'male', whereas the corpse is 'female'. The motif of the 'dead woman' enforces the traditional juxtaposition of the active 'male' speaker or viewer with the 'female' as the superlatively passive image.

5.2.4 More Than a 'Male' Gaze on the 'Beautiful Female Corpse'

In *Otsuka Nene Wears Tuzigahana*, the viewer enters Otsuka's private sphere and looks down at a 'dead' woman lying vulnerably on the floor. He is in a powerful position, investigating the isolated scene and 'penetrating' the 'female' with his stare, while she cannot do anything but passively receive them. Taking these arguments into consideration, the *Landscapes* series reinforces the juxtaposition of the 'female' as an alluring, passive image and the 'male' as an active creator and viewer – a stereotypical gender relation which has been criticised by feminists since the 1970s. Thus, it is not surprising that the German feminist Alice Schwarzer has harshly criticised the *Landscapes* series as 'misogynistic'.[268] However, I would argue that the series goes far beyond showing women as passive sexual objects.

Firstly, Izima uses the 'female image' as an opportunity to visualise 'death'. 'Death' is beyond any human subject's experiential realm and has thus always been the subject of cultural myths. The use of a 'female' to embody this mythical 'death' could be linked with the male artist's desire to see 'death' as ultimate 'alterity'. The image of a beautiful 'dead' woman fascinates the (male)

---

266 BRONFEN (1992): 64.

267 POE (1946): 187.

268 Alice Schwarzer uses Izima's *Shinohara Ryoko Wears Vivienne Westwood* (1996) as an example of 'misogynistic photography'. In her opinion, the photographs of the actress Shinohara lying 'dead' before a long row of urinals in a men's restroom are as 'pornographic' as the work of Helmut Newton and Nobuyoshi Araki. SCHWARZER (2000): 22–28.

viewer because it confronts him with a 'frightening' concept, yet it is the death of 'the Other'. In Bronfen's words:

> Over representations of the dead feminine body, culture can repress and articulate its unconscious knowledge of death which it fails to foreclose even as it cannot express it directly… the interstice between death, femininity and aesthetics is negotiated over the representation of a dead feminine body clearly marked as being other, as being not mine.[269]

'Clearly marked as being other', a woman's 'death' can be fantasised about more easily. It has been argued before that 'death' 'translates' Otsuka Nene into a most 'beautiful' image. However, it could then also be argued that while 'translating' 'death' into a 'beautiful' image, Otsuka Nene simultaneously provides an aesthetic shield against the fear of 'death'. To return to Poe's words, not only does 'death' make a 'beautiful woman' the 'most poetical' motif, the 'woman' also makes 'death' 'poetical'. In other words, the 'beautiful woman' makes the abstract phenomenon of 'death' speakable or viewable. In light of these considerations, the *Landscapes* images do not simply present a sexually attractive female body, but rather use it in order to tease the viewer, inviting him to *imagine* death. The series translates 'inexperiencable death' into an image and presents it as a fantasy.

This brings me to my second argument: that the viewpoints reflected in the images are not only a visualisation of Izima's own dealing with 'death', but also reflect the models' fantasies. The perspective reflected in the artworks is not simply a 'misogynistic' and typically 'active male gaze' on a 'passive female object' but something more complex. As explained in Part 2, Izima asks the women about their death fantasies (a location, designer and story), and interprets their answers as photographic images. According to Susanne Boecker, the fantasies do not show any weakness on the part of the female model.[270] In contrast, Hasegawa Yûko has interpreted the model as 'being "broken" or as a beautiful and strange doll that offers no resistance'.[271] I would suggest that the female subjects of the *Landscape* series are in an ambiguous position: they pose as weak and passive; however, at the same time, they are also strong and active in the artistic production process, embodying their own death fantasies. On the one hand, Otsuka Nene acts as a 'dead' victim, who cannot return the viewer's gaze. On the other hand, her unnatural bearing of her legs and arms as well as her peaceful facial expression are a pose; as her slight smile in *#213* and *#214* indicates, she enjoys acting 'dead'. Furthermore, her name is mentioned in the title of the photographic sequence and a viewer who

---

269 BRONFEN (1992): xi.
270 BOECKER (2001b): 216–217.
271 HASEGAWA (2008): 17.

is familiar with Japanese films recognises the actress, who has appeared in more than forty films and TV dramas. The fact that she is a well-known actress suggests that the weakness within the image is a role; she is used to create cinematic images. As such, the photographs' title with the name of the actress or model influences the way some viewers perceive the woman's role within the images.

Thirdly, the *Landscapes* series references the notions of 'death' and 'female' playfully by using metaphors and tautologies with regard to both the series' motif and medium. Bronfen has summarised Poe's statement convincingly; by dying, i.e. becoming an 'inanimate body', a beautiful woman can become an art object:

> Because her dying figure as an analogy to the creation of an art work, and the depicted death serves as a double of its formal condition, the "death of a beautiful woman" marks the mise en abyme of a text, the moment of self-reflexivity, where the text seems to comment on itself and its own process of composition, and so decomposes itself.[272]

As such, the 'death of a beautiful woman' can be interpreted as a general metaphor for the creation of art. Thus, the motif 'dead woman' references metaphorically the creation of the *Landscapes* series as an artwork. This self-reflexive metaphor is emphasised by the artificial impression of the images, created by the combination of elaborately staged settings, professional models and glamorous clothing in colour-saturated large-sized photographs.

The models and their 'glamorous' designer garments also point at another metaphorical aspect: fashion, by definition, 'dies' at some point and can be interpreted as a symbol of death. As such, the photographs present not only an analogy of 'death' and 'female' but also of 'death' and 'fashion'. Furthermore, it should not be forgotten that the *Landscapes* images are *photographs* with photography being a medium closely intertwined with each moment's 'death'. I will return to these metaphorical arguments in 7.

In conclusion, the female subjects of the *Landscapes* series are shown as 'beautifully' passive and sexually attractive 'corpses'. Their 'teasing' posture might become the starting point for the viewer's reflection on 'death': the 'beautiful female body' as a symbol of alterity offers the (male) viewer a 'screen' for his thoughts on 'death'. Furthermore, the professional models and actresses are 'active' in the photographic production process, and as such, 'strong' women who do not fantasise about 'death' as 'being not mine' but who imagine their *own* death. However, although it is their own 'death', it neverthe-

---

272 BRONFEN (1992): 72.

less is inexperienceable, a colourful and 'fashionable' fantasy. The main reading I propose for the *Landscapes* series therefore is that it draws attention to 'death' as a myth by presenting it simultaneously as both a male and female fantasy image. In addition, by using the 'beautiful female' as an analogy to 'death', Izima highlights both as cultural clichés. The 'beautiful female' functions in a similar way to the motif of 'death' as the motif of 'fashion' and the medium of 'photography': the 'beautiful female', 'fashion' and 'photography' all reference playfully the idea of 'death as an image'.

Izima's 'death images' might be viewed by some as 'misogynistic' and as reiterating existing power relations; however, it cannot be denied that the *Landscapes* series is a complex work with a fascinating, timeless theme. To close in Bronfen's words, 'we can deny neither the powerful fascination emanating from, nor the psychic necessity for these images, even as we seek to disclose them'.[273]

5.3 'Masculinity' in 1990s Japan: Thoughts on *Chromosome XY s. o.*

5.3.1 Anonymous Intimacy – Ishiuchi's Gaze on the Male Body

Up until this section, *Chromosome XY s. o.* has been described as a photograph of a 'naked' body and its aesthetic impression as 'stylised' and comparable to that of a 'torso': it is both a bodily fragment and a self-contained body image. The concept of being a detail and yet also a complete art composition in itself has appeared more relevant to the photograph's almost abstract aesthetic than sexual tensions evident in 'nude' images. Nevertheless, the combination of the symmetric close-up perspective, the black and white aesthetic, and the soft illumination also creates a feeling of sensuality. In addition, it cannot be ignored that in the *Chromosome XY* series, Ishiuchi as a 'female' photographer approached naked 'males', regarded them from close distance and 'transformed' details of their bodies into art motifs. In other words, the specific aesthetic of the 'male' body is a relevant topic in the series, suggesting subtly 'erotic' undertones. What kind of 'masculinity' does *Chromosome XY s. o.* present? Could this 'masculine' body aesthetic be compared or rather contrasted with other works in (art) photography? Does it reflect trends in 1990s Japan?

Chromosome XY s. o. presents the upper body of a stranger; the viewer does not get to know the face of the body's owner or anything about his personal background. Furthermore, the title of both the individual photograph and the complete series refers to the DNA structure of all men in the world; all men

273 Bronfen (1992): xiii.

have the XY chromosomes pairing. As such, the title refers to a biological fact concerning males in its most ubiquitous sense. The image presents the male body anonymously and is concerned with 'the man' on a universal level rather than with individuals.

However, at the same time, the viewer sees the male body from a short distance; the soft photographic focus, the mild light and the harmonious composition evoke a gentle feeling. In Sandra S. Phillips words, the 'general atmosphere' of the series 'is of intimacy and sexuality.'[274] 'Sexuality' here should not be understood as a strong and aggressive power but rather as an interest in the human body and a desire to view it from a very close perspective. This is emphasised in the Japanese title of the 1995 volume of *Chromosome XY* photographs, *Sawaru Chromosome XY* (To Touch Chromosome XY). The term 'to touch' reflects the photographic gaze: the lens is so close it seems to 'touch' the body.

The somewhat contradictory aspect of anonymity and closeness in *Chromosome XY* has also been addressed indirectly in Ishiuchi's following quotation:

> … I'll never be a man and will never understand men entirely… With a bit of exaggeration one might call it an unknown world… I wanted to look at the male body in complete detail. So I went very close to the male skin, as if the camera lens were touching it, licking it. It is not a man with a specific name. 'Chromosome XY' stands for a detail in the bodies of all men. It is also the object of the desire to look at strange men.[275] [sic]

The expression 'the desire to look at strange men' alone corroborates the photograph's ambiguous quality: the word 'strange' emphasises the male subject's anonymity and suggests a feeling of distance, whereas Ishiuchi's 'desire' for intimacy is mirrored in the gentle atmosphere of the photographs. As Ishiuchi's quotation shows, this ambiguous moment is linked with her being 'female', trying to overcome a feeling of distance towards an 'unknown world', namely 'the male'. The method for overcoming this distance is the practise of photography, which is compared to a form of sexual intercourse: 'touching' and 'licking' the male body.

The way in which Ishiuchi's photographic process can be equated with sexual interaction could be juxtaposed ironically with the common cliché of the male photographer symbolically 'penetrating' the female model with the camera lens. A famous adoption of this metaphorical motif can be seen, for instance, in Michelangelo Antonioni's film *Blow Up* (1966) when the main protagonist, the fashion photographer Thomas (David Hemmings), photographs the supermodel Veruschka. It is the *female* body which has been the object of

---

274 PHILLIPS (2005): 131.
275 As cited in MATT and WEIERMAIR (eds.) (1997): 57.

desire for the (male) gaze within the history of art, photography and popular imagery.

5.3.2 'Masculinity' in *Chromosome XY s. o.* and Robert Mapplethorpe's *CHEST* (1986)

There are few examples of female photographers who have been concerned with naked male bodies.[276] Rather, most photographs of naked men which are not taken for documentary purpose are linked to homoerotic imagery; that is to say, a 'male' photographer presents the 'male nude' as a sexual object (for a 'male' audience). In Japan, Takano Ryûdai has been creating large-sized art photographs of Japanese men since the 1990s. In contrast to Ishiuchi's images, the colour photographs are taken from a greater distance and show both the young men's bodies and faces. His models are posing and sometimes still wearing a necklace or a jacket. In short, Takano's artworks exude a completely different aesthetic to the *Chromosome XY* images.

Robert Mapplethorpe's 1980s black and white close-up photographs of male bodies seem more comparable to the *Chromosome XY* series. However, unlike Ishiuchi, Mapplethorpe concentrates on extraordinarily athletic bodies; the models often tense their muscles to emphasise their well-toned form. In addition, numerous photographs reflect a fixation on Black men's bodies; Mapplethorpe expropriates Black 'masculinity' in a fetishist way. In his nude photographs, the notion of 'masculinity' develops from the combination of firm, large muscles, body control, athletic strength, and sexual power, as symbolised by large genitals. In other words, 'masculinity' is equated with strength and potency, embodied stereotypically by 'the Black man'.

To return to *Chromosome XY s. o.*, at first sight, its aesthetic impression seems quite similar to that of Mapplethorpe's photograph *CHEST* (1986), which shows an almost hairless chest of a Black man in a symmetric close-up, black and white composition (fig. 46). However, *Chromosome XY s. o.* also includes the man's navel and parts of his left arm, whereas *CHEST* is a square image focused solely on the chest with its two small nipples and two distinct abdominal muscles. *CHEST* presents Mapplethorpe's typical concept of 'masculinity': the male front does not display any fat; the abdominal muscles and 'well-built' chest reflect ultimate strength. The quadrate size of the photograph creates a compact impression and emphasises this impression of strength. In contrast, the man in *Chromosome XY s. o.* is slim, his chest and arms do not appear muscular or strong; the photograph's upright size emphasises the body's lightweight impression.

---

[276] The few exceptions include works by Leni Riefenstahl and Annie Leibovitz.

This representation of 'masculinity' in *Chromosome XY s. o.* reflects Ishiuchi's statement that she was interested in 'normal men, normal *ojisan* or *onîsan'*. The term '*ojisan'* (literally 'uncle') referring to 'ordinary middle-aged men' and '*onîsan*' (literally 'older brother'), which stands for 'ordinary young men', represent the average Japanese man rather than Mapplethorpe's personifications of force and potency. At the same time, the slender body represents a particularly Japanese notion of 'masculinity' which is less bound to muscular strength and large size, but nevertheless linked to the 'male' and his sexuality. The chest in *Chromosome XY s. o.* may be of an average *onîsan*, however, at the same time, the coupling of its hairlessness and its slim and yet defined form perhaps also represents a Japanese 'masculine ideal'.

5.3.3 A New 'Masculine Ideal' and the Rise of the 'Female' Gaze

From the beginning of Japan's period of high economic growth in the 1960's, the stereotypical image of 'the Japanese man' had been rather 'asexual': he had to be a good company worker, a responsible citizen and a representative of his family. In Laura Miller's words, Japanese men and women evaluated men 'primarily on the basis of character, social standing, earning capacity, lineage and other social criteria'.[277] In addition, the *sararîman* representing the stereotypical Japanese man wears a business suit, which masks his body contours.[278] In contrast to females' business dress, his garments downplay his sexual characteristics, as do requirements for dark colour and an almost identical cut of the suit. All these things considered, sexual and attractive appearance was excluded from the stereotypical 'Japanese man'; rather, he was associated with his work and social responsibility.

However, in the 1990s, a new 'masculinity' began to develop, weakening the 'asexual' *sararîman* image. A new generation of Japanese men started to present 'masculinity' as a sexually alluring aesthetic. This aesthetic has been embodied by the actor and singer Kimura Takuya (abbreviated as Kimutaku), who is regularly voted the most attractive and 'sexy' man in Japan by both men and women.[279] As Miller has noted, Kimutaku 'exudes a frank sexuality that does not so easily endorse an uncomplicated portrayal of traditional masculinity'; however, he is popular among the younger generations and viewed as both

277 MILLER (2006): 37.

278 EICHER and ROACH-HIGGINS (1997): 20.

279 For instance, the young men's magazine *Fine Boys* ranked him number one in a survey of 'Favourite Male Celebrities' in 1998. Similarly, since 1995, female readers of the *An An* magazine have consistently voted Kimutaku the celebrity they viewed as most 'sexy' and 'manly'. MILLER (2003): 37.

'sexy' and 'manly'.[280] Moreover, an increasing number of young men have become concerned with their appearance and sexual attractiveness, be it by going to the gym, colouring their hair, plucking their eyebrows,[281] or using cosmetic products. According to a survey published in the German magazine *Japan Magazin* in 1998, the sales for cosmetic products for men in Japan increased by 70 percent between 1985 and 1995.[282] In men's magazines, such as *Men's No-No* or *Fine Boys*, consumers are encouraged to improve their fashion sense and physical appearance in the same way as women are in women's magazines (see 5.1). These magazines, together with popular culture and the beauty industry, fit a male body image into the minds of young men which pressurizes them to submit to a particular 'masculine ideal'.

In his topless photographs, Kimutaku shows a slender, hairless chest, comparable to the one in *Chromosome XY s. o.*. Since the 1980s, the hairless chest has replaced the ideal of a hairy chest à la Sean Connery.[283] This is evident, for instance, in the increase in hair removal services for men at cosmetic salons: in the late 1990s, the most popular service at the cosmetic salon Men's TBC was body hair removal, and at Men's Joli Canaille Salon, body hair removal topped the list, alongside weight loss.[284]

These new beauty trends have not been welcomed by the majority of older generations of men, many of whom are concerned about what they see as the loss of 'masculinity' and what they perceive as an identity crisis among the Japanese youth who are 'unwilling to carry the "burden" of tradition.'[285] This new, more externalised concept of 'masculinity' has been interpreted as a form of 'feminisation' both in Japan and 'the West'.[286] However, I disagree with this interpretation. Men have become more concerned with their appearance, dying their hair, plucking their eyebrows and following a hairless body ideal like women, however, this does not mean that they copy the previously mentioned 'femininity' concept of *kawaii* (see 5.1). Rather, they present a 'masculine' aesthetic which differs to the 'Western' 'masculine ideal' of muscular strength and power. The comparison of the Japanese male body in *Chromosome XY s. o.* with the Black male body in Mapplethorpe's *CHEST* has once again shown that notions of 'masculinity' differ according to culture, space and time. Mapplethorpe's and Ishiuchi's photographs present different and yet equally 'masculine' bodies and bodily ideals. As R.W. Connell has argued persuasively, there

280 MILLER (2003): 37.
281 According to a survey by the magazine *Seventeen* in 2001, the majority of young men (89 percent) stated to do their eyebrows; MILLER (2006): 145.
282 KÜHNE (1998): 23.
283 For more information on the reception of chest hair in Japan see MILLER (2003): 40–43.
284 MILLER (2006): 133.
285 IIDA (2002): 230.
286 UENO (1997); GETREUER-KARGL (2001): 9.

is no one form of 'masculinity' but rather 'many different masculinities'.[287] I would argue that viewing a slender, non-muscular and hairless body as more 'feminine' than a muscular, wide and hairy one is a rather Eurocentric and contemporary viewpoint.

Considering Japanese pre-modern history, a slender, non-muscular and, from a 'Western' viewpoint, 'feminine' man was often viewed as attractive. In the Heian period (794–1192), fine faces powdered in white were considered a male beauty ideal; in Murasaki Shikibu's *Genji monogatari* (around 1021), the puerile beauty of Genji's soft face, his hair, his clothes, his fragrance and his grace are all described in detail. Furthermore, in the Edo period, the slender *wakashû* ('young man') became an object of desire for both men and women, as is, for example, reflected in his depiction in *shunga* woodblock prints. I will return to this in more detail in 5.4. Although the 'masculine ideal' of 1990s Japan cannot be compared directly with gender ideals in pre-Meiji Japan, the historical background nevertheless shows that the male body used to be a candidate for aesthetic assessment and was viewed as an object for the female (and male) gaze. In other words, the emergence of a male body aesthetic in Japan is not entirely new; rather, it started to fade in the Meiji era when the notion of 'beauty' was taken over by women (see 2.2). Thus, although developed within the structures of 1990s consumption culture, the notion of a 'new masculinity' could nevertheless also be linked to Japanese traditions.

In light of these considerations, I would argue that 'masculinity' in 1990s Japan cannot be interpreted as a trend toward 'femininity' but rather as a 'shift to beautification as a component of masculinity.'[288] Furthermore, as Miller has pointed out, one reason for this 'beautification' is, in fact, the 'female gaze': 'men's beauty consumption is … informed by female desire, while concurrently symbolizing consumption-driven identity and the rejection of their fathers' model of masculinity.'[289] In other words, the new 'masculinity' was born out of a resistance towards their parents' generation as well as out of the desire to respond to young women's expectations. The fashion and cosmetic work of (heterosexual) men is mostly intended to stimulate women's interest.

A new generation of Japanese women values men's looks; the plethora of media images has opened up a space for a 'female gaze' to arise. Photographing a naked young man with a slender, hairless chest from close distance, Ishiuchi indirectly represents the gaze of women who openly view men as aesthetic objects. As such, *Chromosomy XY s.o.* draws attention to a new 'masculine' ideal and to a new confidence among Japanese women to look at men from an aesthetic perspective.

---

[287] CONNELL (1995): 77–81.
[288] MILLER (2006): 126.
[289] IBID: 127.

5.3.4 *Chromosome XY s. o.* as an 'Alternative Nude'

Considering the *Chromosome XY* series, Ishiuchi presents the viewer with a cross-section of body parts belonging to Japanese and Caucasian men, old and young, slim and large, with hairy and smooth skin. As such, the photographs represent the male body in a wide sense. Kasahara Michiko has found the right words when stating: 'facing the body of an individual man, Ishiuchi playfully touches his hair and small patterns on his body with her lens, while looking at every man in this world.'[290] At the same time, *Chromosome XY s. o.* as an individual image shows a hairless, slender chest which could be interpreted as an attribute of a new, more external 'masculinity' of 1990s Japan.

It has been argued that Ishiuchi's 'female' view on the male body can be linked to a new, 'female gaze' on men as aesthetic objects. However, in contrast to most 'nude' photographs of women taken by (heterosexual) men, or 'nude' photographs of men taken by (homosexual) men, including Mapplethorpe's, Ishiuchi's gaze appears concerned with bodily patterns and skin structure, rather than with 'complete' figures. The close-up perspective, the harmonious composition and the mild light resulting in soft contours create a calm photograph, exuding a sense of gentle closeness. In addition, the body is photographed face-on, not from any angle. This results in a 'neutral' and 'respectful' gaze insofar as the camera is not 'looking up' or 'looking down' on the naked body's owner. As such, Ishiuchi's gaze is not a superior one, 'penetrating' or 'fetishising' the body but it rather tenderly analyses its aesthetic. Approaching the body with respect, the photographic lens 'scans' it carefully.

Returning to the aforementioned metaphor of photographic activity as sexual interaction, Ishiuchi never 'abuses' her position as a photographer to solely please herself. Rather, she uses it as an opportunity to find out more about the male body, trying to overcome a distance. Perhaps it is this curious and yet respectful gaze which makes *Chromosome XY s. o.* so different from a conventional 'nude' image. And perhaps this gaze could be an alternative approach for some photographers to view human subjects, whether 'female' or 'male', naked or clothed.

290 KASAHARA (1998): 22.

5.4 'Hybrid' Gender Representations in *Portrait (Futago)* and *Red Marilyn*

5.4.1 Gender 'Hybridity'

Up until this last section of the Gendered Body segment, the body in *Portrait (Futago)* and *Red Marilyn* has been analysed with regard to traditions of 'nude' and 'naked' bodies in 'Western' as well as Japanese art history. It has been stated that by reclining 'nude' on the bed in *Portrait (Futago),* Morimura provides an ironic critique of conventional gender relations (the male gaze vs. the female body) in 'Western' art history, while, at the same time, re-eroticising the Japanese male body, which had started to fade as an aesthetic object of visual art shortly after Manet painted *Olympia.* Furthermore, Morimura's bodily representations in the two artworks have been linked with thoughts on 'national identity' and Japan's relationship with 'the West' since the Meiji era. Self-confidently showing his naked body in large-sized colour-saturated images, Morimura presents the viewer with complex identities which are 'hybrid' culturally and ethnically. However, they are equally complex from a gender perspective: is Morimura a 'male' who presents himself as a 'female' with a 'feminine' gender? Or is this 'gender' 'androgynous', i.e. neither distinguishable 'masculine' nor 'feminine'? This section will offer three different and yet intertwined readings of gender representations in Morimura's works, trying to answer these questions.

5.4.2 First Reading: A 'Man' in the 'Disguise' of a 'Woman'

The simplest interpretation of gender in *Portrait (Futago)* and *Red Velvet, Pose 1* is that Morimura is a 'male' in the disguise of a 'female', presenting a 'feminine' gender. Therefore, it is not surprising that he has been compared with actors of female roles in the *kabuki* theatre (*onnagata*).[291] In *Red Marilyn*, the combination of Morimura's extremely light skin, small eyes with strong black eyeliner and the red mouth slightly open so that, in contrast to Marilyn Monroe in *Red Velvet, Pose 1*, his teeth cannot be seen, are collectively reminiscent of *onnagata* faces. In addition, an *onnagata* appears 'feminine' through his poses. Similarly, Morimura adopts a 'feminine' gender by copying the pose of a pin-up and looking seductively into the camera.

However, in both *Portrait (Futago)* and *Red Marilyn*, Morimura references a 'Western' rather than a Japanese icon. Furthermore, his blatant nakedness and the dynamic of his pose, especially in *Red Marilyn*, contrast with the highly re-

---

291 MATT and WEIERMAIR (1997): 14–15; YOON (2000): 123 etc.

duced, 'quiet' aesthetic that *onnagata* (literally 'woman's manner') are famous for. In general, the *onnagata* aims at smallness 'through compression and restraint, and grace through control, stylization, and simplification bordering on austerity'.[292] His 'femininity' is never exposed as a body of muscle and flesh; rather, it is a construction of shape and line, a stylised image. Although the reference of a 'feminine' gender through alluring, 'typically feminine' body language is a similarity of Morimura's approach and that of *onnagata*, the appropriation of 'Western' art and pop icons and Morimura's naked body contrast strongly with *onnagata*.

In *Red Marilyn*, Morimura not only wears a brassiere with obviously fake breasts, he also does not conceal his defined abdominal muscles and his 'masculine' thighs. Morimura makes his 'disguise' as a 'woman' obvious; his 'male' body contrasts with 'feminine' attributes, revealing them as a 'masquerade'. Therefore, he could be categorised as a 'male in drag' with a 'masculine' body beneath the 'feminine' gender. In contrast, his slender body in *Portrait (Futago)* appears more 'hybrid' with 'masculine' and 'feminine' characteristics blending into each other. Although the flat breasts, 'well-built' stomach and muscles on the thighs suggest that the photographic object is not a woman, the hairstyle, jewellery, make-up, shoes as well as the posture convey a sense of the effeminate. The curvaceousness of many forms within the image, such as the blonde curls, the flowers on the *kimono* and the bouquet create an organic impression associated with the female body. The 'masquerade' is not as obvious as in *Red Marilyn*: is the photographic object a 'feminine' looking 'man' or a 'masculine' looking woman? At least from a contemporary 'Western' viewpoint, the body appears rather 'androgynous'; this impression is rendered all the more emphatic by the fact that Morimura's genitalia are hidden.

For a viewer with a good knowledge of Manet's paintings, Morimura's androgynous body also offers a witty parallel to the body of Victorine Meurent, who is Manet's most famous model. Due to her slender, almost 'androgynous' forms, Manet not only used her as a model for female subjects, such as in *Olympia*, but also in 'masculine' roles, such as a torero in *Mlle. Victorine in the Costume of a Matador* (1862). Moreover, she even sat for the painting *The Fifer*, which shows a prepubescent boy (1866). As mentioned in Part 2, Morimura exhibited *Portrait (Futago)* next to *Portrait (Shonen 1,2,3)* (Young Boy), which appropriates *The Fifer*; as such, he augments the gender play with Meurent in Manet's works.

---

292 MEZUR (2005): 206.

5.4.3 Second Reading: Beyond the Binary of 'Female' and 'Male'

Whether with a 'male' body beneath a 'female masquerade' or with a rather 'androgynous' body, Morimura is present in both 'self-portraits'. As Joonsung Yoon has pointed out, Morimura is comparable to an *onnagata* since he 'never completely disappears.'[293] Indeed, *onnagata* do not simply present a 'feminine' style: their 'male' bodies are also an important part of their transformative gender. As Katherine Mezur has argued persuasively, there is an 'interplay between the male actor body and the *onnagata* gender role, made up of gender acts created by, and with, the male body beneath.'[294] In her extensive study on *onnagata*, Mezur has used the word 'ambiguous' to describe their gender:

> *Onnagata* present an ambiguous kinaesthetic and visual appearance of female-likeness ... At times, an *onnagata* may appear very female-like. At another glance, he may appear slightly male-like, or adolescent-like, or boy-girl-like, or even posthuman, beyond the binary of female and male.[295]

The statement that their gender is 'beyond the binary of female and male' could be linked with my afore-mentioned thesis that the methodology of 'Western' gender studies, i.e. the polarised binary of 'female' vs. 'male', is too narrow for a Japanese context. The Meiji era, in bringing 'Western' influences to Japan, precipitated an alteration of Japanese 'gender' concepts by proclaiming that males should confine to the 'masculine' gender and females to the 'feminine'. Thus, modernisation made bisexuality taboo and 'de-eroticised' and 'de-aestheticised' the male body (see 2.2).[296] In addition, the idea of normative monogamy was transplanted into Japan. However, in pre-Meiji Japan, the notion of gender had been more ambiguous and multiple: a person's gender was less dependent on 'biological' sex. As Chino Kaori has written, 'culture' was, unlike in the 'West', associated with 'courtliness' and 'femininity', whereas 'nature' connoted 'barbarity' and 'masculinity'.[297] Consequently, the court was associated with and represented by a 'feminine' gender. 'Femininity', especially in the Heian era, was a culturally and artistically dominant style which should not be equated with the 'female'; rather, it was the 'feminine embodied by men'.[298] It was only during the Meiji period, that the gender of the Japanese

---

293 YOON (2000): 123.
294 MEZUR (2005): 8.
295 IBID: 141.
296 Homosexuality and androgynous appearance became popular again in the Taishô and early Shôwa era, for instance as a literary topic. However, an analysis of this context is beyond the scope of this thesis.
297 CHINO (1993): 32.
298 IBID: 32.

ruling class, embodied by the Meiji Tennô, became 'masculine' through 'masculine' (body) language and military uniforms.[299]

Given the association of 'femininity' with 'culture' and 'art', it is not surprising that 'feminine' men were considered attractive. For instance, a 'feminine' face with 'soft', round features, powdered in white was a male beauty ideal in the Heian era (see 2.2).

In addition, men, like women, presented themselves as 'erotic' objects for both the male and the female gaze, especially during the Edo period. In certain amusement quarters in Edo, including Yoshiwara, male performers were employed as *otoko no geisha* ('male geisha'), *hôkan* ('jesters'), or *taikomochi* ('drummers'), who 'performed bawdy dances or stripteases for customers in the courtesan brothels.'[300] The fact that both women and men were viewed as alluring images is closely intertwined with the prevalence of a flexible notion of sexuality which involved physical or emotional attraction to both males and females. Pre-Meiji Japan did not condemn 'male-male-sexuality';[301] rather, it was a practice which went in and out of fashion depending on the style of the ruling class and their leaders' sexuality. Pederasty flourished, especially under the rule of the samurai between the 16th and 18th century; love between males as a cultural phenomenon was termed *shudô* (an abbreviation of *wakashû-dô*, literally 'the way of the *wakashû*'). 'Male-male-sexuality' became a commercialised element of urban social life and popular culture. Love and sexual relationships between samurai and their masters, or regents and their pages were not only tolerated but also explored in various literary works, which started to circulate increasingly due to the rapid growth of the publishing industry in the 17th century.[302] As Pflugfelder has explained, the proliferation of *shudô* literature 'brought about far-reaching changes in the organisation of erotic knowledge'.[303] However, most men who were involved in 'male-male-sexuality' in the Edo period were also involved in 'male-female-sexuality': a

---

299 On different transitions of gender notions in the Meiji era, for instance the gender of Empress Jingû or the deity Kannon, see essays by Melanie Trede and Doris Croissant; CROISSANT, MOSTOW and VANCEYEH (2008).

300 MEZUR (2005): 145.

301 Following Gregory M. Pflugfelder's argument in *Cartographies of Desire* (2007), I deliberately use the term 'male-male-sexuality' instead of 'homosexuality' here. This is due to the term 'homsexuality' being a 'Western', scientific term, which associates a connection between male-male and female-female sexual behaviour. However, pre-modern Japan generally did not view a connection between male-male and female-female forms of erotic activities.

302 For instance, *Chigo no sôshi* (Youngboy's Notebook) (1320s); *Aki no yo no naga monogatari* (Long Story for an Autumn Night) (15th century); Ihara Saikaku's *Nanshoku ôkagami* (The Great Mirror of Male Love) (1687); *Nanshoku yamaji no tsuyu* (Nanshoku Dew on a Mountain Path) (early 18th century). For more information see WATANABE and IWATA (1987) and PFLUGFELDER (2007).

303 PFLUGFELDER (2007): 45

great number of men, including well-known figures, such as the poets Matsuo Bashô and Ihara Saikaku, routinely slept with men as well as with women.[304] The fact that this form of 'bisexuality' was prevalent is also evident in Screech's analysis *Sex and the Floating World*, which amalgamates illustrations of varying sexual preferences. Sexual encounters of two men are scattered through *shunga* albums in which most of the other images show male-female intercourse; for instance, it is common to have one or two male-male images within a male-female set.

Not only were men 'sexual objects' for a 'male' (and 'female') gaze, the notions of 'sex' and 'gender' also interacted in flexible and playful ways. This argument can be corroborated by the tradition of 'gender crossing' in the Edo period. At first sight, the *kimono* is a less gender-specific garment than the pants, dress, and skirt of contemporary 'Western' cultures; padded and wrapped in a *kimono*, male and female bodies appear rather straight in shape. As Screech has written, men and women in *kimono* are 'not polarized' but 'hold the majority of their external traits in common'.[305] However, *kimono* have always included distinguishable male and female stylisations, and certain hairstyles or accessories were solely worn by either women or men.

'Crossing', i.e. the adoption of styles which were usually reserved for the other 'sex', can be found not only in theatre, such as the *onnagata* in *kabuki*, but also in the sexual entertainment sector. For instance, in the early 19th century, *haori geisha* in the Fukagawa amusement district started to wear men's 'jackets' (*haori*) and slightly shaved their pate, which was a hairstyle of young men.[306] Similarly, *wakashû jorô* ('*wakashû* female prostitutes') shaved their forelocks, dressed like men and created a *wakashû*-like, 'androgynous' look. In addition, *kagema onna* ('boy prostitute women') as the equivalent of *onnagata*, danced in men's *kimono*, wore swords, and imitated the speech patterns of men. Cross-dressing performers were popular and patronized as prostitutes by both men and women. As Joshua Mostow has concluded, the Kasei era (around 1804–1868) was one of 'exceptional gender ambiguity', even by the ambiguous standards of the Edo period. [307]

Cross-dressing has remained an important characteristic of Japanese theatre, not only with male actors in women's roles in the *nô* and *kabuki* theatre, but also in the Takarazuka theatre which features women acting and singing as male characters. Furthermore, as Wim Lunsing has explained in her essay on transgender practices among Japanese men, in Japan, contrary to the 'West', it

---

304 WATANABE and IWATA (1987): 134; SCREECH (2009): 93.

305 SCREECH (2009): 108.

306 Joshua Mostow has examined the *haori geisha* focusing on Kunisada's print *Tate-hiki sô* (The Competitive Type) from his series *Tôsei sanjûni sô* (A Contemporary Thirty-Two Types) (1822 – 1823); MOSTOW (2008): 398–398.

307 MOSTOW (2008): 412.

is not uncommon for drag queens to be heterosexual men.[308] This once again makes clear that 'Western' gender acts and the relationship of 'gender' and 'sexuality' cannot be taken for granted.

Gender ambiguity and androgynous appearance have also have played a major role in Japanese art history. Firstly, there are Buddhist deities, including Kannon (the Bodhisattva of Mercy), who have been depicted as androgynies. Secondly, the *wakashû* was a popular motif in Japanese art, such as in woodblock prints of *kabuki* actors or *shunga* images.[309] Watanabe and Iwata have highlighted *wakashû*'s androgynous appearance: they 'were not young "men" but young androgynies, one might say'.[310] Thirdly, since 'femininity' was associated with courtliness, and white skin was a 'feminine' beauty ideal, it is not surprising that in picture scrolls, for instance the *Genji monogatari emaki* (Picture Scroll of the Tale of the Genji) (12th century) the skin of the gentry is painted white, in contrast to the brownish skin of the attendants. Their eyes are slim, noses are hooked and their facial and bodily forms are rounded, whereas the servants and the common people appear more slender and with larger eyes. Ikeda Shinobu has explained how the differentiation of social categories leads to gender ambiguity amongst the gentry: 'there is very little gender differentiation'.[311] The relevance of class made gender distinctions rather insignificant; this is also corroborated by Joshua Mostow's lecture *National Erotics, Gender, and the Representation of Sexuality in Heian Japan*, in which Mostow explained that representations of sexuality in art works of the Heian era were limited to the aristocracy.[312] Although lower-class servants are depicted in some works, they did not count as sexual objects; in this way, the difference between people's 'sexual' aura was based firstly on class and then on gender axis. Examining depictions of *nanshoku* ('sexual relation between adult and adolescent males') of late 17th century Japan, Mostow has postulated at least four distinct genders: 'men (*otoko*), wives (*onna*), prostitutes (*jorô*) and youngmen (*wakashû*)'.[313] Both the class distinctions of the Heian era and these four genders of 17th century Edo serve to prove yet again the inadequacy of 'Western'

---

308 LUNSING (2003): 33.

309 For instance, woodblock prints of the series *Men, Boys and Courtesans in a Brothel* (1730–1740) by Ishikawa Toyonobu, the *shunga* hand scroll *Spring Pastimes* (around 1750) by Miyagawa Isshô or Suzuki Harunobu's *Wakashû Looking at a Painting of Mt. Fuji* (18th century).

310 WATANABE and IWATA (1987): 134.

311 IKEDA (2003): 45.

312 The lecture was given as a keynote at the workshop *Representations of Sexualities in Asian and European Cultures* at Heidelberg University on the 8th and 9th of June 2009. The workshop was part of the interdisciplinary project *Rethinking Gender, Sexuality and the Body in a Transcultural Art World* within the cluster of excellence *Asia and Europe in a Global Context* at Heidelberg University.

313 MOSTOW (2003): 65.

concepts of gender duality in the context of Japan: 'we need to try to bracket our own binary thinking'.[314]

Set against this cultural-historical background, Morimura's 'masquerade' in *Red Marilyn* and his androgynous' appearance in *Portrait (Futago)* can be linked with a traditional Japanese 'gender' concept based on non-binary and transformative notions of 'gender' and 'sexuality'. In addition, his 'androgynous' body in *Portrait (Futago)* is reminiscent of the *wakashû* and the *onnagata*, whose multiple gender is 'based on the adolescent beautiful boy body'.[315] Morimura embodies the ideal of a 'feminine man', whose 'femininity' symbolised courtliness and socio-culturally high status.

5.4.4 Third Reading: The 'Western Feminisation' of the Japanese 'Male'

Morimura's androgynous appearance in *Portrait (Futago)* can also be linked to a political motif and a 'Western' viewpoint: the 'European imaginary's feminization of the Asian male'.[316] As Norman Bryson has pointed out, Morimura fits the role of Olympia so well 'not only because he is a great drag artist but because the 'Western' cultural imagery aligns "Asia" and "female" into cognate positions of powerlessness'.[317] Bryson has offered an insightful comparison by highlighting the similarities of *Portrait (Futago)* and David Hwang's drama *M. Butterfly* (1986), written only two years before Morimura completed his photographic artwork.

The drama *M. Butterfly* explores the love between the French diplomat René Gallimard and Liling Song, who is not only an actor of female roles at the Peking opera but also a Chinese spy.[318] Gallimard is obsessively convinced that Song is a woman. The drama ends with a trial, which reveals the deceit and leads to Gallimard committing suicide. The title of the drama makes an ironic reference to Puccini's opera *Madama Butterfly*. The cliché of the powerful White man and the submissive Asian woman as an 'Oriental Butterfly' are inverted. While the illusions of 'the West' lead to the Japanese woman's dramatic suicide in Puccini's opera, Gallimard perishes because of his Orientalist fantasies. The personification of the 'West' as 'masculine' and of 'Asia' as 'feminine', is directly addressed in the fifth act:

---

314 IBID: 70.
315 MEZUR (2005): 142.
316 BRYSON (1995): 74.
317 IBID: 74.
318 For a detailed analysis of the drama see LYE (1995): 260–289.

> Song: You expect Oriental countries to submit to your guns and you expect oriental women to be submissive to your men. That‘s why you say they make the best wives.
>
> Judge: But why would that make it possible for you to fool Monsieur Gallimard? [...]
>
> Song: One, because when he finally met his fantasy woman, he wanted more than anything to believe that she was, in fact, a woman. And second, I am an Oriental. And being an Oriental, I could never be completely a man.[319]

Bryson's comparison of *Portrait (Futago)* with *M. Butterfly* is plausible since the photograph and the drama both draw attention to the Orientalist cliché of the exotic Asian woman by replacing her humorously with a man. Furthermore, they highlight how 'the West' stereotypically regards 'Asian male' bodies as 'feminine' and, at the same time, how this has resulted in the 'Asian man' having a complex towards 'the West': he 'could never be completely a man'.

Posing 'nude' as Marilyn Monroe and as Olympia, Morimura parodies 'Western' expectations: his adoption of 'femininity' as an Asian male highlights the 'Western' viewpoint of Asia and Asians, namely that they are 'feminine' or 'more feminine' than the 'West' and 'the White'. Morimura displays his 'body' and gender confidently and humorously. Returning our gaze unashamedly, it seems as if he were saying to us: 'you want to view us as feminine, there you go. We can almost be as feminine as your best-known female icons!'

My gender analyses have been linked to Japan's history and its relationship with 'the West'. However, Morimura's 'self-portraits' could equally be interpreted as forward-thinking: reproductive technologies are precipitating a fundamental redefinition of 'sex' as well as 'gender'; medical possibilities, including sex changes have increased enormously. Morimura has stated enthusiastically that it would 'just be a matter of time until the differences between female and male disappear';[320] his numerous 'self-portraits' as 'women' reflect his excitement about fluid gender notions in the future.

5.5 Conclusions

It has been argued that the dichotomy of 'male' and 'masculine' on the one side, and 'female' and 'feminine' on the other, is a modern and 'Western' imperative; 'gender' and 'sex' are often more complex. For instance, notions of

---

319 LYE (1995): 274.
320 MORIMURA (2001d): 249.

'femininity' in Japan have traditionally been associated with 'culture' and 'courtliness' and were hence also embodied by aristocratic men.

My analysis of gender representation in the different artworks has corroborated the argument that gender cannot be categorised into a simple binary. For instance, 'femininity' embodied by women is different from 'femininity' embodied by men. Ideal 'femininity' of women in late 20th century Japan is linked with outward appearance: *Elevator Girls 3F* and *Tea Ceremony III* both allude to the importance of women's 'decorative' appearance in Japanese society. In addition, women are generally supposed to be kind, gentle, polite and submissive. These behavioural norms are reflected in Mori's submissive tea-service in *Tea Ceremony III*, whereas the women in *Elevator Girls 3F* break free from these rules, driven by consumerism instead. *Elevator Girls 3F* also highlights the homogenising effect of 'feminine' images and how these lead to women pressurizing themselves. Against the background of the 1990s, both artworks not only reflect Japanese society's expectations of women to embody this pretty, submissive 'feminine ideal', but also communicate *kawaii* as a new 'feminine' quality. This 'femininity' cannot be equated with the 'feminine' beauty trends embodied by an increasing number of Japanese men. Although, from a 'Western' viewpoint, these trends appear 'feminine', the men rather represent a new 'masculinity'.

The central gender theme of Izima's *Landscapes* series is the conjunction of 'the beautiful female' and 'death'; thus, his work reinforces the conventional 'male gaze' vs. the 'female sexualised object'. However, it could be argued that the 'female' and her 'beauty' 'tease' the viewer, making him reflect upon 'death'. The main reading I have proposed for the *Landscapes* photographs is that it draws attention to both 'death' and 'the female' as cultural myths. By featuring 'death' as a simultaneously 'male' and 'female' fantasy image, the series goes far beyond the presentation of men's 'misogynistic' view of vulnerable women. Rather, the 'beautiful female' in connection to death can even be interpreted as a witty motif which self-reflexibly references 'death as an image'.

The *Landscapes* series is concerned with 'death' instead of gender critique. In contrast, *Tea Ceremony III* and *Elevator Girls 3F* could be described as colourful glossy images, and yet 'feminist' statements, criticising social expectations of, and restrictions for, women by means of 'parodical masquerade'.

Both Yanagi and Mori insert 'moments of deconstruction' into the images: *Tea Ceremony III* combines humorously the stereotypical, 'feminine' images *ôeru* and the *kawaii* girl in *manga* or *anime*, while *Elevator Girls 3F* exaggerates 'feminine' ideals and their homogenising effect by displaying similar elevator girls together, being mesmerised by similar shoes.

Red Marilyn and *Portrait (Futago)* present complex gender plays. *Red Marilyn* could be described as presenting a 'male in drag', i.e. a 'male' body adopting a 'feminine' gender, comparable to an *onnagata*. However, as the 'masquerade' is made blatantly obvious with the fake breasts' brassiere, Morimura's 'masculinity' also becomes a relevant part of the gender play. In *Portrait (Futago)*, the borders between 'masculine' and 'feminine' attributes are more blurred, resulting in a more 'androgynous' body. Morimura's appearance can be linked to the somewhat 'masculine' looking female model Victorine Meurent and Manet's use of her as a model for both 'male' and 'female' characters. In both images, Morimura as a 'male' artist is present. The convergence of a 'male' body with a 'feminine' gender has a long tradition in Japanese culture, which can partly be explained with the equation of 'high class' and 'femininity' in the Heian era. Furthermore, 'feminine' looking men have been considered attractive by both men and women; this is evident in Japanese theatre, sexual entertainment and art history. Both men and women were viewed as 'erotic' objects, adopting either 'more feminine' or 'more masculine' characteristics playfully. Against this historical background, Morimura's 'masquerade' as a 'woman' results in a hybrid gender which can be interpreted as a reference to the fluid and non-binary gender concept of pre-modern Japan. However, the appropriated images are 'Western' icons with 'Western' women; hence *Red Marilyn* and *Portrait (Futago)* can also be read as parodies of a Western equation of Asia and Asian men with 'femininity'.

Returning to the social background of 1990s Japan: on the one hand, the 1990s were a time in which 20th century gender notions were still dominant, e.g. women were predominantly supposed to stick to 'feminine' roles. On the other hand, it was also a decade which introduced gender changes. Firstly, women started to increasingly break out of 'feminine' norms. Laura Miller and Jan Bardsley have published a book, *Bad Girls*, which focuses on young women who act and live in a way that would traditionally be considered 'bad' in Japan. The essays in the book show clearly that 'badness' could often be equated with 'manly behaviour'; for instance, girls 'speak loudly on their cell phones in trains and in restaurants' or they are accused of 'eating in the open air, a behaviour thought to be particularly unfeminine' although standing noodle shops in train stations have been used by commuting males for decades.[321]

In addition, young women started to tan their skin in an extremely dark tone (*ganguro*), wear short skirts and extremely bright garments, embodying a provocative and 'un-feminine' style. Secondly, as Morimura's self-portraits and Ishiuchi's *Chromosome XY* series reflect, the 'male' and the 'male body' were increasingly 're-eroticised'. The rise of male beauty aesthetics has done little to

[321] MILLER and BARDSLEY (2003): 8.

change existing power relations between men and women in, for instance, the work sector. However, it has not only brought back the 'man' as a sexually alluring object instead of an 'asexual' company worker, it has also encouraged a female gaze on the 'male', represented by Ishiuchi approaching numerous naked men and 'touching' them with her camera lens.

In addition, gender 'crossings' by both 'females' and 'males' have resulted in an increase of 'hybrid' and multiple gender identities. However, it remains to be seen if Morimura is correct in his assumption that it is 'just a matter of time until the differences between female and male disappear'.[322]

6. The Religious Body

The term 'religious' is derived from the noun 'religion' (Latin: religio), which generally defines a social system of human belief in a deity, deities or other forms of higher power. Furthermore, the term covers concepts and rules which are linked to this belief, as well as various communal practices which reference higher powers through human action, such as praying, meditation or other rituals. As Jonathan Z. Smith has pointed out, 'religion' is not a 'native category' but rather 'imposed from the outside on some aspect of a … culture', therefore it is not a 'theological' but rather an 'anthropological' category.[323] The anthropologist Melford E. Spiro's definition of religion as 'an institution consisting of culturally patterned interaction with culturally postulated superhuman beings'[324] offers a broad definition of 'religion'. However, the term 'superhuman' suggests that the referenced forms of power must be imagined as a higher form of the human species. Thus, religions which believe in power in a wider sense, i.e. in power beyond natural rules, are not included in Spiro's definition. Therefore, I agree with Stark and Bainbridge, who have changed Spiro's definition by using the broader term 'supernatural' instead of 'superhuman'.[325]

The following analysis is primarily concerned with Buddhist concepts and the way in which human subjects and their bodies in art photographs reflect these. However, instead of titling this section the 'Buddhist' body, I have chosen the broader term 'religious' in a sense of Stark and Bainbridge. In this way, I would like to demonstrate that the artworks could be interpreted as being concerned with motifs and ideologies which are relevant not only in Buddhism but also in other religions.

---

322 MORIMURA (2001d): 249.
323 SMITH (1998): 269.
324 SPIRO (1966): 96.
325 STARK and BAINBRIDGE (1987).

6.1 will examine Yamanaka's *Arakan #1* by comparing the homeless man in the photograph with traditional depictions of Buddhist *arakan* in *rakanzu* images. Are there similarities between the photographed man and an *arakan* with regard to their bodies, lifestyle and the way that they are represented? Following this, 6.2 will be concerned with Mori's *Pure Land.* After analysing the Buddhist iconography, I will examine how Mori uses her own body to represent the concept of Buddhist enlightenment. Furthermore, I will consider whether the photograph's visual language, which has been criticised as 'kitsch', is consistent with its theme Pure Land. 6.3 will focus on Izima's *Landscapes* series, examining suicide as one possible interpretation and linking it with an 'aesthetic appreciation' of death in Japanese culture.[326] In addition, the series will be analysed as a Memento Mori and compared with the representation of transience in *jisei* poems, as well as in the artworks *Gyahtei #17* and *SCAR 1983 illness.* Moreover, its motif of the 'corpse' will be compared with the depiction of dead bodies in Buddhist artworks belonging to the *kusôzu* genre.

6.1 Homelessness and Buddhist followers: Thoughts on *Arakan #1*

6.1.1 A Homeless Man as an Enlightened Buddhist Follower

When the economic 'Bubble' burst in Japan in the early 1990s, unemployment began to rise. Since then, homelessness has become a major topic of public debate, and is often viewed as a new social problem. Saga Yoshiko has pointed out that various aspects of the social system, such as unemployment insurance and welfare support, are still insufficient.[327] According to Tokyo City calculations, around 96% of the homeless in Japan in 2003 were male and the average age was 57.3 years.[328] Although these data are of the early 21st century and the photographs of the *Arakan* series were taken in the 1980s, the fact that fifteen out of sixteen photographic objects are middle-aged men also seems representative of the average Japanese homeless person of the late 20th century. At the same time, the homeless of the *Arakan* series all wear extremely old rags, their hair is often matted to dreads and their wrinkled faces reflect a hard life on the street. As such, the series does not represent the mass of homeless people but only those who have been homeless for a long time and who do not look as if they planned to ever return to a 'normal life' in society.

326 PINGUET (1996): 235.
327 SAGA (no year): unnumbered.
328 According to the city of Tokyo council, in the year 2003 there were 5351 male and 173 female homeless in Tokyo. In: TOKYOTO (2004): 5–7.

What does *Arakan* mean? An *arakan* or *rakan* (Sanskrit: Arhat, meaning 'the worthy one') is a Buddhist follower, who is detached from all earthly desires, transcending even life and death. In the Southern schools of Buddhism,[329] it is believed that *arakan* have attained enlightenment and will not be reborn into any samsaric realm but will attain nirvana at death like Buddha. They are the highest of the Four Holy Persons (Ârya-pudgala);[330] for them all suffering has come to an end.

In the early Indian sutras, Shakyamuni asks four Arhats to remain on earth after his death, in order to propagate Buddhist teachings. However, in later sutras from China and Japan, sixteen Arhats are mentioned. The *Fazhuji* (in Japanese *Hôjûki*), which was translated from Sanskrit into Chinese by the monk Xuanzang in 654, includes the names of sixteen Arhats as well as the regions where they lived.[331] According to the Japanese version of this sutra, Buddha ordered sixteen '*dai-arakan*' (principal Arhats) to remain forever in this world to defend and maintain the Buddhist truth.[332]

In China, wall paintings and hanging scrolls which depict these sixteen *arakan* can be traced back to the Tang dynasty (618–907). Their styles, especially the colourful and detailed Riryûmin style, which is named after the artist Ri Ryûmin, and the Zengetsu style, which is more simple and subdued, influenced Japanese artists. In Japanese, the depictions of *arakan* are called *rakanzu* (literally 'images of *rakan*'). They started to develop as an art genre around 736, when the Shômu-Tennô ordered 914 *arakan* portraits.[333] In the Muromachi period (1333–1587) the production of *rakanzu* reached its height;[334] however, artists in the Edo period also created hanging scroll series of the sixteen *arakan* as well as woodblock prints (often caricatures).

By titling a series of photographs with homeless people as '*Arakan*', Yamanaka is making a statement, namely that the photographed people are similar to the enlightened Buddhist followers or the way that these are represented in *rakanzu*. However, are there any similarities between the homeless subjects and *arakan* and if so, what are they?

There are comparable aspects in the ascetic lifestyle of some Japanese homeless people and *arakan*. In urban areas, such as Tokyo and Osaka, most homeless people live in tents and cardboard shacks inside parks, under bridges or in railway stations. In general, they do not attract any attention. They rather collect tins and cans in order to earn money, or search for food in garbage bins.

---

329 The 'Southern' schools are also referred to as the 'Theravada' schools and include the historical Buddhism of Sri Lanka, Thailand, China, India, Bangladesh and Malaysia.

330 For further information on the Four Holy Persons see PREBISH and KEOWN (2007): 54–55.

331 TAKASAKI (1985): 17.

332 IBID: 17.

333 IBID: 23.

334 IBID: 24.

Although they do not live in nature or in abbeys, they are similar to Buddhist disciples in experiencing a life which differs from the average Japanese working life with its general goal of accumulating material wealth. Although for different reasons and often not by choice, they have severed their connection with society like *arakan*. Consequently, Japanese society and, in Foucauldian terms, its 'disciplinary technologies' control their bodies to a lesser extent than compared with the bodies of people who live a 'normal' life in society. Instead of following social ideals and regulatory norms, both the homeless people in Yamanaka's series and *arakan* live with a 'natural' body, rarely considering it from a visual perspective. For instance, the matted hair and long beard of the man in *Arakan #1* show that he has not altered his body by cutting his hair or shaving. Like an ascetic who lives in nature, his starving body is slim, his face is haggard and his hair and beard are unkempt.

Moreover, there are visual similarities between the *Arakan* photographs and *rakanzu* with regard to both the images' iconography and form. The long wide blanket of the homeless person in *Arakan #1*, as well as his aged face with bushy eyebrows and a beard are reminiscent of the iconography which has traditionally been used in various *rakanzu*, including the hanging scroll *Rakanzu* by Setsuzan of the 17th century (fig. 47). For instance, the *arakan* Pindola Bharadvaja is usually depicted as an old man with white hair, a white beard and bushy eyebrows, sitting on a rock.[335] In addition, there are formal similarities between *Arakan #1* and *rakanzu,* especially those in the Zengetsu style. This style is related to the Chinese priest Guanxin (832–912), whose pseudonym was Zengetsu.[336] He became influential in the genre of *rakanzu* particularly with his set of sixteen hanging scrolls *Shinshû kaigyokuzan jûroku rakan*.[337] These ink paintings, which he is said to have created between 880 and 896, represent the typical Zengetsu style.

In all of the sixteen images, the *arakan* is depicted in a large size and positioned in the middle of the picture, sitting on a rock or under a tree. There are no humans in the images and the background is rather neutral. There are hardly any colours used; distinctive black ink and thick ornamental lines bring a sense of two-dimensionality. Similarly, the light and dark contrast in *Arakan #1* and its neutral background create a two-dimensional impression. Similar to Zengetsu's sixteen *arakan* paintings, Yamanaka presents the *Arakan* photographs as a series of sixteen artworks which are all alike in their style and size. There are some characteristics of the Zengetsu style which contrast with the photographic style found in the *Arakan* series. The *arakan* in Zengetsu's *rakanzu* are sitting, whereas some of the homeless people in Yamanaka's series, such as

---

335 McArthur (2004): 83.
336 In Japanese, he is also known as Kankyû.
337 Takasaki (1985): 39.

Arakan #1, are standing. Furthermore, the parallel lines and expressively drawn wrinkles in Zengetsu's sixteen *rakanzu* as well as in Setsuzan's work create a somewhat caricature-like style, which is different to the aesthetic of a photograph. However, the focus on the men's wrinkled faces and their somewhat wise expression is an important similarity between Zengetsu's sixteen *rakanzu*, Setsuzan's *Rakanzu,* and *Arakan #1*. I agree with Hasegawa Yûko, who has pointed out that the men's wrinkles in the *Arakan* photographs could be viewed as 'signs of asceticism and spiritual awakening'.[338]

A formal similarity between the *Arakan* photographs, *rakanzu* and Buddhist portraits of priests in general, is their vertical size. Although Setsuzan's hanging scroll *Rakanzu* is smaller than *Arakan #1*, the relationship between height and width is similar in both works (*Rakanzu* is 119. 4 x 52. 4 cm and *Arakan #1* is 180 x 90cm). Furthermore, the *Arakan* photographs are mounted on wooden panels when presented in exhibitions. This further emphasises that they reference Buddhist artworks.

In this way, the *Arakan* series adapts Buddhist iconographic and formal methods of representation which have traditionally been used for socially and religiously respected people. In other words, it elevates 'social outcasts' to the ranks of the enlightened.

Yamanaka has explained the difficulties he had in finding the right people for the series: 'the people I was looking for are not concerned with our world anymore; thus, they are not very helpful. I offered them money or bread but those who would accept it are no *arakan* yet.' Out of around 500 photographs, Yamanaka chose sixteen. 'But out of these, I'm only satisfied with around five. This means that the others are not completely at that *arakan* state yet'. These quotations emphasise that Yamanaka was only interested in those who had severed their connections to society and worldly pursuits and gained a somewhat ascetic appearance, exuding something like a spiritual wisdom. The images do not represent the average Japanese homeless person but rather those few who matched Yamanaka's idea of *arakan*. As Aileen Torres put it aptly, Yamanaka 'chooses his subjects according to how well they personify certain tenets of Buddhism...'[339] As such, Yamanaka has projected his own religious associations on to the bodies of homeless people. In other words, the homeless man in *Arakan #1* might be a 'social outcast' and less touched by society's bodily norms, nevertheless, by being compared to *arakan*, his appearance is viewed within a certain social context, namely the field of religious imagery.

---

338 HASEGAWA (2001): 5.

339 TORRES (2005): unnumbered.

6.1.2 *Arakan #1* and Christian Iconography

Although the title *Arakan* is a term only used in Buddhist terminology, the series is concerned with religious asceticism and enlightenment on a more universal level. Firstly, the way the man in *Arakan #1* is presented in the black and white vertical portrait evokes an impression of timelessness. His blanket, the long hair and beard, his wrinkled face, and above all his intense look create a sense of sageness, which could be also compared to Christian images, for instance of John the Baptist.[340] Secondly, the homeless man in *Arakan #1* may not be a Buddhist but of another religion. Moreover, he might be an atheist. Contrary to a religious disciple, he may not consciously pursue enlightenment or any spiritual goals. However, he experiences a comparably austere lifestyle outside of society, renouncing worldly pursuits. This abstinence from society and his extremely simple living conditions lead to a different understanding of his body and his life, including a greater freedom from aesthetic judgements and social compulsions. As such, he may (subconsciously) live out religious ideas and has perhaps achieved a peace of mind that many religions or philosophies teach – be it Buddhism, Christianity or Yoga.

Although the viewer sees the homeless man's soiled rags and matted hair, the large size of the photograph, its black and white aesthetic, the portrait-like position of the man in front of a neutral background and his 'wise' facial expression create an atmosphere which makes the viewer look up to him respectfully rather than despise or pity him. Like an Arhat or 'a Buddha statue'[341], the man radiates a somewhat 'holy' grace. Considering this, it is not surprising that art critics and journalists often praise Yamanaka's work as not 'violating' or 'devastating' their subjects in a voyeuristic way.[342] By representing 'social outcasts' as religious followers, Yamanaka re-interprets their haggard bodies and soiled rags; in the photographs, these signs of homelessness become part of a religious iconography. As such, the series proves how the same bodily appearance can be read differently depending on its social context.

---

340 See for example Dietrich Bout's painting *Johannes in der Landschaft* (John in the Landscape) (1470), Matthias Grünewald's *Isenheim Altarpiece* (1512); Hans Baldung Grien's drawing *Kopf des Johannes* (John's Face) (1516) or Hieronymus Bosch's painting *Meditierender Johannes der Täufer* (Meditating John the Baptist) (1504–1505).

341 ASAHI SHINBUN (09. 12. 1989): 15.

342 For example HASEGAWA (2001): 5 and FINKH (2001): 3.

6.2 Enlightenment in 'Pop Land': Thoughts on Mori's *Pure Land*

6.2.1 The Buddhist Iconography of *Pure Land*

The iconography of Mori's *Pure Land* includes different Buddhist motifs and symbols. These will be analysed in their religious and art historical context, before examining how Mori uses her own body to represent a deity. Furthermore, the relationship of the artwork's theme and its style will be of interest.

Mori's robe, like the dresses of noblewomen in the Tang Dynasty, her shawl, fluttering in the wind, her headdress with a wheel in the middle of her forehead, the lotus bloom and the lotus bud gem in her left hand make it obvious that Kichijôten images were a major source of inspiration. Kichijôten is a deity who was brought into Buddhism from Hinduism, known as the Hindu goddess Mahasri (Sanskrit for 'great fortune') or Laksmi (Sanskrit for 'prosperity'). In Buddhist texts she is described as a beautiful goddess of prosperity and welfare, who either stands on a lotus-shaped platform or holds a blooming lotus in her hand. Moreover, in the *Darani-shû-kyô*, Kichijôten is described as holding a coloured ball in her left hand; it is a symbol of fulfilment of desire.[343] According to Carol Eliel, Mori's costume is inspired by a late-twelfth-century wood sculpture, 'well known in Japan' of Kichijôten.[344] Eliel's argument refers to a polychrome wood sculpture, held at the Jôruri-ji temple in Nara. The sculpture's decorated robe and shawl are indeed similar to Mori's costume. However, a similar costume can be found in a Kichijôten painting on hemp cloth of the 8th century in the Yakushi-ji temple in Nara (fig. 48). Therefore, it seems that Mori references more than one specific artwork.[345]

The pose of Mori's right hand is common in Buddha and Bodhisattva images, and known as the Vitarka mudra.[346] This hand gesture stands for turning the wheel of Dharma, which symbolises the teachings of the Buddhist doctrine.[347]

The lotus bud gem and the huge lotus bloom floating in the centre of the image refer to the Buddhist belief of rebirth in paradise, where one is born from a lotus. Furthermore, the lotus is also a symbol of enlightenment in general.

---

343 BAKSHI (1979): 130. For further information on Kichijôten see IBID: 127–134 or KIMURA (1987): 236–239.

344 ELIEL (1998): 31.

345 Other well-known artworks depicting Kichijôten include images in Tôdai-ji's Hokke-dô, the Golden Hall of the Hôryû-ji in Nara, the Hôzan-ji in Nara, the Daigô-ji in Kyoto etc.

346 MCARTHUR (2004): 55; mudras are ritualized hand gestures, performed, for instance, during meditation. They have specific meanings, often referring to an event in Buddha's life.

347 The Wheel of Dharma (in Sanskrit: Dharmacakra) is a symbol of Buddha's teaching of the path to enlightenment. Buddha's teachings (Dharma is Sanskrit for 'law, rule, doctrine') are likened to a wheel that moves from country to country in accordance with changing conditions. The chariot wheel has globally been used as a symbol of Buddhism.

Just as the beautiful lotus flower grows out of mud, Buddhists believe in the possibility of experiencing enlightenment in this imperfect world.

The conical spire of the somewhat 'futuristic' object in the background is similar to Tibetan stupas.[348] This reference is relevant insofar as the stupa also symbolises enlightenment, which is the goal of every Buddhist (Buddha meaning 'the enlightened one'). Both the lotus and the stupa are thus connected to the title of the artwork: the Pure Land could be defined as both paradise and a peaceful state of mind, guaranteeing enlightenment. Furthermore, Mori as the main photographic subject literally 'embodies' the idea of enlightenment. She uses her own body in the photograph in order to represent a beautiful goddess of prosperity. There are no 'interruptive elements' to somewhat disillusion Mori's 'masquerade'; rather, Mori's body and Kichijôten's are inseparably one. Consequently, within the artwork *Pure Land*, Mori *is* a deity and thus enlightened.

In addition to the lotus, the stupa and Mori as Kichijôten, the alien-like figures and their musical instruments also reference Buddhist traditions. The figure in the far background on the left hand side is playing the hour glass drum (*tsuzumi*), the one floating before him is playing the lute (*biwa*), and the one in the front is playing a mouth organ (*shô*). The musicians on the right hand side are playing cymbals (*hachi*), a Buddhist bell (*inkin*), and the flute (*fue*). In other words, they play instruments that are used in Buddhist ceremonies. According to Gijs van Tuyl,[349] the musicians resemble an orchestra of Apsaras.[350] In the famous Hôôdô hall (also known as Phoenix hall) in the Byôdô temple in Uji there is a relief with fifty-two Apsaras, sitting on clouds and playing various instruments (fig. 49). They can be seen in the background of a huge statue of Amida-Buddha, sitting on a lotus bloom.

Regardless of which specific artworks Mori used as her main references, it is a fact that different traditional Buddhist images have inspired the artwork. *Pure Land* freely mixes various figures and symbols, and adapts them into a pastel-coloured computer-generated scene. This pastel-coloured landscape could be described as a tranquil-looking sea with islands. According to Eliel, it refers to the Dead Sea, which is the lowest point on earth. She also suggests that the protruding spit of sand at the bottom of *Pure Land* refers to the myth of Japan's creation, in which the sun goddess Amaterasu touched her spear into

---

[348] A stupa (Sanskrit for 'mound') is a mound-like monument containing Buddhist relics. It symbolizes the enlightened Buddhist mind, and the path to its realisation. According to Carol Eliel, the architecture of the object in the background of *Pure Land* recalls the shape of Tibetan stupas; ELIEL (1998): 30.

[349] VAN TUYL (1997): 12.

[350] Apsaras (Sanskrit for 'nymph') are supernatural female beings of Hindu and Buddhist mythology, living as servants in the palace of the goddess Indra. They dance to music and entertain various gods.

the water and created the islands of Japan.[351] Eliel's assumptions may be right: Mori combines different symbols of Buddhism freely – it could be that she also incorporated elements of Japanese mythology into the artwork. However, there are no explicit details in the landscape and no definitive information about the place. The title *Pure Land* corroborates this: the image does not depict a specific place on earth, such as the Dead Sea, but rather a religious concept: the paradise Pure Land.

6.2.2 *Pure Land* as 'Pop Land'

Pure Land Buddhism in Japan is connected to the schools Jôdo Shû and Jôdo Shinshû, which are among the most popular Buddhist denominations in Japan today. It is a subset of the Mahâyâna branch of Buddhism, teaching that through devotion to the Buddha Amida (Sanskrit: Amitâbha), not only monks who know complicated meditation rituals, but also ordinary people will be reborn in the Pure Land.

Mori's works have been criticised as 'Techno-Pop' – either positively, mostly in exhibition catalogues,[352] or negatively as 'kitsch'.[353] In Japan, curators and critics object to the way Mori interprets elements of traditional culture in a pop-like way through the use of cutting edge technology.[354] Furthermore, some critics have, in Dave Beech's words, viewed Mori as a 'star-struck innocent who wants everyone to be happy and has no conception of the obstacles standing in our path to Utopia'.[355] Indeed, the pastel-pink aesthetic of *Pure Land* could be described as 'kitsch'. In contrast to *Tea Ceremony III*, *Pure Land* does not reflect contemporary issues of Japanese society. It does not mirror any criticism but rather allures the viewer by presenting a harmonious, bright fantasy image. The use of religious iconography in a popular kitsch style could be considered offensive. Moreover, Mori's embodiment of a goddess floating within a computer-generated alien-orchestra might appear naïve as well as religiously abusive.

---

351 IBID: 30.

352 For positive critics of her work as 'Techno-Pop' see: CORRIN (1998): 24; KING (1998): 39; MOLON (1999): 15–28.

353 MORGAN (1996): 27–33; ROBERTS (1997): 78; CORRIN, (1998): 19; HEROLD (06/1999).

354 SHIODA (2002): 81; Kitamura Junko has said it was difficult for her to judge Mori's art because of Mori's 'fixation on Japanese tradition'; Kasahara Michiko has stressed the importance of the Western reception of Mori's art: 'she is obviously loved because she is seen with an orientalist gaze'; Iida Shihoko has explained: 'the use of Shintoism and high technology, and this modelling as *miko* stuff were just a clever marketing strategy towards Americans.'

355 BEECH (1998): 35.

However, the motif of a beautiful goddess, the pop aesthetic and the medium of impressive photo technology all suit the subject of Pure Land. Kichijôten has traditionally been imagined and depicted as a beautiful woman, wearing a head-dress and richly decorated robe.[356] In other words, the idea of prosperity and luck was visualised across a bodily image of a human woman, which was then worshipped as that of a goddess. By 'embodying' this divine image, Mori returns the deity back into the human realm. On the one hand, this could be interpreted as disrespectful towards the deity; on the other hand, it could be understood as an attempt to get closer to her. In the artwork *Pure Land*, Mori becomes Kichijôten, and as such, achieves enlightenment.

One important idea of Pop Art is to equalise Low and High Art by using popular images, which are easy for everybody to understand. Similarly, the main accomplishment of Mahâyâna Buddhism is the idea that, unlike in Hinâyâna Buddhism, anybody who follows Buddha's teachings has the opportunity of reaching enlightenment – regardless of social position, intelligence or education. Why should it be wrong to please a large audience with a young woman, wearing beautiful garments and floating in a pastel-coloured landscape? Why should this harmonious composition not be realised in large size with impressive technology? The choice of a colourful pop language and impressive technology might be a better way to express the idea of a peaceful paradise for everybody than the creation of rather complicated conceptual art. Considering the fact that Pure Land Buddhism is not only for elite monks but also for ordinary people, the artwork's centring on Mori as an appealing 'young goddess' as well as its alluring visual language are consistent with the teaching of this Buddhist school.

In summary, Mori uses her own young model body, which is generally considered 'beautiful', and combines it with religious iconography, primarily attributes of Kichijôten. In this way, she elevates her status to that of an enlightened deity and yet, at the same time, embodies Kichijôten as a human. The divine body and the human body become one – Mori personifies the idea of enlightenment. By using a colourful pop-like visual language, computer-generated images and impressive technology, she offers a contemporary interpretation of the religious concept of Pure Land Buddhism. The artwork's form is consistent with its content: enlightenment is for everybody.

---

[356] See Kichijôten images in Tôdai-ji's Hokke-dô, the Golden Hall of the Hôryû-ji in Nara, the Hôzan-ji in Nara, the Daigô-ji in Kyoto etc.

6.3 The Impermanent Body in Buddhist Culture: Thoughts on *Otsuka Nene Wears Tuzigahana*, *Gyahtei #17* and *SCAR 1983 illness*

6.3.1 Three Different 'Memento Mori'

The three artworks in the title above share a common focus on the human body as an impermanent object – they show it as something which changes and eventually dies. As such, the photographs could be categorised as 'Memento Mori': they have the purpose of 'reminding' us of 'our death'. This Latin term has been in fine arts as well as literature, mostly in a Christian context. Since medieval times, numerous artworks have highlighted mortality by depicting dance macabres or still lifes with death symbols including skulls, hourglasses and burnt-out candles. However, in the following section, the Memento Mori theme is understood in a wider sense and will be examined in the context of Japanese culture and Buddhist religion.

Humans die due to different reasons which could be divided into three main fields: firstly they die of old age, secondly they die due to an illness, and thirdly they die due to other internal or external human factors, such as an accident, suicide or murder. The three artworks of this section are concerned with one of these death causes each. Whereas *Gyahtei #17* shows an old woman as an allegory of old age, *SCAR 1983 illness* shows, as the title suggests, how an illness has left a scar on a human body. *Otsuka Nene Wears Tuzigahana* features a woman who appears as if she could either have been killed through poison or taken an overdose of medicine. She could have taken the medicine or poison accidentally or on purpose. As such, the artwork is evocative of what I have categorised as the third cause of death (due to murder, accident or suicide).

Before 'projecting' the Memento Mori theme on to the three mentioned photographs and examining the images in the context of Buddhist teachings and artworks, the motif of suicide as one possible interpretation of *Otsuka Nene Wears Tuzigahana* and the *Landscapes* series in general will be examined. Furthermore, it will be linked to a Japanese 'death aesthetic'.

It could be argued that this rather broad analysis of suicide and impermanence is not directly connected to the overall religious topic of this subchapter. However, death plays a fundamental role in any religion and, conversely, religion determines cultural views on death. Buddhist concepts of rebirth are interwoven with the Japanese aesthetic of suicide; Buddhist concepts of impermanence are interwoven with cultural motifs. As such, this section will examine the 'impermanent body' in both a broadly religious as well as religiously influenced, cultural context.

6.3.2 Suicide and the Aesthetic Appreciation of Death

In Japan, the 1990s are often referred to as the 'Lost Ten Years' (see Part 1). Between the years 1990 and 2000 the suicide rate increased as many employees (mostly male) were made redundant. In the year 2000, the rate increased significantly with 21.656 men and 8595 women committing suicide.[357] This means that 23.1 in 100.000 inhabitants committed suicide, whereas in comparison, there were 14.3 in 100.000 in Germany one year later.[358] One important reason for the high suicide rate in Japan is the general fear of becoming a burden on society and a disgrace to one's family. To lose one's job is synonymous with loss of pride and has therefore led to suicide more often than in 'Western' countries. Furthermore, compared to 'Western', Christian viewpoints, suicide in Japan is less scrutinised, due to Buddhist tradition. I will return to this argument later in this section. The proliferation of websites that promote suicide as well as Tsurumi Wataru's bestseller book of 1993, *Kanzenjisatsu manyuaru – The Complete Manual Of Suicide*, have generated concern that the media may be fuelling this phenomenon.[359]

As the title suggests, Tsurumi's book is a manual on how to commit suicide, giving information about drugs and hanging techniques and providing maps of areas where people have successfully committed suicide. In the foreword, Tsurumi compares his book to the drug Angel Dust, which some people 'carry around their neck in a small golden capsule'. They live with a 'cheerful feeling, knowing that if it comes to the worst, they can take the drug and die … this book should be something like this'.[360]

The book is divided into eleven chapters, explaining different suicide methods. Each method is ranked according to six criteria: 'pain, time of preparation, unsightliness, inconvenience caused, impact and fatality'. The criteria 'unsightliness', 'inconvenience' and 'impact' deal with the people who see the act of suicide or find the corpse. For example, throwing oneself in front of a train leaves the corpse in an 'unsightly' state and causes more inconvenience for others than taking an overdose. Furthermore, there are passages which use the terms 'beautiful' or 'ugly', mirroring the author's concern with the aesthetic of the corpse. For instance, Tsurumi explains that gas poisoning and freezing are said to leave the 'most beautiful' corpses.[361] He also states that the only

---

357 WORLD HEALTH ORGANIZATION (2004a).

358 WORLD HEALTH ORGANIZATION (2004b).

359 MCNEILL (2005).

360 TSURUMI (1993): 8.

361 IBID: 133, 174; There are many more passages. For instance, there is a section which starts with the question of whether a hanged body looks 'ugly'. Tsurumi answers this by stating that 'compared to someone who jumped from a high building or threw himself in front of a train, a hanged person's corpse looks much more beautiful' (IBID: 61–62). In the tenth

disadvantage of gas poisoning is the risk of incontinence, concluding sarcastically: 'people who want to look good when they are found should go to the toilet first.'[362] Other sections deal with the scenario that the dead body is found in; for example the first chapter starts with a description of a scene with 'beautiful' pills and capsules in 'red, green and yellow' strewed next to the corpse.[363] As such, the *Manual Of Suicide* is concerned with suicide from an aesthetic and sometimes macabre, humorous viewpoint.

Tsurumi's descriptions of the dead body's aesthetic seem to be connected to a Japanese tradition of 'beautiful deaths'. To begin with, there is a history of dramatic deaths found in literature as well as in *nô*- and *kabuki*-theatre. One central motif in *kabuki* plays, especially in scenes with female-role actors (*onnagata*), is the 'beauty of torture' (*zankoku no bi*). As Katharine Mezur has explained, *onnagata* have created a 'variety of stylized techniques to compose … acts of pain into refined, attractive, and sensually pleasurable representations of violence. These … stylization techniques of *zankoku no bi* are designed to make the violence enacted on the female-like characters beautiful.'[364] Similarly, Ôshima Nagisa's film *Ai no korîda* (In the Realm of the Senses) (1976) or films by Kitano Takeshi, such as *Hana-Bi* (1997) and *Zatôichi* (2004), exemplify a stylised aesthetic of blood and death in Japanese film culture.[365] As Maurice Pinguet concludes, there is an 'aesthetic appreciation' of death in Japanese culture.[366]

European art critics and journalists mainly view the *Landscapes* series as either 'shocking' or 'beautiful'.[367] I would argue that the aesthetic of the images and the 'dead' models is more relevant than the shock effect. The images of the *Landscapes* series are perfectly arranged, and the models look 'fresh', as if they had only just died. Otsuka Nene's skin looks as if she were still alive, and her body does not show any injuries. More dramatic images using a large amount of 'blood', such as *Akikawa Risa Wears Chanel* (1994), are too colourful and detailed to look 'real'. Furthermore, Izima employs large-format cam-

---

chapter he explains that although a frozen body 'looks beautifully white', the appearance of the corpse depends on the season when it is found (IBID: 174).

362 IBID: 113.

363 IBID: 14.

364 MEZUR (2005): 164.

365 There are also numerous examples of European and American films in which death and violence are stylised. When asked why his film *Pierot Le Fou* (1965) featured so much blood, Jean-Luc Godard famously corrected the journalist of the *Cahiers du Cinema*, stating that 'it's not blood, it's red'. This quotation highlights the cinematic approach of stylising violence – the artificiality of the film image is not concealed, what Godard presents to the viewer is not 'reality' ('blood') but a film ('red').

366 PINGUET (1996): 235.

367 For criticism of Izima's work as shocking see e.g. HOFFMANN (2003): unnumbered or NEDERLANDS FOTO INSTITUUT (2001): 6–7; For critics of his work as 'beautiful' see e.g. REGENER (2000): 38–39 or HORNY (2000): 57.

eras in order to include the whole scenario in the image. This viewpoint not only contrasts with the perspective of photographs taken with a smaller camera for documentary purpose, but it also makes clear that the photographs must have been elaborately prepared. As such, the images do not conceal their artificiality and thus are not as shocking. Indeed, the extensively staged images of the *Landscapes* series reflect an 'aesthetic appreciation' of death.

Izima has denied in my interview that these images glamorise death or suicide. He has emphasised that he is 'against suicide' and 'disappointed that viewers misunderstand some of the photographs'. However, many images of the *Landscapes* series do not explain the cause of the 'death': as mentioned before, the reason for Otsuka Nene's 'death' is unclear. Since there are two tangerine peelings on the table, there may have been a murderer in the room who ate one tangerine after Otsuka Nene had eaten the other one. However, there is a possibility that Otsuka Nene ate both tangerines. Since there are no apparent injuries on her body, it appears that she either took a drug overdose or that the tangerines were laced with poison. Hence, the *Landscapes* series does not definitively exclude suicide. It also does not reflect Izima's critical view on suicide.

Furthermore, it is a fact that Buddhism sees death as not the end of life, but a transition to another life. Thus, suicide should not be interpreted as ending one's life but rather as entering another realm, which could even mean achieving the state of enlightenment. Early Buddhist texts include cases of suicide, which Buddha either accepted or condemned, depending on the person's state of mind.[368] When asked about the morality of committing suicide in order to achieve nirvana, Buddha does not criticise suicide per se. Rather, he emphasises that only the unperturbed mind is able to move on towards nirvana. This shows that from a Buddhist point of view, it is the state of one's mind which determines the rightness or wrongness of suicide. Carl B. Becker has summarised this: 'Buddhism has long recognized persons' rights to determine when they should move on from this existence to the next. The important consideration here is not whether the body lives or dies, but whether the mind can remain at peace ...'[369]

This Buddhist viewpoint on death and suicide has led to a value system in Japan, which appreciates peace of mind and dignity more than the length of one's life. There are countless examples of suicide in Japanese history, committed in order to preserve one's dignity, to approach the Pure Land, or done in

[368] For instance, the disciples Vakkali and Channa both committed suicide in the context of painful and terminal illness. Buddha accepts their suicides since their selfless and enlightened minds legitimated their passing. BODHI (2000): 938–941; 1164–1167.

[369] BECKER (1990): 548.

sympathy with a departed emperor.[370] Most suicides in Japan in the 1990s were not committed due to a direct religious reason; however, they are still reminders that the Buddhist perspective does not scrutinise suicide. Besides, although it is a crime under Japanese law to assist or encourage a suicide, one's own suicide has never been considered illegal.[371] As such, the motif of suicide as one possible interpretation of some *Landscapes* images seems not as 'shocking', 'immoral' or unusual in its Japanese context as in a European society, influenced by Christian principles.

If the images had included suicide fantasies, would this change the way in which I interpret the series? The images provide room for the viewer's assumptions on the model's 'death' – they present hints, such as the tangerines on Otsuka Nene's table or the scissors in Akikawa Risa's chest, but they never tell the complete story. As pointed out before, the 'corpse' is young and 'beautiful' and elaborately draped in a scenario which looks either peaceful, such as *Otsuka Nene Wears Tuzigahana*, or dramatic, such as *Akikawa Risa Wears Chanel*. Either way, the scenes never conceal their artificiality. In addition, the title of each artwork includes the model's name and the fashion label of her clothing, but it does not give any information on her death fantasy. The fashion label and the name of the model or actress emphasise the stagedness of the 'death' scene. As such, the images do not focus on the manner of death but on the aesthetic of a 'death scene'; it does not seem relevant if the 'back story' features the model being killed by someone else or by herself. The images do not portray any moral attitude towards suicide; their importance lies in the aesthetic and the mode of death does not appear to be significant.

This attitude enables the *Landscapes* series to deal with death as an aesthetic motif. There are images which treat death even in a sarcastic manner; for example in *Natsuki Mari Wears Luisa Beccaria* (2003), the model lies absurdly within a sea of ripe tomatoes. This aspect of dark humour could be linked to Tsurumi's *Manual of Suicide* as well as Japanese death poems (*jisei*).[372] Many poets have chosen to end their lives with a *kyôka*, which is a satirical poem in the short *tanka* form.[373] The poems describe an entertaining afterlife, taking off another poet's well-known *jisei*,[374] or they make fun of death in general. The following poem mocks another man's death scene:

---

370 For further examples and a details explanation see BECKER (1990): 548–549.

371 This contrasts to European law in medieval times; for instance in the U.K. and Germany suicide was considered a sin in a Christian context and prohibited.

372 Death poems (*jisei*), which have been popular amongst Zen monks and many *haiku* poets, are usually written near the time of one's own death.

373 The *tanka* (short poem) is a verse of thirty-one syllables in five lines; the syllables are distributed in the pattern 5-7-5-7-7.

374 For example there is Bashô's *haiku*:
On a journey, ill: My dream goes wandering over withered fields.

The dying priest
looks as if
he knew it all [375]

The description is not as extensive and dark as some of the *Landscapes* images, however, its humorous way of dealing with death is certainly comparable to some descriptions in Tsurumi's book as well as the *Landscapes* photographs.

6.3.3 The Human Body's Impermanence as an Aesthetic Concept

The sometimes humorous element of the *Landscapes* series as well as its colourfully staged narrative and sometimes dramatic style contrast with the rather subdued black and white aesthetic of *Gyahtei #17* and *SCAR 1983 illness*. Needless to say, the three mentioned works focus on human death in contrasting styles and from different perspectives. However, they are similar in their concern with the human body's impermanence. Before analysing the human body as a Memento Mori motif and connecting it with Japanese art history, the theme of impermanence will be examined briefly in the more general context of Japanese aesthetic.

The aesthetic principles of *mono no aware* and *wabi sabi*, which are fundamental to Japanese art, are connected to the Buddhist concept of impermanence. The Buddhist doctrine teaches that everything and everybody is in a constant state of change (*mujô*). The only realm which overcomes this flux is nirvana. In a passage of the *Vakkali Sutta*, mentioned before in the context of Buddhist views on suicide, Buddha asks his ill disciple Vakkali if he views his body as something permanent or impermanent. When Vakkali answers that his body, feelings, perceptions and consciousness are all impermanent, Buddha praises him.[376] Vakkali has achieved a peace of mind and can thus move into the realm of Pure Land. This is one of the countless examples which show how the understanding of impermanence is seen as one of the most relevant insights in Buddhism, leading to the believer's salvation.

Mono no aware is connected to this idea of everything being impermanent: it is an aesthetic concept which could be described as a melancholic awareness of the transience of all things.[377] For instance, cherry blossoms and autumn foliage, symbolising life's fleeting nature, have been used as motifs in visual art

This was ironically adapted by an unknown poet as follows:
Locked in my room: my dream goes wandering over brothels. HOFFMANN (1986): 82.

375 IBID: 83.

376 NHAT HANH (1991): 431

377 The term is derived from the word '*mono*' ('things') and '*aware*' ('sensitivity'); it was used in the Heian period as an exclamation such as 'ah', expressing a 'sensitivity' of the transience of all 'things', and a melancholic feeling at their passing.

and literature in order to express *mono no aware*. Some of the *Landscapes* images directly reference these traditional motifs, for example *Nagasaku Hiromi Wears Louis Vuitton* (1999), as it shows the young woman under a blooming cherry tree (fig. 51–53). The image almost visualises a death poem by the famous poet Saigyô (1118–1190):

> I wish to die
> in spring, beneath
> the cherry blossoms,
> whilst the springtime moon
> is full[378]

Some of the cherry petals have fallen down on Nagasaku Hiromi and the ground is full of petals. Like the withering cherry blossoms and like Nagasaku Hiromi, whose 'corpse' is sitting under the tree, everything is impermanent. In addition, cherry trees are thought to be the conduit between the world of the dead and that of the living.[379] As such, the tree seems to symbolise that Nagasaku Hiromi's 'spirit' travelled to another realm.

Gyahtei #17 and *SCAR 1983 illness* are good examples of the aesthetic concepts of *wabi sabi*, which are connected to the idea of the impossibility of perfection and the ephemeral nature of things. *Wabi* and *sabi* became especially popular in Zen Buddhism since the Kamakura era (1185–1333). For instance, the tea master Sen no Rikyû states in the *Nanpôroku* (1690) that 'it is desirable for every utensil [in the tea room] to be less than adequate. There are those who dislike a piece when it is even slightly damaged; such an attitude shows a complete lack of comprehension'.[380] His quotation exemplifies how the *wabi* aesthetic values utensils with minor imperfections – sometimes even more highly than the ostensibly perfect ones. The term *sabi* can be found in the poem collection *Manyôshû* (around 759), where it is associated with desolateness as well as something that has aged well and acquired an aesthetic comparable to 'patina' (written in other Chinese characters, '*sabi*' also means 'rust').

Although it is rather precarious how Yamanaka took the *Gyahtei* photographs, his view on the old female body in the stylised black and white photographs is a respectful one. Moreover, representing old age and decay, the woman in *Gyahtei #17* is 'beautiful'. As the word *wabi* connotes imperfection, and *sabi* is a beauty that comes with age and decay, the woman personifies this aesthetic concept. Similarly, the scar within healthy skin in *SCAR 1983 illness* represents human imperfection and ephemerality. However, it is part of a harmonious composition and as such 'beautiful'.

---

[378] As cited in HOFFMANN (1986): 48.
[379] OHNUKI-TIERNEY (2002): 37.
[380] HIROTA (1995): 226.

6.3.4 The Human Body as a Buddhist Memento Mori

The motif of a large scar on a human body in *SCAR 1983 illness* could be considered a symbol of human vulnerability and thus, mortality. As such, both the scar and its photograph could be described as a Memento Mori. Furthermore, like the photographic medium, scars could be described as obvious 'traces' of time since they testify to an event in the past. In this way, the scar and the photograph are tautological; I will return to this in 7.1. In this section, I will rather focus on *Gyahtei #17* and *Otsuka Nene Wears Tuzigahana*.

Both the *Gyahtei* series and the *Landscapes* series could be compared and contrasted with Buddhist doctrines and artworks, teaching the ephemerality of human life. The most famous use of the Buddhist term *gyatei* is in the last verse of the *Heart Sutra*:[381] *gya tei gya tei ha ra gya tei ha ra sô gya tei. Bo ji so wa ka.*'[382] There are various translations and explanations; however, one possible interpretation of *gya tei* (Sanskrit: Gate) is 'to go beyond' or 'to pass'. Edward Conze has translated the mantra[383] as follows: 'Gone, gone, gone beyond, gone altogether beyond, oh what an awakening, all-hail!'[384] This 'going beyond' can be interpreted in many ways; however, one possible meaning is 'going beyond life' and moving towards enlightenment which seems most relevant for the *Gyahtei* series. The frail and old body of the woman in *Gyahtei #17* seems to announce her passing to another world. Hasegawa has put it aptly when saying that the *Gyahtei* images capture the final bodies of the women before they 'disappear as material beings'.[385]

Like birth and sickness, ageing and dying in Buddhism are seen as suffering and are thus connected to the first doctrine of the *Four Noble Truths*: life is suffering.[386] In other words, life is indirectly equated with ageing and, eventually, dying. In the *Maha Dukkhakkhanda Sutta*, there is a passage where Buddha describes a young girl, whose beauty and charm is at its height, referring to the sensual gratification one would get from her.[387] Following this, Buddha

381 The *Heart Sutra* (Japanese: *Maka Hannya Haramita Shingyô*) is not only the shortest but also one of the most popular and famous sutras of Mahayana Buddhism. Consisting of fourteen verses in Sanskrit and 260 Chinese characters, the *Heart Sutra* is the most abbreviated sutra of the *Perfection of Wisdom Sutras* (Sanskrit: Prajñā Pāramitā). It teaches the doctrine of emptiness and is regarded as the summation of the wisdom of Buddha. The Heart Sutra is a relevant text since it is chanted at various occasions in different Buddhist schools' temples.

382 DESHIMARU-RÔSHI (1988): 28.

383 A mantra is a sacred word or a group or words, which are chanted in religious ceremonies, during meditation or in a prayer.

384 CONZE (1960): unnumbered.

385 HASEGAWA (2001): 5.

386 The *Four Noble Truths* form the cornerstone of the Buddhist doctrine, encapsulating Buddha's understanding of the human predicament and its solution.

387 The *Maha-dukkhakkhandha Sutta* (The Great Mass of Stress) is part of the *Sutta Pitaka* (The Basket Of Discourses), which covers sermons and utterances by Buddha and his close disci-

says that the same girl as a woman of ninety or one hundred years old would be crooked, scanty-haired and wrinkled. He explains that one might also see the same woman subject to an illness, lying helplessly in her urine and excrement, and finally dead and thrown onto the charnel ground where hyenas devour her flesh and blood. Lastly, her bones would be scattered everywhere.[388] Both the *Four Noble Truths* and the passage of the *Maha Dukkakkhanda Sutta* are examples of the Buddhist doctrine teaching the inevitability of ageing and dying. In the *Maha Dukkakkhanda Sutta* the motif of the female body is used to demonstrate the transience of form. Although *Gyahtei #17* does not show the old women helplessly lying in urine or excrement, her naked body could be interpreted as a visualisation of this description of the old woman in the sutra. The motif of death is prominent in her old decaying body, which could thus be interpreted as a Memento Mori.

In contrast, *Otsuka Nene Wears Tuzigahana* shows the 'death' of a young woman. However, this motif of a young female 'corpse' can also be linked to Buddhist exercises and artworks. Since the fifth century, there have been Buddhist texts which use the image of a decaying corpse as a subject for devotional exercise. The process of decay is described in nine different stages (*kusôkan*). This form of contemplation of death first appeared in the sutra *Kanbutsu zanmai kaikyô* (Sutra on the Samâdhi Contemplation of the Oceanlike Buddha) (around 400) or in the *Dai chidoron* (Discourse on the Great Wisdom) (402–405).[389] The practice could be described as a meditation on impurity (*fujôkan*), aiming at the devotee's overcoming of worldly attachments, especially sexual desires.[390]

There are numerous examples in medieval literature which mention monks meditating on these nine decay stages of both male and female corpses. For instance, the monk and founder of the Shingon sect, Kûkai, wrote poems on the topic (*kusôkanshi*) in the 8th century.[391] In addition, a tale in the *Kankyo no tome* (A Companion in Solitude) (1216) by Keisen, describes an anonymous monk, who meditated on a decomposing corpse.[392] In one tale of Kamo no Chômei's *Hosshinshû* (A Collection of Tales of Religious Awakenings) (after 1208), the monk Genpin Sôbu falls in love with the wife of a chief councillor. In order to overcome his feelings, he meets her and gazes on her for two hours, contemplating the decay of her corpse.[393]

---

ples. The *Sutta Pitaka* is an important scripture in Theravada Buddhism, which is the oldest surviving Buddhist school.

388 BHIKKHU (2005): unnumbered.

389 KANDA (2005): 24.

390 IBID (2005): 24.

391 IBID (2005): 24.

392 SHIGEKATSU (1974): 111–119.

393 MIKI (1988): 179–182.

In art history, the decay of a female corpse can be found in the genre of *kusôzu* ('images of the nine stages of a decaying corpse'). Artworks belonging to this genre were created from the 13th century through to the 19th century in different formats, such as hand scrolls, hanging scrolls and book illustrations.[394] A famous example is the painting *Nindô fujôsôzu* (or *Jindô fujôsôzu*) (Signs of the Impurity of the Human Path), which is part of the hanging scrolls set *Rikudôe* (or *Rokudôe*) (Painting of the Six Paths) of the Kamakura era (1185–1333).[395] Nine images of a female corpse are arranged on the painting in a zigzag form, depicting the process of its decomposition: in the first image, the corpse still looks rather 'fresh', it then ruptures, blood exudes, it is consumed by birds (fig. 50) and finally its bones return to the ground. Both Kanda Fusae and Hasegawa Yûko have emphasised convincingly the artwork's 'cruel' and 'realistic' way of dealing with the motif of death.[396]

However, it is more relevant in this context that the woman is said to be a 'stunning beauty' and in the first image 'as alluring as a sleeping beauty'.[397] One art-historical theory states that she represents Ono no Komachi, a famous poet of the early Heian period, who has become a symbol of Japanese 'feminine beauty'. According to Kanda this theory is based on a misidentification, which is linked to interpretations in the 18th and 19th century; she has highlighted the unlikeliness of a Buddhist devotional image centring on a specific poet.[398] The interpretation, nevertheless, emphasises that the corpse has been viewed as belonging to a beautiful, aristocratic woman. This enhances the contrast of the first image in which the body still looks 'alluring', with the last one, depicting just its bones. This shocking contrast is not surprising when considering that male monks viewed the image in order to tame their sexual desire.

The emphasis on the woman's beauty seems relevant when comparing *Nindô fujôsôzu*, representing the traditional genre of *kusôzu*, with Izima's *Landscapes* series. The depiction of the 'corpse' of an attractive woman in a surrounding without any other human beings provides an obvious parallel. In addition, both *Nindô fujôsôzu* and, for example, *Otsuka Nene Wears Tuzigahana* create a visual narration within the artwork by being composed of

---

394 KANDA (2005): 24.

395 *Rikudôe* (or *rokudôe*) literally means 'Picture of the Six Paths'. According to Buddhist thought, all living beings are caught in an endless cycle of birth, death, and rebirth into one of the 'six paths', also called 'six realms'. The only way to escape is by breaking from desire and achieving enlightenment. The artwork referred to, *Rikudôe, nindô fujô sôzu,* was created during the Kamakura period (1185–1333) and is held in the Shôjuraigô-ji Temple in the prefecture Shiga. A series of fifteen hanging scrolls visualises the six paths, devoting four scrolls each for the realms of humans and hells; for a detailed examination of the *Nindô fujôsôzu* see KANDA (2005): 29–35.

396 KANDA (2005): 29; HASEGAWA (2008): 16.

397 TERAMOTO (2000): 196.

398 KANDA (2005): 3.

numerous images. However, at the same time, it is this narrative element which highlights the difference of the two works with regard to their form, content and function: In *Nindô fujôsôzu*, the narration can be found within one painting; in contrast, the narration in *Otsuka Nene Wears Tuzigahana* is most evident in the artwork's composition of four separate images. In addition, the narrative element is connected to the presentation of different viewpoints, which show Otsuka Nene's 'dead' body over a short period of time. Consequently, her 'corpse' looks equally 'fresh' in each photograph. In contrast, *Nindô fujôsôzu* depicts a narration over a long period time – it shows how a corpse gradually decays.

With regard to the function of the narrative element, *kusôzu* use it in order to emphasise how the woman's beauty vanishes as her body decays. This helps the Buddhist viewer to *overcome* his sensual desires. However, *Otsuka Nene Wears Tuzigahana* uses the narrative element to *create* a feeling of suspense, comparable to a criminal story (see Part 2). Moreover, the viewer enters Otsuka Nene's house, gets closer to her 'beautiful' 'dead' body and as such, experiences a somewhat 'intimate' perspective. Needless to say, the photographs do not show any decay and do not appear to be realistic but staged. As such, the narration does not help to defeat a sexual viewpoint on the female body but rather enhances it. Thus, the Memento Mori approach of *Otsuka Nene Wears Tuzigahana* could be interpreted as contrasting with that of traditional *kusôzu* in its dealing with sexuality: *kusôzu* juxtapose the sexual attractiveness of a young woman with her body's decay – sexuality and death are interpreted as opposing elements, the latter is supposed to help overcome the former. In contrast, the *Landscapes* series uses the motif of death not as a docile element to 'shock' the viewer but rather intertwines it with sexuality (see 5.2).

In summary, like traditional *haiku*, *jisei* poems and Buddhist artworks, the *Landscapes* as well as the *Gyahtei* and *SCARS* series are concerned with the ephemeral nature of life. They reflect a 'beauty of impermanence', which is connected to a tradition in Japanese culture, influenced by Buddhist views on life, death and rebirth. Furthermore, the *Landscapes* series can be compared and contrasted in its depiction of 'dead' bodies with *kusôzu*: the 'aesthetic appreciation' of death and its erotic associations seems to be a more relevant characteristic of the *Landscapes* series than any moral attitude. As such, it contrasts with the *kusôzu* and their educational function of subduing the viewer's craving for sensual pleasure. Nevertheless, the young women's 'death' is a striking and eye-catching feature; it contrasts with the deserted surroundings, be it an old, traditional house, a cherry blossom tree, or a sea of tomatoes. It is this juxtaposition of female beauty, death and tranquillity that fascinate the viewer as an aesthetic image and reminds him of ephemerality in equal measures.

6.4 Conclusions

Arakan #1, *Gyahtei #17*, *Pure Land* and *Otsuka Nene Wears Tuzigahana* all reflect a more or less direct influence of Buddhism and Buddhist culture.

Arakan #1 focuses on a homeless man, who has completely given up on his appearance and freed himself from social regulatory norms; Yamanaka presents him as a Buddhist follower by using formal and iconographic characteristics of *rakanzu*. Formal similarities between the *Arakan* photographs and *rakanzu* include the two-dimensional style, the vertical size of the images and the fact that the pictures are presented as a series of sixteen. Iconographically, the haggard man in *Arakan #1* is presented on his own, he wears a loose robe, and his hair and beard are long. The photograph focuses on his wrinkled face and its somewhat wise expression, reminiscent of an *arakan*. As such, signs of homelessness are re-interpreted as religious signs; the man is viewed respectfully and, moreover, is elevated to the ranks of the enlightened.

At the same time, the man's body appears weak, mirroring his hard and 'ascetic' life. Although presented as an Arhat and thus as 'enlightened,' the man is still part of 'our world', possessing a vulnerable, human body. As Buddha's disciple, he has to remain on earth and teach the Buddhist doctrine. This contrasts with the way that Mori presents enlightenment as the colourful paradise *Pure Land*.

Mori features herself as the goddess Kichijôten within a digitally created, colourful surrounding using various symbols of Buddhist enlightenment. As such, she 'embodies' divinity and enlightenment. The pop-like style, the large size and the impressive technology address a wide audience by presenting a rather uncomplicated visual language. Thus, the artwork's form and the theme of the Pure Land seem consistent: everybody can achieve enlightenment and find peace in another realm – in the Pure Land.

The idea of either achieving nirvana in the Pure Land or being reborn into another samsaric realm has strongly influenced the Buddhist view of human ephemerality. Death and suicide have been less scrutinised than in Christian cultures and have been used as aesthetic motives in various aspects of Japanese culture, be it in *kabuki* plays, literary works or films. This cultural context is relevant in the analysis of the *Landscapes* series, which views death from an aesthetic viewpoint – by dramatically, calmly or humorously staging it and 'appreciating' it as an image.

The *Landscapes* series can be viewed both in its contemporary aesthetic context as well as within a Japanese tradition. In the 1990s, the increase of suicide, internet groups which encouraged suicide, and Tsurumi's *Manual of Suicide* led to heated debates about suicide, death and Japanese society's responsibility. Both the *Manual of Suicide* and the *Landscapes* series view death from an aesthetic and sometimes even humorous perspective. In addition, it has been argued that the aesthetic impression of the *Landscapes* images contrasts with *kusôzu* pictures, which present decay in a 'shocking' contrast to sexual attractiveness, in order to tame the viewer's desires. However, it cannot be denied that the elaborately staged scenes with a 'dead' young woman, such as Otsuka Nene, go beyond an 'aesthetic appreciation' of death. The images also remind the viewer of how suddenly all humans can die – 'memento mori'.

All images could also be viewed without any Buddhist background. Although titled *Arakan*, the series convinces on a rather universal level: which religion the man in *Arakan #1* believes in does not seem relevant. Rather, his wrinkled face and tattered clothes exude a freedom from earthly desires, which could be considered relevant in many religious doctrines. Furthermore, it goes without saying that death is a central issue in any religion. For instance, the afore-mentioned context of the term 'Memento Mori' illustrates how human mortality has played an important role in Christianity. Religion is closely intertwined with human mortality and people have used it as a barrier to their fear. The concept of enlightenment and nirvana is perhaps most associated with Buddhist belief. Yet, the idea of a peaceful paradise and the depiction of this in art can obviously also be found in a Christian context. However, a comparison of the Pure Land in Mori's photograph and other Buddhist artworks on the one hand, and depictions of paradise in Christian artworks on the other, is beyond the scope of this thesis.

7. The Body and Photographic Discourse

Most academics would agree on the centrality of certain texts by contributors such as Roland Barthes, John Berger and Susan Sontag to the discourse on photography. However, there is no 'photo theory' in the sense of a methodology. This is mainly due to the fact that these contributors come from various academic fields, such as semiotics, literature and philosophy, and thus offer very different perspectives, often focussing on only one characteristic of photography. For instance, Charles Peirce's definition of photography as an 'indexical sign', which I will examine further in 7.1, is inextricably intertwined with his semiotic theory. Roland Barthes' famous *Camera Lucida*, which has been considered a major work of photographic discourse, is a collection of rather subjective thoughts primarily concerned with the affective impact of photographs. It does not provide a theory but offers philosophic arguments and personal ideas which could also be read from a non-academic perspective. Susan Sontag emphasised at the very beginning of her speech *Photography Within The Humanities* in 1975 that she does not consider herself 'a critic, and

... above all not a critic of photography.'[399] As such, most authors who are cited in this thesis are not 'critics of photography' but rather writers of other fields. Consequently, the following section considers 'photographic discourse' in a broad and rather non-methodological sense.

In this last section, I will focus on two ideas which were striking when examining the *SCARS* series and the *Landscapes* series, primarily considering the relationship of their themes with the photographic medium. First, the motif of the scar on a human body in *SCAR 1983 illness* will be examined in relation to photography's indexical nature as well as symbolic meaning. Following this, *Otsuka Nene Wears Tuzigahana,* representing the *Landscapes* series, will be interpreted by questioning the motif of 'dead' bodies in relation to photography and well-known discourses on photography. Furthermore, the motifs of fashion and death seem to be connected; the theme of 'death' will be related to fashion as well as fashion photography and popular imagery in the 1990s.

7.1 The Photograph as an 'Index' and a 'Symbol': Thoughts on *SCAR 1983 illness*

The photographic motif of *SCAR 1983 illness*, i.e. a scar on a human body, and the photographic medium reference each other on two levels which could be defined as 'indexical' and 'symbolic'.

7.1.1 The Indexical Reference

The 'indexical' reference is connected to the way photography somewhat 'records' reality through a light process: simply put, light passes through the lens and diaphragm of a camera and transforms sensitive emulsion on a photographic negative. Thus, an analogue photograph could be described as a 'trace of light'. In Susan Sontag's words, it is 'something directly stencilled off the real, like a footprint or a death mask';[400] Jean Baudrillard has compared the photographic medium with a crime always leaving a trace.[401] Similarly, Philippe Dubois has argued that photography is a 'trace of reality' and an 'indexical sign' in a Peircean sense.[402] The philosopher and semiotic Charles Peirce defined the photograph as an 'indexical sign' at the end of the 19th century: his understanding of 'indexicality' depends on there being a 'real' and 'physical

399 SONTAG (1975): 59.
400 SONTAG (1979): 154.
401 BAUDRILLARD (1995): 127–132.
402 DUBOIS (1983): 48; 60–62.

connection' between the items involved.[403] With regard to photography, 'indexicality' thus refers to the direct physical relationship between the photographed object and the photographic image.

This indexical character of photographs led to the once prevalent belief that photography is a medium more reliable in showing reality than traditional art media. For instance, André Bazin believed that photography is rather 'objective'[404] arguing that, contrary to a painting or sculpture, a photographic or film image is formed scientifically without the subjective intervention of man. Photography almost evaporates the artist's human touch and thus, 'confers on [an image] a quality of credibility'.[405] As such, the argument that a photograph is a 'light trace' has led to the idea that a photograph could be viewed as evidence to something like a historical truth. Similarly, a scar could be interpreted as an evident trace of a historical incident. In this way, the photographic medium and the scar on the human body are in a tautological relationship: both appear to be 'objective' visual traces and in Peirce's terms, 'indexical signs', testifying to the existence of something in the past.

At the same time, it should not be forgotten that any 'objective' trace, be it a footprint, a scar or a photograph, is embedded in a subjective context. For instance, the 'light trace' is just one moment in the photographic process: Ishiuchi's choice of the individual body in *SCAR 1983 illness* and of the photographic section of the buttocks and thigh, as well as the development of the film and the display of the image in a photo gallery or art museum, all add to the final artwork as well. Besides, photography has lost its claim of being an indexical sign and a 'record of truth' due to the digital revolution (at the latest): a digital photograph may be manipulated, or even created entirely by means of a computer programme. As the photography critic Ôshima Hiroshi has written, this has resulted in 'a shift' in the way we view photographs; photography should be re-thought of and seen from a viewpoint which has 'nothing to do with the theory of photography as a trace'.[406] Considering such statements and the great increase in digital photography, Ishiuchi's decision to use analogue black and white photography seems rather 'old-fashioned' and emphasises the motif of the scar as a document of the *past.* This brings me to the reference of scars and photographs on a 'symbolic' level.

403 PEIRCE (1958a): 558; PEIRCE (1958b): 335; COLAPIETRO and OLSHEWSKY (1996).

404 BAZIN (1967); note that in the French original, the term 'objectif' can be read as 'objective' in the sense of 'not subjective' as well as in the sense of 'through a camera objective'.

405 BAZIN (1967): 13.

406 ÔSHIMA (2004): 25.

7.1.2 The Symbolic Reference

Peirce has defined three different kinds of signs: In contrast to 'indexical signs', references through similarity, for instance in a painting, are defined as 'iconic signs'.[407] Representation through associations and conventions are 'symbolic signs'. In this Peircean context, a photograph as well as its motifs could also be interpreted as a 'symbolic sign'.

On such a symbolic level, the image of a scar suggests a bittersweet ineluctability of time leaving its traces. Both the scar on a human body and the photographic medium could be interpreted as symbolising past moments – moments that we either regret or enjoy remembering but which we can never return to. With regard to the aesthetic of *SCAR 1983 illness*, the long curved scar dominates the photograph. It is reminiscent of an illness, a rather threatening incident in the past. Yet, it blends into the pattern of new pores and small wrinkles harmoniously. This composition, the soft focus, and the medium of analogue photography all evoke a 'natural' atmosphere. As such, the scar as well as the photograph symbolise events in our *past* and yet, also forms a natural part of our *present*.

Ishiuchi has explained her passion for scars referring to the similarities of the motif and the photographic medium: 'I cannot stop [taking photographs of scars] because they are so much like a photograph. ... Both the scars and the photographs are the manifestation of sorrow for the many things that can never be retrieved and love for life as a remembered present.'[408] The last sentence of Ishiuchi's quotation summarises neatly what this section has tried to explain: both scars and photographs are 'indexical signs', testifying to events in the past. Furthermore, they symbolise past moments, which may evoke a certain sorrow, but which can never be retrieved. At the same time, both scars and photographs represent how memories are intertwined with our present life. As the harmonious impression of *SCAR 1983 illness* as well as Ishiuchi's expression 'love for life' suggest, our history can be considered, in its most optimistic sense, an inevitable part of our present.

---

[407] COLAPIETRO and OLSHEWSKY (1996).

[408] As cited in PHILLIPS (2005): 132.

7.2 (Fashion) Photography and 'Death': Thoughts on *Otsuka Nene Wears Tuzigahana*

7.2.1 Death and the Photographic Medium

The history of all artistic media is closely related to an 'externalisation' of the human subject and thus also to its death. This refers to any written documents, records of human voices as well as any paintings. Images are a 'trace' of their creator and reflect a certain moment of the past; they are thus reminiscent of the ending of all things. In the 1990s, Hans Belting and Martin Schulz analysed this connection of art images and death in the project *Bild und Tod* (Image and Death); according to the scholars, the human awareness of death is our original motivation to create images.[409] Referring to Jean Baudrillard's theory of a *Symbolic Exchange*, Schulz has explained that the visual image of a human being could be interpreted as a double of his physical body. The image is a medium which gives the mortal body an opportunity to 'gain immortality'.[410]

In photography, this idea of 'keeping' a mortal body is even more obvious; as 'indexical signs' of reality, photographs are often taken to 'freeze' a moment of a person's life. Yet, any photograph which tries to 'preserve' life 'creates' death at the same time. This particular relationship of the photographic medium with death has often been discussed in texts on photography. For instance, it can be found in Susan Sontag's essay collection *On Photography*: Sontag has stated that all photographs are 'Memento Mori' since they 'testify to time's relentless melt'.[411] However, the most famous example is Roland Barthes' *Camera Lucida*, in which the author examines various photographs, such as a private photograph of his mother as a young girl in a winter garden. He has reflected on how every photograph of a person returns the dead:

> ... if Photography seems to me closer to the Theater, it is by way of a singular intermediary ...: by way of Death. We know the original relation of the Theater and the cult of the Dead: ... Now it is this same relation which I find in the Photograph; however 'lifelike' we strive to make it ... Photography is ... a kind of *Tableau Vivant*, a figuration of the motionless and made-up face beneath which we see the dead.[412]

409 SCHULZ (2002): 742; for more information see also BELTING (2001a).
410 SCHULZ (2002): 743.
411 SONTAG (1979): 15.
412 BARTHES (1981): 31 – 32.

Although Memorial Photography exists as an independent genre,[413] it goes without saying that photographs of the dead are not as common as photographs of living subjects. Schulz has pointed out that there are a few publications about Memorial Photography as if there was something indecent or even perverted about it.[414] Photographs of people have originally been used as documents of life; as Barthes' has put it, we 'strive' to make the images look as 'lifelike' as possible.

In this context Izima's *Landscapes* series could be interpreted as an ironic comment on the photographic medium itself and on photographic discourse. Following Barthes' metaphorical definition of photography as a kind of 'tableau vivant' and a 'made-up face', the *Landscapes* series references the photographic medium within the images: it could be argued that *Otsuka Nene Wears Tuzigahana* shows a scene as staged as a tableau vivant; the viewer sees 'the dead' beneath the 'motion-less' woman and her 'made-up face'. In contrast to Barthes' quotation, however, Izima does not strive to make the photographic scene as 'lifelike' as possible but rather stages it as 'deadlike'. He uses 'death' not as a *motivation* for his photographs but rather as a *motif*: instead of taking photographs in order to preserve a person's life, he accepts his/her 'death'. As such, both the motif of the artworks and their medium represent 'death'.

Out of the fifty young models of the *Landscapes* series, Fukasawa Elisa († 2004) and Barbara Rudnik († 2009) died a few years after the photographs were taken. Izima has emphasised in my interview that the photographs of Fukasawa at the amusement park Nihon Land mirror her liveliness while pretending to be dead; 'compared to some snapshot of her laughing, these photographs seem more alive.' This statement is highly subjective and can thus not be corroborated by an academic analysis of the photographs. However, Izima's quotation is interesting insofar as it could be juxtaposed with Barthes' statement that producing 'lifelike' effects in photographs is connected to fear of death: '… as if the (terrified) Photographer must exert himself to the utmost to keep the Photograph from becoming Death.'[415] Ôshima Hiroshi has linked Barthes' quotation with Izima's *Landscapes* series by pointing out that many 'terrified' fashion photographers try to make their work look alive, so as never to encounter death. He has argued that Izima, however, is not a 'terrified photographer', but one who is able to 'turn around and amiably shake hands

413 The genre Memorial Photography refers to photographs of corpses which are taken as a last document before the bodies decay. On Memorial Photography see: BURNS, Stanley B. (1990): *Sleeping Beauty. Memorial Photography in America*. Altadena: Twelvetrees Press; RUBY, Jay (1995): *Secure the Shadow. Death and Photography in America*. Cambridge: MIT Press; SYKORA, Katharina (2009): *Die Tode der Fotografie* [The Deaths of Photography]. München: Willhelm Fink.

414 SCHULZ (2002): 756.

415 BARTHES (1981): 14.

with Death.'[416] Indeed, by narratively, extensively and humorously staging 'death scenes', Izima offers a photographic viewpoint, which seems less 'terrified' of death. Moreover, by appreciating the motif of 'death' on an aesthetic level within the images, the *Landscapes* series references also the photographic medium's characteristic of 'creating' death.[417]

7.2.2 Death in (Fashion) Photography

Death as a motif in Fashion Photography is a rather controversial issue that should be given some historical context. Firstly, fashion and death can be connected on a metaphorical level since each fashion trend comes, by definition, to an end. Walter Benjamin has explained that there is a connection between the rapid change of fashion and death:

> … fashion has never been anything but the parody of the colourfully decorated corpse, the provocation of death through the woman …. That is fashion. For this reason, she changes so rapidly, teasing death, already becoming somebody else again, somebody new, as death looks about for her to strike her down.[418]

As such, the transience of fashion symbolises the ending of life: as every fashion has to die, every human life has to end. Wearing Chanel or Louis Vuitton, the models in the *Landscapes* series are 'up to date' and linked to their immediate present. Being 'dead', however, they symbolise the sudden change of what is considered fashionable. By staging their own death in a 'fashionable' way, the models seem to be brave enough not only to 'tease' death but also to accept the ending of both fashion trends and their lives.

Secondly, an increasing number of designers opted to show symptoms of decay and sickness ('heroin chic') in the 1990s.[419] In 1995, the American fashion designer Jeremy Scott showed a collection in Paris, which was inspired by

---

416 ÔSHIMA (2000): 52.

417 The topic of death and its relation to (photographic) images has become a popular field of study within cultural studies of the last two years. I could not include the new extensive publications by Katharina Sykora and Dominik Groß and had to eliminate parts of my interpretations due to space limitations. SYKORA, Katharina (2009): *Die Tode der Fotografie 1–2* [The Deaths of Photography]. München: Wilhelm Fink; GROSS, Dominik (ed.) (2010): *Todesbilder. Studien zum gesellschaftlichen Umgang mit dem Tod 1–3* [Death Images. Studies On the Social Handling of Death 1–3] Frankfurt: Campus Verlag.

418 BENJAMIN (1989): 4

419 Images of death and danger became popular in fashion photography in the 1990s but were already introduced to Fashion Photography in the 1970s, e.g. by Guy Bourdin and Helmut Newton. Susan Sontag explained in 1979 that 'in an apparent revulsion against the beautiful, recent generations of photographers prefer to show disorder…' SONTAG (1979): 102.

car crash victims. He explained that he liked the idea of women in a car accident being 'chic'ed out in couture' and being 'sexy'.[420] The fashion industry employed shock-techniques in its marketing campaigns and created fashion images of crime, decay and death that Rebecca Arnold has categorised as 'fashion noire'.[421] Renzo Rosso's advertisement for Diesel in the early 1990s is a good example of this category. It shows a crash of four cars with 'dead' models, who are harmoniously arranged across the road and on top of the cars. Three men are standing at the side, photographing the 'dead'. The image is reminiscent of Andy Wahol's print *Saturday Disaster* (1963/1964) from his *Death in America* series. The colourful, sharp advertisement photograph with classic cars and the improbable poses of the models contrasts with the doubled and screen-printed newspaper photograph in Warhol's work. However, the motif evokes both mass media disaster images and Warhol's appropriation of these. I will return to Warhol's prints later in this section. Another example is Graham Fink's photograph for John Pearse *Go Out in Style* (1997), which depicts a staged murder and a man lying on the floor with blood on his face and a pistol in the foreground.

Izima started his *Landscapes* series in the 1990s, when the use of such 'shocking' fashion commercials caused heated debates among members of the public. The controversy generated by Oliviero Toscani's advertisement for Benetton,[422] for example featuring images of military uniforms covered in blood, was so intense that some retailers stopped stocking Benetton products. Izima, who has worked in the field of advertising, was undoubtedly aware of these images. He has explained, however, that he was 'inspired by newspaper photos of accidents, thinking that if the dead person was wearing the latest fashion or interesting clothes by coincidence, the images could be fashion photography.'[423] This quotation can be linked to the plethora of images and 'media overkill', which has produced a fundamental change in the way in which we consume images. Images of accidents, disasters and dead bodies have become part of our everyday consciousness.

However, using such images in art or fashion advertisement, rather than in the news, takes them out of their usual context. Andy Warhol was one of the first artists who worked with mass-produced disaster, death and police images, such as of car accidents, race riots, mug shots and electric chairs.[424] He critically appropriated and mechanically reproduced the pictures in the same way

420 As cited in EVANS (2003): 106.

421 ARNOLD (2001): 32–62.

422 For more information on Toscani's images for Benetton see PAGNUCCO SALVEMINI (2003).

423 As cited in BOECKER (2001b): 218.

424 For further information on Andy Warhol's work concerned with images of death and disaster see FOGLE, Douglas (ed.) (2006): *ANDY WARHOL/SUPERNOVA: Stars, Deaths, and Disasters, 1962–1964*. New York: Distributed Art Publishers.

he used other media images, such as those of Marilyn Monroe. As artworks we look at his death images from a different perspective, focussing on their aesthetic qualities and their critical message.

One image that Warhol adapts and multiplies in a print titled *Suicide (Fallen Body)* (1962) demonstrates parallels with the images of the *Landscapes* series and reflects Izima's afore mentioned quotation. The photograph, taken by the photographer Robert Wiles, was published in the May 12th 1947 edition of the *Life* magazine as the 'picture of the week' (fig. 54).[425] It shows a 23-year old woman, Evelyn Mchale, who committed suicide by jumping from the Empire State Building and who landed atop a limousine. She lies on her back with her legs crossed. Her face does not show any injuries; her eyes and mouth are softly closed. Wearing a grey two-piece dress, a white blouse, white gloves and lipstick, the young woman's style epitomizes elegance. The fact that she does not look injured, her peaceful expression, her young and delicate features, and her elegant garments all create an aesthetic impression which is comparable to that of *Otsuka Nene Wears Tuzigahana*. In addition, a short article about the suicide in the *New York Times*, which probably also featured the photograph, almost seems like a template for Izima's fictional articles in *zyappu*:

> On the observation deck, Detective Frank Murray of the West Thirtieth Street station, found Miss McHale's gray cloth coat, her pocketbook with several dollars and the note, and a make-up kit filled with family pictures.[426]

As in Izima's fictional articles, the newspaper details the woman's clothes and objects as described in the police report. In this way, there are striking similarities between the *Landscapes* images (and the way that these were presented in the *zyappu* magazine) and 'real' photographs of dead people (and the accompanying articles) in the newspaper.

Returning to Fashion Photography in the 1990s, Caroline Evans sees a connection between the fascination with the dark side of life in fashion images in the 1990s and fashion's emphasis on idealised bodies. She makes an insightful point when saying that the standardised bodies and stereotypes are 'only half the picture, so we are drawn to the negated or neglected other side, be it cultural otherness or death.'[427] In such images, fashion functions as 'a symptom to evoke its opposite, so that glamour masks decay, but the latter returns as the repressed of the former.'[428] Similarly, it is this extreme clash of glamour

---

425 I am grateful to Chad Fahs for drawing my attention to this image and for giving me the details of its publication. LIFE MAGAZINE (1947): 42–43.

426 NEW YORK TIMES (02. 05. 1947): 23.

427 EVANS (2003): 227.

428 IBID: 227.

and decay, of life and death, of Eros and Thanatos, which evokes a somehow erotic and 'beautiful' aesthetic in the *Landscapes* photographs.

Images of 'dead' people in Fashion Photography are more unexpected than in the news and also in works of art. Fundamental principles of the advertising system are turned upside down: the brand is not linked to something desirable but to a dark, controversial image. However, the question of whether it is morally justifiable to advertise using the motif of death does not seem relevant for this thesis. Firstly, I would like to stress again that Izima's *Landscapes* photographs are 'artworks' which can be viewed in the 'art world' or, in Japan, in the 'photography world'. Unlike any Benetton campaign, the images are not presented as posters to a wide public. Secondly, although the titles name fashion labels, the *Landscapes* images do not sell anything apart from themselves. 'Death' is an art motif and not connected to the marketing strategy of a fashion label.

According to Britta Sachs, no one can say if Izima wants to shock or criticise the fashion world, and Yannick Vigouroux sees the *Landscapes* photographs as 'parodies' of the Fashion Photography of recent years.[429] The *Landscapes* series uses exaggeration and contrast stylistically to evoke amusement comparable to a parody. However, the images are no 'parody of fashion photography' insofar as the colourful and extensively composed scenarios, the pretty women and their designer clothes employ a Fashion Photography aesthetic. Although the women pose as if they were 'dead', their faces and bodies are never unsightly or deformed. Hence, the artworks reflect an 'aesthetic appreciation of death' rather than a critique of Fashion Noir Photography.

7.3 Conclusions

Both *SCAR 1983 illness* and *Otsuka Nene Wears Tuzigahana* reference the photographic medium through their motifs. Scars as well as photographs could be interpreted as 'indexical signs' in a Peircean sense, testifying to events in the past. The motif of the 'dead' woman in the *Landscapes* series references how every photograph 'becomes death'.[430] These interpretations are based on the same argument, namely that a photograph is a 'trace': a 'trace of light' as well as a 'trace of a human'.

However, both artworks go beyond the tautological relationship of their motifs with the photographic medium. *SCAR 1983 illness* also presents the scar as an element of the present: as the harmonious impression suggests, the scar symbolises how past moments are intertwined with our present in a rather

---

429 SACHS (2000); VIGOUROUX (2004): 137–138.
430 BARTHES (1981): 14.

optimistic sense. In *Otsuka Nene Wears Tuzigahana*, Izima offers a viewpoint which does not appear to be belonging to a 'terrified photographer'. Rather, he accepts 'death' aesthetically. Using fashion as a metaphor of death in the images and employing a 1990s Fashion Photography style, the *Landscapes* series presents 'death' as an inevitable part of our everyday imagery and, moreover, of our life.

Conclusions

1. Summary of the Main Findings

My study had two main purposes: firstly, to explore different contexts of art photography in 1990s Japan, and, secondly, to examine the various ways in which specific artworks featuring human subjects reflect socio-cultural problems related to the 'body'.

Through the examination of Japanese publications concerned with the foundations of 'art' and the 'art system' in Japan, as well as the analysis of in-depth interviews with artists and 'art specialists', I have gained insights into the local backgrounds and problems surrounding art in 1990s Japan. These insights have been presented in Part 1. It has been explained how the notion of 'art' being introduced to Japan as a 'Western' concept remains problematic until today: the opinion of 'the West' plays an important role in a Japanese art system that finds it difficult to appreciate its contemporary art. This is one reason why some artists, such as Morimura Yasumasa, were acknowledged in exhibitions in North America and Europe before being exhibited in Japan. Although new museums and galleries featuring contemporary art were established in the 1990s, and collaborations between 'Western' and Japanese museums increased, it was still difficult for artists to have a career in Japan. It was only during the last twenty years that a Japanese infrastructure for contemporary art started to develop.

In addition, I have highlighted the problems that Japanese (as well as other 'non-Western') artists have faced in an international art market which is dominated by 'the West'. My questions could not be fully answered in this study; rather, they address complex areas of debate which are relevant in our post-colonial and globalised present in various fields of culture. For instance, how can Japanese artists avoid making use of Japonism and yet present 'Japanese' artworks? Moreover, who should decide which works are included as 'art' in an international, yet 'Western' art system? What criteria can justify the exclusion of works without disrespecting 'non-Western' notions of 'art'?

Part 1 has also described the establishment of what I have called the 'photography world' in Japan; after photography was introduced to Japan, it developed into an economically powerful web of camera companies, photography galleries, amateur clubs and magazines. I have traced back the different paths that 'photography' on the one side and 'art' on the other have followed in Japan, arguing that the distinction of 'photographs' and 'photographic works of art' is mostly based on the context that the works are presented in rather than visual criteria.

It was only in the 1990s that the paths of 'photography' and 'photographic art' started to overlap. Japanese photographic art has increasingly become acknowledged in 'Western' as well as Japanese art museums. Moreover, images which were categorised as 'photographs' in Japan, for instance by Yamanaka Manabu and Izima Kaoru, have been displayed within the 'Western' art system as 'works of art'. In addition, recent winners of the *Kimura Ihei Award* symbolise how the boundaries between 'photography' and 'art photography' have become blurred within Japan. The consequences this might have on photographic art could be an interesting topic of future research.

After an introduction to the photographic work of six artists, Part 2 described and analysed ten photographs as case studies. Following this, in Part 3, the photographs' bodily representations were linked to socio-cultural issues concerning art historical traditions, national identity, social behavioural norms, gender constructions and religious topics. The expression 'screen' in the title of the third chapter (and the title of this thesis) has been used for 'projections' on three different levels: first, the photographs have revealed socio-cultural 'inscriptions' on the human body; second, they have revealed critical messages by the artists; third, my interpretations of the artworks have included my own projections as a scholar. Every section of Part 3 has ended with conclusions; I will not repeat these again. Rather, I would like to return to the ten artworks by briefly summarising the most relevant interpretations.

Portrait (Futago) references the European tradition of the female nude as well as its adoption in Japan. Morimura Yasumasa parodies and deconstructs the gender binary of the 'Western' art genre, while, at the same time, reclaiming the male as an 'erotic' object in Japanese imagery. Furthermore, *Portrait (Futago)* highlights colonial history: Morimura not only dresses up as a Black servant, he also uses the medium of photography which is reminiscent of modern pictures of 'the colonised'. The word '*futago*' ('twins') in the artwork's title highlights the equally subordinated position of White prostitutes and Black servants in late 19th century France. Set against Japan's historical background, *Portrait (Futago)* offers two readings: the first concerns Japan's definition of its national identity through the gaze of 'the West' since the Meiji period. The second concerns the EuroAmerican 'Orientalist' perspective, namely the romantisation as well as devaluation of Japan as an 'exotic petite geisha'. Furthermore, the influence of Japanese culture on 'Western' art, which is reflected in Manet's painting *Olympia*, is emphasised in *Portrait (Futago)* through numerous 'Japanese' props. In this way, *Portrait (Futago)* offers interpretations connected to the historical background of Manet's time both in France and Japan.

At the same time, the large-sized colourful image draws attention to the contemporary relationship of Japan with 'the West'. Morimura's discernible

'Japanese' body, the 'Japanese' props and the photographic medium, which can be associated with Japan, suggest that Morimura did not aim at a complete identification with the 'Western Other'. Rather, he presents us self-confidently with 'hybrid bodies' and a 'hybrid artwork': gender goes beyond the binary of 'female' and 'male', national identity goes beyond dichotomies of 'Japan' and 'the West' and the artwork is a photograph of a tableau vivant with a painted background. It is up to the viewer if he sees (historical) binaries or if he accepts the artwork as a cheerful sign of (future) 'hybridity'.

Red Marilyn is similar to *Portrait (Futago)* in drawing attention to conventional gender structures of 'Western' imagery by presenting the viewer with a 'male' artist in a 'feminine masquerade'. *Red Marilyn* challenges the female nude in popular pin-up imagery, and, moreover, combines it with traditional Japanese concepts of feminine male 'beauty'. Furthermore, *Red Marilyn* emphasises the influence of American icons on Japan in the post-war era: Hollywood films and their most famous actresses, including Marilyn Monroe, re-enforced the Japanese fascination with 'Western' culture and body ideals. *Red Marilyn* also shows that the filmstar's Caucasian looks and 'Western' lives were out of the reach of the Japanese post-war audience. However, the colourful image does not create a complex-loaded impression but rather, like *Portrait (Futago)*, a powerful aesthetic of 'hybridity'.

Yamanaka Manabu's *Arakan #1* contrasts with Morimura's works as it is a black and white photograph of a homeless man who seems to have completely given up on his appearance. He is equated with a Buddhist follower through formal and iconographic characteristics of *rakanzu* images: formally, the two-dimensional style, vertical size and the series of sixteen images are all reminiscent of *rakanzu*. Iconographically, the man is presented on his own, he wears a loose robe, his hair and beard are long, and his face exudes a somewhat wise expression. The haggard body reflects the homeless man's hard life; however, presented in a stylised black and white photograph in front of a neutral background, this body turns into that of an Arhat – an enlightened disciple, who has to remain on earth and teach the Buddhist doctrine. In this way, Yamanaka re-interprets signs of homelessness as religious signs and presents us with the power of images: within an art image, the homeless stranger can be elevated to the ranks of the enlightened.

Gyahtei #17 has been interpreted as a Buddhist Memento Mori. Through the aestheticised presentation of an old body in a black and white photograph with bright artificial lighting, Yamanaka transforms the female subject into a somewhat 'beautiful' symbol of decay and transience. The woman embodies old age, announcing her death as *gya tei* – 'going beyond' life.

Mori Mariko's *Tea Ceremony III* questions what I have defined as 'social codes' in 'subsystems' of Japanese society. Mori dresses like a *ôeru* and follows the prescribed tea-serving rules for women in offices, using a submissive, respectful body language. Juxtaposing herself with business men walking by, she alludes to women's structural discrimination in the Japanese 1990s business sector. Furthermore, wearing a silver *kosupure*-like costume underneath the *ôeru* dress, Mori exposes the neat secretary outfit as nothing but a masquerade creating the social identity of decorative 'office ladies'. At the same time, the *kosupure* aspect alludes to cute female images in popular *manga* or *anime.* Although *Tea Ceremony III* is a colourful glossy image, it can be interpreted as a feminist parody, criticising social expectations of and restrictions for women. Mori inserts an unexpected moment of deconstruction in the image by combining the 'feminine' stereotypes of '*ôeru*' and '*kawaii manga* girl'.

In *Pure Land,* Mori is less concerned with socio-criticism as she presents herself as the goddess Kichijôten within a digitally created, pastel-coloured fantasy surrounding. Various symbols reference traditional Buddhist iconography of enlightenment. Embodying a goddess, even Mori herself represents enlightenment. The pop-like style, the large size and the impressive technology of the photograph address a wide audience. Hence, the artwork's form and theme seem consistent: everybody can achieve enlightenment and find peace in the realm of the Pure Land.

Ishiuchi Miyako's *Chromosome XY* series is interesting in its focus on the naked male body in stylised black and white photographs. The close-up perspective reflects Ishiuchi's attempt to get closer to the body of the Other sex. The slender young chest in *Chromosome XY* has also been interpreted as alluding to a new 'masculine ideal' of 1990s Japan, evident in increasing numbers of Japanese men being concerned with their outward appearance. This is intertwined with the rise of a 'female gaze' on 'the male body'. Ishiuchi's close-up approach to naked male bodies reflects this, inverting the conventional art dichotomy 'male gaze' vs. 'female nude'. Juxtaposed with a work by Robert Mapplethorpe, the chest in *Chromosome XY* appears rather 'feminine'; however, this reflects my 'Western' viewpoint. Within a Japanese context, *Chromosome XY* as well as the new body consciousness of Japanese young men rather represent a re-aestheticised 'masculinity'.

SCAR 1983 illness also features the human body in a close-up image, viewing it from an aesthetic perspective. The photograph is reminiscent of a landscape in presenting us with a self-contained composition of organic forms, which, nevertheless, continue outside the artwork's frame. Moreover, a large curved scar, i.e. a body part which is usually not focussed on in artworks, is elevated to the main motif of a photograph. As such, the motif references the medium: scars as well as photographs could be interpreted as 'indexical' and 'symbolic signs' in a Peircean sense, testifying to events in the past and symbolising transience and memory.

In Yanagi Miwa's *Elevator Girls 3F,* elevator girls let go of their prescribed body language by sitting on the floor and staring at shoes. In this way, Yanagi deconstructs the standardised 'social codes' of department store employees, especially elevator girls. At the same time, the photograph shows women as consumers who are fixated on buying branded goods. Both the decorative inside of the department store system, represented by elevator girls, and the outside, represented by the same young women staring at shoes, are female. *Elevator Girls 3F* could thus also be described as a 'feminist' critique: firstly, like *Tea Ceremony III*, the image alludes to the importance of women's 'decorative' appearance in Japanese society; secondly, Yanagi criticises 'parasite' women, who are driven by consumerism. Third, she exaggerates 'feminine' ideals and their homogenising effect by displaying numerous similar looking girls being mesmerised by similar shoes. Set against the 1990s background, the artwork criticises not only society's expectations of women to embody a submissive 'feminine ideal', but also women's blind imitation of a similarly *kawaii* style.

The 'erotic' associations of this helpless *kawaii* femininity are reflected in Izima Kaoru's *Otsuka Nene Wears Tuzigahana* in a superlative form: a young actress lies on the floor and appears to be 'dead'. Presenting a conjunction of 'the beautiful female' and 'death', the work could be criticised for reinforcing the conventional dichotomy of the 'male gaze' vs. the 'female sexualised object'. However, I have argued that the image goes far beyond the depiction of a 'vulnerable beautiful female' – the women's 'erotic passivity' is just the 'teaser' making the viewer reflect upon 'death'. In the 1990s, the increase in suicide, suicide groups on the internet, and Tsurumi Wataru's *Manual of Suicide* led to heated debates about suicide, death and Japanese society's responsibility. Both the *Manual of Suicide* and Izima's *Landscapes* series view death from an aesthetic and even partly humorous perspective. This references a tradition of 'aesthetic appreciation' of death in Japanese culture influenced by Buddhist views on death and rebirth. However, the main reading I have proposed for the *Landscapes* photographs is that they draw attention to both 'the female' and 'death' as cultural myths; 'death' becomes simultaneously a 'male' (Izima's) and 'female' (the models') fantasy image. Moreover, a 'dead' and yet 'beautiful' female wearing 'the latest fashion' can be interpreted as a witty motif which self-reflexively references 'death as an image'. Similarly, the motif of the 'dead' woman symbolises how every photograph 'becomes death'.

Given space constraints, it was with regret that I had to eliminate many issues from this final thesis, for instance the progress of digital image technologies, which have increasingly been assimilated into photographic practice since the 1990s. New technologies have led to debates on the 'crisis for photographic truth' and the beginning of a 'post-photographic' era in the 1990s.[1] It would be interesting to examine these debates and link them to a Japanese context; many Japanese photographers experiment with the newest software programmes and camera equipment. Eric C. Shiner has linked the technology 'hype' in contemporary Japanese culture to photographic artworks by Morimura Yasumasa, Yanagi Miwa and Sawada Tomoko, stating that the technology allows the artists to 'expand boundaries' of bodies and realities.[2] In addition, the context of Japanese *manga*, *anime* and game culture, and their relationship with photography is another interesting topic that could not be examined in this study. The influence of Japan's economic success in the *manga* and computer gaming sector seems to have led to a new 'national' self-confidence; in my interviews the relevance of game culture since the 1990s has been addressed several times. For instance, Nanjô Fumio has stated that Morimura's self-portraits probably started as 'something like a game', explaining this with the fact that 'Japan is the land of games'. The influence of new technologies, games and gaming culture on Japanese photography would be a relevant topic for further research.

2. 20th Century Binary Structures vs. 21st Century Hybridity

The summary of the main findings has shown that the ten photographs display the human subject and its body in different ways: some images are directly concerned with socio-cultural issues, while others focus on the body as an aesthetic motif. For instance, *Tea Ceremony III* addresses a range of socio-cultural problems, intertwining them with the human body and body language, whereas *Gyahtei #17* focuses on an old female body as an aesthetic symbol of age. Hence, it is not surprising that some images have been examined repeatedly in this thesis, each time from different viewpoints, while others offered one clear interpretation. This makes it difficult to present general conclusions. Rather, I would like to address one interesting problem that this thesis – and the topic of 1990s Japanese photographic art in general – captures: the paradox of 'hybridity'.

The flexible structure of Part 3 and, moreover, the entire thesis has purposely referenced the 'postmodern', multiple and fluid concept of the 'body': it has offered one possible arrangement amongst many others. The overlaps and flows between the diverse body sections have been emphasised in numerous cross-references. Nevertheless, within the individual sections, I have ended up using 'modern' binary categorisations: for instance I have compared the 'nude'

---

1 See for example MITCHELL (1992).
2 SHINER (2008): 187.

with the 'naked', contrasted 'Western' and 'Japanese' motifs, differentiated between a system's 'inside' and 'outside', and juxtaposed the 'male' with the 'female' body. This was necessary for methodological reasons. Moreover, it was due to the analysed artworks all 'looking back' on 20th century Japan (or even earlier historical Japan): by appropriating or referencing images of art history and popular culture explicitly (Morimura, Yamanaka) or implicitly (Mori, Izima), by expressing criticism of a long tradition of women's discrimination at work (Mori, Yanagi) or by showing bodies and body parts which have been rather repressed in 20th century imagery (Ishiuchi, Morimura, Yamanaka).

At the same time, however, it has become clear that these modern binary structures are either parodied or criticised within the images themselves, or that they have become blurred. For example, the photographs analysed in the second section of Part 3 all had in common that they contrast images of erotic 'nude' bodies on the one hand with neutrally 'naked' bodies on the other. They illustrate how the categorisations 'naked' and 'nude' are no longer persuasive; new terms are needed to define the different shades that exist between 'nude' and 'naked'. In addition, the fifth sub-chapter of Part 3 has shown that most of the photographs either criticise narrow notions of gender or show gender as something flexible. This is linked with 1990s Japan; in the 1990s women were still predominantly supposed to stick to 'feminine' roles and men to follow the ideal of the responsible *sararîman*; however, the decade also introduced changes. Young women started to increasingly break out of 'feminine' norms, often acting more 'manly'. Furthermore, as Morimura's self-portraits and Ishiuchi's *Chromosome XY* series reflect, the 'male' and the 'male body' were 're-eroticised'. The rise of male beauty aesthetics brought back the 'man' as a sexually alluring object instead of an 'asexual' company worker, while, at the same time, encouraging a female gaze on the 'male'.[3] Gender 'crossings' by both 'females' and 'males' have resulted in an increase of multiple gender identities; reproductive and gender realignment technologies have been improved enormously. In this way, the modern gender binary has blended. This fusion of gender binaries is reflected in Morimura's *Red Marilyn* and *Portrait (Futago).* Furthermore, *Portrait (Futago)* also references issues of 'national' identity in a blended form; *Arakan #1* presents us with a homeless man who is equated with a Buddhist Arhat; *Tea Ceremony III* presents Mori as a mix of a secretary and a cute *manga* girl; *Elevator Girls 3F* features females who appear human and yet

3 The new 'masculinity' ideal and the 'rise of the female gaze' not only alludes to Japanese history but can also be found in 'the West', where men, including the British footballer David Beckham, have promoted a 'male' image with 'feminine' attributes. The increase of heterosexual men's concerns for their appearance, especially in large cities, led to the coining of the term 'metrosexuality' in the early 21st century.

robotic or doll-like; *Scar 1983 illness* presents a scar as if it were an element of a landscape image or an abstract painting. Taking these arguments into account, I suggest that the analysed artworks encourage us to re-evaluate the 20th century binary ways in which we comprehend human subjects and their bodies by presenting us with a blending of these. In other words, the presented bodies, their identities and the overall impression of the photographic compositions often appear 'hybrid' or even 'super-hybrid'.

'Hybridity' in a cultural context is a term which has first been used in postcolonial studies, referring to 'the creation of new transcultural forms' originally within the contact zone produced by colonisation.[4] As Homi Bhabha argued in his *Location of Culture* in 1990, 'hybridisation' subverts the narratives of colonial cultures; the formerly-excluded 'colonised' subjects enter into the discourse of the dominating culture. Thus, 'hybridity' in postcolonial discourse could be defined as a counter-narrative, a critique of the canon's exclusion of other narratives. An analysis of 'hybridity' as a controversial notion of postcolonial studies is beyond the scope of this thesis. However, in cultural commentary and art critique, the term has been used in a wider sense, defining the blending of cultural identities due to globalisation. Unfortunately, it has often been used in a rather indifferent way to describe any works of art created by, for instance, African, Aboriginal or Native American artists who are working in a 'Westernised' context. Nicholas Thomas has criticised this: 'the interest in hybridity enables critics and curators to celebrate their own capacity for acknowledging cultural difference, while refraining from engaging with the stories and works that emerge from ground remote from their own'.[5] According to Thomas, concepts of hybridity are 'too general and reactive to contribute to … the understanding … of cultural forms.'[6] I agree with Thomas that visual culture which emerges from ground remote from our own, should not simply be described as 'hybrid' but rather analysed within its context; I have tried to do this throughout this study.

However, for want of an alternative term, I would still like to use the term 'hybridity', but in a non-judgmental and rather literal sense: a 'hybrid' is the result of the crossing of two (or more) factors. I suggest that the term 'hybrid' in this sense well describes a somewhat paradoxical characteristic of the photographs that I have analysed in this thesis: the photographs reference binaries while, at the same time, blending them and, moreover, often leading them ad absurdum. Morimura's *Portrait (Futago)*, for instance, is 'hybrid' in presenting a fusion of the 'Asian male' and the 'Caucasian female'. However, as argued in the third chapter, the notion of the 'Asian male' itself could be described as

4 Ashcroft, Griffith and Tiffin (2003): 118

5 Thomas (1996): 9

6 Ibid: 9

being 'hybrid' and intertwined with the 'female'. Moreover, in the photograph, 'Western' and 'Japanese', 'male' and 'female' are cultural constructions which are inextricably interlinked; it is difficult, if not impossible to demarcate them from each other. However, if the term 'hybrid' suggests that the two factors from which it originated can be identified clearly, I would argue that *Portrait (Futago)*, like contemporary Japanese photography and culture, should better be described as 'super-hybrid'. This term was coined by Jörg Heiser in an article in *Frieze* in 2010: Heiser uses the prefix 'super' as 'a reflection of how hybridization has moved beyond the point where it's about a fixed set of cultural genealogies ...'[7] I believe the photographs in this study, as well as my interpretations, reflect a cultural process of moving beyond fixed binaries into a conglomerate of multiple influences; as such, they do indeed represent 'super-hybridization'.

Morimura might be correct in his assumption that it is 'just a matter of time until the differences between female and male disappear'.[8] Perhaps, the analysed photographs should encourage us to step away from dichotomies and simply accept 'super-hybridity' as the future normative in many cultural contexts: distinctions I have used for methodological reasons, such as the 'Asian male' and the 'Caucasian female', might fade completely in the future. The effects that the increase of globalisation and 'super-hybridization' might have on future images produced in 'Japan' remain to be seen. I am convinced, however, that the human body will, whether 'hybrid', 'super-hybrid' or not, remain a motif of visual culture.

---

7 HEISER (2010): 13

8 MORIMURA (2001d): 249.

Appendix

Bibliography (Primary and Secondary Sources)

ALLOULA, Marek (1986): *The Colonial Harem*. Minneapolis: University of Minnesota Press

AMY, Michael (2000): Manabu Yamanaka at Stefan Stux. In: *Art in America, May 2000*, URL: http://findarticles.com/p/articles/mi_m1248/is_5_88/ai_62111804 (10. 03. 2010)

ANDERSON, Benedict (1991): *Imagined Communities: Reflections on the Origin and Spread of Nationalism. Revised Edition*. London and New York: Verso

AOKI, Tamotsu (1990): *Nihon bunkaron no henyô* [The Historical Change of the Japan Discourse]. Tokyo: Chûô Kôronsha

ARAKAWA, Chihiro and Kanji BANDO (2001): *Manekineko no hakurankai* [An Exhibition Of Manekineko]. Tokyo: Shiroishishoten

ARENAS, Amelia (1998): *Naze, kore ga âto na no?* [Why is this Art?] Kyoto: Tankôsha

ARKSEY, Hilary and Peter KNIGHT (1999): *Interviewing for Social Scientists*. London: Sage Publications

ARNOLD, Rebecca (2001): *Fashion, Desire and Anxiety*. London and Oxford: Tauris & Co

ASAHI SHINBUN (1989): Hito purasu ichi. Arakan wo totta Yamanaka Manabu san [People Plus One. Yamanaka Manabu Who Took Photographs Of Arakan]. In: *Asahi shinbun (Tokyo), 09. 12. 1989,* 15

ASHCROFT, Bill, Gareth GRIFFITH and Helen TIFFIN (eds.) (2003): *Post-Colonial Studies: The Key Concepts*. London: Routledge

BACHMAYR, Eva (1990): ‚Gequälter Engel'. Das Frauenbild in den pornographischen Comics ['Tortured Angel'. The Image of Women in Pornographic Comics]. In: LINHART, Ruth and Fleur WÖSS (eds.) (1990): *Nippons neue Frauen* [Nippon's New Women]. Hamburg: Rowohlt Verlag, 205–225

BAKSHI, Dwijendra Nath (1979): *Hindu Divinities in Japanese Buddhist Pantheon. A Comparative Study*. Calcutta: Benten

BARDSLEY, Jan and Hiroko HIRAKAWA (2003): Branded: Bad Girls Go Shopping. In: MILLER, Laura and Jan BARDSLEY (eds.) (2005): *Bad Girls of Japan*. New York: Palgrave, 111–125

BARTHES, Roland (1981): *Camera Lucida. Reflections on Photography*. New York: Hill and Wang

BATE, David (1993): Photography and the Colonial Vision. In: *Third Text, Vol. 7, issue 22*, 81–91

BAUDRILLARD, Jean (1998): The Finest Consumer Object: the Body. In: FRASER, Mariam and Monica GRECO (eds.) (2005): *The Body. A Reader*. London and New York: Routledge, 277–282

BAUDRILLARD, Jean (1995): *Le crime parfait* [The Perfect Crime]. Paris: Galilee

BAYER, Frauke (2009): *Mythos Ophelia* [The Myth Ophelia]. *Literatura 21*. Würzburg: Ergon

BAZIN, Andre (1967). The Ontology of the Photographic Image. In: BAZIN, Andre (1967): *What Is Cinema? Vol. 1.* Translated from the French by Hugh Gray. London: University of California Press. 9–16

BECKER, Carl B. (1990): Buddhist Views of Suicide and Euthanasia. In: *Philosophy East and West, V. 40 No. 4 (October 1990)*, 543–555

BEECH, Dave (1998): Mariko Mori. Serpentine Gallery. In: *Art Monthly, 09/98, 219*, 35–36

BELTING, Hans (2001a): Bild und Tod. Verkörperung in frühen Kulturen [Image and Death. Embodiments in Early Cultures]. In: BELTING, Hans (ed.) (2001): *Entwürfe für eine Bildwissenschaft* [Drafts for Visual Studies]. München: Fink

BELTING, Hans and Andrea BUDDENSIEG (eds.) (2009): *The Global Art World.* Ostfildern: Hatje Cantz

BELTING, Hans (2009): Contemporary Art as Global Art: A Critical Estimate. In: BELTING, Hans and Andrea BUDDENSIEG (eds.) (2009): *The Global Art World.* Ostfildern: Hatje Cantz, 38–73

BELOW, Irene and Beatrice VON BISMARCK (eds.) (2005): *Globalisierung/Hierarchisierung. Kulturelle Dominanzen in Kunst und Kunstgeschichte* [Globalisation/Hierarchization. Cultural Predominance in Art and Art History]. Marburg: Jonas

BENJAMIN, Walter (1989): *Gesammelte Schriften VI*. Frankfurt a. M.: Suhrkamp

BENL, Oscar (1966): *Die Geschichte vom Prinzen Genji. I und II. Altjapanischer Liebesroman, verfaßt von der Hofdame Murasaki* [The Tale of Prince Genji I and II. Old Japanese Love Story, Written by the Court Lady Murasaki]. Zurück: Manesse

BERGER, John (1972): *Ways of Seeing*. Harmondsworth: Penguin

BERGER, Klaus (1992): *Japonisme in Western Painting from Whistler to Matisse*. Cambridge: Cambridge University Press

BERNDT, Jacqueline (2005): Beweglich, flächig, glatt: "Japan" und "Manga" in den Arbeiten des Künstlers Murakami Takashi [Flexible, Flat, Slick: 'Japan' and 'Manga' in the Work of the artist Murakami Takashi]. In: KÖHN, Stephan and Martina SCHÖNBEIN (eds.) (2005): *Facetten der japanischen Populär- und Medienkultur 1* [Facets of Japanese Popular Culture and Media Culture 1]. Wiesbaden: Harrassowitz, 5–36

BERNDT, Jacqueline (2008): Nationally Naked? The Female Nude in Japanese Oil Painting and Posters (1890s–1920s). In: CROISSANT, Doris, Joshua S. MOSTOW and Catherine VANCEYEH (eds.) (2008): *Performing Nation: Gender Politics in Literature, Theatre and the Visual Arts in China and Japan, 1880–1940*. Leiden: Brill, 307–346

BHABHA, Homi (1994): *The Location of Culture*. London and New York: Routledge

BHIKKHU, Thanissaro (2005): *Maha-dukkhakkhandha Sutta. The Great Mass of Stress Translated from Pali*
URL: http://www.accesstoinsight.org/tipitaka/mn/mn.013.than.html (20. 08. 2008)

BIJUTSU TECHO (1989): Topics. Itte tanoshî, mite tanoshî, sankashite tanoshî [Topics. It is Fun to Go There, to See It and to Participate]. In: *Bijutsu techo, Vol. 50, Nr. 754*, 199

BLAIR, Dike (1996): Mariko Mori. Deitch Projects. In: *Flash Art, No 189, 13*, 131–132

BLOOM, Lisa (2000): Gender, Race and Nation in Japanese Contemporary Art and Criticism. In: *n. paradoxa international feminist art journal, Volume 5, 2000*, 35–43

BODHI, Bikkhu (2000): *The Connected Discourses of the Buddha. A Translation of the Samyutta Nikaaya*. Boston: Wisdom Publications

BOECKER, Susanne (2001a): Die Schönheit dient ihm als Faustpfand. Exzentrische Kunstwerke von Izima Kaoru [Beauty Is A Dead Pledge For Him. Excentric Artworks By Izima Kaoru]. In: *Kölner Stadt-Anzeiger Nr. 23, 27/28. 01. 2001*, 39

BOECKER, Susanne (2001b): Das Gefühl haben, dass das mit dem eigenen Tod schon ganz in Ordnung war im Nachhinein [To Have The Feeling That After All Your Own Death Was Not Too Bad]. In: *Kunstforum, Bd. 157, Nov.–Dez. 2001*, 213–225

BOECKER, Susanne (2004): Zeitgenössische Japanische Fotografie [Contemporary Japanese Photography]. In: *Kunstforum International, Bd. 168*, 193–247

BOEHM, Gottfried (1985): *Bildnis und Individuum. Über den Ursprung der Porträtmalerei in der italienischen Renaissance* [Image and Individual. On the Origin of Portrait Painting in the Italian Renaissance]. München: Prestel

BOEHM, Gottfried (2004): Gegenwart und Zukunft der Kunstgeschichte. Teil 3 [Presence and Future of Art History. Part 3]. In: *KAb 12 2004*, 59–62

BONNET, Anne-Marie (1997): Körper-Bild / Bild-Körper. Das Geschlecht der Kunst [Body-Image / Image-Body. Gender in Art]. In: NAGELSCHMIDT, Ilse (ed.) (1999): *Frauenforscherinnen stellen sich vor. Ringvorlesung Teil V, Sommersemester 1996, Wintersemester 1996/97* [Female Scientists Introduce Themselves. Lectures Part V, Sommer Term 1996, Winterterm 1996/1997]. Leipzig: Leipziger Universitätsverlag, 69–84

BONNET, (2004): *Kunst der Moderne. Kunst der Gegenwart. Herausforderung und Chance* [Modern Art. Contemporary Art. A Challenge and Chance]. Köln: Deubner

BONNET, Anne-Marie, Willibald SAUERLÄNDER, Victoria SCHMIDT-LINSENHOFF and Beat WYSS (2004): Gegenwart und Zukunft der Kunstgeschichte. Teil 1 [The Presence and Future of Art History. Part 1]. In: *KAb 7/8 2004*, 81–88

BORGGREEN, Gunhild (2003a): Gender in Contemporary Japanese Art. In: MOSTOW, Joshua S. and Norman BRYSON and Maribeth GRAYBILL (eds.) (2003): *Gender and Power. In the Japanese Visual Field.* Honolulu: University of Hawaii Press, 179–200

BORGGREEN, Gunhild (2003b): Cultural Clichés in Contemporary Art: The Reception of Mori Mariko's Work. In: *Review of Japanese Culture and Society, Vol. XV, Japanese Art: The Scholarship and Legacy of Chino Kaori*, 88–89

BORNOFF, Nicholas (2002): Sex and Consumerism: the Japanese State of the Arts. In: LLOYD, Fran (ed.) (2002): *Consuming Bodies. Sex and Contemporary Japanese Art.* London: Reaktion Books, 41–68

BRONFEN, Elisabeth (1992): *Over Her Dead Body: Death, Femininity and the Aesthetic.* Manchester: University Press

BRONFEN, Elisabeth (2003): *Nackte Berührung – Disfiguration und Anerkennung im weiblichen Akt* [Naked Touching – Disfiguration And Appreciation in the Female Nude].
URL: http://www.bronfen.info/index.php/archive/46-archive2003/95-Disfiguration-und-Anerkennung.html (23. 09. 2009)

BUNETTI, John (1998): Yasumasa Morimura. Deconstructing Cultural Myths. In: *nd[re]view 6*
URL: http://www.nd.edu/~ndr/issues/ndr6/morimura/morimuratxt.html (25. 04. 2006)

BRYSON, Norman (1994): Art in Context. In: BAL, Mieke and Inge E. BOER (eds.) (1994): *The Point of Theory: Practices of Cultural Analysis*. Amsterdam: Amsterdam University Press, 66–78

BRYSON, Norman (1995): Morimura: 3 Readings. In: *Art and Text, No. 52*, 74–79

BRYSON, Norman (1998): Cute Futures. Mariko Mori`s Techno-Enlightenment. In: *Parkett, No. 54, 1998/1999*, 74–80

BRYSON and Maribeth GRAYBILL (eds.) (2003): *Gender and Power. In the Japanese Visual Field*. Honolulu: University of Hawaii Press

BRYSON, Norman (2003): Westernizing Bodies: Women, Art, and Power in Meiji Yoga. In: BRYSON, Norman und Maribeth GRAYBILL und Joshua S. MOSTOW (eds.) (2003): *Gender and Power in the Japanese Visual Field*. Honolulu: University of Hawai'i Press, 89–118

BUTLER, Judith (1990): Bodily Inscriptions, Performative Subversions. In: PRICE, Janet and Margrit SHILDRICK (eds.) (1999): *Feminist Theory and the Body. A Reader*. New York: Routledge, 416–422

BUTLER, Judith (1993): *Bodies that Matter: On the Discursive Limits of 'Sex'*. New York: Routledge

BUTLER, Judith (1999): *Gender Trouble. Feminism and the Subversion of Identity*. New York and London: Routledge

CAMPELL, Clayton (1999): Miwa Yanagi. In: *Flash Art, Vol. XXXII, Number 204, jan–febr, 1999*, 88

CHAPMAN, Christine (1993): Auf dem Weg zur Gleichheit [On Their Way to Equality]. In: *Japan aktuell, Juni/Juli 1993*, 16–17

CHERRY, Kittredge (1987): *Womansword. What Japanese Words Say About Women*. Tokyo and New York: Kôdansha International

CHIBA, Shigeo (1989): Bijutsu as Genus. In: MUNROE, Alexandra (ed.) (1994): *Japanese Art After 1945: Scream Against the Sky*. New York: Harry N Abrams, 388

CHINO, Kaori (1993): Gender in Japanese Art. In: MOSTOW, Joshua S. and Norman BRYSON and Maribeth GRAYBILL (eds.) (2003): *Gender and Power. In the Japanese Visual Field*. Honolulu: University of Hawaii Press, 17–34

CHINO, Kaori (1999): Bijutsukan, bijutsushigaku no ryôiki ni miru jendâ ronsô: 1997–1998 [Gender Debates as Seen in the Realms of Museums and Art History: 1997–1998]. In: CHINO, Kaoru and Takaaki KUMAKURA (eds.) (2001): *Onna? Nihon? Bi? Aratana jendâ hihyô ni mukete* [Women? Japan? Beauty? Towards a New Gender Critique]. Tokyo: Keio Gijuku Daigaku, 117–154

CHINO, Kaori and Takaaki KUMAKURA (eds.) (2001): *Onna? Nihon? Bi? Aratana jendâ hihyô ni mukete* [Women? Japan? Beauty? Towards a New Gender Critique]. Tokyo: Keio Gijuku Daigaku

CLARK, Kenneth (1972): *The Nude. A Study in Ideal Form*. New York: Pantheon Books

CLARK, Thomas James (1978): Un realisme du corps. 'Olympia' et ses critiques en 1865 [A Realism of the Body. 'Olympia' and her Critics in 1865]. In: *Histoire et Critique des Arts, May 1978*, 139–160

CLARK, Timothy (1993): *Demon of Painting. The Art of Kawanabe Kyôsai*. London: The British Museum Press

CLARK, Timothy (1997): Mitate-e: Some Thoughts, and a Summary of Recent Writings. In: *Impressions 19, 1997*, 6–27

CLARKE, Graham (1997): *The Photograph. Oxford History of Art*. Oxford: Oxford University Press

COHEN, Michael (1997): Mariko Mori. Plastic Dreams in the Reality Bubble. In: *Flash Art No 194, May/June 1997*, 94–97

COLAPIETRO, Vincent M. and Thomas M. OLSHEWSKY (eds.) (1996): *Peirce's Doctrine of Signs. Theory, Applications, and Connections*. Berlin and New York: Mouton de Gruyter

COLEMAN, Arthur and Robert MAPPLETHORPE (ed.) (1992): *Mapplethorpe*. München: Schirmer-Mosel

CONNELL, R. W. (1995): *Masculinities*. Sydney: Allen and Unwin

CONZE, Edward (1960): *The Heart Sutra*. Digital International Buddhism Organization. URL: http://kr.buddhism.org/zen/sutras/conze.html (04. 08. 2008)

CORRIN, Lisa (1998): Mariko Mori's Quantum Nirvana. In: MORI, Mariko and Dominic MOLON (ed.) (1998): *Mariko Mori*. Chicago: Chicago Museum of Contemporary Art, 19–24

COTTON, Charlotte (2004): *The Photograph as Contemporary Art*. London: Thames and Hudson

CREIGHTON, Millie R. (1995): Imaging the Other in Japanese Advertising Campaigns. In: CARRIER, James G. (ed.) (1995): *Occidentalism. Images of the West*. Oxford: Clarendon Press, 135–160

CRIMP, Douglas (1979): Pictures. In: *October 8, 1979*, 75–88

CROISSANT, Doris and Misako WAKABAYASHI-OH (1991): *Linden bijutsukansô Baelz Collection. Nihon kaiga 2* [The Baelz Collection in the Linden Museum. Japanese Painting 2]. Tokyo: Kôdansha

CROISSANT, Doris, Joshua S. MOSTOW and Catherine VANCEYEH (eds.) (2008): *Performing Nation: Gender Politics in Literature, Theatre and the Visual Arts in China and Japan, 1880–1940*. Leiden: Brill

CROISSANT, Doris (2008): From Madonna to Femme Fatale: Gender Play in Japanese National Painting. In: CROISSANT, Doris and Joshua S. MOSTOW and Catherine Vance YEH (ed.) (2008): *Performing "Nation". Gender Politics in Literature, Theater, and the Visual Arts of China and Japan, 1880–1940*. Leiden and Boston: Brill, 265–306

DALBY, Liza (1993): *Kimono: Fashioning Culture*. Hew Haven: Yale University Press

DASGUPTA, Romit und Mark MCLELLAND (eds.) (2005): *Genders, Transgenders, and Sexualities in Japan*. New York: Routledge

DEITCH, Jeffrey (ed.): (1993): *Post Human: Neue Formen der Figuration in der zeitgenössischen Kunst*. [Post Human: New Forms of Figuration in Contemporary Art]. Feldkirchen: Oktagon

DELANK, Claudia and Philip MARCH (2002) (eds.): *Abenteuer Japanische Fotografie 1860–1890* [The Adventure of Japanese Photography 1860–1890]. Heidelberg: Kehrer

DESHIMARU-RÔSHI, Taisen (1988): *Hannya Shingyô. Das Sutra der Höchsten Wahrheit* [Hannya Shingyô. The Sutra of the Highest Truth]. Leimen: Kristkeitz

DIPIETRO, Monty (1998): Yasumasa Morimura at the Tokyo Museum of Contemporary Art. In: *AssemblyLanguage Tokyo Avant-garde Culture and Japanese Contemporary Art. Reviews.*
URL: http://www.assemblylanguage.com/reviews/Morimura.html (30. 02. 2009)

DLK COLLECTION (2009): *Izima Kaoru, New Work @ Von Lintel.* URL: http://dlkcollection.blogspot.com/2009/04/izima-kaoru-new-work-von-lintel.html (30. 04. 2009)

DOWNER, Lesley (2003): *Madame Sadayakko. The Geisha Who Bewitched the West.* New York: Gotham

DOY, Gen (2005): *Picturing the Self. Changing Views of the Subject in Visual Culture.* London and New York: I.B. Tauris

DUBOIS, Philippe (1983): *L'acte photographique* [The Photographic Act]. Paris & Bruxelles: Nathan/Labor

DUERR, Hans Peter (1992): *Nacktheit und Scham* [Nudity and Shame]. Frankfurt a. M.: Suhrkamp

DUFWA, Jacques (1981): *Winds from the East: A Study in the Art of Manet, Degas, Monet and Whistler, 1856–86.* Stockholm: Almqvist and Wiksell International

DRÜCK, Patricia (2004): *Das Bild des Menschen in der Fotografie. Die Porträts von Thomas Ruff* [The Image of the Human in Photography. Portraits By Thomas Ruff]. Berlin: Reimer

EDWARDS, Elisabeth (ed.) (1992): *Photography and Anthropology 1860–1920.* New Haven: Yale University Press

EIBLMAYR, Silvia (1993): *Die Frau als Bild: Der weibliche Körper in der Kunst des 20. Jahrhunderts* [The Woman as an Image: The Female Body in the Art of the 20th Century]. Berlin: Reimer

EICHER, Joanne B. and Mary Ellen ROACH-HIGGINS (1992): Definition and Classification of Dress. In: BARNES, Ruth and Joanne B. EICHER (eds.) (1997): *Dress and Gender. Making and Meaning*. Oxford: Berg, 8–28

ELIAS, Norbert (1969a): *Über den Prozeß der Zivilisation. Band* 1 [The Civilizing Process. Volume 1]. Bern: Francke

ELIAS, Norbert (1969b): *Über den Prozeß der Zivilisation. Band* 2 [The Civilizing Process. Volume 2]. Bern: Francke

ELIEL, Carol S. (1998): Interpreting Tradition: Mori's Nirvana. In: MOLON, Dominic and Mariko MORI (ed.) (1998): *Mariko Mori*. Chicago: Chicago Museum of Modern Art, 27–32

ELKINS, James (ed.) (2007): *Is Art History Global?* New York and London: Routledge

EVANS, Caroline (2003): *Fashion at the Edge. Spectacle, Modernity and Deathliness.* New Haven and London: Yale University Press

FEHER, Michel with Ramona NADDAFF and TAZI, Nadia (eds.) (1989): *Fragments for a History of the Human Body. Vol. 1–3.* New York: Zone

FINKH, Gerhard (ed.) (2001): *Manabu Yamanaka. Museum Morsbroich Leverkusen 27. 3.–6. 5. 2001.* Leverkusen: Museum Morsbroich

FOLIE, Sabine and Michael GLASMEIER (eds.) (2002): *Tableaux vivants. Lebende Bilder und Attitüden in Fotografie, Film und Video* [Tableaux Vivants. Living Images and Attitudes in Photography, Film and Video]. Vienna: Kunsthalle Wien

FOREMAN, Kelly (2003): Bad Girls Confined: Okuni, Geisha, and the Negotiation of Female Performance Space. In: MILLER, Laura and Jan BARDSLEY (eds.) (2005): *Bad Girls of Japan.* New York: Palgrave, 33–47

FORMANEK, Susanne (2005): *Die "böse Alte" in der japanischen Populärkultur der Edo-Zeit* [The 'Evil Old Woman' in the Japanese Popular Culture of the Edo Period]. Wien: Österreichische Akademie der Wissenschaften

FOUCAULT, Michel (1978): *The History of Sexuality, Vol I: An Introduction.* Translated from the French by R. Hurley. Harmondsworth: Penguin

FOUCAULT, Michel (1991): *Discipline and Punish. The Birth of the Prison.* Translated from the French by Alan Sheridan. London: Penguin Books

FRITSCH, Ingrid (2000): Distanz, Aura, Differenz. "Zwischenräume" der japanischen Kultur [Distance, Aura, Difference. The 'In-between' in Japanese Culture]. In: *Universitas, Februar 2000, 644*, 167–176

FRITSCH, Lena (2008): *Yasumasa Morimura's Self-portrait as Actress. Überlegungen zur Identität* [Thoughts on Identity]. Saarbrücken: VDM

FRÜHSTÜCK, Sabine (1997): Fragmente zum Studium des japanischen Körpers I: Das Gesicht [Fragments on the Study of the Japanese Body I: The Face]. In: *Minikomi 1/1997*, 15–19

FUKAGAWA, Masafumi (1993): Den Modernismus durchqueren [Crossing Modernism]. In: KUNSTHAUS ZÜRICH (ed.) (1993): *In die Felsen bohren sich Zikadenstimmen* [Cicada Voices Boring Into Rocks]. Zürich: Kunsthaus Zürich, 13–22

FUKAGAWA, Masafumi (2007): *Hikari no Purojekuto* [A Project of Light]. Tokyo: Seikyûsha

FUSE, Hideto (1991): Art of Arts. Man Among Men. Morimura Yasumasa. In: *Taiyô, Nr. 357*, 159–165

FUSE, Hideyoshi (1999): Bi no hyôhonshitsu [A Preparation Room For Art]. In: *Mainichi shinbun (Tokyo), 06. 08. 1999, Evening Edition*, 10

FRIZOT, Michel (ed.) (1998): *Neue Geschichte der Fotografie* [New History of Photography]. Köln: Könemann

GEIMER, Peter (ed.) (2002): *Ordnungen der Sichtbarkeit. Fotografie in Wissenschaft, Kunst und Technologie* [Organisations of Visibility. Photography in Science, Art and Technology]. Frankfurt a. M.: Suhrkamp

GETREUER-KARGL, Ingrid (2001): Sich einen schönen Körper geben. Überlegungen zur sozialwissenschaftlichen Körperforschung [To Get a Beautiful Body. Thoughts on Sociological Body Research]. In: *Minikomi Nr. 62, 04. 2001*, 5–12

GIACOMUZZI, Renate (2000): Wo die Kulturen sich nähern, trennen sich die Geschlechter: Interkulturalität und Geschlechterdifferenz am Beispiel westlicher Japanliteratur [When Cultures Approach Each Other, Gender Separates Them: Interculture and Gender Difference Using the Example of Western Literature on Japan]. In: ARIIZUMI, Yasuo and Kenchi ONO and Karl Anton SPRENGARD (eds.) (2002): *Deutschland und Japan im 20. Jahrhundert. Wechselbeziehungen zweier Kulturnationen* [Germany and Japan in the 20th Century. Mutual Relationships Between Two Nations of Culture]. Wiesbaden: Harrassowitz, 163–173

GODZIK, Maren (2007): *Avantgarde Männersache? Künstlerinnen im Japan der 50er und 60er Jahre des 20. Jahrhunderts* [Avantgarde For Men? Female Artists in Japan in the 50's and 60's of the 20th Century]. München: Iudicium

GOLDSTEIN-GIDONI, Ofra (1999): Kimono and the Construction of Gendered and Cultural Identities. In: *Ethnology, Vol. 38, No. 4, Fall 1999*, 351–370

GONZALEZ-FOERSTER, Hans Ullrich OBRIST and Miwa YANAGI (2003): Interview. In: DEUTSCHE BANK (ed.) (2004): *Miwa Yanagi. Sammlung Deutsche Bank.* Ostfildern-Ruit: Hatje Cantz, 40–53

GOTO, Shigeo (2002): *Miwa Yanagi: My Grandmothers*. Kyoto: Art Beat Publishers

GRIFFIN, Tim (2001): Izima Kaoru. Traffic Accident. In: *Artext, No 74, August–October 2001*, 30–32

GROOS, Arthur (1999): Cio-Cio-San and Sadayakko. Japanese Music-Theater in Madama Butterfly. In: *Monumenta Nipponica, Vol.54, no.1*, 41–73

GROSZ, Elisabeth (1994): *Volatile Bodies. Towards a Corporeal Feminism*. London: Routledge

GROSZ, Elisabeth (1995): Bodies – Cities. In: PRICE, Janet and Margrit SHILDRICK (eds.) (1999): *Feminist Theory and the Body. A Reader*. New York: Routledge, 381–387

GUMPERT, Lynn (1996): Glamour girls. In: *Art in America 84.7,* 62–65

GUNJI, Pegio-Yukio (1998): Mumokuteki na nôdôsei [Senseless Activiy]. In: KAWAI, Hayao and Shinichi NAKAZAWA (1998): *Genda inihon bunkaron 1. watakushi to wa nanika* [Studies on Contemporary Japanese Culture I. On the Self.]. Tokyo: Iwanamishoten, 171–222

HAMMOND, Anna (2001): Manabu Yamanaka at Stefan Stux. In: *Art in America, May 2001*
URL: http:// www.findarticles.com/p/articles/mi_m1248/is_5_89/ai_74439429 (13. 08. 2009)

HANDELSBLATT (2007): Demografie trifft Japan mit Wucht [Demography Hits Japan]. In: *Handelsblatt, 20. 08. 2007*
URL: http://www.handelsblatt.com/politik/international/demografie-trifft-japan-mit-wucht;1311166 (01. 06. 2010)

HANDY, Ellen (1998): Japonisme and American Postcard Visions of Japan. In: GEARY, Christraud and Virginia-Lee WEBB (eds.) (1998): *Delivering Views: Distant Cultures in Early Postcards*. Washington and London: Smithsonian Institute, 91–113

HASEGAWA, Yûko (1997): Pachinko, Mandala and Merry Amnesia. In: NOEVER, Peter (ed.): *Japan today. Kunst, Fotografie, Design*. Wien: MAK, 16–21

HASEGAWA, Yûko (2001): Doshi, Arakan, Gyahtei and Fujohkan. In: FINKH, G. (ed.) (2001): *Manabu Yamanaka. Museum Morsbroich Leverkusen 27. 3. – 6. 5. 2001*. Leverkusen: Museum Morsbroich, 4–5

HASEGAWA, Yûko (2002): Post-identity Kawaii: Commerce, Gender and Contemporary Art. In: LLOYD, Fran (eds.) (2002): *Consuming Bodies. Sex and Contemporary Japanese Art*. London: Reaktion Books Ltd, 127–141

HASEGAWA, Yûko (2008): Landscapes With A Corpse. In: HATJE CANTZ (2008): *IZIMA KAORU. Landscapes With A Corpse*. Ostfildern Ruit: Hatje Cantz, 14–19

HEISER, Jörg (2010): What is 'Super-Hybridity'? In: *Frieze, issue 133, September 2010*, 13

HENDRY, Joy (ed.) (1990): *Unwrapping Japan*. Honolulu: University of Hawaii Press

HENDRY, Joy (ed.) (1993): *Wrapping Culture: Politeness, Presentation, and Power in Japan and Other Societies*. Oxford: Oxford University Press

HENNING, Michelle (2004): The Subject As Object. Photography and the Human Body. In: WELLS, Liz (ed.) (2009): *Photography: A Critical Introduction. Third Edition*. London and New York: Routledge, 159–192

HEROLD, Thea (06/1999): Nirwana ist auch nur ein Foto. Jetzt auch im deutschen Entwicklungsland: Die Techno-Schamanin Mariko Mori [Even Nirvana is Just a Photo. Now in the German Developing Nation: the Techno-shaman Mariko Mori]. In: *Zeit Online 06/1999*
URL: http://www.zeit.de/1999/06/199906.mori_.xml (20. 05. 2008)

HIGA, Karin (1996): Some Thoughts on National and Cultural Identity. Art Contemporary Japanese and Japanese American Artists. In: *Art Journal, Vol. 55, Fall 1996*, 6–7

HIROTA, Dennis (ed.) (1995): *Wind in the Pines: Classic Writings of the Way of Tea as a Buddhist Path*. Fremont: Asian Humanities Press

HOFFA, Susan (2000): Persuasive Images. Speaking in Tongues. Addressing Questions of Identity in the University Art Collection. In: *University at Albany, University Art Museum, Past Exhibitions*
URL: http://www.albany.edu/museum/wwwmuseum/persuasive/js/TONGUES.html (25. 04. 2006)

HOFFMANN, Justin (2003): Der Tod trägt Designermode. “Terror Chick” und “Viertes Reich”: provozierende Kunst in vier Galerien [Death Wears Designer Clothes. “Terror Chic” and “Fourth Reich” Provoking Art in Four Galleries]. In: *Süddeutsche Zeitung, 23. 09. 2003*

HOFFMANN, Yoel (1986): *Japanese Death Poems. Written by Zen Monks and Haiku Poets on the Verge of Death.* Tokyo, Rutland, Vermont and Singapore: Tuttle Publishing

HORNY, Tinga (2000): Fotoausstellung in Münchner Galerien. Die Anziehungskraft des Exotischen [Photography Exhibition in Galleries in Munich. The Attraction Of The Exotic]. In: *Kunstmarkt, Nr. 40, 25./26. 02. 2000*, 57

HUBER, Jörg (1996): Vorwort [Preface]. In: BRONFEN, Elisabeth and Jörg HUBER and Alois Martin MÜLLER (eds.) (1996): *Die Wiederkehr des Anderen* [The Return of the Other]. Basel/Frankfurt a. M.: Stroemfeld, 7–16

IIDA, Shihoko (2008): Contemporary Trace Elements. In: TOKYO OPERA CITY ART GALLERY (ed.) (2008): *Trace Elements. Spirit and Memory in Japanese and Australian Photomedia*. Tokyo: Hakkôbijutsu, 36–44

IIDA, Yumiko (2002): *Rethinking Identity in Modern Japan. Nationalism as Aesthetics*. London and New York: Routledge

IKEDA, Shinobu (2002): Zeichen der Unterscheidung von „Selbst" und „Anderen". Darstellungen der Haut in der japanischen Malerei [Signs of Difference Between 'Self' and 'Others'. Images of Skin in Japanese Paintings] Translated from the Japanese by Alexander Hofmann. In: GEISSMAR-BRANDI, Christoph, Irmela HIJIYA-KIRSCHNEREIT und Sato NAOKI (eds.): *Gesichter der Haut* [Faces of the Skin]. Frankfurt a. M. und Basel: Stroemfeld, 77–91

IKEDA, Shinobu (2003): The Image of Women in Battle Scenes: "Sexually" Imprinted Bodies. In: BRYSON, Norman, Joshua S. MOSTOW und Maribeth GRAYBILL (eds.) (2003): *Gender and Power in the Japanese Visual Field*. Honolulu: University of Hawai'i Press, 35–48

IIZAWA, Kôtarô (1992): *Nihon shashinshi wo aruku* [Walking Through the History of Japanese Photography]. Tokyo: Shinchôsha

IIZAWA, Kôtarô (1994): The Shock of the Real. Early Photography in Japan. In: STEARNS, Robert (ed.) (1994): *Photography and Beyond in Japan. Space, Time and Memory*. Tokyo: Hara Museum of Contemporary Art, 37–49

INAGA, Shigemi (1999): To Kitahara, Megumi Reading Art Activism #22. Letters to Editor section. In: *Impaction 112, 1999*, 170–173

ISHIUCHI, Miyako (1995): *Sawaru Chromosome XY*. Tokyo: Shinchôsha

ISHIUCHI, Miyako (2005): *SCARS*. Tokyo: Sôkyusha

ISHIUCHI, Miyako and MEGURO ART MUSEUM (eds.) (2008): *Hiroshima Yokosuka. Ishiuchi Miyako*. Tokyo: Meguro Art Museum

IZIMA, Kaoru (1992): *Izima Kaoru Shashinshû – Kaoru Izima Color Photographs*. Tokyo: Kôrinsha

IZIMA, Kaoru (1994): *Hairmode*. Tokyo:

IZIMA, Kaoru (1995): *New Beauty II. Colored Beauty*. Tokyo: Kôrinsha Press

IZIMA, Kaoru (1999): Sin Renzoku Zyoyû satuzin ziken 1. Otsuka Nene no Sitai, Tiba no akiya de hakken. Kite ita no wa Tuzigahana no kosode [New Case of the Actress-

Murder-Series. 1. Otsuka Nene's Corpse Found in Akiya in Chiba. She Was Wearing a Tuzigahana Kosode-Kimono]. In: *zyappu, 21, 1999*, 18–21

IZIMA, Kaoru (2001*): Landscapes With a Corpse 1999–2000*. Friedrichshafen: Gessler

IZIMA, Kaoru (2003): *Neru Matsuyuki Yasuko* [Sleeping Matsuyuki Yasuko]. Tokyo: Asahi Press

JAPAN PHOTOGRAPHIC SOCIETY (2009): *Kai no ayumi, katsudô* [The Development and Activities of the Club]
URL: http://www.jp-photo.gr.jp/history/index.html (23. 03. 2009)

JARMAN, Francis (1998): *The Perception of Asia. Japan and the West. Hildesheimer Universitätsschriften Bd. 5*. Hildesheim: Universität Hildesheim

JMPA (2009): *Magajin dêta* [Magazine Data].
URL: http://www.j-magazine.or.jp/data_001/commonness_3.html (25. 03. 2009)

JOLLY, Margaret (1997): From Point Venus to Bali Ha'i: Eroticism and Exoticism in Representations of the Pacific. In: MANDERSON, Lenore and Margaret JOLLY (eds.) (1997): *Sites of Desire, Economies of Pleasure*. Chicago and London: The University of Chicago Press

JONES, Amelia (1998): *Body Art. Performing the Subject*. London and Minneapolis: University of Minnesota Press

JUGAKU, Akiko (1990): *Nihongo to onna* [Japanese and Women]. Tokyo: Iwanamishoten

KANDA, Fusae (2005): Behind the Sensationalism: Images of a Decaying Corpse in Japanese Buddhist Art. In: *The Art Bulletin, 2005, 87*, 24–49

KANO, Ayako (2003): Women? Japan? Art?: Chino Kaori and the Feminist Art History Debate. In: *Review of Japanese Culture and Society, Vol XV, December 2003*, 25–38

KASAHARA, Michiko (1998a): Shôzô (Futago) [The Portrait (Twins)]. In: KOBAYASHI, Yasuo und Akira TATEHATA (eds.): *Gendaiâtonyûmon: Ima ni deau yorokobi* [The Introduction of Contemporary Art: The Joy of Encountering the Present]. Tokyo: Heibonsha, 212–223

KASAHARA, Michiko (1998b): Love's Body – Rethinking Naked and Nude in Photography (translated by Gavin Frew). In: TOKYO METROPOLITAN MUSEUM OF PHOTOGRAPHY (ed.) (1998): *Love's Body – Rethinking Naked and Nude in Photography*. Tokyo: Tokyo Metropolitan Museum of Photography, 185–194

KASAHARA, Michiko (1998c): *Nûdo no poritikkusu. Josei shashinka no shigoto* [Politics of the Nude. The Work of Female Photographers]. Tokyo: Chikumashobô

KASAHARA, Michiko (1999): Ishiuchi Miyako – hifu no kioku [The Memory of Skin]. In: KASAHARA, Michiko (2002): *Shashin, jidai ni kô suru mono* [Photography, Something Which Resists History]. Tokyo: Seikyûsha, 305–310

KASAHARA, Michiko (2001): Kiss in the Dark: Contemporary Japanese Photography. In: TOKYO METROPOLITAN MUSEUM OF PHOTOGRAPHY (ed.) (2001): *Kiss in the Dark: Contemporary Japanese Photography.* Tokyo: Tokyo Metropolitan Museum of Photography, iii–xi

KASAHARA, Michiko (2002): *Shashin, jidai ni kô suru mono* [Photography, Something Which Resists History]. Tokyo: Seikyûsha

KASAHARA, Michiko (2005): Ishiuchi Miyako: Traces of the Future. In: THE JAPAN FOUNDATION (ed.) (2005): *Ishiuchi Miyako Mother's 2000–2005: Traces Of The Future.* Tokyo: Tankôsha, 122–133

KASAHARA, Michiko (2007): Contemporary Japanese Women's Self-Awareness. In: REILLY, Maura and Linda NOCHLIN (ed.) (2007): *Global Feminisms. New Directions in Contemporary Art.* London and New York: Merrell, 97–105

KASAHARA, Michiko (2008): On Your Body: Contemporary Japanese Artists. In: TOKYO METROPOLITAN MUSEUM OF PHOTOGRAPHY (ed.) (2008): *On Your Body: Contemporary Japanese Photography.* Tokyo: Tokyo Metropolitan Museum of Photography, 139–143

KAWAI, Hayao (1997): Owari ni. Kazoku no mirai [End. The Future of the Family]. In: ÔBA, Minako and Hayao KAWAI (eds.) (1997): *Gendainihon bunkaron. Kazoku to sei.* [Studies on Contemporary Japanese Culture. Family and Gender]. Tokyo: Iwanamishoten, 231–25

KAWAI, Hayao (1998): Owari ni. 'watashi' sagashi [End. Searching For the 'Self']. In: KAWAI, Hayao and Shinichi NAKAZAWA (1998): *Gendainihon bunkaron 1. watakushi to wa nanika* [Studies on Contemporary Japanese Culture I. On the Self.]. Tokyo: Iwanamishoten, 252–274

KEELAN, Siumee Helen (2001): Paradox in a Postmodern Paradise. In: LLOYD, Fran und Melanie ROBERTS (eds.) (2001): *Sex and Consumerism. Contemporary Art in Japan.* Brighton: University of Brighton, 57–97

KEMP, Wolfgang, Huber LOCHER, and Regine PRANGE (2004): Gegenwart und Zukunft der Kunstgeschichte. Teil 2 [The Presence and Future of Art History. Part 2]. In: *KAB 9 2004*, 55–60

KEMP, Wolfgang and Hubertus von AMELUNXEN (eds.) (2006): Die komplette Theorie der Fotografie in einem Band [The Complete Theory of Photography in One Volume]. München: Schirmer/Mosel

KENT, Rachel (2002): Futurescape. The Surreal Vision of Miwa Yanagi. In: *Art AsiaPacific, 35, 2002*, 50–57

KIMURA, Shôshû (ed.) (1987): *Nihon butsuzô zuki* [Encyclopaedia of Japanese Buddhist Images]. Tokyo: Kokushokankôkai

KIMURA, Bin (1995): *Zwischen Mensch und Mensch. Strukturen japanischer Subjektivität* [Between One Human and Another. Structures Of Japanese Subjectivity]. Darmstadt: Wissenschaftliche Buchgesellschaft

KINDLER, Simone (2004): *Ophelia – Der Wandel vom Frauenbild und Bildmotiv* [Ophelia –Variations of the Image of a Woman and a Motif]. Berlin: Reimer

KING, Margery (1998): Mori Pop. In: MORI, Mariko and Dominic MOLON (eds.) (1998): *Mariko Mori*. Chicago: Chicago Museum of Contemporary Art, 33–40

KINSELLA, Sharon (1995): Cuties in Japan. In: SKOV and MOERAN (eds.) (1995): *Women, Media, Consumption*. Honolulu: University of Hawaii Press, 222–228

KISHIMOTO, Yasushi (1996): *Go on the Stage Morimura. Morimura Yasumasa 1985–1996. Slide Show Self-portrait as Actress.* (Documentary DVD) Kyoto: Ufer! Art Documentary

KITAHARA, Megumi (1998): The Debate around 'Just Only': Gender Difference in the Japanese Art World from 1997–1998. In: *Impaction 110, 1998*, 96–107

KITAZAWA, Noriaki (2003): *'Nihonga' no ten'i* [The Shift of 'Nihonga']. Tokyo: Brücke

KITAZAWA, Noriaki (2005): *Kyôkai no bijutsushi* [An Art History of Borders]. Tokyo: Brücke

KLEIBER, Karina (1990): Geishas und andere Frauen. Stereotype in der deutschsprachigen Japanliteratur nach 1945 [Geisha and Other Women: Stereotypes in the German Literature on Japan After 1945]. In: LINHART, Ruth and Fleur WÖSS (eds.) (1990): *Nippons neue Frauen* [Nippon's New Women]. Hamburg: Rowohlt, 44–53

KÔGEI TOKYO POLYTECHNIC UNIVERSITY (2009): *History*.
URL: http://www.t-kougei.ac.jp/e/about/history.html (26. 03. 2009)

KOKATSU, Reiko and KAGAWA, Mayumi (eds.) (2007): *Kioku no kômoku wo taguru. Âto to genda wo meguru taiwa* [Pulling in the Web of Memory. Conversations on Art and Gender]. Tokyo: Saikisha

KONDO, Dorinne K. (1990): *Crafting Selves. Power, Gender, and Discourses of Identity in a Japanese Workplace*. Chicago: University of Chicago Press

KRELL, Alan (1996): *Manet and the Painters of Contemporary Life*. London: Thames and Hudson

KUDÔ, Megumi (2003): 'Hakujin' imêji no tairyôshôhi [The Mass Consumption of the 'Whites' Image]. In: IMAGE AND GENDER KENKYÛKAI (ed.) (2003): *Image and Gender Vol. 4, 12. 2003*, 56–70

KÜHNE, Ariane (1998): Gesellschaft. Japans schöne Männer [Society. Japan's Beautiful Men]. In: *Japan Magazin, 2/ 99, 29. 01. 1998*, 20–26

KUMAGAI, Isako (1995): The Last Ten Years of Contemporary Japanese Art. In: MUSEUM OF CONTEMPORARY ART TOKYO (1995): *Nihon no Gendaibijutsu 1985–1995* [Japanese Contemporary Art 1985–1995]. Tokyo: Museum of Contemporary Art, 35–39

KUNSTFORUM (ed.) (2001): Fotografie. Mörderische Phantasien [Photography. Murderous Fantasies]. In: *Kunstforum, 165, Jan/Feb 2001*, 211

KURAHASHI, Shigefumi and Haruo ÔTSUKA (1997): *Geijutsu shakaigaku josetsu* [Introduction to Art Sociology]. Kyoto: Kôyô Shobô

KURIYAMA, Shigehisa (2000) (ed.): *The Imagination of the Body and the History of Bodily Experience. International Symposium*. Kyoto: International Research Centre for Japanese Studies

LAFLEUR, William R. (1998): Body. In: TAYLOR, C. Mark (ed.) (1998): *Critical Terms for Religious Studies*. Chicago and London: The University of Chicago Press, 36–54

LEACH, Mark Richard (1994): Origins? Quotations? Translations? A Westerner's Meditations on Contemporary Japanese Photography. In: THE LIGHT FACTORY PHOTOGRAPHIC ARTS CENTER (ed.) (1994): *Inside Out. Contemporary Japanese Photography*. Charlotte: The Light Factory Photographic Arts Center

LEUPP, Gary P. (1995): *Male Colours. The Construction of Homosexuality in Tokugawa Japan*. Los Angeles and London: University of California Press

LEVY, Dana and Frank B. GIBNEY and Lea SNEIDER (1983): *Kanban Shop. Signs of Japan*. New York and Tokyo: Weatherhill

LEW, Christopher Y. (2005): All About My Mother. Miyako Ishiuchi. In: *Art AsiaPacific, 45, 2005*, 52–55

LIFE MAGAZINE (1947): Picture of the Week. In: *Life Magazine, 12. 05. 1947*, 42–43

LINHART, Sepp (1999): Warum sind die erotischen Holzschnitte Japans zum Lachen [Why are the Erotic Woodprints of Japan Funny]? In: EDER, Franx (ed.) (1999): *Neue Geschichten der Sexualität* [New Histories of Sexuality]. Wien: Turia und Kant, 117–143

LINHART, Sepp (2000): *Okina kara ijiwaru obâsan e. Nihon ni okeru rôjin no shakaishi* [From the Old Man to the Nasty Old Woman. The History of Old People in Japan's Society]. In: MIYATA, Noboru and Takanori SHINTANI (eds.) (2000): *Ôjôkô. Nihonjin no sei, rô, shi* [Thoughts on Death/A Peaceful Passing. The Japanese' Live, Age, Death]. Tokyo: Shôgakukan, 67–80

LINHART, Sepp (2007). The Western Discovery of Nudity in Japan and its Disappearance. In: MURAKAMI-GIROUX, Sakae (ed.) (2007): *Actes du troisième Colloque d'Etudes Japonaises de L'Université Marc Bloch. La rencontre du Japan et de l'Europe* [The Encounter of Japan and Europe]. Aurillac: Colloque d'Etudes Japonaises

LLOYD, Fran (2001): Foreword. In: LLOYD, Fran und Melanie ROBERTS (eds.): *Sex and Consumerism. Contemporary Art in Japan*. Brighton: University of Brighton, 11–15

LLOYD, Fran (2002): Introduction: Critical Reflections. In: LLOYD, Fran (ed.) (2002): *Consuming Bodies. Sex and Contemporary Japanese Art*. London: Reaktion Books, 8–21

LO, Jeannie (1990): *Office Ladies/Factory Women: Life and Work at a Japanese Company*. New York: M.E. Sharpe

LOKE, Margarett (2000): Photography Review; Moments of Ravaging Time. In: *New York Times, 19. 05. 2000*
URL: http://query.nytimes.com/gst/fullpage.html (21. 08. 2008)

LONG, John Luther (1905): *Madame Butterfly. Purpe Eyes. A Gentleman of Japan and a Lady. Kito Glory*. London: Methuen & Co

LOTI, Pierre (n. y.): *Madame Chrysanthème*. Paris: Calmann-Lévy

LUHMANN, Niklas (2002): *Einführung in die Systemtheorie* [Introduction to the System Theory]. Darmstadt: Wissenschaftliche Buchgesellschaft

LUNSING, Wim (2003): What Masculinity? Transgender Practices among Japanese 'Men'. In: ROBERSON, James E. und Nobue SUZUKI (eds.) (2003): *Men and Masculinities in Contemporary Japan: Dislocating the Salaryman Doxa*. London und New York: Routledge, 20–36

LURY, Celia (1996): *Consumer Culture*. New Brunswick: Rutgers University Press

LYE, Colleen (1995): *M. Butterfly* and the Rhetoric of Antiessentialism. Minority Discourse in an International Frame. In: PALUMBO-LIU, David (ed.) (1995): *The Ethnic Canon. Histories, Institutions, and Interventions.* Minneapolis und London: University of Minnesota Press, 260–289

LYNE, Sandra (2002): Consuming Madame Chrysantheme: Loti's Dolls to Shanghai Baby. In: *Intersections (2002), issue 8*, unnumbered
URL: http://intersections.anu.edu.au/issue8/lyne.html (23. 09. 2009)

LYOTARD, Jean-François (1979). *La condition postmoderne: rapport sur le savoir.* Paris: Minuit

MACKIE, Vera (2005): "Understanding Through the Body": the Masquerades of Mishima Yukio and Morimura Yasumasa. In: MCLLELAND, Mark und Romit DASGUPTA (eds.) (2005): *Genders, Transgenders and Sexualities in Japan*. London and New York: Routledge, 126–144

MAE, Michiko (2001): Japans Frauenbewegungen: Frauen kämpfen um ihre Rechte [Japan's Women's Movement: Women Fighting for their Rights]. In: *Japan Magazin, 07/01*, 6–9

MANEKI NEKO CLUB (n. y.): *History of Maneki Neko*.
URL: http://www.amy.hi-ho.ne.jp/ ~mono93/cat/english/index_e.html (28. 06. 2005)

MASUDA, Rie (1999): The Texture of Time – Photographic Works by Miyako Ishiuchi. In: NATIONAL MUSEUM OF MODERN ART TOKYO (1999): *Miyako Ishiuchi: Time Textured in Monochrome.* Tokyo: National Museum of Modern Art Tokyo, 98–102

MATT, Gerhard und Peter WEIERMAIR (eds.) (1997): *Japanische Photographie. Lust und Leere.* [Japanese Photography. The Desire and the Void]. Wien: Edition Stemmle

MCARTHUR, Meher (2004): *Reading Buddhist Art: An Illustrated Guide to Buddhist Signs and Symbols*. London: Thames & Hudson

MCNEILL, David (2005): Drop-dead gorgeous. In: The Japan Times Online, 10. 04. 2005, unnumbered
URL: http://search.japantimes.co.jp/print/fl20050410x1.html (10. 05. 2008)

MCVEIGH, Brian J. (2000): *Wearing Ideology. State, Schooling and Self-Presentation in Japan*. Oxford and New York: Berg

MEZUR, Katharine (2005): *Beautiful Boys/Outlaw Bodies. Describing Kabuki Female-Likeness*. New York: Palgrave

MIESSGANG, Thomas (2006): Marilyn Monroe. In: KUNSTHALLE WIEN and BA-CA KUNSTFORUM (eds.): *Superstars. Das Prinzip Prominenz von Warhol bis Madonna* [Superstars. The Phenomenon of Fame from Warhol to Madonna]. Ostfildern-Ruit: Hatje Cantz, 124–145

MIKI, Sumito (1988): *Hôjôki* [An Account From My Hut] *Hosshinshû* [Collection of Tales of Religious Awakening]. Tokyo: Shinchôsha

MILLER, Laura (2003): Male Beauty Work in Japan. In: ROBERSON, James E. und Nobue SUZUKI (eds.) (2003): *Men and Masculinities in Contemporary Japan: Dislocating the Salaryman Doxa*. London und New York: Routledge, 37–58

MILLER, Laura and Jan BARDSLEY (eds.) (2005): *Bad Girls of Japan*. New York: Palgrave

MILLER, Laura (2006): *Beauty Up. Exploring Contemporary Japanese Body Aesthetics*. Berkeley, Los Angeles and London: University of California Press

MITA, Haruo (1994): Morimura Yasumasa – Renburando no heyaten. Kowareyuku jiga wo yûmoresu ni [Morimura Yasumasa – The Exhibition Rembrandt's Room. Don't Take the Breaking Down of the Ego Too Seriously]. In: *Mainichi shinbun (Tokyo), 26. 09. 1994, Evening Edition*, 6

MITCHELL, W. J. T. (1992): *The Reconfigured Eye: Visual Truth in the Post-photographic Era*. Cambridge: The MIT Press

MITCHELL, W. J. T. (2003): Interdisziplinarität und visuelle Kultur [Interdisciplinarity and Visual Culture]. In: WOLF, Herta (ed.) (2003): *Diskurse der Fotografie. Fotokritik am Ende des fotografischen Zeitalters* [Discourses of Photography. Photography Critique at the End of the Photographic Era]. Frankfurt a. M.: Suhrkamp, 38–50

MOLON, Dominic (1999): Countdown to Ecstasy. In: MORI, Mariko (ed.) (1999): *Esoteric Cosmos*. Ostfilden Ruit: Cantz, 15–28

MORGAN, Rober C. (1996): Le statut du kitsch [The Status of Kitsch]. In: *Art Press 217, 1996*, 27–33

MORI, Mariko und Dominic MOLON (eds.) (1998): *Mariko Mori*. Chicago: Museum of Contemporary Art

MORIMURA, Yasumasa und Noriyuki TANAKA (1994): *Kisekae ningen dai ichi gô* [The The Paper Human Number One]. Tokyo: Shôgakkan

MORIMURA, Yasumasa (1998): *Geijutsuka M no dekiru made* [Before the Artist M Functioned]. Tokyo: Chikumashobô

MORIMURA, Yasumasa (2000): *Kûsô shûgiteki geijutsuka sengen* [The Artist's Imaginative Manifesto]. Tokyo: Iwanamishoten

MORIMURA, Yasumasa (2001a): *Bijutsu no kaibôgaku kôgi* [Lectures On the Anatomy of Art]. Tokyo: Chikumashobô

MORIMURA, Yasumasa (2001b): *Joyûka M no monogatari – A Story of M's Self-portraits.* Tokyo: Asahishinbunsha

MORIMURA, Yasumasa (2001c): *Mâ, eegana' no kokoro* [The 'Well, it'll be fine' – Mindset]. Tokyo: Tankôsha

MORIMURA, Yasumasa (2001d): Onna? Nihon? Bi? Nôto [Women? Japan? Beauty? Some Notes]. In: KUMAKURA, Takaaki und Kaori CHINO (eds.) (2001): *Onna? Nihon? Bi? Aratana jenda hihyô ni mukete* [Women? Japan? Beauty? Towards a New Gender-critique] Tokyo: Keio Gijuku Daigaku Shuppankai, 243–263

MORIMURA, Yasumasa (2002): *Joyûka M engi no hanamichi* [The Play Of the Actress M on the *hanamichi*]. Tokyo: Shôbunsha

MORIMURA, Yasumasa (2003a): *Daughter of Art History*. New York: Aperture

MORIMURA, Yasumasa (2003b): *Kawarime kô. Geijutsuka M no shakaikengaku* [Thoughts On Transitions. Sociological Research of the Artist M]. Tokyo: Shôbunsha

MORIMURA, Yasumasa (2005): *Toki wo kakeru bijutsu. Geijutsuka M no kûsô gyareri* [Art over Time. The Artist M's Phantasy Gallery]. Tokyo: Kôbunsha

MOSTOW, Joshua (2003a): Introduction. In: MOSTOW, Joshua S. and Norman BRYSON and Maribeth GRAYBILL (eds.) (2003): *Gender and Power. In the Japanese Visual Field*. Honolulu: University of Hawaii Press, 1–15

MOSTOW, Joshua A. (2003b): Gender of *Wakashu* and the Grammar of Desire. In: BRYSON, Norman, Joshua S. MOSTOW und Maribeth GRAYBILL (eds.) (2003): *Gender and Power in the Japanese Visual Field*. Honolulu: University of Hawai'i Press, 49–70

MOSTOW, Joshua S. (2008): Utagawa Shunga, Kuki's Chic' and the Construction of a National Erotics in Japan. In: CROISSANT, Doris and Joshua S. MOSTOW and Catherine Vance YEH (eds.) (2008): *Performing "Nation". Gender Politics in Literature, Theater, and the Visual Arts of China and Japan, 1880–1940*. Leiden and Boston: Brill, 383–424

MUSEUM OF CONTEMPORARY ART TOKYO (ed.) (2002): *Mariko Mori Pure Land*. Tokyo: Museum of Contemporary Art Tokyo

NAJAMABADI, Afsaneh (2006): Beyond the Americas. Are Gender and Sexuality Useful Categories of Historical Analysis? In: *Journal of Women's History, Spring 2006, Vol. 18, No 1*, 11–21

NAKAJIMA, Masatoshi and Reiko TOMII (1994): Readings in Japanese Art after 1945. Translated by Reiko Tomii. In: MUNROE, Alexandra (ed.) (1994): *Japanese Art After 1945: Scream Against the Sky*. New York: Harry N Abrams, 369–391

NANJÔ, Fumio (1991): After Word. Nature and Culture in Japan. In: TATE GALLERY LIVERPOOL and THE JAPAN FOUNDATION (eds.) (1991): *A Cabinet of Signs. Contemporary Art from Post-Modern Japan*. Liverpool: Tate Gallery, 13

NAPIER, Susan (1998): Vampires, Psychic Girls, Flying Women and Sailor Scouts: Four Faces of the Young Female in Japanese Popular Culture. In: MARTINEZ, Dolores. (ed.) (1998): *The Worlds of Japanese Popular Culture. Gender, Shifting Boundaries and Global Culture*. Cambridge: Cambridge University, 9–109

NATSUME, Sôseiki (1911): The Civilization of Modern-day Japan. In: NATSUME, Sôseki (1992): *Kokoro / a Novel and Selected Essays*. Translated from the Japanese by Edwin McClellan. Lanham: Madison Books, 257–283

NATSUME, Sôseki (1996): *Ich der Kater. Aus dem Japanischen übertragen und mit einem Nachwort versehen von Otto Putz* [I Am A Cat. Translated from Japanese and with an Epilogue by Otto Putz]. Frankfurt a M.: Insel

NEAD, Lynda (1992): *The Female Nude. Art, Obscenity and Sexuality*. London and New York: Routledge

NEDERLANDS FOTO INSTITUUT (2001). *NFI news, Surface 11/11/2001. – 06/01/2002. Contemporary Photography and Video from Japan*, 4–7

NEW YORK TIMES (1947): Empire State Leap Ends Life. In: *New York Times, 02. 05. 1947,* 23

NHAT HANH, Thich (1991): *White Clouds. Walking in the Footsteps of Buddha.* Translated from the Vietnamese by Moby Ho. Berkeley: Parallax Press

NOCHLIN, Linda (1971): Why Have There Been No Great Women Artists? In: NOCHLIN, Linda (1988): *Women, Art, and Power and Other Essays*. New York: Harper and Row Publishers, 145–178

NOMURA, Masaichi (1990): Remodeling the Japanese Body. In: NOMURA, Masaichi and M. MOERMAN (eds.) (1990): *Culture Embodied.* Osaka: National Museum of Ethnology, 259–274

OGUIBE, Olu (1995): Kunst, Identität, Grenzen: Postmodernismus und zeitgenössische afrikanische Kunst [Art, Identity, Boundaries: Postmodernism and Contemporary African Art]. In: WEIBEL, Peter (ed.) (1996): *Inklusion/Exklusion. Kunst im Zeitalter von Postkolonialismus und globaler Migration* [Inclusion/Exclusion. Art in the Era of Postcolonialism and Global Migration]. Köln: Dumont, 91–97

OHNUKI-TIERNEY, Emiko (2002): *Kamikaze, Cherry Blossoms and Nationalisms.* Chicago and London: The University of Chicago Press

OKABE, Aomi (2003): *Âto to josei to eizô* [Art and Women and Images]. Tokyo: Saikisha

ÔNISHI, Wakato (1999): Kôshô dakara âto na no ka [Is It Art Because It Is Sublime?]. In: *Asahi Shinbun (Tokyo), 09. 11. 1999, Evening Edition*, 5

ORBAUGH, Sharalyn (2003): Busty Battlin' Babes: The Evolution of the Shôjo in 1990s Visual Culture. In: MOSTOW, Joshua S. and Norman BRYSON and Maribeth GRAYBILL (eds.) (2003): *Gender and Power. In the Japanese Visual Field.* Honolulu: University of Hawaii Press, 201–228

ÔSHIMA, Hiroshi (2000) Izima Kaoru Tod des Todes. Death of Death. In: *European Photography, Art Magazine, number 66, volume 20, issue 2, winter 1999/2000*, 52–59

ÔSHIMA, Hiroshi (2004): *Konseki no ronri. Shashin wa onore wo nani to kokoroeru no ka* [The Logic of a Trace. How Photography Views Itself]. Tokyo: Natsumeshobô

OSTERLOH-GESSAT, Elke and Marion PETRI (eds.) (1997): *"Der größe jetzt lebende japanische Maler"* ['The Greatest Living Japanese Painter'] *Kawanabe Kyôsai.* Bietigheim-Bissingen: Stadtmuseum Hornmoldhaus

PAGNUCCO SALVEMINI, Lorella (2003): *United Colors: The Benetton Campaigns*. London: Scriptum Editions

PANTZER, Peter (ed.) (2005): *Japanischer Theaterhimmel über Europas Bühnen. Kawakami Otojirô, Sadayakko und ihre Truppe auf Tournee durch Mittel- und Osteuropa 1901/1902*. [Japan's Theatre Sky Above the Stages of Europe. Kawakami Otojiro, Sadayakko and Her Troupe on Tour Through Mid and Eastern Europe 1901/1902]. München: Iudicium

PEIRCE, Charles Sanders (1958a): *Collected Papers VI*. Cambridge: Harvard University Press

PEIRCE, Charles Sanders (1958b): *Collected Papers VIII*. Cambridge: Harvard University

PFISTER, Thomas (1999): Between Exoticism and Banality. The Documentary Photograph as Art. In: DOSWALD, Christoph (ed.) (1999): *Missing Link. The Image of Men in Contemporary Photography*. Zürich: Edition Stemmle, 21–28

PFLUGFELDER, Gregory M. (1999): *Cartographies of Desire*. Berkeley: University of California Press

PHILLIPS, Sandra (1997): *Police Pictures: The Photograph as Evidence*. San Francisco: Chronicle Books

PHILLIPS, Sandra S. (2005): Between Substance and Essence: the Art of Ishiuchi Miyako. In: ISHIUCHI, Miyako (ed.) (2005): *Mother's 2000–2005. Traces of the Future*. Tokyo: Tankôsha, 128–133

PINGUET, Maurice (1996): *Der Freitod in Japan. Geschichte der japanischen Kultur* [Suicide in Japan. A History Of Japanese Culture]. Frankfurt a. M.: Gatza

POE, Edgar (1946): The Philosophy of Composition. In: THOMPSON, G. R. (ed.) (1984): *Edgar Allan Poe. Essays and Reviews. Literary Classics of the United States*. New York: Library of America

PREBISH, Charles S. and Damien KEOWN (eds.) (2007): *Introducing Buddhism*. London and Oxford: Routledge

PRIELER, Michael (2006): *Racial Divide in Japanese TV Ads: Othering, Racial Hierarchies, and Identity Construction*
URL:http://visualculture.hanyang.ac.kr/Prieler_Racial%20Divide%20in%20Japanese%20TV%20Ads.pdf (24. 09. 2009)

PROCHASKA, David (1991): Fantasia of the Phototheque: French Postcard Views of Senegal. In: *Africa Arts, October 1991, Vol. 24, No. 4,* 40–47

PUSTOLLA, Astrid (2006): *Kunstmuseen in Japan und Deutschland* [Art Museums in Japan and Germany]. Berlin: Logos

RABINOW, Paul (ed.) (1984): *The Foucault Reader*. London: Penguin

REGENER, Susanne (2000): Verbrechen, Schönheit, Tod. Tatortfotografien [Crime, Beauty, Death. Crime Scene Photographs]. In: *Fotogeschichte. Beiträge zur Geschichte und Ästhetik der Fotografie* [The History Of Photography. Contributions to the History and Aesthetic of Photography], *20, 78, 2000*, 27–42

REX, John (1974): *Approaches to Sociology. An Introduction To Major Trends in British Sociology*. New York and London: Routledge

ROBERSON, James E. und Nobue SUZUKI (eds.) (2003): *Men and Masculinities in Contemporary Japan: Dislocating the Salaryman Doxa*. London und New York: Routledge

ROBERTS, James (1997): Sweet Nothings. In: *Frieze 36, Oktober 1997*, 78–79

ROBERTS, Melanie (2001): In Conversation – Eight Artists from Japan. In: LLOYD, Fran und Melanie ROBERTS (eds.) (2001): *Sex and Consumerism. Contemporary Art in Japan*. Brighton: University of Brighton, 16–46

ROMANO, Gianni (2000): Miwa Yanagi. In: *Zoom International, 39, 2000*, 60–63

ROSKILL, Mark (1968): *Dolce's "Aretino" and Venetian Art Theory of the Cinquecento*. New York: New York University Press

RYÛICHI, Kaneko (1999): Eine kurze Geschichte der Fotografie in Japan [A Short History of Photography in Japan]. In: NBK (ed.) (1999): *Zeitgenössische Fotokunst aus Japan* [Contemporary Photographic Art from Japan]. Heidelberg: Umschau Braus, 8–25

SACHS, Britta (2000): Kunstmarkt, Izima Kaoru [Artmarket, Izima Kaoru]. In: *Frankfurter Allgemeine Zeitung, 05. 02. 2000*

SAGA, Yoshiko (n.y.): Hintergrund zur Obdachlosigkeit in Japan [The background of homelessness in Japan]. In: *Goethe-Institut Japan*, unnumbered
URL: http://www.goethe.de/INS/JP/lp/prj/obd/jap/deindex.htm (09. 08. 2008)

SAID, Edward (1979): *Orientalism*. New York: Vintage Books

SANDA, Maruo (1997): Jôkyô kô 3: karimono no shisô, chi, shudai wo megutte [Thoughts on the Situation 3: On Borrowed Thoughts, Knowledge and Themes]. In: *LR, No 3, August 1997*, 22–23

SANTE, Luc (1992): *Evidence*. New York: Atlantic Book

SATÔ, Dôshin (1996): *Nihonbijutsu tanjô, Kindainihon no 'kotoba' to senryaku* [The Birth of Japanese Art. The Words and Strategies in Modern Japan]. Tokyo: Kodansha

SATÔ, Dôshin (1999): *Meiji kokka to kindaibijutsu* [The Meiji Nation and Modern Japanese Art]. Tokyo: Yoshikawa Kôbunkan

SAWARAGI, Noi (1992): An Anomaly Called Bijutsu: Laterally-Written Japanese Contemporary Art. In: MUNROE, Alexandra (ed.) (1994): *Japanese Art After 1945: Scream Against the Sky*. New York: Harry N Abrams, 388

SAWARAGI, Noi (1998): *Nihon – Gendai – Bijutsu* [Japan – Contemporary – Art]. Tokyo: Shinchôsha

SCHMIDT-LINSENHOFF, Victoria (2005): Das koloniale Unbewusste in der Kunstgeschichte. In: BELOW, Irene and Beatrice VON BISMARCK (eds.) (2005): *Globalisierung/Hierarchisierung. Kulturelle Dominanzen in Kunst und Kunstgeschichte* [Globalisation/Hierarchization. Cultural Predominance in Art and Art History]. Marburg: Jonas, 19–38

SCHNEIDER, Angela (2006): Körper im Raum. Fotografien aus Tokyo und Berlin [Bodies in Space. Photographs from Tokyo and Berlin]. In: SCHNEIDER, Angela et. al. (eds.) (2006): *Berlin Tokyo Tokyo Berlin*. Berlin: Hatje Cantz, 246

SCHULZ, Martin (2001): Spur des Lebens und Anblick des Todes. Die Photographie als Medium des abwesenden Körpers [The Trace of Life and the View of Death. Photography as a Medium of the Absent Body]. In: *Zeitschrift für Kunstgeschichte 64, 2001*, 381–396

SCHULZ, Martin (2002): Die Thanatologie des Photographischen Bildes. Bemerkungen zur Photographie [A Thanatology of the Photographic Image. Comments on Photography]. In: ASSMANN, Jan and Rolf TRAUZETTEL (eds) (2002*): Tod, Jenseits und Identität* [Death, Afterlife and Identity]. Freiburg/München: Karl Alber, 740–763

SCHWARZER, Alice (2000): Pornografie. Der Sexualisierte Menschenhass. Newton-Ausstellung in der Berliner National-Galerie [Pornography. Sexualised Hate Towards the Human Being. Newton-Exhibition in the Berlin National Gallery]. In: *Emma, November/Dezember 2000*, 22–28

SCREECH, Timon (1996): *The Western Scientific Gaze and Popular Imagery in Later Edo Japan: The Lens Within the Heart*. Cambridge: University Press

SCREECH, Timon (2009): *Sex and the Floating World. Erotic Images in Japan 1700–1820. 2nd Edition*. London: Reaktion Books

SELENKA, Emil and Lenore (1925): *Sonnige Welten. Ostasiatische Reise-Skizzen* [Sunny Worlds. EastAsian Travel-Sketches]. Berlin: C. W. Kreidel

SERRANO, Andres (2004): *America and Other Work*. Köln: Taschen

SHIGEKATSU, Minobu (ed.) (1974): *Kankyo no tomo* [A Companion in Solitude]. Tokyo: Miyai

SHIMADA, Shingo (1994): *Grenzgänge – Fremdgänge. Japan und Europa im Kulturvergleich* [Borders and the Other Side. A Cultural Comparison of Japan and Europe]. Frankfurt a. M.: Campus

SHIMIZU, Akiko (2008): *Lying Bodies. Survival and Subversion in the Field of Vision. Gender, Sexuality, Culture, Vol. 8*. New York: Peter Lang

SHINER, Eric C. (2008): Focus and Cross: Thoughts on the Changing Face of Japanese Contemporary Photography. In: KELSEY, Robin and Blake STIMSON (eds.) (2008): *The Meaning of Photography*. London and New Haven: Yale University Press, 186–189

SHINOHARA, Kishin (1998): Morimura Yasumasa. Kûsobijutsukan 1. kanpeki na sagishi no shigoto ni kanmei [Fantasy Art Museum 1. Deeply Impressed By the Work of a Perfect Copycat]. In: *Asahi shinbun (Tokyo), 22. 04. 1998, Morning Edition*, 34

SHIODA, Junichi (2002): Thoughts on Mariko Mori: Journey to Somewhere Away from Here. In: MUSEUM OF CONTEMPORARY ART (ed.) (2002): *Mariko Mori Pure Land*. Tokyo: Museum of Contemporary Art Tokyo, 79–83

SHIRASUGI, Etsuo (2000): Envisioning the Inner Body in Edo Japan: The Inshoku Yôjô Kagami (Rules of Dietary Life) and Bôji Yôjô Kagami (Rules of Sexual Life). In: KURIYAMA, Shigehisa (2000) (ed.): *The Imagination of the Body and the History of Bodily Experience. International Symposium*. Kyoto: International Research Centre for Japanese Studies, 31–49

SIEDENBERG, Sven (2001): Modefotografie. Der Tod und das Mädchen [Fashion Photography. Death and the Maiden]. In: *Süddeutsche Zeitung, Extra Ausstellungen, 25. 04. 2001*, 3

SINGER, Robert T. (1994): Japan's Persisting Traditions. A Premodern Context for Postmodern Art. In: STEARNS, Robert (ed.) (1994): *Photography and Beyond in Japan. Space, Time and Memory*. Tokyo: Hara Museum of Contemporary Art, 15–35

SKIRL, Krestina (2007a): Performing Identity/Performing Gender: A Reading of Miwa Yanagi's Artistic Series Elevator Girls and My Grandmothers. In: *Cross Sections Vol. 1.* Kyoto: National Museum of Modern Art

SKIRL, Krestina (2007b): *Performativity and Translatability in Miwa Yanagi's Art Practice* (unpublished paper of the 7th conference of the Nordic Association of Japanese and Korean Studies, Visual Culture Section Copenhagen, August 24th–26th 2007)

SMITH, Jonathan Z. (1998): Religion, Religions, Religious. In: TAYLOR, Mark C. (ed.) (1998): *Critical Terms for Religious Studies*. Chicago: University of Chicago Press, 269–284

SMITH, Roberta (21. 09. 2001): Art in Review. Yasumasa Morimura. In: *The New York Times* URL: http://query.nytimes.com/gst/fullpage.html (02. 05. 2008)

SONTAG, Susan (1975): Photography Within the Humanities. In: WELLS, Liz (ed.) (2003): *The Photography Reader*. London and New York: Routledge, 59–66

SONTAG, Susan (1979): *On Photography*. Harmondsworth: Penguin

SPIELMANN, Heinz (1985): *Die japanische Photographie. Geschichte, Themen, Strukturen* [Japanese Photography. History, Themes, Structures]. Köln: Dumont

SPIELVOGEL, Laura (2003): *Working Out in Japan*. Durham: Duke University Press

SPIRO, Melford E. (1966): Religion: Problems of Definition and Explanation. In: BANTON, Michael (ed.) (1966): *Anthropological Approaches to the Study of Religion*. London: Tavistock, 85–126

STARK, Rodney and William S. BAINBRIDGE (1987): *A Theory of Religion.* New York: Peter Lang

STRATZ, C. H. (1925): *Die Körperformen in Kunst und Leben der Japaner. Vierte Auflage* [Bodily Forms in the Art and Life of the Japanese. Fourth Edition]. Stuttgart: Ferdinand Enke

STREIFF, David (1993): Einführung und Dank [Introduction and Acknowledgment]. In: KUNSTHAUS ZÜRICH (ed.) (1993): *In die Felsen bohren sich Zikadenstimmen* [Cicada Voices Boring Into Rocks]. Zürich: Lars Müller, 7–21

SUMMER, David (2003): *Real Spaces: World Art History and the Rise of Western Modernism*. New York: Phaidon

SUZUKI, Takao (1986): Language and Behavior in Japan: The Conceptualization of Personal Relations. In: SUGIYAMA LEBRA, Takie and William P. LEBRA (eds.) (1986): *Japanese Culture and Behavior. Revised Edition*. Honolulu: University of Hawaii' Press, 142–157

SUZUKU, Tokiko, Kaori CHINO and Akiko MABUCHI (eds.) (1997a): *Bijutsu to jenda – hitaisho no shisen* [Art and Gender. The Asymmetrical Gaze]. Tokyo: Brücke

SUZUKU, Tokiko, Kaori CHINO and Akiko MABUCHI (eds.) (1997b): *Bijutsu to jenda – kooza suru shisen* [Art and Gender. Intersecting Visions]. Tokyo: Brücke

TAKASAKI, Fujihiko (1985): *Nihon no bijutsu 234. rakanzu* [Japanese Art 234. *Rakanzu*]. Tokyo: Shibundô

TAKEHATA, Tetsu (1991): Yuragu orijinariti shinwa [The Declining Myth Of the Original]. In: *Asahi shinbun (Tokyo), 14. 11. 1991, Evening Edition*, 7

TANIZAKI, Junichirô (1977): *In Praise of Shadows*. Translated from the Japanese by Thomas J. Harper and Edward G. Seidensticker. New Haven: Leete's Island Books

TAWADA, Yoko (1996): Leicht wie ein Schiff [Light as a Ship]. In: VON WYSOCKI (ed.) (1996): *Fremde Bühnen. Mitteilungen über das menschliche Gesicht* [Unknown Stages. Notifications About the Human Face]. Hamburg: Europäische Verlagsanstalt, 219–223

TERAMOTO, John (2000): Problems of Corporeality in Japanese Painting. In: KURIYAMA, Shigehisa (ed.) (2000): *The Imagination of the Body and the History of Bodily Experience*. Kyoto: International Research Center for Japanese Studies, 193–216

THE ALL-JAPAN ASSOCIATION OF PHOTOGRAPHIC SOCIETIES (2009): *Yoku aru shitsumon* [Frequently Asked Questions].
URL: http://www.photo-asahi.com/faq/ (25. 03. 2009)

THE JAPAN PROFESSIONAL PHOTOGRAPHERS' SOCIETY (2009): *JPS nit suite. Jigyô katsudô* [On JPS: The society's activities].
URL: http://www.jps.gr.jp/about/public_utility.html (16. 07. 2009)

THE PHOTOGRAPHIC SOCIETY OF JAPAN (2009): *Setsuritsushushi to soshiki* [The Club's Establishment and its Structure].
URL: http://www.psj.or.jp/profile/index.html (16. 03. 2009)

THOMAS, Nicholas (1999): Cold Fusion. In: *American Anthropologist 98, 1996*, 9–16

TOKYO METROPOLITAN MUSEUM OF PHOTOGRAPHY (ed.) (1995): *The Founding and Development of Modern Photography in Japan*. Tokyo: Tokyo Metropolitan Museum of Photography

TOKYO UNIVERSITY OF THE ARTS (2009): *About Us. A Brief History of the University*. URL: http://geidai.ac.jp/english/about/history.html (30. 03. 2009)

TOKYOTO (ed.) (2004): *Hômuresu no jiritsu shitsuensaku ni kansuru Tokyoto jisshi keikaku* [The City of Tokyo's Support Plan for the Independence of Homeless People]. Tokyo: The City of Tokyo

TORRESS, Aileen (2005): Culture. The Art of Manabu Yamanaka. In: *NYC-Plus, Volume 1, issue 2, May 2005*, unnumbered
URL: http: // www.nyc-plus.com/nycp2/theartofmanabuyamanaka.html (13. 08. 2009)

TSURUMI, Wataru (1993): *Kanzenjisatsu Manyuaru – The Complete Manual Of Suicide*. Tokyo: Ôta Shuppan

TURNER, Bryan S. (1984): *The Body and Society: Explorations in Social Theory*. Oxford: Blackwell

UEDA, Shizuteru (1998): Watashi wa aruka [If the 'I' exists]. In: KAWAI, Hayao and Shinichi NAKAZAWA (1998): *Gendainihon bunkaron 1. Watakushi to wa nanika* [Studies on Contemporary Japanese Culture I. What does the 'Self' mean?]. Tokyo: Iwanamishoten, 33–66

UENO, Chizuko (1997): In the Feminine Guise: a Trap of Reverse Orientalism. In: *US-Japan Women's Journal 13*, 3–25

VAN DAMME, Wilfried and Kitty Zijlmans (eds.) (2008): *World Art Studies: Exploring Concepts and Approaches*. Amsterdam: Valiz

VAN TUYL, Gijs (1997): Einführung: Mariko Moris Esoterischer Kosmos oder Die Entführung aus der Realität [Introduction: Mariko Mori's Esoteric Cosmos Or The Kidnapping From Reality]. In: MORI, Mariko (ed.) (1999): *Esoteric Cosmos*. Ostfilden Ruit: Cantz, 9–14

VAN WOLFEREN, Karel (1990): *The Enigma of Japanese Power*. New York: Vintage

VIGOUROUX, Yannick (2004): Ces photographes qui font leur cinema… [These Photographs Which Make a Film]. In: *Reponses Photo, Automne-Hiver 2004*, 134–144

VOLKENANDT, Claus (ed.) (2004): Kunstgeschichte und Weltgegenwartskunst [Art History and Contemporary World Art]. Berlin: Reimer

VON SCHLABRENDORFF, Eva (1990): Eher Puppen als Menschen. Das Bild der Japanerin in der europäischen Literatur 1850–1910 [More Dolls Than Humans. The Image of the Japanese Woman in European Literature 1850–1910]. In: LINHART, Ruth and Fleur WÖSS (eds.) (1990): *Nippons neue Frauen* [Nippon's New Women] Hamburg: Rowohlt Verlag, 32–43

WAKAKUWA, Midori (2000): *Shôchô toshite no joseizô: Jendashi kara mita kafuchô sei shakai ni okeru josei hyôshô* [The Image of the Woman as a Symbol: The Image of Women in the Patrialistic Society from a Gender History Perspective]. Tokyo: Chikumashobô

WAKASA, Mako (2001): Interview with Miwa Yanagi. In: *Journal of Contemporary Art, 2002*
URL: http://www.jca-online.com/Yanagi.html (22. 03. 2010)

WALTON, Abby (30. 09. 2004): East weets West, with a twist: The art of Morimura Yasumasa. In: *The Sophian*
URL: http://www.smithsophian.com/media/paper587/sections/20040930Arts.html (16. 04. 2006)

WANKE, Carola (2008): Feministischer Zynismus. Weiblichkeit und Repräsentation im Werk von Yanagi Miwa [Feministic Cynicism. Femaleness/Femininity and Representation in the Work of Yanagi Miwa]. In: *OZ, Neue Serie, Nr. 15, Frühjahr 2008*, 41–49

WATANABE, Tsuneo and Junichi IWATA (1987): *The Love of the Samurai. A Thousand Years of Japanese Homosexuality*. Translated by D.R. Roberts. London: GMP

WATANABE, Sachiko (1994): Soshiki ni ubawareru "jiko kettei ken": "josei nomi" seifuku no shûhen" ["The Right of Self-Determination" Deprived by the Organisation: The Circumference of "Only Women Wear Uniforms"]. In: *Kikan joshi kyôiku mondai* [Women's Education Issues Quarterly], 59, April, 18–23

WEIBEL, Peter (ed.) (1997): *Inklusion: Exklusion. Versuch einer neuen Kartografie der Kunst im Zeitalter von Postkolonialismus und globaler Migration* [Inclusion: Exclusion. Redefining the Cartography of Art in an Era of Postcolonialism and Global Migration]. Köln: Dumont

WEIBEL, Peter (1997): Jenseits des weißen Würfels. Kunst zwischen Kolonialismus und Kosmopolitismus [Beyond the White Cube. Art Between Colonialism and Cosmopolitanism]. In: WEIBEL, Peter (ed.): *Inklusion: Exklusion. Versuch einer neuen Kartografie der Kunst im Zeitalter von Postkolonialismus und globaler Migration.* [Inclusion: Exclusion. Redefining the Cartography of Art in an Era of Postcolonialism and Global Migration]. Köln: Dumont, 8–13

WEIBEL, Peter (2009): Global Art: Rewritings, Transformations, and Translations. Thoughts on the Project GAM. In: BELTING, Hans and Andrea BUDDENSIEG (eds.) (2009): *The Global Art World.* Ostfildern: Hatje Cantz, 74–87

WEIERMAIR, Peter (2008): Everybody Dies Someday. In: HATJE CANTZ (2008): *IZIMA KAORU. Landscapes with a Corpse*. Ostfildern Ruit: Hatje Cantz, 6–7

WELLS, Liz (ed.) (2004): *Photography: A Critical Introduction. Third Edition*. London and New York: Routledge

WICHMANN, Siegfried (1999): *Japonisme: The Japanese Influence on Western Art since 1858*. London: Thames and Hudson

WILKES-TUCKER, Anne and Dana FRIIS-HANSEN and Kaneko RYÛICHI (eds.) (2003): *The History of Japanese Photography*. New Haven and London: Yale University Press

WORLD HEALTH ORGANIZATION (2004a): *Number of Suicides By Age Group and Gender. Japan, 2000*
URL: http:// www.who.int/mental_health/media/en/327.pdf (08. 08. 2008)

WORLD HEALTH ORGANIZATION (2004b): *Suicide Rates by gender and age. Germany, 2001*
URL: http://www.who.int/mental_health/media/en/324.pdf (08. 08. 2008)

WÖSS, Fleur (1983): Einstellung zum Tod in Japan [Attitudes Towards Death in Japan]. In: LINHART, Sepp (ed.) (1983): *Japanische Geistesströmungen*. [Japanese Trends of Thought]. Wien: Literas, 57–68

WRIGHT JASINOWSKI, Rosemary (2001): *Morimura Yasumasa. A Cross Cultural Study in the Self-Portrait, Self Definition and the Creative Process*. New York: New York University

YAKUSHIJI (ed.) (2006): Genjô sanzô ingaran kenritsu jûgoshûnen kinen. Taihô zôden tokubetsu kôkai. Genjô sanzô to tonkôkyô [The 15 Year Anniversary of the Genjôsanzôingaran Temple Building. Special Exhibition of the Treasures. Genjô's Tripitaka and the Sutras of Dunhuang]. Nara: Yakushiji

YAMAMOTO, Kazuhiro (1987); Photography as Art Medium. In: YAMAMOTO, Kazuhiro (ed.) (1987): *Gendaibijutsu ni natta Shashin* [Photography That Has Become Contemporary Art]. Utsunomiya: Tochigi Prefectural Museum of Fine Art, 16–20

YAMAMOTO, Kazuhiro (1990): Toward Art in Practice or Art Economics. In: SOH GALLERY: *Yoshihara Tomoaki. Koyama Hotaro. Morimura Yasumasa* (pamphlet for an exhibition with the same title). Tokyo: Soh Gallery, unnumbered

YAMAMOTO, Kazuhiro (1991): Kettai na amari ni kettai na kachi no tenpuku. Art of Arts, Man Among Men [A Crazy, Absolutely Crazy, Yet Valuable Turning Point. Arts of Arts, Man Among Men]. In: *Art & Critique, Nr. 15, 2.*, 16–17

YAMAMOTO, Taketoshi and Toshihiro TSUGANESAWA (1992): *Nihon no hôkoku. Hito jidai hyôgen* [Japan's Advertisement. People, Eras, Expressions]. Tokyo: Sekaishisôsha

YANAGI, Miwa (2007): *Fairy Tale Miwa Yanagi*. Kyoto: Seigensha

YOKOHAMA MUSEUM OF ART (ed.) (1996): *Morimura Yasumasaten. Bi ni itaru yamai – joyû ni natta watashi* [Morimura Yasumasa Exhibition. Sickness Unto Beauty – When I Became an Actress]. Yokohama: Yokohama Museum of Art, 163–167

YOON, Joonsung (2000): *The Emperor's New Clothes. Gender, Culture and Self in Photographic Self-Portraiture*. New York: New York University

YORÔ, Takeshi (1996): *Nihonjin no shintaikan no rekishi* [The history of Japanese People's Bodily Feeling]. Tokyo: Hôzôkan

ZEIT-FOTO SALON (2010): *Zeit-Foto Salon*.
URL: http://www.zeit-foto.com/about/index_e.html (20. 11. 2010)

ZIJLMANS, Kitty (2004): Die Welt im Blickfeld. Unterwegs zu einer global orientierten Kunstgeschichte [A Focus on the World. Towards a Global Art History]. In: VOLKENANDT, Claus (ed.) (2004): *Kunstgeschichte und Weltgegenwartskunst* [Art History and Contemporary World Art]. Berlin: Reimer

ZIJLMANS, Kitty (2007): An Intercultural Perspective in Art History: Beyond Othering and Appropriation. In: ELKINS, James (ed.) (2007): *Is Art History Global?* New York and London: Routledge, 289–298

Interviews with the Artists

The original interviews were all conducted in Japanese; the following texts are the most relevant excerpts translated into English.

Excerpts of the Interview with Morimura Yasumasa
(13. 12. 2008 in Morimura's studio in Osaka)

Lena Fritsch:
I'm currently trying to get an overview of the 1990s art scene in Japan. I have the impression that, originally, there was a strong division between fine art and photography. This started to get blurred in the last ten years. Could you tell me about your experience?

Morimura Yasumasa:
Indeed, in Japan, fine art and photography are two different worlds. When I was nominated for the Kimura Ihei Award in the mid-nineties, this led to a big debate among the jury members… [laughs] … some argued that my photographs of the *Actress* series 'are no photographs', others said 'of course they are photographs' … in the end, I didn't get it; my work was considered inappropriate for the award. In the mid-nineties, the *Kimura Ihei* award was reserved for photography and considered inappropriate for works coming from the fine art world. But then, a couple of years later, people like Sawada Tomoko and Nagashima Yurie got the award for their self-portraits or images of their family.

LF:
That's funny, isn't it? Like you, Sawada Tomoko 'disguises' herself and presents herself in front of the camera; she does not push the shutter herself …

MY:
[laughs]… you know, in the past, photography was always photography; even art photography was photography. The idea of using photography as a medium to create art simply didn't exist. People who took photographs were active within the photography world … photographers exhibited their work within the context of camera companies, such as Nikon or Canon, which owned photography galleries. In Japan, there are so many amateur photographers … this has changed quite a lot actually but amateur photographers used to be the base of the photography world. Also, there were professional photographers and many camera magazines. To these people, things like limited editions were unknown and they didn't exhibit their photographs like artworks and try to sell them. And then, clubs, for instance the Nikon salon, would organise joint photo

shootings and all the photographers would go somewhere together or take photographs of the same model. I once participated in such an event and professional photographers commented on my work. I also met Araki there for the first time… [laughs] … I was told that I'm a genius … [laughs] … well, at the time there was this photography world on the one side and the art world on the other. … In my case, I have taken the medium of photography into the art world and people didn't know how to judge that. At the beginning of the 90s, people still argued that my work was not photography… However, digitalisation has weakened the base of amateur photography. You know, most amateur photographers were men and they were in love with the technical aspect of photography, collecting cameras, lenses etc. The photography clubs were not so much for photography-lovers but perhaps even more for camera-lovers …[laughs] … But now, since the progress of digital photography, everybody can easily take nice photographs and the world of photography has been weakened… Within this context, the attitude towards photography has changed. People now think that photography can be used more freely; thus, increasing the numbers of 'artists' who have been awarded the *Kimura Ihei* award.

LF:
Returning to the 1990s, there were few galleries for contemporary art in Japan – was it hard to get exhibition spaces and have you used rental galleries?

MY:
The first time I had a proper exhibition was in 1985. That was in Kyoto and yes, it was a rental gallery. There were no alternatives. Well, there were some galleries in Nagoya, such as the Akira Ikeda gallery or the Takagi gallery. They were huge, rich galleries. Of course there were also some in Tokyo, at the Ginza or so. But they were rather conservative. Therefore, in Japan, if you wanted to do something a little avant-garde-like, you had to use a rental gallery. You pay money, get the space, have an exhibition and then, that's it … [laughs] … between 1985 and 1990, I basically used such rental spaces. In 1990, I had the *Daughter of Art History* exhibition at the Saga Exhibit Space; that was no rental gallery, but some alternative space. In the 1980s, more art students started to exhibit contemporary art. At the same time, gallerists and art critics appeared on the scene; for instance, Nanjô Fumio and Kasahara Michiko. In fact, Kasahara was the one who wrote a critique for my exhibition at the Saga Exhibit Space in 1990. She was the only critic in Japan who viewed my works from the perspective that you are interested in, Lena: from a gender viewpoint. I would say that the changes and developments of the Japanese art scene started in the 1980s and became bigger and more obvious in the 1990s. And now, everything is getting commercialised, it's not even funny… so yes, the 1990s

are an interesting time, a decade which is exactly in-between the starting points of the 1980s and the 21st century with its commercialisation.

LF:
Let's talk about *Portrait (Futago*). I have found out that *manekineko*[1] were introduced to Geisha houses in the Meiji period when a law was enacted that prohibited the making, selling and displaying of anything resembling genitals. They were seen as symbols of Geishas and the sex business before becoming a general sign of luck and business success. *Portrait (Futago)* is full of signs and symbols. Did you choose all of them consciously to create a synthesis of 'Japanese' and 'Western' signs?

MY:
Well, today the *manekineko* is a symbol of business. However, the black one contrasts with the white one. The black one definitely possesses some dark power. The white *manekineko* is the most common one but, whenever I see a black one, I feel a strong power. That is the power of darkness. In the context of selling one's sex, in this world where the sun doesn't really shine, the black cat and its power fit perfectly. And in my case, I needed a black cat because the cat in Manet's *Olympia* is black as well… this also has something to do with the characteristics of the black *manekineko* that I just mentioned. The funny thing about photography is that you need real, concrete objects. And all these objects contain some information. Therefore, my works carry a lot of information … [laughs] … because I chose all the different objects … At the time, a little gallery in Osaka planned an exhibition on *manekineko*. Some producer of *manekineko* from Kyoto made similar blank *manekineko* and gave them to different artists, who could paint and design them. And I participated in this playful exhibition. Therefore, I had the *manekineko* at home.

LF:
Did you design and paint it for the exhibition or for the artwork then?

MY:
Well, I had the unpainted one at home and decided to paint it black so I could also use it in the painting. You know, I needed something which isn't associated with Japanese high class culture but rather with folk culture… something that many people grew up with. I wanted to insert such a folk element into Western art history. It's not part of Shintô or Buddhism but some weird superstition, something which developed within the world of the common people. And with regards to the *kimono*, well, Manet used a more Chinoise

1 A *Manekineko* is a 'beckoning cat' and a popular sign of good luck, which can be found in the entrances of shops and restaurants in Japan.

cloth, I think. But I chose this very colourful *hanamishô*,[2] something with gold and silver which is also part of folk instead of elite culture. I wanted to insert as many of these folk elements into the artwork as possible. *Olympia* itself appeared provocative in its contemporary Western, art academy context. I wanted to transfer this idea to contemporary Japanese culture and thus inserted folk elements like the *manekineko*.

LF:
Portrait (Futago) is also interesting in its reference to Western culture and body ideals within a Japanese context. The same applies to *Red Marilyn*… I get the impression that Western ideals are still omnipresent in Japan and have led to a complex towards 'the West'. Could you comment on that?

MY:
Don't you think contemporary Japan has changed, Lena? But you are right – in the 1990s that was still a big issue. I created a photograph in reference to Brigitte Bardot and also another one referencing Asaoka Ruriko, a Japanese actress, who was popular in the 60s. While doing the make-up and the style for Asaoka Ruriko, I realised that it was the same as Brigitte Bardot's; her hairstyle and garments were exactly like Brigitte Bardot… [laughs] … and Audrey Hepburn was very influential too… you know, I think even more than the Meiji period, World War II had a huge influence on the Japanese people and led to a complex towards the West … when the Tennô announced Japan's defeat on the radio that was a real shock. And then, there is this famous photo, which I always wanted to make an artwork about…

LF:
The one with the Tennô and the American general, who looks really big and powerful next to him?[3]

MY:
Yes, with the American general, MacArthur, and the Shôwa Tennô. The photograph had a shocking impact on many Japanese people. This is due to MacArthur looking really tall in the photograph. There is just an extreme bodily difference. This seems to somewhat symbolise the extreme power gap between the countries, Japan and America. And then, from the same country, America, films came to Japan, for instance *Roman Holidays* with Audrey Hepburn. That film became extremely popular. She was adored by many Japanese … for common Japanese people, Western things became symbols of a good life; they

---

2 A *hanamishô* is a cloth with a flower pattern.

3 The photograph of General MacArthur and Emperor Hirohito was taken at the American Embassy in Tokyo in 1945.

were independent of the real country. I guess, that's also because people adored the fictional Paris or New York of films; they mostly couldn't go to the real Paris anyway… Japan had been basically isolated from other countries for a long time and the Japanese nation was said to be an ethnically homogenous nation with the Tennô at its top. But all this changed in the 20th century… and art has changed as well. And to return to the 1990s, I think the movements of Japanese culture and art are inextricably intertwined. Women used to adore Audrey Hepburn and cut their hair short. Or they would colour their hair and eyebrows light … they used to do many things to look Western. But, in the late 1990s, in the context of globalisation, blond or brown hair has gained a different meaning. This meaning is *anime*. It is definitely *anime*. People are influenced by the hair colour, eye size and garments of *anime* characters. Blond and brown are just like blue or red; they are variations of *anime* styles. And this change happened in the 1990s … it is linked with *kosupure*.[4]

LF:
Perhaps the very girly, *kawaii*[5] make-up of young Japanese women or the style of young Japanese men could also be explained with this *anime* trend. In Europe, such a cute style would seem like too much …

MY:
When I created the *Actress* series in the 1990s, I had to buy a lot of make-up, very long eyelashes etc. It was very difficult to get all that since normal people didn't buy it; I had to go to special theatre and film make-up shops. But now, normal shops sell these long eyelashes; even the 100 Yen shops sell them,[6] you can buy them for a cheap price. This is because many people wear a lot of make-up. This is probably *anime*-make-up … Even the government says now that Japan's way should be *anime* and games. Japanese *anime* has become so popular worldwide…

LF:
I see this among the students who study Japanese at German universities these days … there are increasing numbers of students who are into *anime* and *kosupure* and therefore become interested in Japan…

4 *Kosupure* comes from the English 'costume play' and refers to a popular trend which developed in the 1990s, namely masquerading as *manga* or *anime* heroes, characters from video games and fantasy films.

5 *Kawaii* means 'cute' or 'lovable'.

6 100 Yen Shops are comparable to One Euro Shops in Europe or One Pound Shops in the United Kingdom.

MY:
Japan today can be equated with *anime* and games. For instance, at the Venice Film Festival, they show Miyazaki Hayao … all this might be good or bad; however, Japan has gained a lot of self-confidence from that. Today, Japan can show the world something: *manga* and *anime*. And as you said, one characteristic is *kawaii*. One important criterion is if you are *kawaii* or not. Things have to be *kawaii* or they don't sell. There are people who view this as something positive, and there are people who view it as something negative. Women often see it positively. In general, feminine things in Japan today are girly things. People adore girly things that would appear in a *manga* … it might be a harsh way of saying it, but: if you want to live cheerfully in Japan today, you just need to use the word *kawaii*. Even if you are an adult, as long as you have something *kawaii*, you can live with that. Men have to find something to fit in this *kawaii* context in some way; they have to participate. Kids who can't participate in this *kawaii* world, become *otaku*:[7] they can't participate and therefore, they dream of it, for instance, looking at images and sitting at home at their computers. These kids are not so *kawaii* … [laughs] ... well, to return to the girls, the girls don't act like grown-up women but like characters from an *anime*. Boys are either inside of the girl's *kawaii* world or they are outside… but, you know, I think it is precarious that people are o.k. with that …

LF:
Well, *kawaii* means being infantile … it's precarious to see a merit in being infantile …

MY:
Exactly… but on the other hand, people adore the infantile now because they used to feel a pressure that they had to be adults. This is complicated … on the one hand, yes, as you said, people don't grow up and they don't develop any critical attitude … but, on the other hand, most young Japanese today are ok and confident with that. This new self-confidence has affected the relationship of Japan with the West. You know, becoming an adult used to be something that Japan sought to do … since the Meiji government, Japanese elites told the people that they should grow up. Novelists, film directors etc told people to grow up culturally and as people so they could conquer their complex toward the West. That has resulted in Japan adopting Western elements on the one side, and, emphasising its 'Japanese' elements on the other. But the complex of being infantile remained. However, the word *kawaii* changed everything! As a metaphor one could say that the children achieved what the adults couldn't… the children say: 'we don't mind that we are infantile … because it's *kawaii*!'

---

7 An '*otaku*' is a passionate *manga* and *anime* fan; he is considered to be 'geek' or 'maniac'.

[laughs] … that's the attitude of Japan today, I think. Therefore, we should perhaps reconsider the idea of growing up…

LF:
Returning to the medium of photography, in the last twenty years, many photographers from Japan have been successful in the Western art world. Why do you think that is? Is photography maybe more neutral than *nihonga* and *yôga* for Japanese artists?[8]

MY:
Indeed, it might be more neutral. Photography is independent of Japanese *nihonga* and also independent of the Western art history since Michelangelo. In this way, it is a very neutral medium … and also, the photography of the late 1960s and 1970s is linked with German photography, German 'neutral' photography… By the way, some Japanese photographers who were active in the 1970s, like Ishiuchi and Moriyama, were rather ignored in the 1980s. However, they have had a big revival since the 90s. Ishiuchi wasn't that big in the 70s but now she gets a lot of attention. Araki gets a lot of attention as well. It is funny how the world around them has changed in the last forty years… I think they both never dreamt of being in such a position as they are now … you know, they have thought of themselves as photographers. I think they never expected to find their work exhibited in an art museum or at the Venice Biennale. [smiles]

---

8 '*Nihonga*' means 'Japanese painting', constrasting with '*yôga*', 'Western painting'.

Excerpts of the Interview with Yamanaka Manabu
(06. 11. 2008 in a conference room in Tokyo)

Lena Fritsch:
I'm currently trying to get an overview of the 1990s art scene in Japan. Could you tell me about your experience? How did you become an artist?

Yamanaka Manabu:
In Tennôji in Osaka, there is a school which also teaches photography; the name of the school is Osaka Shiritsu Kôgei Kôtô Gakkô.[9] I graduated from the high school, proceeded to its college and then, after three years, I graduated and became a fashion photographer's assistant. While working as an assistant, I learnt a lot about photography and also started getting my own jobs. These photographs were done with stylists and models, and had a certain concept. They are commercial images, taken within the context of advertisements; they are not artworks. I was dissatisfied with that and thought that my photographs should look different. That's when I started taking other photographs as well. I got various awards for my commercial photographs but you know, commercial photographs are so short-lived: they just don't last. I thought I should find my own photographic themes …

LF:
Where did you present your photographs? I was told that there are few galleries for contemporary art in Japan – has it been hard to get exhibition spaces and have you used rental galleries?

YM:
The first time I presented my work, the *Arakan* series, was in the Asahi gallery in Yûrakuchô,[10] which is a large space owned by the Asahi newspaper. They use it for the exhibition of photographs as well as for other events. And then I walked around the Ginza,[11] searching for a gallery. But, my photographs are large and there was no gallery which was large enough and willing to exhibit them. Therefore, I ended up renting a space.

LF:
Could you tell me more about the edition of your works? And your works are always analogue photographs, aren't they?

---

9 The official English translation of the school's name is Osaka City Kogei High School.

10 Yûrakuchô is a district in Tokyo.

11 The Ginza is a district and a street in Tokyo, which is especially known for its upscale fashion boutiques and department stores.

YM:
Most photographs have an edition of five and one artist print. And yes, I only take analogue photographs. I don't really like digital photography, I want to take orthodox photographs.

LF:
What was the trigger for the *Arakan* series? I read in an interview that you saw images with sixteen disciples of Buddha who looked like beggars with rags. Was that a specific artwork and, if so, which one?

YM:
Arakan are enlightened people who have given up any worldly desires and concerns. I saw Zengetsu's sixteen *rakanzu*.[12] Their style is rather subdued. And I thought, I want to create such a series of *rakanzu* … At that time, I had just come to Tokyo and was still young … the Ginza was not so posh but rather dirty. There would be homeless people sleeping in the subway stations.

LF:
Were all of the photographs taken here around the Ginza?

YM:
Yes, here around the Ginza and also in Osaka. You have lived in Osaka, I'm sure you know the areas Tennôji, Umeda and Namba…[13]

LF:
Yes, I know them… in the late 1980s, my mum and I used to go to the temple and the flea market in Tennôji and we would pass the homeless people in their cardboard shacks. So when did you take the photographs and how did you meet the homeless people?

YM:
The photographs were taken between the years 1983 and 1989. I lived in Roppongi at the time and could just walk to the Ginza. They would turn up around five or six o'clock in the morning when most people were still sleeping … you know, before the refuse collection service and the street cleaning cars arrive … they would search for food in the garbage in front of MacDonalds or the Sushi bars. Garbage is an important source of food for them. And when I realised that the early morning hours are the times when they are most active, I

12 '*Rakanzu*' are 'depictions of *arakan*'. The Chinese priest Zengetsu (832–912) became influential in the genre of *rakanzu* particularly with his simple and subdued style in the set of hanging scrolls *Shinshû kaigyokuzan jûroku rakan* (approximately 880–896).

13 In the 1980s and 1990s, numerous homeless people lived in cardboard shacks in parks and subways around these areas in Osaka.

started to hang out there and to approach some of them … it took me six years…

LF:
And in those six years, you also worked as a photographer of advertisement images?

YM:
In Japan, there are not many artists who are able to make a living through their art. The market is small. Yes, during that time, I took many photographs of TV stars and pop singers.

LF:
The background of the photographs looks always quite 'neutral' and similar. Where were the photos taken?

YM:
In the areas where I met the homeless people, I looked for white walls … for instance, I had noticed that there was a white wall around the corner from the Shiseido gallery … and they would sleep under some bridge or so … so, how do you convince them to come with you and to have their photograph taken? I developed different strategies … [laughs] … it's never like: 'I would like to take a photo of you' and the homeless person saying: 'yes, sure.' … I really struggled…

LF:
It seems that you were interested in some kind of a spiritual wisdom that these men exuded. Can you tell me more about that idea of homeless people looking like *arakan*?

YM:
Well, it's difficult … there are just no people that you could worship and regard as saints … and I couldn't take that many photos; I only have around two or three negatives of each person … and there were not many good moments to take a photograph. Even when I convinced a homeless person to come with me and stand in front of a white wall, they are no models, you can't ask them to turn right and then turn left … it's difficult. And most of these people don't want any contact with society. The people I was looking for are not concerned with our world anymore, thus, they are not very helpful. I offered them money or bread but those who would accept it are no *arakan* yet. [laughs]

LF:
Your *Arakan* series consists of sixteen images. How many photographs did you take?

YM:
Out of around 500 or 600 photographs, I chose these sixteen. But out of these, I'm only satisfied with around five. This means that the others are not completely at that *arakan* state yet … [laughs]

LF:
Andres Serrano's *The Nomads* series (1990) consists of portraits of homeless people in New York. The *Arakan* series reminded me of Serrano's work because both series could be described as a melange of documentary photography and portrait photography, presenting one homeless person in each photograph. Placed in front of a neutral background, the subjects seem somewhat 'elevated', almost like sages. Do you know Serrano's series?

YM:
I didn't know the series when I took the *Arakan* photographs. But I met Serrano at a party at the Stux gallery and found out about his *Nomad* series. I had this image of *rakanzu* in mind and looked for people who would suit that particular image. I don't know where Serrano's 'majestic' image comes from but I think that he probably came up with it when taking the photographs.

LF:
Let's talk about your *Gyahtei* series…

YM:
Yes, that series is also at the Stux gallery in New York; it can hardly be exhibited here in Japan because of censorship reasons…

LF:
Where did you meet the women and could you tell me more about the context of the *Gyahtei* series?

YM:
Well, the reason for the *Gyahtei* series is connected to death. You know, death as a natural death, not due to an accident or an illness but a death chosen by God … I was interested in the bodies of people who have come that far in life. I thought they would be somewhat beautiful. I became interested in the way that bodies look like just before they pass away … but, well, how do you take such photographs … [laughs]… First, I asked my own grandma: 'can I take a photograph of you?' She said: 'you fool, of course not!'… She is a woman and

wouldn't want to show her naked body to anybody but her husband, especially not in a photograph … Then, I checked newspapers. Newspapers often announce the 88th or 90th birthday of random people and then the old people get a cushion or something from the council. Reading these congratulation announcements, I would find out that there is an 88-year old woman living in, for example, Nakano-ku[14] … but, how do you get in touch with such an old women?

LF:
Well, how did you approach them?

YM:
What I came up with is this: I became a voluntary nurse for the elderly. Nowadays there are many organisations doing this but ten years ago that wasn't so common in Japan. I became a voluntary nurse, bathed the old women, fed them, took them to the toilet etc. I met them twice or thrice a week, talked to them and, while bathing them, we would talk and get to know each other better. And when I saw them in the bath, I would pay attention to their bodies and choose the right women. But, it took me around two years until I had a close relationship with the old women.

LF:
So the youngest women were in their late eighties?

YM:
Most of them were over ninety. There are many very old women in Japan.

LF:
The backgrounds in the *Gyahtei* series are white; they are as neutral as the ones in the *Arakan* series. Did you search for the right white wall inside the women's homes and ask them to get naked for your photographs? How did you take the photographs?

YM:
That would have been the best way… but again, I struggled, it was difficult. I was a voluntary nurse … I could not suddenly tell them that, in fact, I'm a photographer…

LF:
At the beginning, you didn't tell them that you were a photographer and then you slowly explained that to them … ?

---

14 Nakano-ku is a ward of Tokyo, close to Shinjuku.

YM:
I would rather not talk about the details, let's say it's a business secret.[15] The loving relationship between me, who was in his thirties at the times, and the ninety year old women made the photographs possible. The old women can't do anything by themselves, when approaching death, defecating can become something like a insurmountable obstacle … When helping them to defecate or when bathing them, I needed to become somebody who they felt totally comfortable with; thus, I could also take photographs of them. I genuinely and wholeheartedly cared for them; after a year or so there wouldn't be any feeling of shame between us anymore. The photographs could be defined as the 'outcome of my love'; I think, this is the reason why the photographs express tenderness and naturalness.

LF:
Do the women know that their photographs have been exhibited? Have they seen the images?

YM:
They don't know. They haven't seen the photographs. I think, by now, they are all in heaven…

LF:
The *Gyahtei* series shows *naked* women. I know it has been a problem in Japan to show photos of the pubic area. You have had problems with your photographs, for example, galleries or museums not wanting to exhibit them because of censorship reasons, haven't you?

YM:
Even when Fuji TV filmed them for a TV documentary, they only showed the women's faces … In Japan, I have exhibited the photographs only once when I got an award. When I send the photographs overseas they often don't get through customs because you can see the female genitals … but should I censor them by putting a black stripe on the pubic area? That wouldn't make sense… yes, censorship is a problem.

LF:
In Western art history there has been a tradition of symbolising age and decay by showing the wrinkled naked bodies of old women, often by juxtaposing them with young women…

---

15 Yamanaka told me about the photo shootings and I have used the information in my study; however, we have agreed to take the detailed explanations out of this interview.

YM:
Really? I didn't know that. I also took photographs of men. But since men's bodies have less fat, their skin just doesn't hang as much. Their skin doesn't look as impressive as women's. And on average, they die earlier; around ten years earlier than women.

LF:
I would like to talk a little about the medium of photography. Why have you chosen photography as your artistic medium?

YM:
I think, the greatest thing about photography is that you have to be there to take it. You can imagine a picture in your head but still, you have to be there. You can imagine in your head how the old woman's naked body looks like but you have to approach her, spend time with her and be there if you want to create such an image. It is this photographic reality which I'm fascinated with ...

LF:
So you are fascinated with finding the right 'real' photographic moment? But you also stage it …

YM:
Yes, I would prepare a white paper-background … I do not simply search but also have a certain purpose. I have a purpose, like taking photographs of naked old women, and turn that purpose into a reality.

LF:
In the last twenty years, many photographers from Japan have been successful in the Western art world. Why do you think that is? Is photography a 'typically Japanese medium'?

YM:
I don't know much about that. But I would agree that the Japanese art market has gradually grown. People like Morimura, you know, people from the art scene who are using photography, have brought Japanese photographic art into the world. … What do you think of my photographs of these tiny dead embryos? [points at his photographs of the series *Wukong Mang Mang Ran*] I think we have all been embryos and then, just because of the right timing, we were born… but these ones were not lucky. These are just thrown away like garbage and if I don't take a photograph, nothing remains.

LF:
I understand your point. I just think it might be more difficult to exhibit such

photographs … some people might view this as a strategy to get attention through presenting 'scandalous' images.

YM:
You think people won't give them a chance as art images.

LF:
I like how you present the objects in black and white and in front of a white background, but still, I find the series a little precarious ...

YM:
I chose a white background because I didn't want to present them as something very important. Rather, I wanted them to look like little toys… you know, in the past we used to have those little machines which sold toys in small capsules for hundred Yen … [laughs] … I wanted to present the little embryos like that, in a very 'light' way. But I'm fighting for the series right now, in many ways … I want to exhibit the photographs but it's not easy …

LF:
I guess it's almost impossible to exhibit the series here in Japan, isn't it?

YM:
I'm thinking that maybe I could just publish them as a book… the size would be reminiscent of those little toys … maybe a book is more appropriate than an exhibition with large-sized images.[16]

[16] In 2009, the series *Wukong Mang Mang Ran* was published in Yamanaka's volume of photographs *Gyahtei*; the book is a rather small, square book.

Excerpts of the Interview with Mori Mariko
(14. 09. 2009, e-mail from Mori, answering a short questionnaire)

Lena Fritsch:
After studying at the Bunka Fashion College in Tokyo, you moved to London to study art. When did you decide to become an artist and why didn't you study in Japan?

Mori Mariko:
While travelling London, I had seen some installation art and realised that it would just be the ideal place to study contemporary art.

LF:
Could you quickly describe your work in your studio in New York and in Japan? How many people work for you and is collaboration with architects and designers important to you?

MM:
In Tokyo, I don't have any fixed staff. In New York, there are three to four people. The collaborations are not just important as a concept; rather, they are necessary. My large-sized artworks couldn't be realised without the help of numerous specialists, including engineers and scientists.

LF:
Could you tell me why you chose photography as your artistic medium in the 1990s?

MM:
I had worked as a fashion model during the 1980s and therefore, I was very familiar with the photographic medium. To express a certain concept through an image was the quickest and easiest method.

LF:
I'm interested in the *Tea Ceremony* series: what was the trigger for the images?

MM:
At the time, many women had to do *ochakumi*[17] and I wanted to express socio-criticism.

LF:
As far as I know, the *Tea Ceremony* photos have often been individually

---

17 *Ochakumi* is a fixed term for women's serving tea in offices.

exhibited. Have they ever been exhibited all together? If yes, when and where was that?

MM:
They have never been exhibited together.

LF:
Could you tell me more about *Tea Cermony III*? In the image, you are standing in front of the Tokyo Fashion School, offering tea to men who do not seem to notice you. Have you digitally inserted yourself in the image or did you actually go there? How did the people react to you?

MM:
At the time, CG was not yet accessible to most people. The artworks are based on guerrilla-like performances; that was part of my concept for the photographs.

LF:
In the work *Pure Land*, you seem to be inspired by various Buddhist artworks and symbols, such as the goddess Kichijôten, an orchestra of Apsaras and Tibetan Stupas. You freely mix different symbols of Buddhism and Shintoism in a futuristic pop image. Is this freedom of combining various religious elements to be viewed in the context of our postmodern times?

MM:
Due to our globalised media society, today, not only Buddhism and Shintoism but also many other philosophies are able to coexist. Partly in consequence, our cultural identity is experiencing a crisis and people are worried that the belief in our country's religion is evaporating. However, on the other hand, it could be argued that contemporary art is going beyond the barrier of words – it has become an alternative belief for our contemporary society.

LF:
I find that Pure Land Buddhism being a religion not only for educated monks but also for common people, the colourful pop style of your work *Pure Land* suits the concept of the Pure Land well. Was this consistency between the topic of the image and its style intended?

MM:
This is a very good question. The works of this series express ideas of Buddhist theory in a contemporary style. I tried to explain these ideas through images so they would also be understood in a Western cultural context which does not

know much about East Asian thought. In this way, indeed, there might be a parallel with the Jôdoshû's teaching approach.

Excerpts of the Interview with Ishiuchi Miyako
(02. 12. 2008, in the Meguro Museum of Art, Tokyo)

Lena Fritsch:
I'm currently trying to get an overview of the 1990s art scene in Japan. Could you tell me about your experience as a photographer? How did you start?

Ishiuchi Miyako:
The first time I had a solo exhibition was when I was thirty years old. Before that, I had participated in group exhibitions; however, my real debut was with *Yokosuka Story*. When I was a student, I wanted to become a designer. But I failed as a design student; it didn't go well at all. Then, I changed to the weaving class and met various people. You know, these were the years of the 70s demonstrations against the Security Treaty between the United States and Japan. I always wanted to do something but didn't really know what to do. After four years, I quit school. Friends often took me to photography exhibitions and a friend had all the photography equipment, like films, developers and everything. I thought I would like to try taking photographs too. And then, by coincidence, there was a group exhibition and I was asked if I wanted to show my photographs as well … and then, I was told that mine were the best … I never thought of becoming a photographer but I enjoyed photography. I really loved the dark room. Even more than taking photographs, I enjoyed developing the images in the dark room. The images slowly develop and you can be by yourself and think about many things. This has always meant a lot to me … and thus, I have continued taking photographs.

LF:
It's interesting; most Japanese artists and photographers I have talked to so far, have started doing something different … design, installation art etc…

IM:
That might be a similarity among many Japanese photographers … there are not too many who have started right away with photography.

LF:
You just said, you continued photography since you enjoyed being in the dark room… However, after your series *Endless Night* (1981) there was a long pause until your next series *1·9·4·7* (1989). Did you not take photographs during that time? Why is there such a long pause?

IM:
I never stopped taking photographs. At that time, I took photographs of buildings, for instance in Yokohama. But yes, there is a feeling of blankness when I

think of that time. I thought, that perhaps there is no need to take any more photographs; I thought I have other things to do and didn't think I would become a photographer. And then, I turned forty.

LF:
So you always did other work as well?

IM:
Yes, I was employed in an office for many years... [laughs] ... I thought I should just take photographs for myself. You know, there are many jobs for photographers, for instance to take photos for magazines ... after I was awarded with the *Kimura Ihei* award, I got so many job offers from magazines and also went overseas. But it was so boring; anybody could have taken these photographs. There was no need for me to take them. But, at least I tried it. I took photographs for magazine covers, went to America for one week ... [laughs] ... I even took photographs of a model, can you believe it?! I did that once when I was in my mid-thirties; but it doesn't suit me. That's why I thought, if there is nothing I want to take photographs of, I should just leave it. And then, I turned forty ... and got this weird feeling ... [laughs] ... I asked myself where are all those years; has this time been recorded somewhere? And I thought, perhaps it is reflected in people's hands and feet ... and I started to take photographs of the hands and feet of women who were also forty years old.[18] I also took photos of their faces but I didn't use these images in my photo book. I have gradually started to exhibit them sometimes though.

LF:
I have read articles about your work written by European critics but I would also be interested in the reactions to your work in Japan; I haven't found too many interesting articles yet. How has your work been received?

IM:
[laughs] For instance, *1·9·4·7* has been featured in many newspaper and magazine articles; however, there hasn't been much criticism ... no negative criticism and no critical articles in general. In Japan, if you take photographs, you are a photographer and not an artist. Overseas, you are an artist though ... [laughs] ... it's weird, isn't it. The way that photography is viewed within Japan is quite special ...There are so many camera magazines and so many amateur photographers. For them it seems hard to acknowledge photography as art. And there is a tradition that the art world does not like to acknowledge photography as art either ... Things are changing though ... I don't have much contact with the photography world; I mean, we are meeting in an art museum

[18] This photographic series were later titled *1·9·4·7* (1989).

right now and I have an exhibition here in an art museum; I don't care how people categorise me. However, it seems that there is a real hostility between art and photography; this is connected to the history of photography in Japan and that there is no tradition of using the medium of photography as art. I was even told that I 'should please come back to the world of photography' … [laughs] … at the same time, there is a real discrimination against the term 'photographer'… Japan is weird. But, the borders are slowly getting wider on both the photography and the art sides.

LF:
When I talked to curators and other people from the Japanese art system about your work, it's quite interesting how one person would categorise you as a 'photographer', and another would say you're an artist … or you would be 'somewhere in-between'…

IM:
It's strange how they think they could judge … [laughs] … these categorisations don't have much to do with the photographic expressions, do they? Japan has developed weird categorisations. Here in the Meguro Art Museum, I am completely regarded as an artist…

LF:
Do you think, these categorisations are connected to the fact that 'art' as a concept was brought to Japan by 'the West' during the Meiji period?

IM:
Yes. In addition, Japan doesn't have a tradition of self-expression. To merit self-expression might also be a Western idea and to regard art as a way to express oneself seems rather Western to me as well. These ideas are connected to identity. Well, I don't care; I just do what I like … [laughs] …

LF:
Let's talk about the *Scars* series: what was the trigger for the series?

IM:
While taking photographs for the *Chromosome XY* series, I saw one man with a huge scar … and then, he started talking and talking about that scar. And I thought it was like looking at an old photograph. And I realised that scars are a bit like old photographs, they bear many old memories and, at the same time, they are part of the present as well.

LF:
That brings me to my next question: I see a connection of the *Scars* series to

many of your other series. On the whole it appears that the motif of human skin as physical memory has been relevant in your work since the 1990s: *1·9·4·7*, *Hands, Feet, Flesh, and Body: Hiromi 1955*, *1906 to the skin*, *Chromosome XY* …

IM:
Yes, that's right. Perhaps that's the topic I was searching for… I'm interested in the way that time records itself into things and people. I have taken more and more photos of scars … at the beginning, their owners were all male. So the trigger for the series is connected to the male body. Later, I also took photographs of women's scars.

LF:
I like the way you curiously and intimately depict the male body in the *Chromosome XY* series. Could the series also be seen as a playful comment on the male gaze on women in many art works and photographs?

IM:
Yes, I intended that. And connected to that, there are so many nude photographs of women and the few photographs of men are mostly related to some homosexual context. There are stereotypical nude photographs but no photographs of average male bodies. And I don't really know the male body; I haven't seen it often. Thus, I was interested in finding out more about the male body. I was interested in the bodies of normal men, normal *ojisan* or *onîsan* …[19]

LF:
How did you meet them? Are they friends and acquaintances?

IM:
Yes, basically they are friends. But most of them are not really famous. I wanted to get away from stereotypical, sensual nude photographs. Most men don't want to see such images though, they say it feels like looking at themselves and they don't like that; I guess that's because there is no history of nude men.

LF:
Your abstract, reduced, soft aesthetic has been interpreted as 'typically Japanese'. Have you been influenced by traditional Japanese art? And what do you think about this interpretation of your work as being 'Japanese' … I came

[19] An '*ojisan'* is one's 'uncle' or a 'middle-aged man next door'; *onîsan* is the 'older brother' as well as a 'young man next door'. Ishiuchi uses both terms in the latter meaning.

across such interpretations in Western exhibition catalogues, for instance, I read that your series *1·9·4·7* reflects a Japanese, more natural relationship with feet …

IM:
[laughs] … well, to be honest, in Japan you should not show your feet… It is the absolute opposite of a natural relationship – when I took photographs of women's feet, two husbands of the photographed women protested [laughs] … showing women's bare feet is considered rather a disgrace in Japan. But, I'm not concerned with them as something disgraceful; rather, I show the feet as bearing traces of time … I don't like exoticism but sometimes, when I go overseas and see my work there, it seems quite 'Japanese' to me as well. When I'm in Japan, I don't realise this but when I go overseas I feel that I'm Japanese. That is an interesting experience. In this way, the idea of my photographs reflecting something 'Japanese' is perhaps not that wrong. This is mainly due to the fact that photographs transmit information and memory. And there are the hands and feet of Buddhist sculptures: maybe my photographs are also reminiscent of these.[20] I just take photos, I don't really think … but as time passes, the way you see photographs changes, doesn't it. I like to consider photographs from different viewpoints. So when you say there is something Japanese about my photographs of feet, I don't mind … I just think, yes maybe, that's interesting … [laughs]

LF:
You obviously don't use 'Japanese' aspects as a marketing strategy…

IM:
Yes, definitely not. Rather, I take my photographs from a perspective which is not very Japanese at all. For instance, the subject of naked bodies is not very Japanese.

LF:
How you see things is always linked to your own context anyway, isn't it.

IM:
Exactly. Photographs especially are linked to contexts. They are connected to a certain atmosphere and history. Therefore, I enjoy exhibiting my photographs at different places. The way you see them changes so much.

---

20 Ishiuchi probably refers to Dōmon Ken's well-known black and white photographs of hands and feet of Buddha statues.

LF:
Here in the museum, your work looks different to your work exhibited in a photo gallery…

IM:
Definitely. I also have an exhibition at the Zeit-Foto Salon right now … to present my work in such small gallery rooms is completely different.

Excerpts of the Interview with Yanagi Miwa
(11. 11. 2008, in Yanagi's studio in Kyoto)

Lena Fritsch:
I'm currently trying to get an overview of the 1990s art scene in Japan. Could you tell me about your experience? You studied at the Kyoto Shiritsu Geijutsu Daigaku and started with *kimono*, screens and then fibre installations before focussing on photography, is that right?

Yanagi Miwa:
Isn't that typical for artists in Japan today? Photographers perhaps have a camera in their hands right from the start; however, people doing art in Japan tried out something else and then they have ended up doing art. For example, they would have tried writing a novel and then do visual art or … like Murakami Takashi: he was a *nihonga* artist before doing the somewhat kitschy *anime* works he does now … and Morimura used to be a designer. And the same applies to me: first, I studied crafts, then *kimono* and, after that, I created installations which are a bit comparable to Christo's. I took photographs of these though. I did that for two or three years … and then I also had a phase in which I didn't create any artworks. That was necessary for me, I think. It was right after I graduated from the art academy: I taught in companies and at universities.

LF:
What did you teach? Was it contemporary art or *kimono*?

YM:
I was a lecturer of art history; you know, teaching art history to normal people. At that time, I got the idea to do something with elevator girls … without that I would probably never have started to use the medium of photography …

LF:
I was told that there were few galleries for contemporary art – has it been hard to get exhibition spaces and have you used rental galleries?

YM:
Until the mid-nineties, there were few commercial galleries. There were only rental galleries especially here in the Kansai area; in Tokyo it was a bit different. But here, you had to use rental galleries: you paid money for a week or two. Young artists in the Kansai area couldn't do anything but exhibit their works in rental galleries. I did not even know commercial galleries existed and

that it would be possible to sell my works. The first time that I sold an artwork was in Germany, in Frankfurt.[21] I was really surprised …

LF:
This is probably connected to the dominance of *nihonga* and 'traditional' Japanese art in Kyoto, isn't it?

YM:
Yes, here in Kyoto there exists an art scene with a very specific hierarchy of *nihonga* and arts and crafts … it's complicated. At the same time, there are five art academies … [laughs] … and they teach contemporary art. However, young artists had to rent rooms and pay money… well, that was until the concept of commercial galleries for contemporary art came over from Tokyo in the 90s and young artists had been introduced to the art world overseas. They have been taken to Germany or France or to New York … it is a bit ironic that there are so many art academies here in Kyoto but no opportunities to show contemporary art here. Artists have had to go to Tokyo and from there out into the world. But, as you might have heard, three new galleries have just opened in Kyoto … because the art market here is growing … Americans and Europeans come here to buy art. The galleries are not selling art to people from Kyoto … [laughs]

LF:
I'm very interested in your *Elevator Girls* series: what was the trigger for the series?

YM:
When I worked as a lecturer, I commuted to Osaka everyday; at Osaka main station, there are many department stores. I guess you know that area: you know, Umeda station, where the Hankyû department store is.

LF:
Yes, there used to be department girls in the 80s. I went the other day though and didn't see any anymore.

YM:
They have been sacked I guess … [laughs] … due to Japan's economic crisis, they disappeared at the end of the 90s. But there were many of them until then. And as soon as the economy recovers, you will be able to see them again. At the Takashimaya department store in Kyoto, there are still some. There, they

21 This was in 1996; the first work of art that Yanagi sold was a photograph of the *Elevator Girls* series.

even have the same hair … [laughs] … When I worked in Tokyo in the early 90s, the Takashimaya there also had elevator girls. Well, I got really interested in the fact that they spent so much time inside an elevator. The girls don't call the elevator 'elevator' – they call it 'casket'. I got to know them, talked to them and became friends with them. I thought, I was a bit like them: they used those ceremonial words and I gave lectures; they were in this 'casket' all day and I was inside a small class room… in the end, it's kind of the same. And I thought, I want to do an exhibition with the motif of elevator girls.

LF:
At the beginning, you created a performance, didn't you?

YM:
Yes, it was a performance. I didn't really know about photography at the time. I brought some elevator girls to a small gallery and let them stand there … you know, a little Vanessa Beecroft-like.

LF:
The *Elevator Girls* photographs are face-mounted on acrylic and presented in darkened spaces with dramatic spotlight, reminiscent of Jeff Wall's work. Why did you choose that technique? You didn't know Jeff Wall's work when you created *Elevator Girls*, did you?

YM:
At the beginning, I didn't know his work. But when I went to Frankfurt in March 1996 and had my first exhibition overseas, Jeff Wall's work was exhibited next to my photographs. There were some other 'big names' in the exhibition, like Sam Taylor Wood and Cindy Sherman. But at the time, I really had no clue. Now Jeff Wall has also had exhibitions in Japan … I find his work and his huge light boxes interesting but with regards to the motifs and concepts, our work is very different. How should I say … his work is rather 'cool'. Some images might be dramatic; however, these dramatic motifs seem to be presented from a distant viewpoint. I find that really interesting though.

LF:
Can you tell me more about the uniforms that the subjects of *Elevator Girls* wear? I heard that they are usually designed by the department stores? How did you get them or did you create your own uniforms?

YM:
Basically I created them myself, trying to make something similar. I didn't want any help from the department stores; my works are an antithesis to the concept of department stores.

LF:
Could you tell me more about the photographic technique in *Elevator Girls*? In my thesis, I focus on the work *Elevator Girls 3F*: which parts are digitally manipulated and what is 'real'?

YM:
Well, I created this glass whole with the shoes etc, and the girls are really there. However, the background is taken from another image … you know, I usually combined different images; I took photographs of European and Japanese department stores and combined them in digital collages. Department stores are quite similar – the Japanese ones basically copy old European ones, like La Fayette in Paris.

LF:
You have explained in an earlier interview that you were critical of standardisation in Japanese society but you were also comforted by it because of being used to it. To me you being torn between two positions can also be seen in your *Elevator Girls* photographs. I interpret them as 'in-between' social criticism and fascination. On the one hand, you are critical of materialism and the behaviour of some women that elevator girls stand for, but on the other hand you use the same visual means as the advertisement world: The photographs are huge, shiny and seductive in their colours and 'beauty'. Would you agree with me in this point?

YM:
Yes, I agree. Moreover, I think art has to be like that. You can't just say: 'this is wrong' and express a negative attitude … such works are mostly not interesting. For example, elevator girls are adored by Japanese women: they wear this uniform, have a similar face, are beautiful … but they don't have any identity, which is dangerous I think. This loss of identity is seductive … and yet, dangerous. These two things are connected. You know, I find feminism in art often boring … well, not only feminism, but also anti-capitalism – art which is strongly based on criticism. I think art should be different: people should look at it and then think. In other words, the works should be interesting and beautiful from a visual point of view. And then, people will be seduced by this visual beauty … well, they won't be seduced completely but suddenly start thinking … that's my opinion. Don't get me wrong: there are great feminist artworks but there are also many boring ones.

LF:
It's difficult to create feminist art without simply re-enforcing the issues that one criticises, such as the male gaze on women …

YM:
I like Judy Chicago's *Dinner Party*; I think that one is amazing because it has a feminist message and, yet, it has this hand-made quality, referencing Western male art history. I think, feminist art is complicated. To create something interesting within the context of feminism is really difficult.
There is a feminist, who has written about my art … Ueno Chizuko … [laughs] I think, she is an amazing feminist. However, she doesn't know too much about art … she likes to combine some female artist's work with her 'personal trauma'… for example, Niki de St. Phalle's work reflects her father's violent treatment of her and the trauma that she went through with that … [laughs] …

LF:
That's a little old-fashioned I would say …

YM:
It is. And it is so boring … [laughs] … well, there are some texts about me which go into that direction… [laughs]

LF:
Talking of feminism, how do you see the role of women in Japanese Society? It seems hard for women in Japan to be accepted as a woman if they are not *kawaii*.[22] Are you critical of that *kawaii*-culture and women purposely acting like helpless little girls? Have there been changes since the 1990s?

YM:
There have been changes for sure; however, some things still haven't changed. Japanese women think they have to be lovable and are always concerned with how much they are valued by people around them and how much they are loved by them. They don't see themselves through their own eyes but through other people's eyes … it's an illness.

LF:
This might get even stronger in the future through all the internet and media images …

YM:
That's right. But at the same time, there have been interesting trends, such as the *gyaru*[23] … they use such extreme make-up and in the end, they all look alike; however, they don't do it because they think that boys find them cute

---

22 *Kawaii* means 'cute' or 'lovable'.

23 *Gyaru* are 'gals': young women who wear extreme make-up and often a strong dark tan (*ganguro*); in general, they are more interested in fashion, make-up and a fun life than marriage and work.

with that make-up … they just do it because they think it's *kawaii* … it's really interesting.

LF:
Returning to the medium of photography, in the last twenty years, many photographers from Japan have been successful in the Western art world. Why do you think that is? And is photography a 'typically Japanese medium'?

YM:
I think Western people like the photographic artworks best among Japanese contemporary art. And Japan has many camera companies … a Japanese artist who comes from this strange country with a huge camera industry … I guess it works well together [laughs] … You said in the last twenty years – Japanese artists have painted pictures and created sculptures long before that; however, these Japanese things mostly didn't get acknowledged in the West. If Japanese people create things which are not 'Japanese' but rather copy European things, they don't get much respect for that in the wider world. And since the Meiji period, when Western things came to Japan, Japan has had a complex.

LF:
Would you agree that photography is more 'neutral' than *nihonga* or *yôga* then?

YM:
Yes, that's a good expression. Photography is more neutral because it is new … and if we look at *purikura* or other strange photography customs,[24] it seems as though photography somewhat fits in our society … Painting and sculpture are connected to such a long history, if you exhibit paintings in the European art world, people always compare you to some European artist or school and then they sometimes add some exoticism to it. When you do photography that happens less.

24 *Purikura* (from the English 'print club') are photographs taken in photo sticker booths. After taking photographs, users can digitally alter and decorate them on small screens inside or next to the booths and finally print them out as small stickers. *Purikura* stickers have been popular in Japan since the middle of the 1990s, especially among young women.

Excerpts of the Interview with Izima Kaoru
(12. 11. 2008, in Izima's studio in Tokyo)

Lena Fritsch:
You started as a fashion photographer and attracted the Western art world in the 1990s with your *Landscapes with a Corpse* series. At the beginning, the images were presented as a feature in your magazine *zyappu*. How did they come to be shown as art works in galleries?

Izima Kaoru:
My friend Roland Hagenberg, who also wrote an article for my magazine *zyappu*, edited an art magazine and featured the *Landscapes* series in his magazine. The Büro für Fotos gallery[25] from Cologne saw the photographs and offered to exhibit my photographs in an art event titled *Tokyo Shock*.

LF:
The series *New Beauty I* and *New Beauty II* were both published in a book. Were they also exhibited in a gallery? Do you think that the publication of so many photo books in Japan is due to the fact that few galleries are showing contemporary photographic art and it is therefore a way to reach a broader audience?

IK:
For *New Beauty I*, a book seemed like the right medium and *New Beauty II,* as it's a follow-up also had to be a book. But thinking about it now, after I exhibited the photographs of *New Beauty II* as large-sized prints, the book could also be viewed as an exhibition catalogue. And yes, in Japan the idea of buying contemporary art and photography is not very popular yet. People might go to a museum to look at it but they usually don't buy it. Therefore, it is common for artists to publish books like my *New Beauty I*. I also published the books *Nemuru Matsuyuki Yasuko* and the magazine *zyappu* … although *zyappu* is a magazine it also is one of my artworks. For example, after a while, I started using *rômaji*[26] for the articles to express my opinion on the Japanese language and its future…

LF:
So, *zyappu* is an artwork which extends the borders of the art system of galleries and art museums … that reminds me of a long tradition among artists, for instance in the 1960s.

---

25 The gallery Büro für Fotos changed its name in 2007 when the gallerists Kudlek and van der Grinten combined their business; today it is the Kudlek Van der Grinten gallery.

26 *Rômaji* are Romanised Japanese letters.

IK:
Yes, at first, the *Landscapes* series was nothing but a photo series in a magazine … but then I realised how important the topic is for Japanese people and I hoped that people would look at the images and think about death within their own families etc. Therefore I published some images in volumes of photographs … however, people in Japan just interpreted them as photographs of *tarento*[27] … they thought it was just a weird series of star photos … they didn't think properly about the reasons why the models are shown as dead etc. I had thought that using famous people would make more people look at the images … and yes, many people saw them, but unfortunately … well, but that was the intention and the reason why I didn't want to exhibit the photographs in a gallery. I wanted normal people to buy the books, maybe even by mistake and then get interested. However, that plan didn't really work. And with *zyappu* it is kind of the same: I wanted normal people to look at the photographs, not only those typical art collectors and the art scene … but it didn't really work. They didn't accept *zyappu* as a fashion magazine…

LF:
I have read articles about your work written by European critics but I would also be interested in the reactions to your work in Japan. How has it been criticised?

IK:
Japanese photography critics and art critics have not commented on my work yet. They either ignore me on purpose or they don't know me.

LF:
Returning to your *Landscapes* series, how would you categorise it? Were the images originally meant to be fashion photography and then they became art works by being exhibited in galleries? Or have they maybe always been both? Are you seeking to blur the boundaries between those two?

IK:
Originally, I didn't think of them as artworks. However, most of my works have in common that they try to destroy fixed terms and obsessions. I want to highlight the secrets and constraints which are hidden inside of our conventions … and the *Landscapes* series is based on that idea as well.

LF:
I have read that you have a waiting list of women who want you to photograph

27 *Tarento* (from the English 'talent') are famous in Japan as TV stars, actors / actresses and models.

their ideal death fantasy. Is that true and are you still working on new photographs for the *Landscapes* series?

IK:
Well, a waiting list might be a bit exaggerated but yes, there are many people who want to do it. However, the women's fantasies are not always easy to realise … it takes time and you need money … so some of the projects are pending.

LF:
The *Landscapes* series is reminiscent of different genres: fashion photography, Japanese landscape photography and police photography. I read in an article that you looked at photographs taken by the police. Can you tell me more about Japanese police photography? Does it also have a long tradition and a typical aesthetic like American or European crime photography?

IK:
In Japan, you can't view any police photographs; they don't get published. But I have looked at police photographs from overseas.

LF:
The use of crime photography as inspiration is not new in the art world. Within the photographic art of the last ten years, I have found similarities between your *Landscapes* series and Yann Toma's *Crimes sur Commande* (1998–2005) and Annika von Hausswolff's *Back to Nature* (1992–1993). Do you know their works?

IK:
I have seen Yann Toma's series but I had never heard of Annika von Hasswolff. I checked on the Internet but unfortunately I could only find one or two images from that series.

LF:
What are your views on fashion photography of the 1990s or even earlier? There are various photographers who used the extreme clash of glamour and decay to create fashion images, such as Guy Bourdin, Helmut Newton and Renzo Rosso (for instance, the Diesel-advertisement).

IK:
I can't really answer the first part of your question but I guess showing decay is a way to somehow escape it …

LF:
You mean escaping death by showing it as something beautiful? If you were just escaping, you would not have to show it at all.

IK:
Yes, that might be a different form of escape. In my case, the 'corpse' within the context of fashion is a visually shocking element. You get attention when doing that in fashion photography. At the same time, the 'dead' body is sexy or somewhat erotic since it is passive … in this way, it suits fashion photography as a motif … [laughs] … and after I started taking such photographs, after around four years, I increasingly thought about death and realised that I was scared of death, and reflected upon my own death … you know, when asking the models about their own death fantasy I started thinking about my own death too and that if I got cancer, I would like to know it etc. And I think it would be good if people in general thought a bit more about their own death. It is easier to start thinking about that with a visually beautiful image of death … it's like: 'wow, this scene is beautiful … but oh, the person is dead' … then, it's easier for the viewer to reflect upon death. That's why I reduced the amount of blood and brutal elements in the *Landscapes* images … at the beginning there is more blood … [laughs] …

LF:
I have noticed that … in the later images it is less obvious that the subject is 'dead', it's a bit more ambiguous…

IK:
Yes, you don't really know if they are dead or if they are alive … well, it's all within a world of images anyway and it's clear that they are supposed to be dead by now … it's like going to a *kabuki* theatre play and when somebody gets stabbed, some red cloth comes out. [laughs]

LF:
In the 1990s there were heated debates about shocking fashion advertisement images, such as Oliviero Toscani's images for Benetton. What do you think about using dark images with corpses which we see in the news everyday in fashion photography?

IK:
Fashion photography is part of fashion … thus, it always searches for something new and unknown, destroying the old … something new also means something which does not meet the viewers' expectations but rather surprises them. Therefore, images which show something which is unexpected are often the most successful.

LF:
My next question might be a typical art historian statement: I cannot help but quote Roland Barthes, who said that nothing would be funnier than the terrified

photographers' contortions to produce effects that are 'lifelike' in the photographs – which always fails. You don't use the photographic medium to keep a certain moment of *life* but to show a *death* scene – if I think about Barthes' and the photographic medium trying to keep traces of life, I find that funny. Do you see such kind of humour in your work?

IK:
Since the beginning of the series, I've created around fifty sequences and one of the models actually died a few years after her photographs were taken. I always thought, what should I do if they all start dying after I stage their death … [laughs] … but you know, when I see her photographs now, I don't see any connection to her real death. She was so lively ... compared to some snapshot of her laughing, these photographs seem more alive. If I saw a normal snapshot of her, I would probably be sadder. In other words, the photographs as images are not linked with the model's real death; they are just interesting as artworks.

LF:
I found the aspect of intimacy very important in the series, for instance in *Otsuka Nene Wears Tuzigahana:* The viewer enters a house to find himself in the private room of a woman, looking down on her, vulnerably lying on the floor. At the same time the scene is staged, in other words it only *pretends* to be an intimate moment. Would you agree with me that this ambiguity is an important quality of the work?

IK:
There is also another way of viewing the sequence: the close-up image comes first, then the viewer gradually retreats from the corpse until the scene is far away. This is the perspective of the dead person's soul. The soul leaves to another world and looks back. So the very last image is the photograph which is taken from far away. The soul sees how beautiful her dead body looks like and can leave feeling relieved … at the beginning I didn't see the sequences in this way though … I wanted people to see the distant image and think 'oh, what's that?' and gradually get closer to the dead person. I think, it's good that there are two possible viewpoints.

LF:
Do you sell the photographs of *Otsuka Nene Wears Tuzigahana* and other works of the *Landscapes* series always as a series or also as single, individual images?

IK:
One sequence is one artwork. However, at the beginning I was told that I wouldn't be able to sell them like that … especially the large editions. Thus,

it's best when museums buy my work. But yes, unfortunately, some were sold as single images … although they should be together as a sequence [laughs]

LF:
The 1990s in Japan are also called the 'Lost 10 Years' and the suicide rate was extremely high. How are your views on suicide?

IK:
I think suicide is a sad thing; I'm against suicide. The best way of dying is to live the life that is given to you. Therefore, the *Landscapes* series doesn't feature suicide. But some people still connect it with suicide; I'm disappointed that viewers misunderstand some of the photographs.

LF:
But it is a fact that Japan has a very special death aesthetic, wouldn't you agree? I think, the depiction of death is intertwined with culture … for instance, the way that Japanese TV dramas, such as Kayô Sasupensu show death is completely different to the European equivalents.[28] In German TV, a person would usually get shot but here, they always get stabbed with a knife … visually, there are differences…

IK:
[laughs] good point … yes, the Japanese love that …

LF:
… and then, they always go to the sea …

Izima Kaoru's assistant Hosoya Yuiko:
That's true … if you ask Japanese women about the way they want to die, they often say in the sea or in a lake …

IK:
Well, we live on an island. In addition, as an image, I guess water has a somewhat calming effect. And returning to the specific death aesthetic, Japanese people love this 'boom' effect: it's like in a *manga*. They like to exaggerate death visually so that it goes beyond reality; it's unreal right from the beginning.

LF:
… like your obviously staged photographs…

28 *Kayô sasupensu* literally means 'Tuesday suspense'; it was a popular crime drama series of the TV channel Nippon Terebi and aired on Tuesdays from 1981 until 2005.

IK:
Yes, maybe they are a bit like *manga* images.

LF:
In Japanese culture, death has played an important aesthetic role. Do you think that the principles of *mono no aware* and *wabi sabi* have influenced your *Landscapes* series, such as the cherry tree in *Nagasaku Hiromi Wears Louis Vuitton*?[29]

IK:
Well, I wouldn't agree that death in Japan is always as aestheticised as people in America or Europe think. However, it is true that Japanese culture often deals with death through a *wabi sabi* aesthetic. I think that Nagasaku Hiromi's wish to die beneath a cherry tree is surely influenced by that.

LF:
I know you learnt photography at a photography school in Tokyo … how did you study photography there?

IK:
At the times, photography was rarely taught at art academies. There were no photography classes at art academies; only the Nihon University offered photography within their art branch. And there were some special photography schools. The school I went to, the Tokyo College of Photography, focussed on photographic techniques. After that I became a fashion photographer's assistant, then I travelled America for a year and had my first photography exhibition when coming back. That was at the Nikon Salon, *It's a Beautiful Day*. However, these works do not exist anymore. After that, I did some other work for around five years until I could make a living through photography jobs in the fashion and music business. I never even dreamt of being able to make a living through selling my art … [laughs]

LF:
Coming to Japan, I got the impression that there are quite strict categorisations here: 'art' vs. 'photography', 'artist' vs. 'photographer' … What are your views on that?

---

[29] The concepts of *mono no aware* and *wabi sabi* are connected to the Buddhist notion of impermanence. '*Mono no aware*' is derived from the words '*mono*' ('things') and '*aware*' ('sensitivity'); it was used in the Heian period as an exclamation such as 'ah', expressing a 'sensitivity' of the transience of all 'things' and a melancholic feeling at their passing. *Wabi and sabi* are connected to the idea of the impossibility of perfection and the ephemeral nature of things.

IK:
In Japan, photography and art are two different genres. However, normally, photography is 'straight photography' … my photographs as well as Morimura Yasumasa's work or Yanagi Miwa's work is not categorised as photography… people view it as something which uses photography as a medium … but you know, I don't really care … [laughs] … I thought about all these categorisations just recently. It's complicated. If I think of myself, it sounds most natural to me to call myself a 'photographer'… I express my thoughts through the medium of photography and then, I present these photographs as works … in this way, I'm a photographer … [laughs]

Illustration Acknowledgements

I would like to thank the following individuals and institutions who have kindly given permissions to reproduce the illustrations listed below. Every effort has been made to trace copyright-holders but in a few cases this has not been possible. Any omissions brought to my attention will be remedied in future editions.

Fig. 1: Morimura Yasumasa, *Portrait (Futago)* (1988–1990). Courtesy of the artist.
Fig. 2: Édouard Manet, *Olympia* (1863). Courtesy of the Musée d'Orsay, Paris.
Fig. 3: Detail of *Portrait (Futago).*
Fig. 4: Detail of *Olympia.*
Fig. 5: Detail of *Portrait (Futago).*
Fig. 6: Detail of *Olympia.*
Fig. 7: Morimura Yasumasa, *Self-portrait (Actress) / After Faye Dunaway1* (1996). Courtesy of the artist.
Fig. 8: Morimura Yasumasa's Photographs *Black Marilyn, White Marilyn* and *Red Marilyn* in his exhibition *The Sickness unto Beauty – Self-portrait as Actress* at the Yokohama Museum of Art in 1996. Courtesy of the artist and UFER! ART DOCUMENTARY.
Fig. 9: Morimura Yasumasa, *Self-portrait (Actress) / Red Marilyn* (1996). Courtesy of the artist.
Fig. 10: Tom Kelley, *Red Velvet, Pose 1* (1949). Courtesy of Tom Kelley Junior and Pacific Licensing Ltd.
Fig. 11: Zoe Leonard, *Pin-up #1 (Jennifer Miller does Marilyn Monroe)* (1995). Courtesy of the artist.
Fig. 12: Yamanaka Manabu, *Arakan #1* (1988). Courtesy of the artist.
Fig. 13: Yamanaka Manabu, *Gyahtei #17* (1995). Courtesy of the artist.
Fig. 14: Andres Serrano, *The Model* (1994). Reproduced from SERRANO (2004): unnumbered
Fig. 15: Mori Mariko, *Tea Ceremony III* (1994). Courtesy of the artist.
Fig. 16: Mori Mariko, *Pure Land* (1998). Courtesy of the artist.
Fig. 17: Ishiuchi Miyako, *Chromosome XY s. o.* (1995). Courtesy of the artist.
Fig. 18: Ishiuchi Miyako, *SCAR 1983 illness* (1994). Courtesy of the artist.
Fig. 19: Yanagi Miwa, *Sleeping Beauty* (2004). Courtesy of the artist.
Fig. 20: Yanagi Miwa, *Elevator Girls 3F* (1998). Courtesy of the artist.
Fig. 21: Izima Kaoru, *Natsuki Mari Wears Luisa Beccaria #362* (2003). Courtesy of the artist.

Fig. 22: Izima Kaoru, *Koike Eiko Wears Gianni Versace #423* (2004). Courtesy of the artist.
Fig. 23: Izima Kaoru, *Akikawa Risa Wears Chanel #22* (1994). Courtesy of the artist.
Fig. 24/25: Izima Kaoru, *Otsuka Nene Wears Tuzigahana # 211–212* (1999). Courtesy of the artist.
Fig. 26/27: Izima Kaoru, *Otsuka Nene Wears Tuzigahana # 213–214* (1999). Courtesy of the artist.
Fig. 28: Two photographs in Izima Kaoru's book *Neru Matsuyuki Yasuko* (2003). Courtesy of the artist.
Fig. 29: Araki Nobuyoshi, *Untitled* (2004). Courtesy of the artist.
Fig. 30: Cindy Sherman, *Untitled #153* (1985). Courtesy of the artist, Metro Pictures and Sprüth Magers Berlin and London.
Fig. 31: Ochiai Yoshiiku, *Imayô nenjû gyôji* (mid – late 19th century). Private Photograph of Postcard.
Fig. 32: Kawanabe Kyôsai, *Shichifukujin* (Seven Lucky Gods) (1881). Reproduced from STRATZ (1925): 166
Fig. 33: Two images of Maruyama Ôkyo's *Jinbutsu seisha sôhon* (1770). Reproduced from HYOGOKENRITSU REKISHI HAKUBUTSUKAN (1994): 34. Courtesy of Tenri University Library in Nara.
Fig. 34: Kuroda Seiki, *Chi Kan Jô* (1897). Reproduced from KURODA MEMORIAL HALL (2010), URL: http://www.tobunken.go.jp/kuroda/gallery/japanese/tikanjo01.html. Courtesy of the National Research Institute for Cultural Properties Tokyo.
Fig. 35: Sapporo Beer Poster (1908). Courtesy of Sapporo Breweries Ltd.
Fig. 36: Sketch by Katsushika. Reproduced from STRATZ (1925): 155.
Fig. 37: Hans Baldung Grien, *Die Drei Lebensalter des Weibes und der Tod* (1510). Reproduced from WIKIMEDIA COMMONS (2011), URL: http://en.wikipedia.org/wiki/File:Hans_Baldung_009.jpg
Fig. 38: Utagawa Kuniyoshi, *Kanzeon reigen. Hitotsuya no kyûji* (1839–1840). Reproduced from WIKIMEDIA COMMONS (2011), URL: http://ja.wikipedia.org/wiki/%E3%83%95%E3%82%A1%E3%82%A4%E3%83%AB:Kuniyoshi_Kanzeon_reigen.jpg
Fig. 39: Tsukioka Yoshitoshi, *Hitotsuya rôba* (1872). Reproduced from MUIAN (2010), URL: http://www.muian.com/muian04/04yoshitoshi03001.jpg
Fig. 40: Illustration in the first volume of Santô Kyôden's *Udonge monogatari* (1808). Reproduced from FORMANEK (2005): 206. Courtesy of Susanne Formanek and OAW.

Fig. 41: A white and black *manekineko*. Private photograph.
Fig. 42: Polychromed *manekineko* Wood Sign. Reproduced from LEVY, Dana and Frank B. GIBNEY and Lea SNEIDER (1983): 126, ©Jonathan Whitman, San Francisco.
Fig. 43: Iwakura Tomomi with statesmen, London (1872). Reproduced from WIKIMEDIA COMMONS (2011), URL: http://en.wikipedia.org/wiki/File:Iwakura_mission.jpg
Fig. 44: Filmstills of the TV drama *Moto kare* (2003), 00:07:45 and 00:07:39 of episode 2, 00:06:09 of episode 1. Reproduced from Fuji Television.
Fig. 45: Kawanabe Kyôsai, Untitled Hanging Scroll (1871). Reproduced from OSTERLOH-GESSAT, Elke and Marion PETRI (1997): 37. Courtesy of the Stadtmuseum Hornmoldhaus and Linden-Museum Stuttgart.
Fig. 46: Robert Mapplethorpe, *CHEST* (1986). © Robert Mapplethorpe Foundation. Used by Permission.
Fig. 47: Setsuzan, *Rakanzu* (17th century). © 2011, Museum of Fine Arts, Boston. Used by Permission.
Fig. 48: *Kichijôten* (8th century). Reproduced from YAKUSHIJI (2006): unnumbered. Courtesy of the National Research Institute for Cultural Properties Tokyo.
Fig. 49: Amida Nyôrai in front of a relief with fifty-two Bodhisattvas (Apsaras) (1053). Reproduced from SCHUMACHER, Mark (1995–2009) URL: http://www.onmarkproductions.com/html/bosatsu-on-clouds-apsaras.html
Courtesy of Mark Schumacher, Byôdôin Temple and PFU Ltd.
Fig. 50: Detail *Rikudôe, nindô fujô sôzu* (late 13th century). Courtesy of Nara National Museum and Shoji Raigoji Temple.
Fig. 51–53: Izima Kaoru, *Nagasaku Hiromi Wears Louis Vuitton #221–223* (1999). Courtesy of the artist.
Fig. 54: Robert Wiles, Photograph of Evelyn Mchale (1947). Reproduced from LIFE (1947): 43

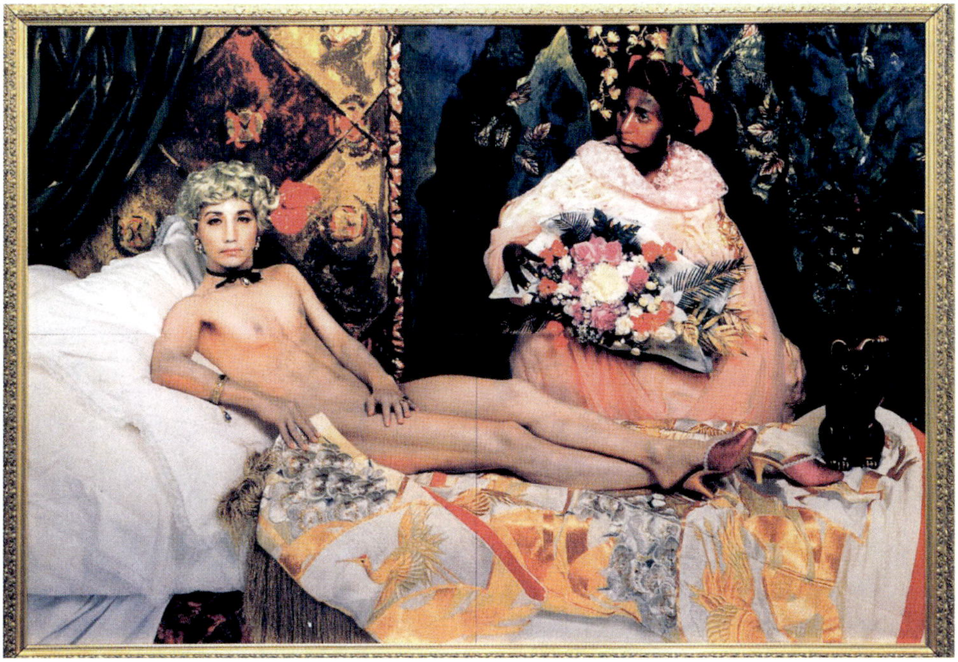

Fig. 1 Morimura Yasumasa, *Portrait (Futago)* (1988–1990). Colour Photograph, 94.5 x 133.7 cm (edition of five) and 266 x 366 cm (edition of three).

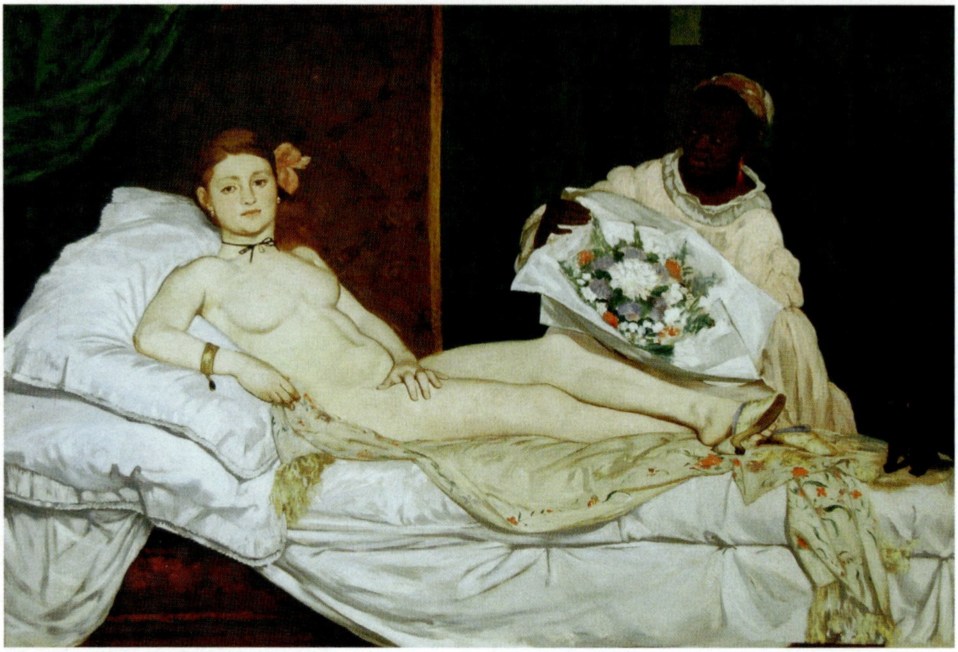

Fig. 2 Édouard Manet, *Olympia* (1863). Oil on Canvas, 130.5 x 190 cm, Musée d' Orsay, Paris.

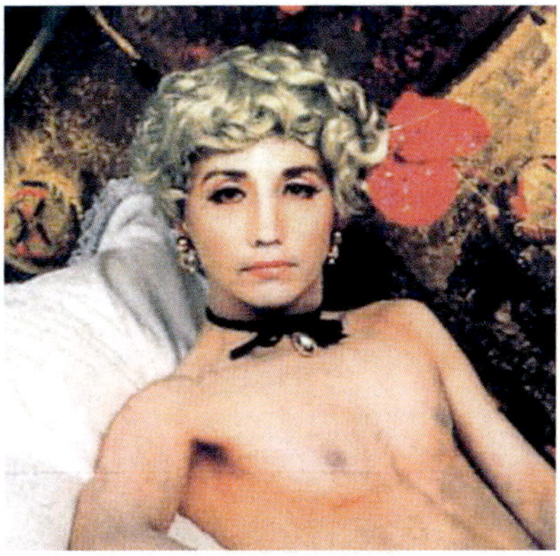
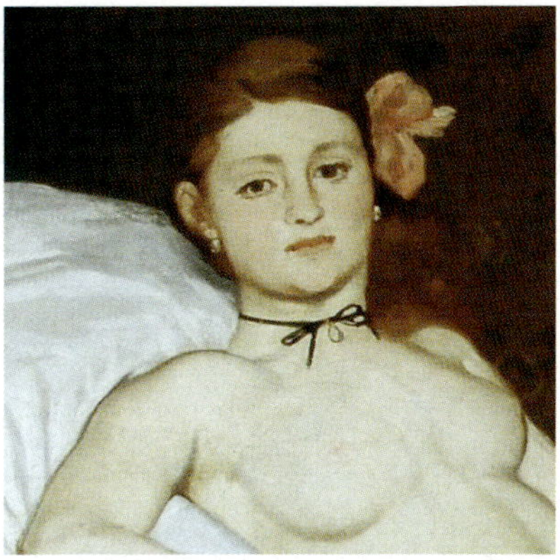

Fig. 3 and **4** Details of *Portrait (Futago)* and *Olympia.*

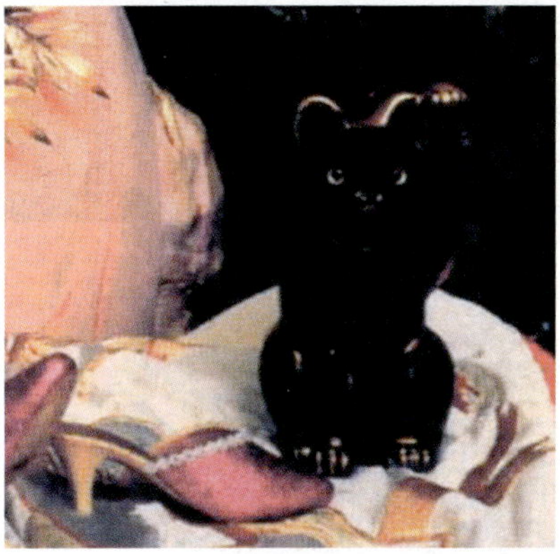
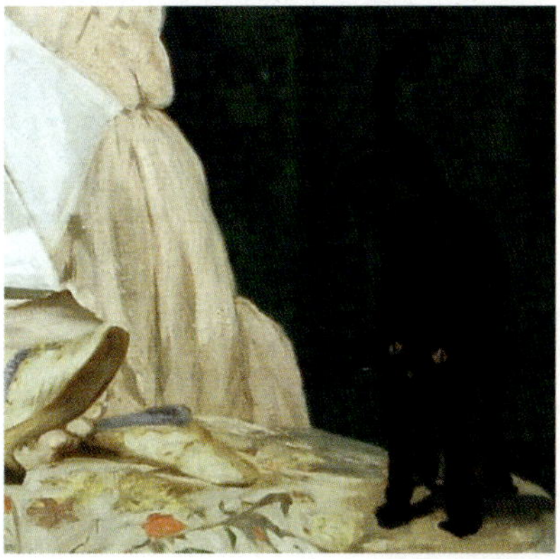

Fig. 5 and **6** Details of *Portrait (Futago)* and *Olympia.*

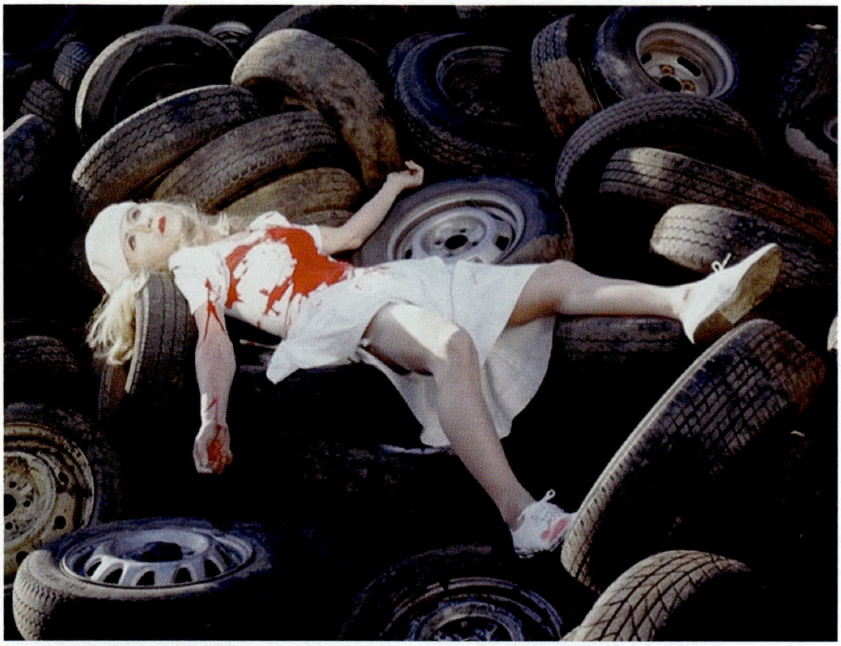

Fig. 7 Morimura Yasumasa, *Self-portrait (Actress) / After Faye Dunaway 1* (1996). Ilfochrome Photograph, 95 x 120 cm (edition of five).

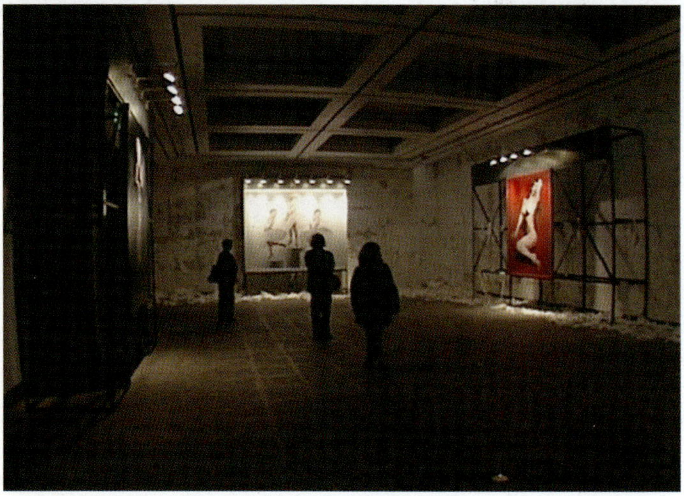

Fig. 8 Installation View of *Black Marilyn, White Marilyn* and *Red Marilyn* in Morimura's exhibition *The Sickness unto Beauty – Self-portrait as Actress* at the Yokohama Museum of Art in 1996.

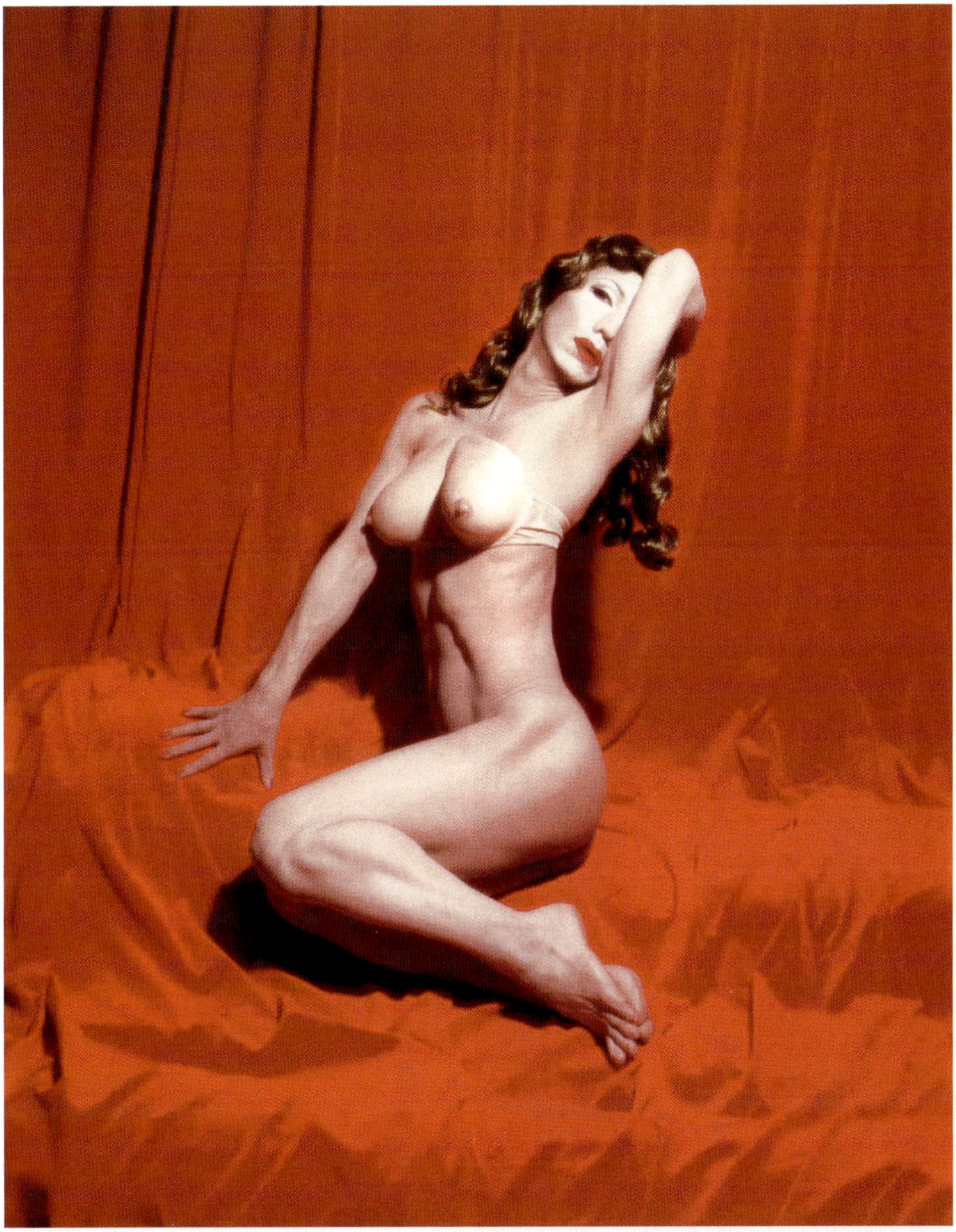

Fig. 9 Morimura Yasumasa, *Self-portrait (Actress) / Red Marilyn* (1996). Ekta Colour Ultra II Photograph, 120 x 95 cm (edition of five), 220 x 167 cm (edition of three).

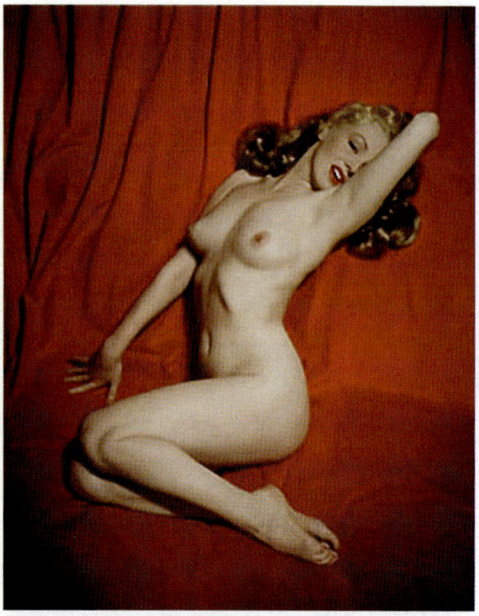

Fig. 10 Tom Kelley, *Red Velvet, Pose #1* (1949). Colour Photograph.

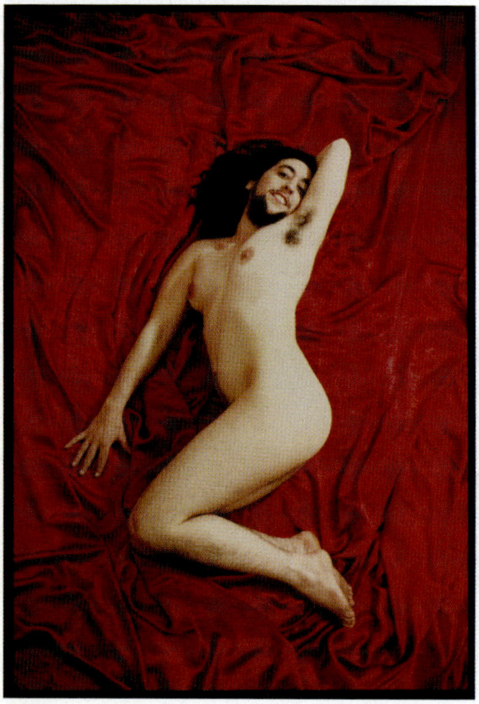

Fig. 11 Zoe Leonard, *Pin-up #1 (Jennifer Miller does Marilyn Monroe)* (1995). Cibachrome, 127 x 84.5 cm.

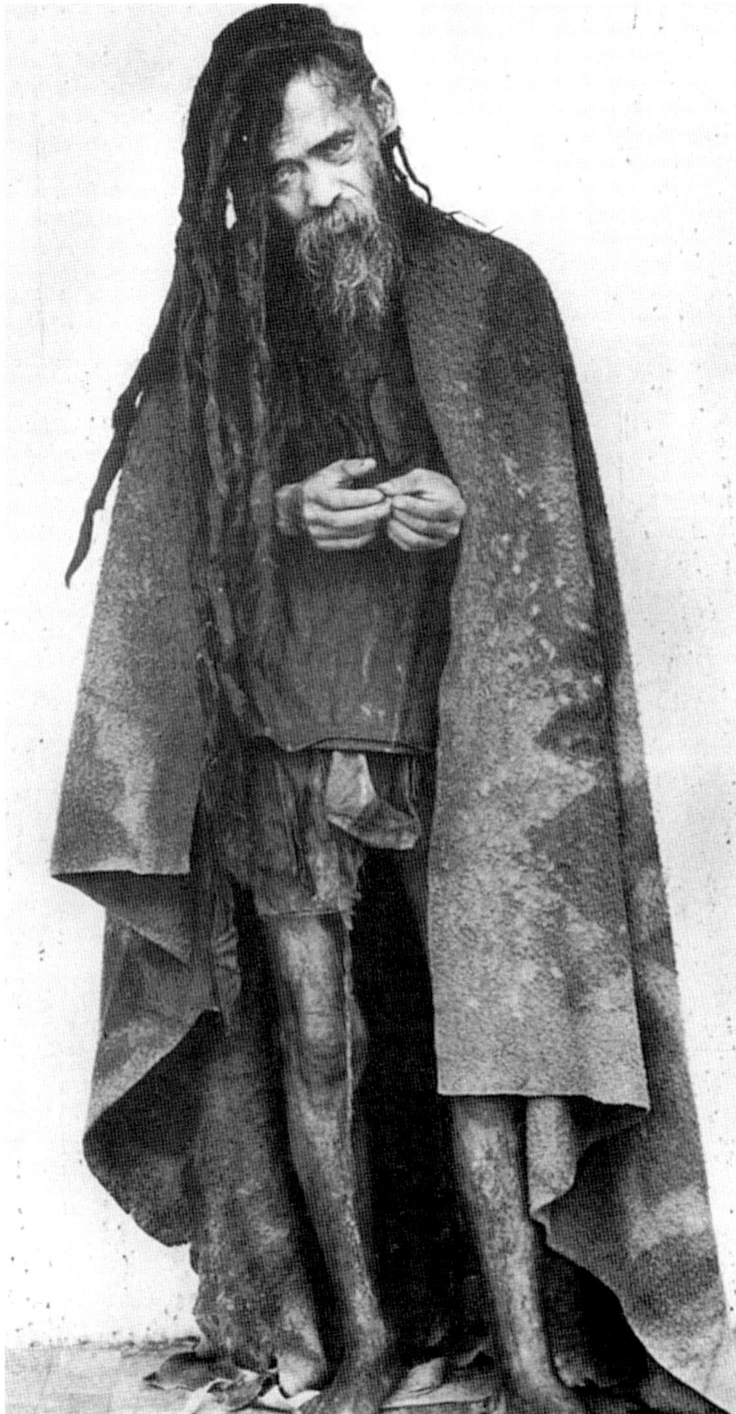

Fig. 12
Yamanaka Manabu, *Arakan #1* (1988). Gelatin Silver Print on Wooden Panel, 180 x 90 cm (edition of six).

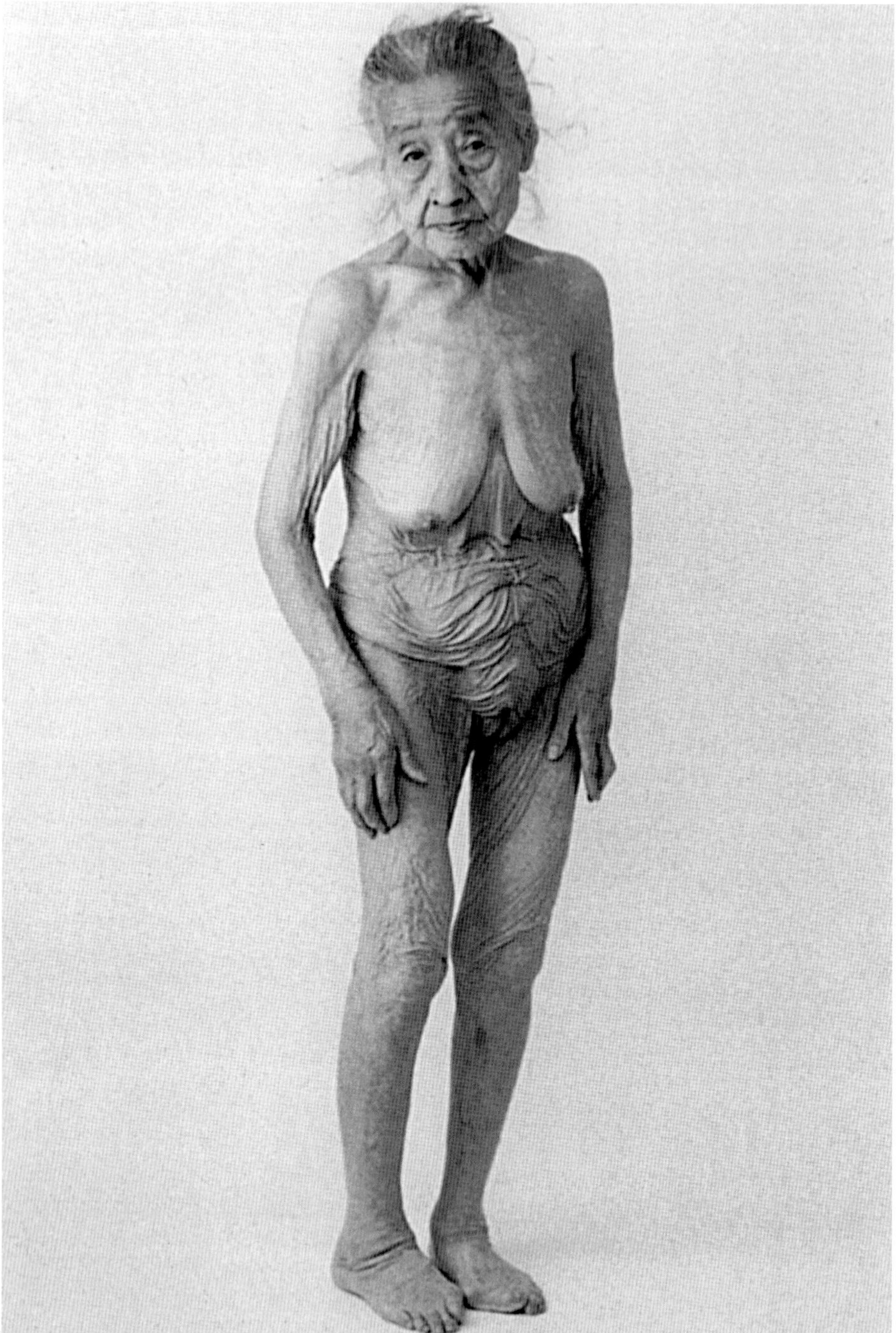

Fig. 13 Yamanaka Manabu, *Gyahtei #17* (1995). Gelatin Silver Print on Wooden Panel, 182 x 92 cm (edition of six).

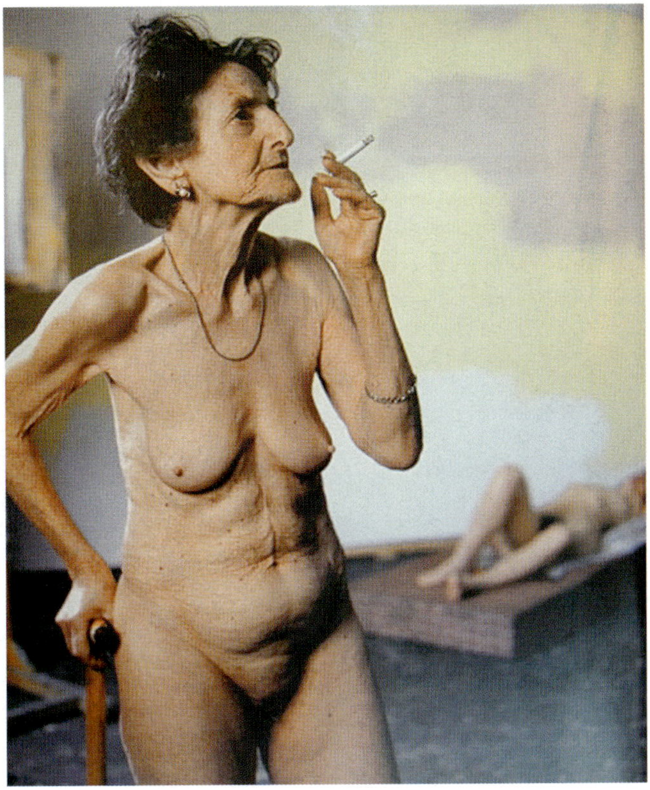

Fig. 14
Andres Serrano,
The Model (1994).
Cibachrome Print,
101.6 x 82.6 cm
(edition of seven).

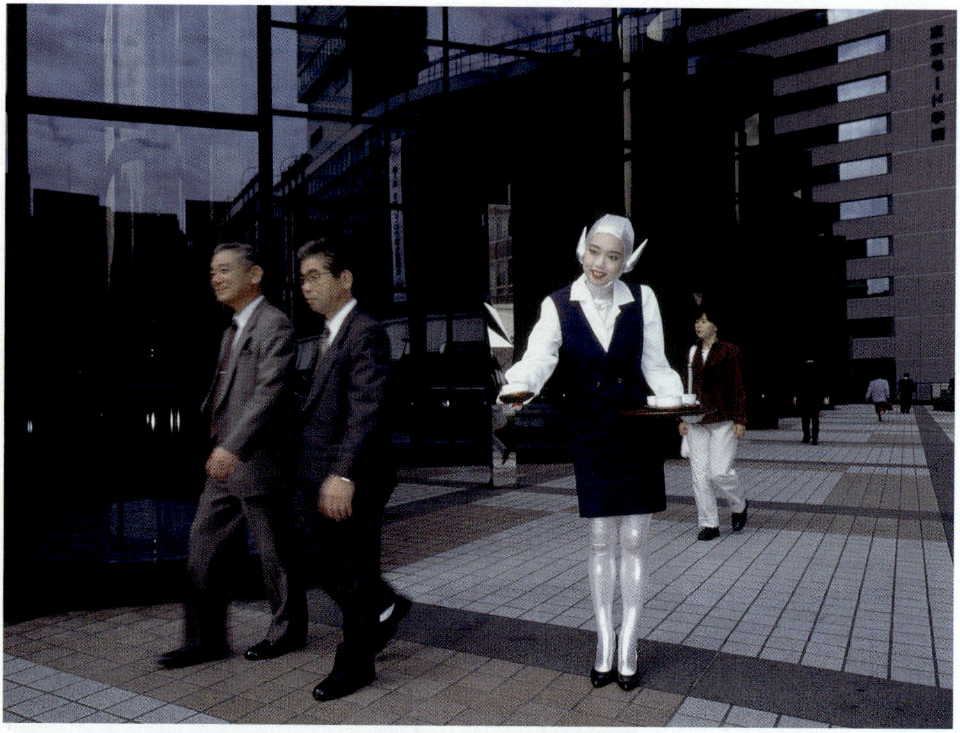

Fig. 15 Mori Mariko, *Tea Ceremony III* (1994). Cibachrome Print on Aluminium, 122 x 153 x 6 cm (edition of four and artist's print).

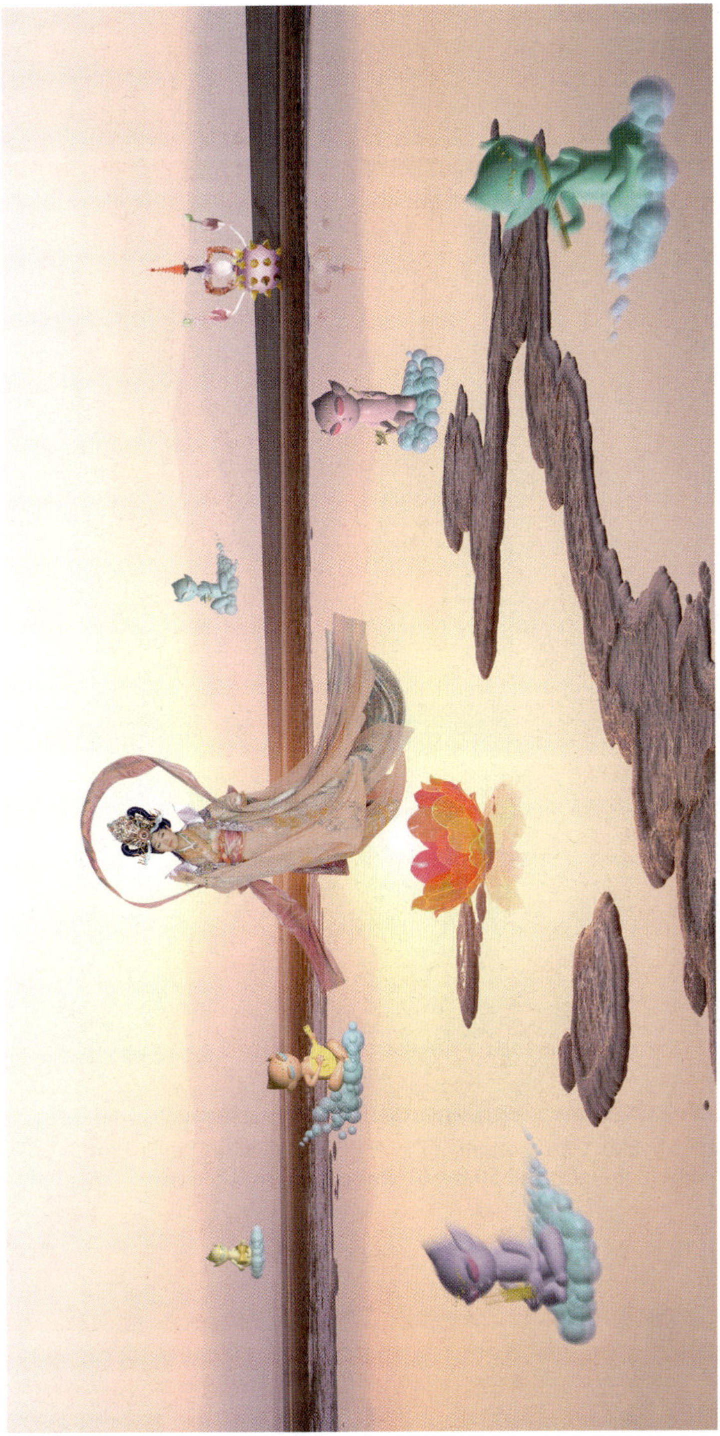

Fig. 16 Mori Mariko, *Pure Land* (1998). Glass with Colour Photograph Interlayer, 305 x 610 x 2.2 cm (edition of three and artist's print).

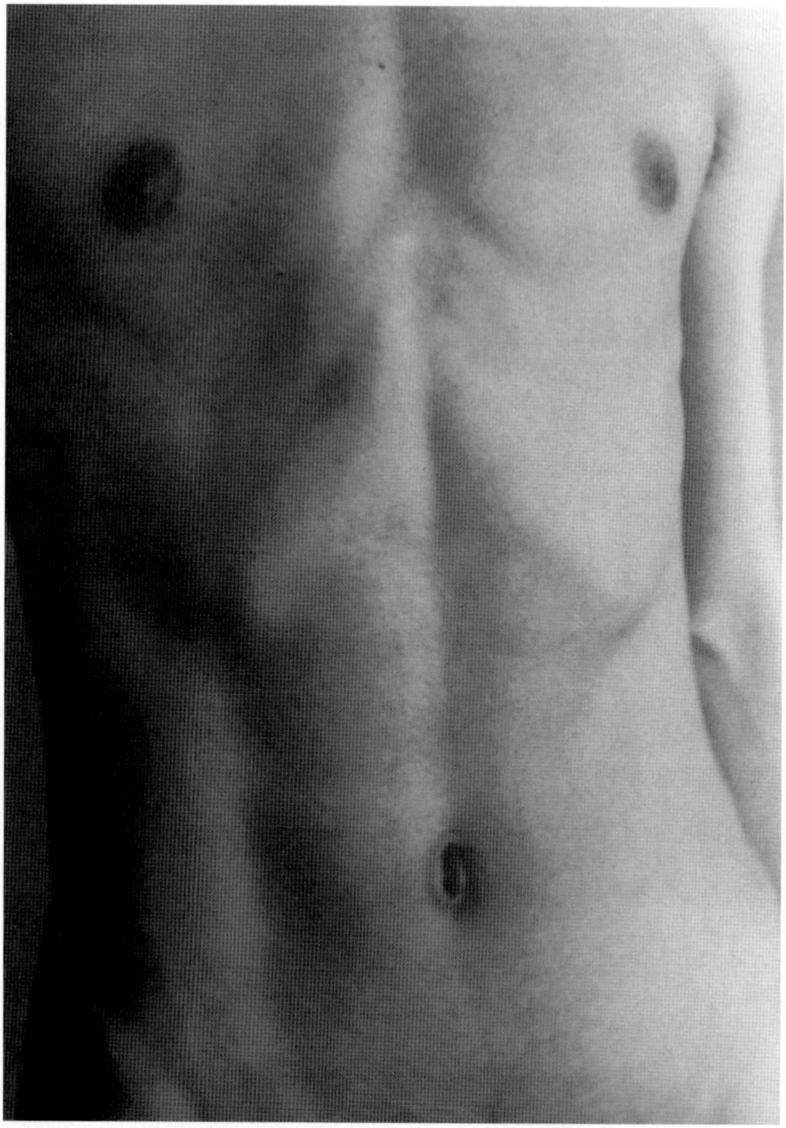

Fig. 17 Ishiuchi Miyako, *Chromosome XY s. o.* (1995). Gelatin Silver Print, 105 x 73 cm (edition of eight) and 50.8 x 61 cm (edition of fifteen).

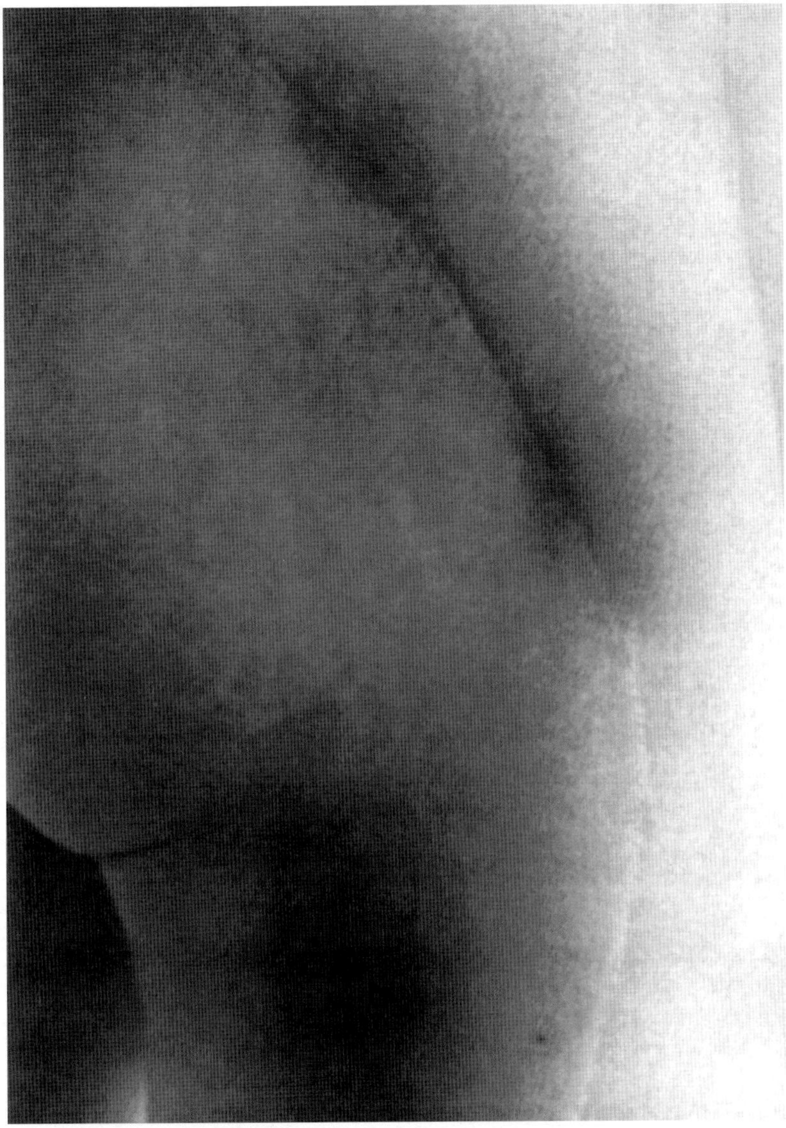

Fig. 18 Ishiuchi Miyako, *SCAR 1983 illness* (1994). Gelatin Silver Print, 108 x 74 cm (edition of ten).

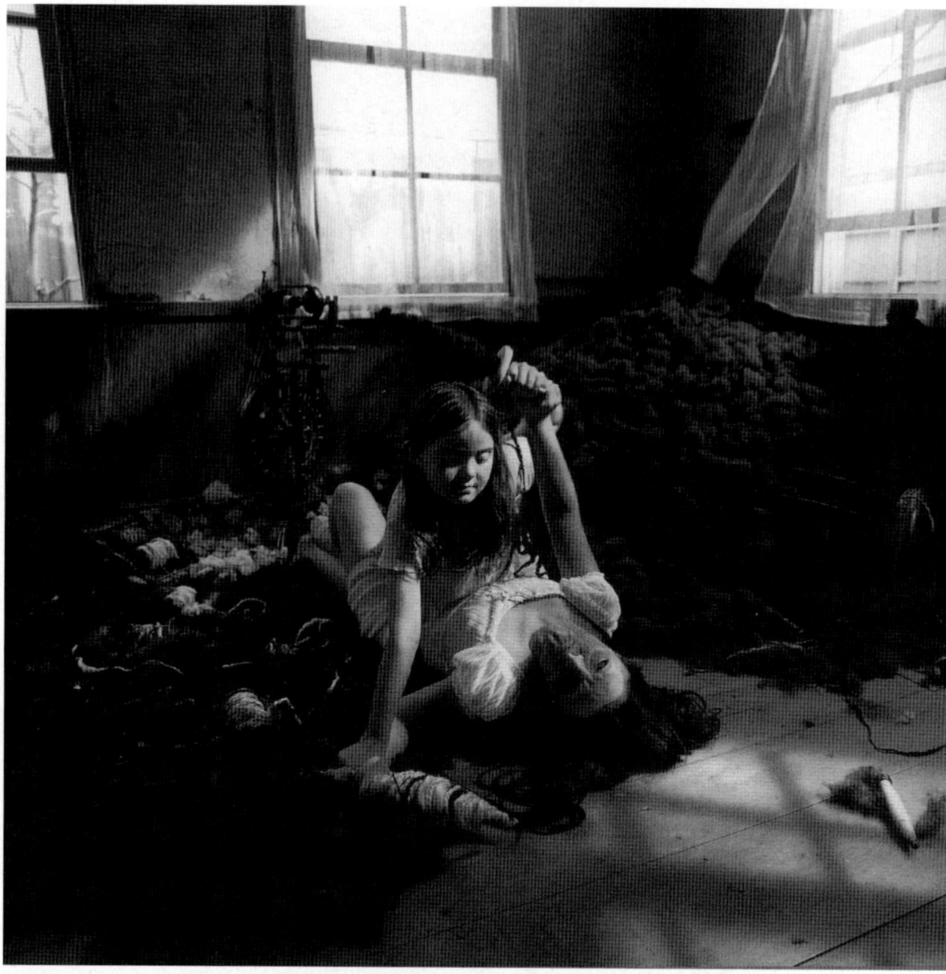

Fig. 19 Yanagi Miwa, *Sleeping Beauty* (2004). Gelatin Silver Print, 140 x 100 cm.

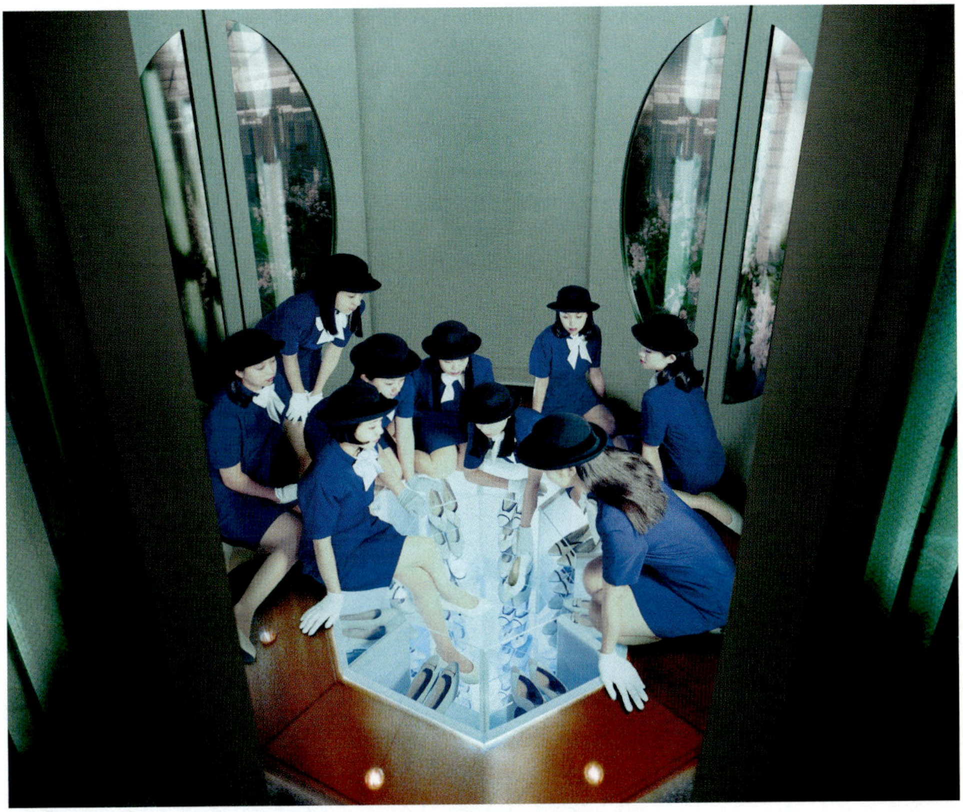

Fig. 20 Yanagi Miwa, *Elevator Girls 3F* (1998). C-Print, Diasec, 180 x 213 cm (edition of five) and 90 x 106.6 cm (edition of fifteen).

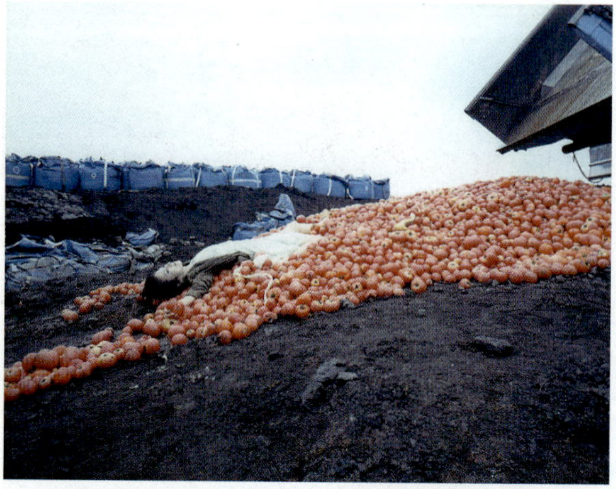

Fig. 21 Izima Kaoru, *Natsuki Mari Wears Luisa Beccaria #362* (2003). C-Print, Face-mounted on Plexiglas, 124 x 104 cm.

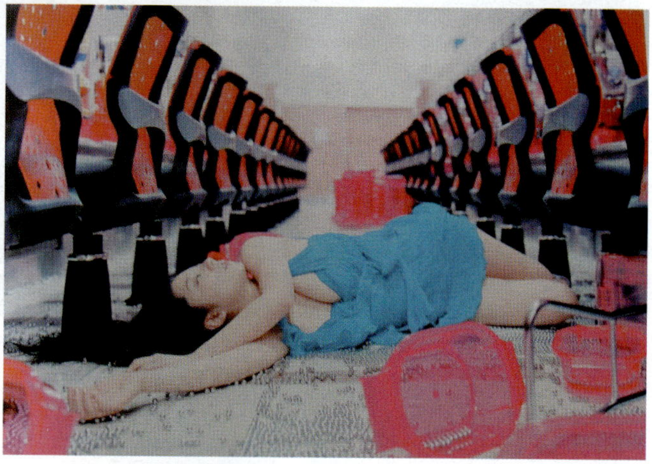

Fig. 22 Izima Kaoru, *Koike Eiko Wears Gianni Versace #423* (2004). C-Print, Face-mounted on Plexiglas, 180 x 240 cm.

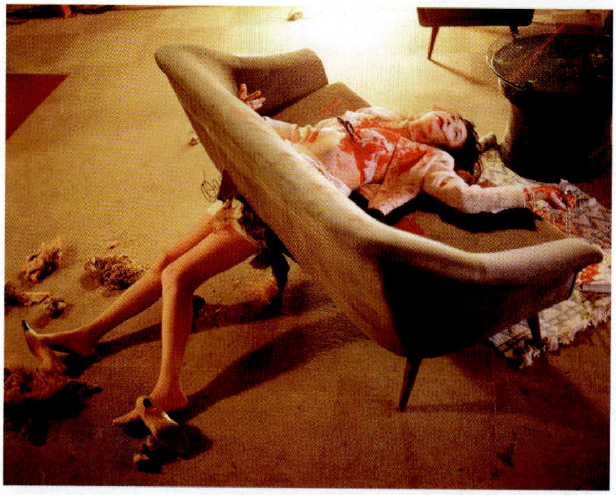

Fig. 23 Izima Kaoru, *Akikawa Risa Wears Chanel #22* (1994). Photograph in Izima's magazine *Zyappu.*

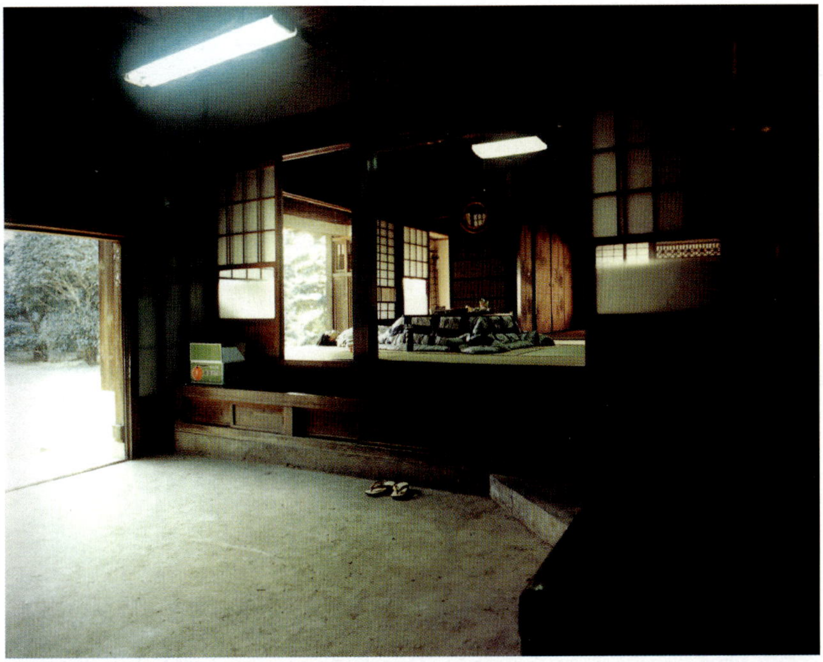

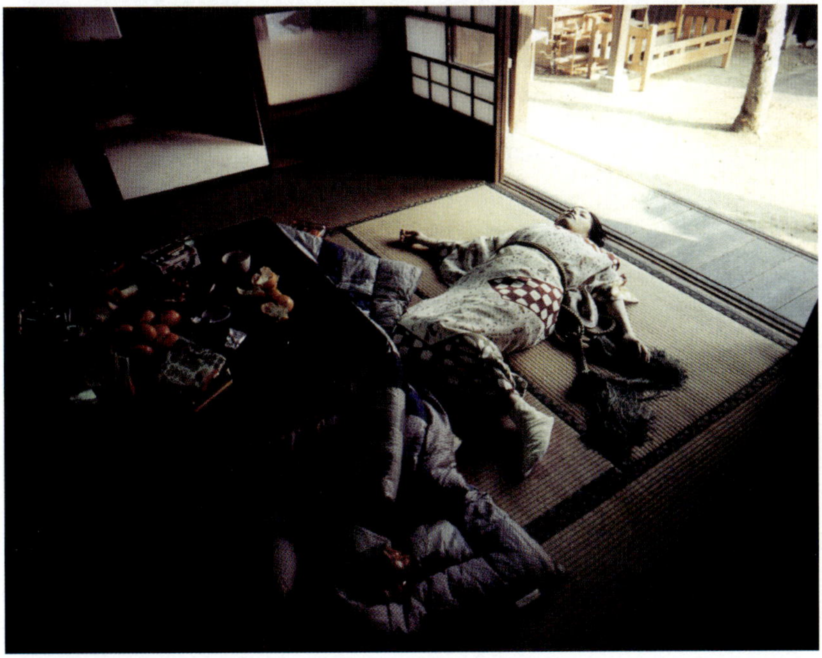

Fig. 24 and 25 Izima Kaoru, *Otsuka Nene Wears Tuzigahana # 211–212* (1999). C-Prints, 100 x 127 cm (edition of five, mounted on acryl and behind glass) and 53.5 x 43 cm (edition of ten, mounted on acryl in wooden frame).

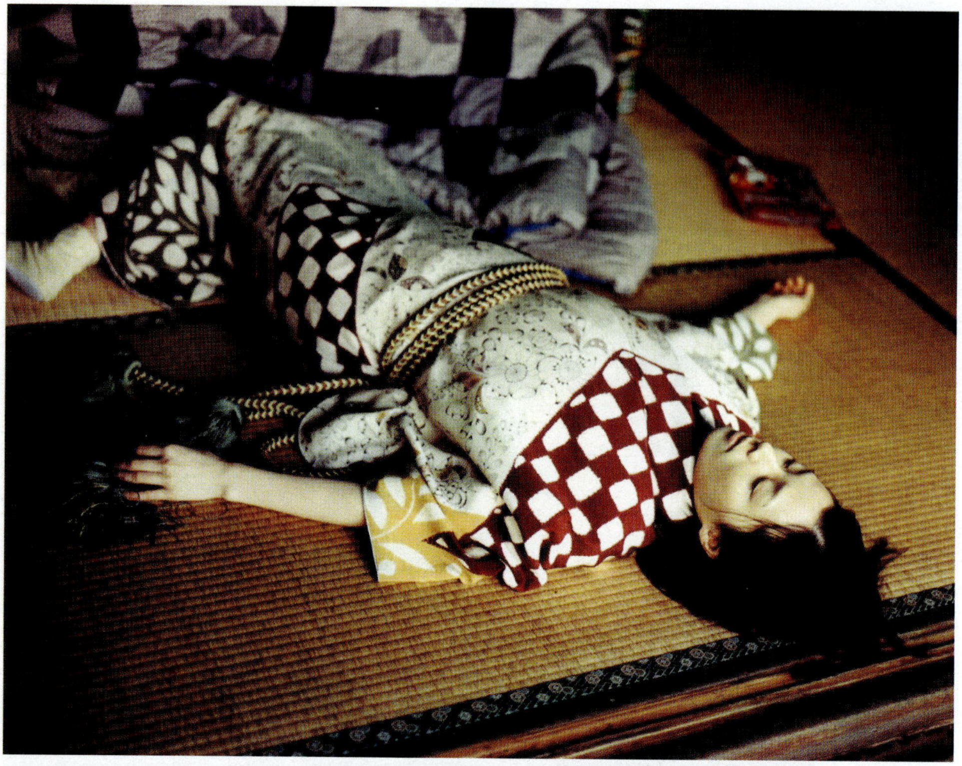

Fig. 26 Izima Kaoru, *Otsuka Nene Wears Tuzigahana # 213* (1999), C-Prints, 100 x 127 cm (edition of five, mounted on acryl and behind glass) and 35.5 x 43 cm (edition of ten, mounted on acryl in wooden frame).

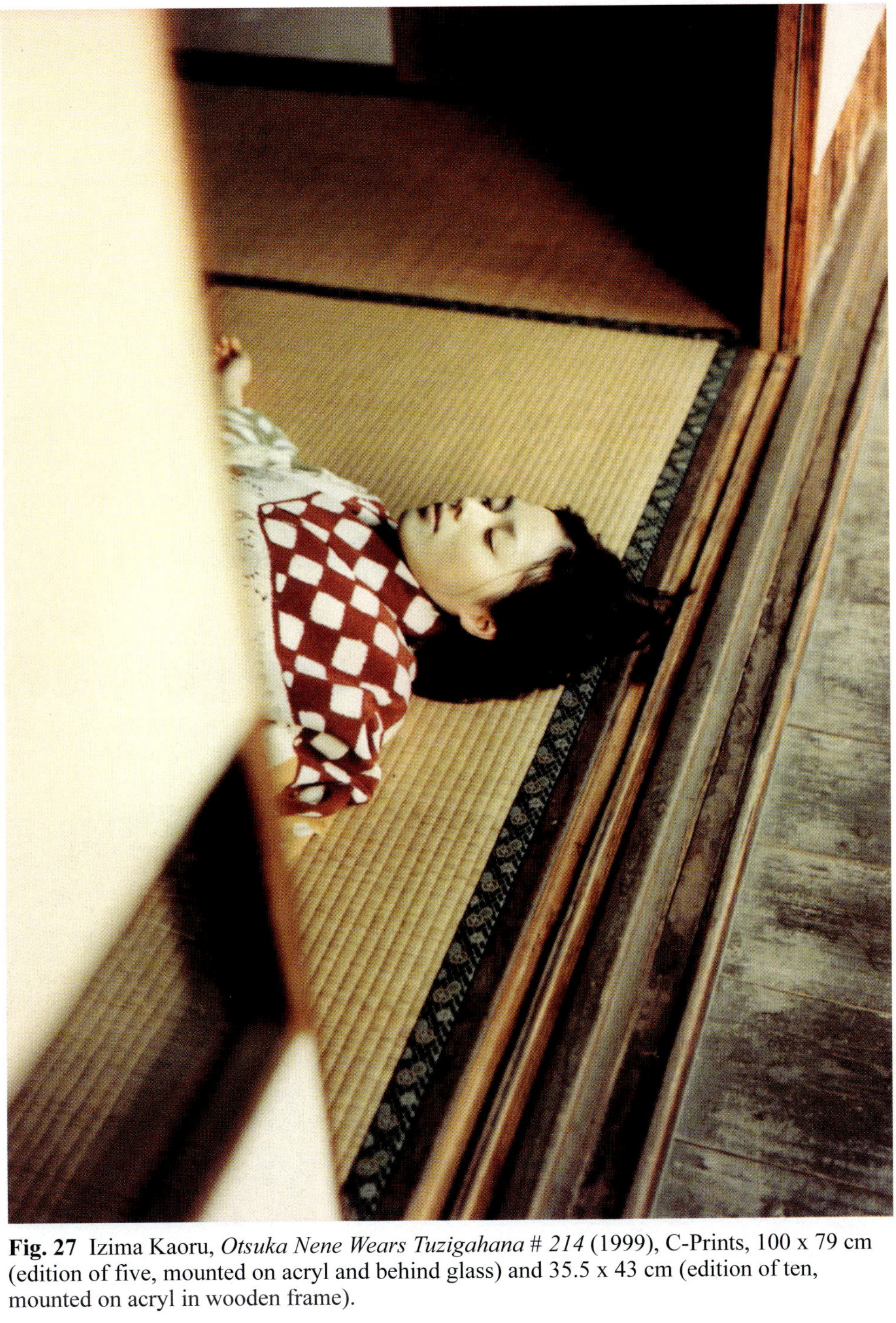

Fig. 27 Izima Kaoru, *Otsuka Nene Wears Tuzigahana # 214* (1999), C-Prints, 100 x 79 cm (edition of five, mounted on acryl and behind glass) and 35.5 x 43 cm (edition of ten, mounted on acryl in wooden frame).

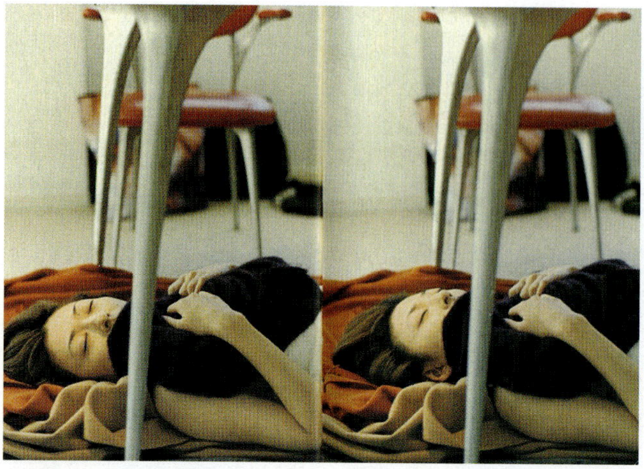

Fig. 28 Two photographs in Izima Kaoru's book *Nemuru Matsuyuki Yasuko* (Sleeping Matsuyuki Yasuko) (2003).

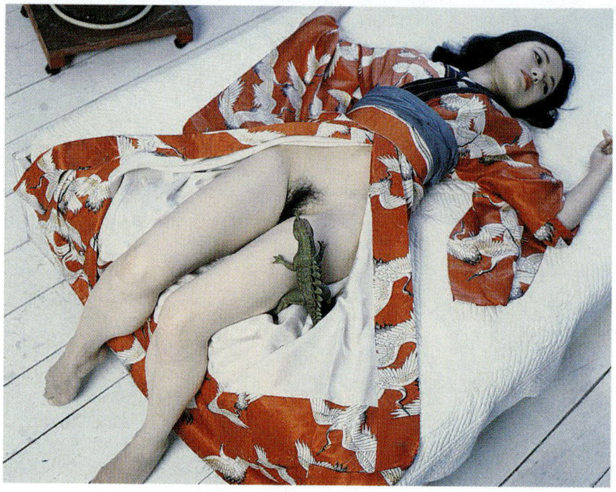

Fig. 29 Araki Nobuyoshi, *Untitled* (2004). Colour Photograph, 39.8 x 49. 7 cm (edition of hundred).

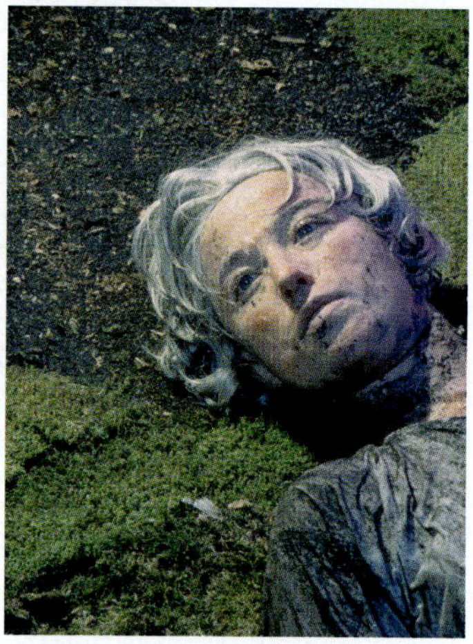

Fig. 30 Cindy Sherman, *Untitled #153* (1985). Chromogenic Colour Print, 170.8 x 125.7 cm.

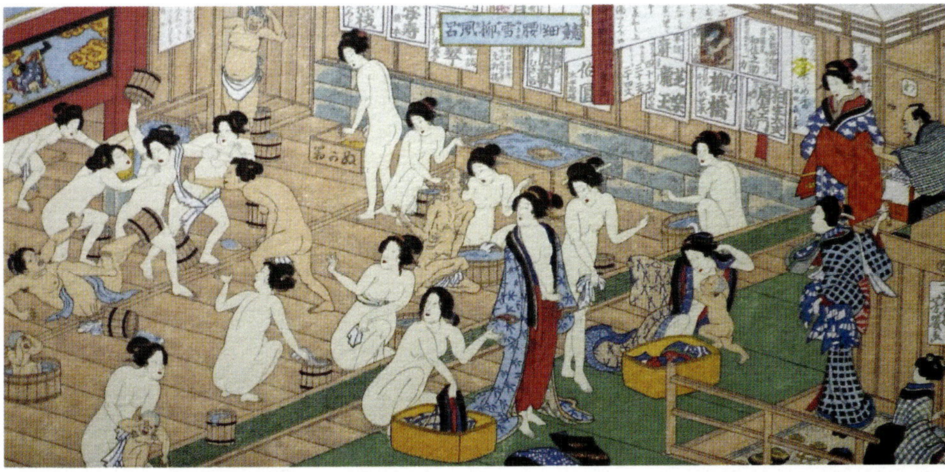

Fig. 31 Ochiai Yoshiiku, *Imayô nenjû gyôji* (Modern Annual Events) (mid–late 19th century), Woodblock Print.

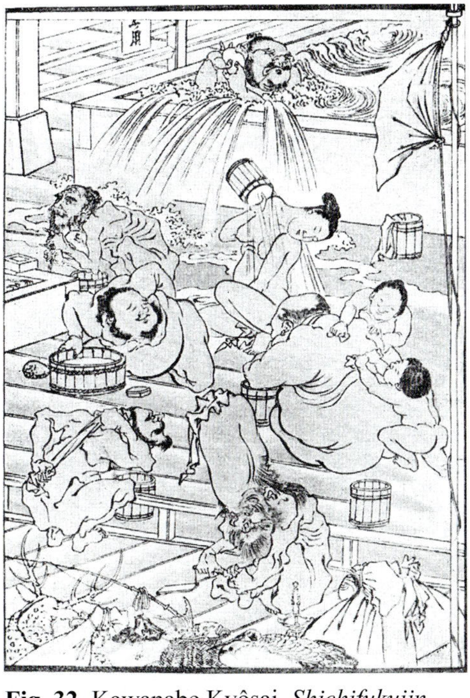

Fig. 32 Kawanabe Kyôsai, *Shichifukujin* (Seven Lucky Gods) in *Kyôsai manga* (1881). Ink on Paper.

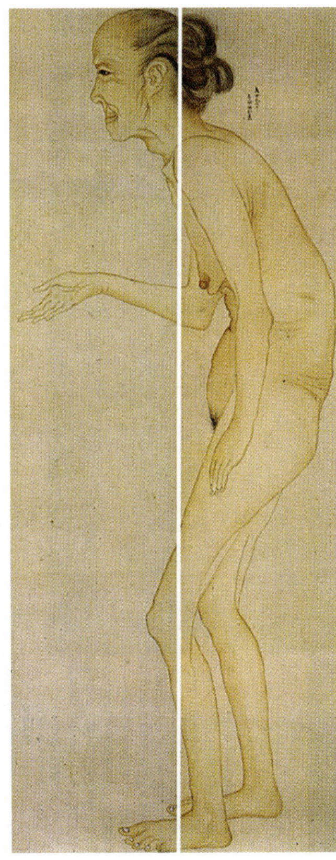

Fig. 33 Image in Maruyama Ôkyo's *Jinbutsu seisha sôhon* (Complete Folio of True Figure Studies) (1770). Ink and Light Colours on Paper Scrolls, 31.4 x 992 cm, Library of Tenri University, Nara.

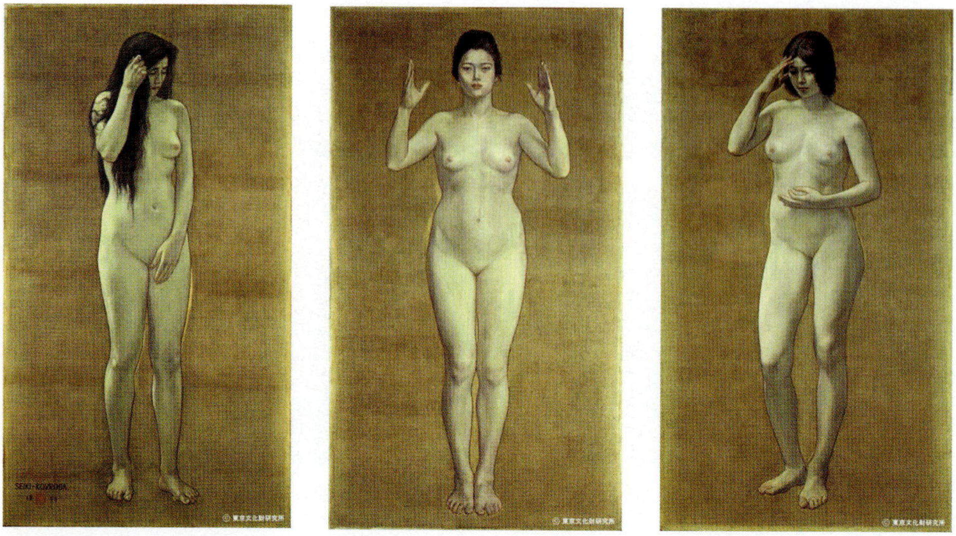

Fig. 34 Kuroda Seiki, *Chi Kan Jô* (Wisdom, Impression, Sentiment) (1897). Oil on Canvas, 180.6 x 99.8 cm, Kuroda Memorial Hall, National Research Institute for Cultural Properties, Tokyo.

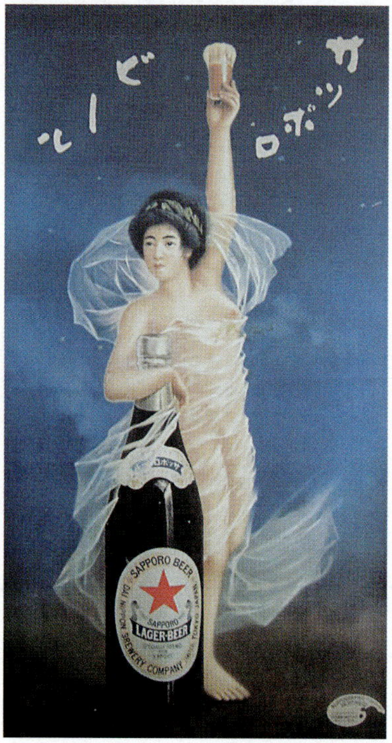

Fig. 35 Sapporo Beer Poster (1908).

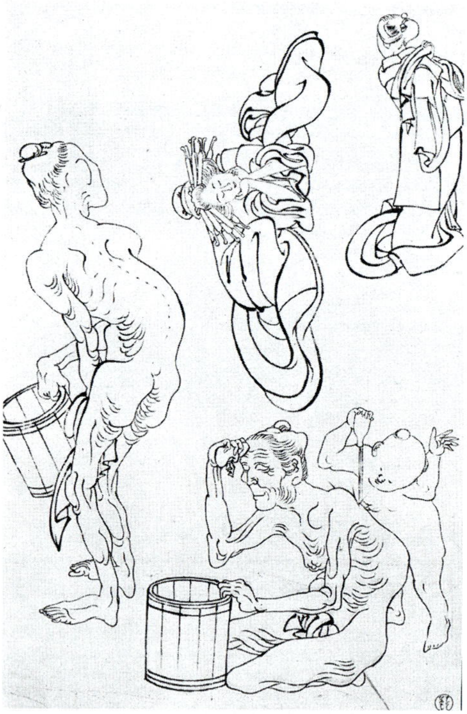

Fig. 36 Sketch by Katsushika Hokusai (late 18th, early 19th century). Ink on Paper.

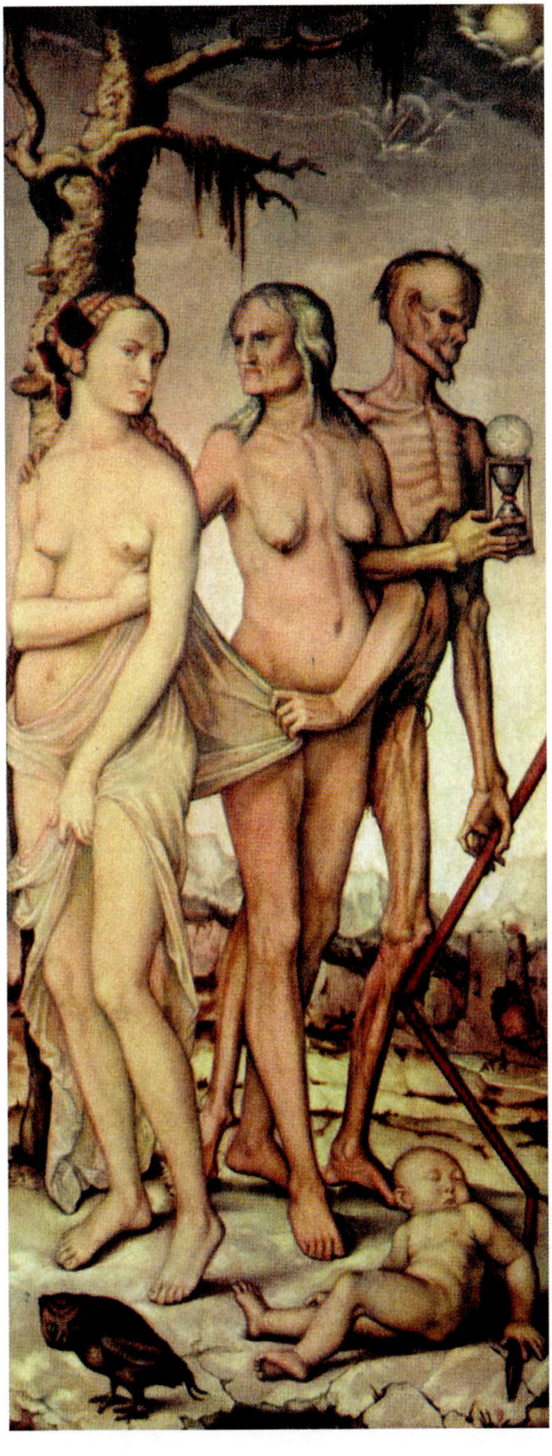

Fig. 37 Hans Baldung Grien, *Die Drei Lebensalter des Weibes und der Tod* (The Three Ages of the Woman and Death) (approximately 1510). Oil on Panel, 151 x 61 cm, Museo del Prado, Madrid.

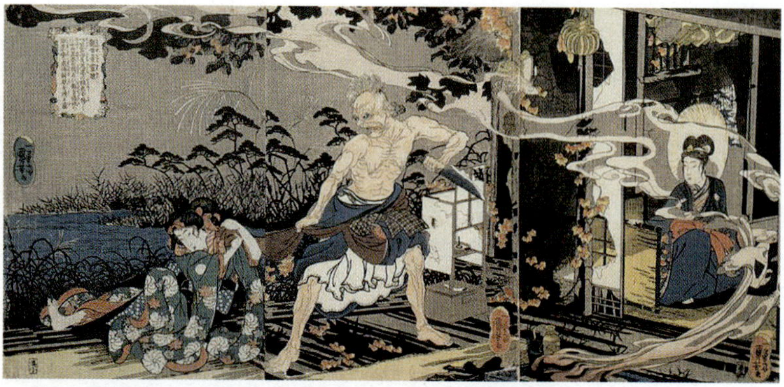

Fig. 38 Utagawa Kuniyoshi, *Kanzeon reigen. Hitotsuya no kyûji* (Kannon's Miraculous Virtue. The Old Tale of the Hitotsuya Hut) (1839–1840). Woodblock Print Triptych, each print 24 x 36 cm.

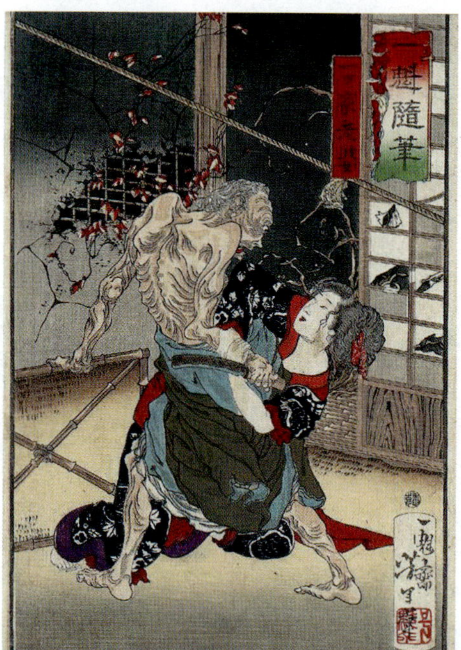

Fig. 39 Tsukioka Yoshitoshi, *Hitotsuya rôba* (The Old Woman of the *Hitotsuya* Hut) (1872). Woodblock Print, 24 x 36 cm.

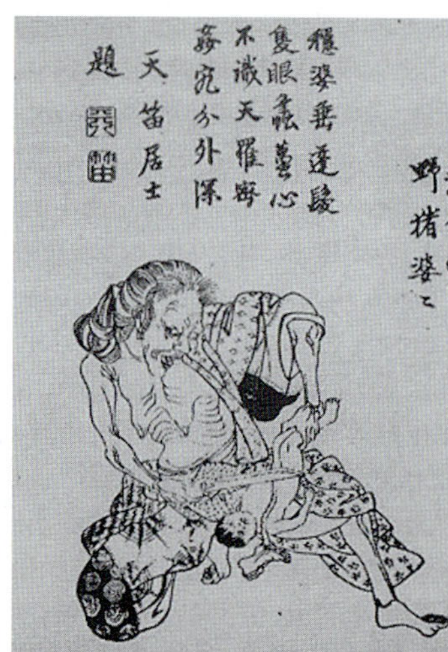

Fig. 40 *Kuchie* ('entrance image', first image), illustration in the first volume of Santô Kyôden's *Udonge monogatari* (The Tale of the three Thousand Year Flower) (1808).

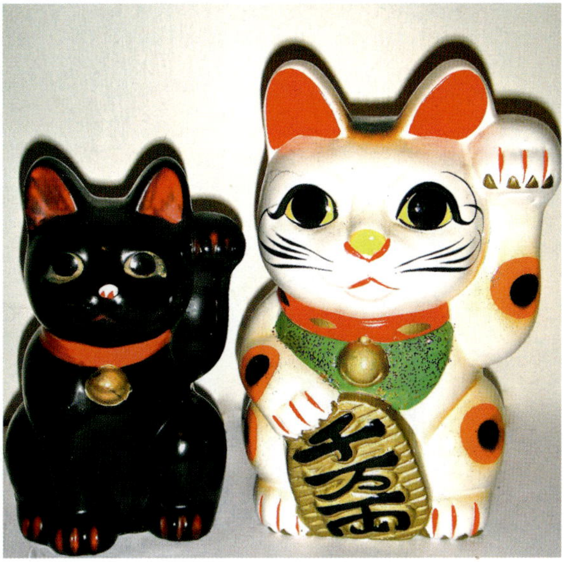

Fig. 41 Black and White *Manekineko.*

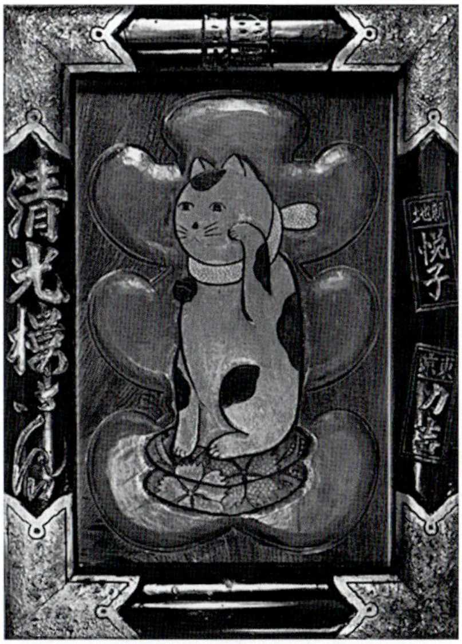

Fig. 42 Polychromed *Manekineko* Wood Sign (Meiji era), 61 x 44.5 cm.

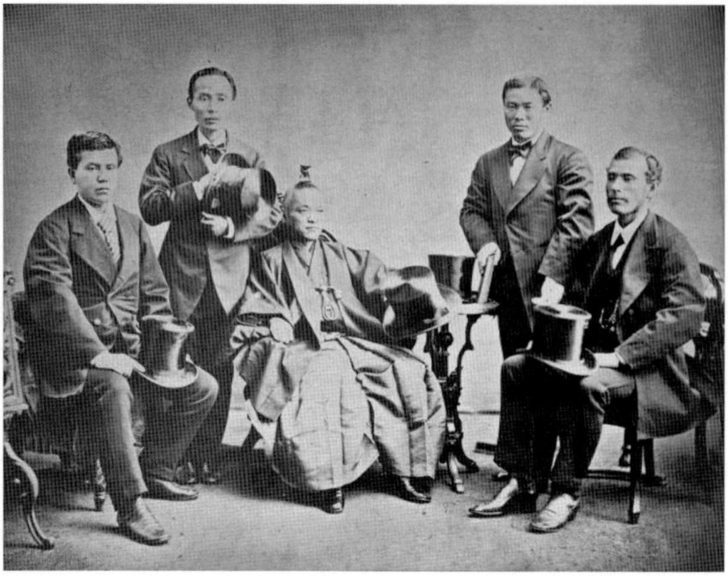

Fig. 43 Iwakura Tomomi with statesmen, London (1872).

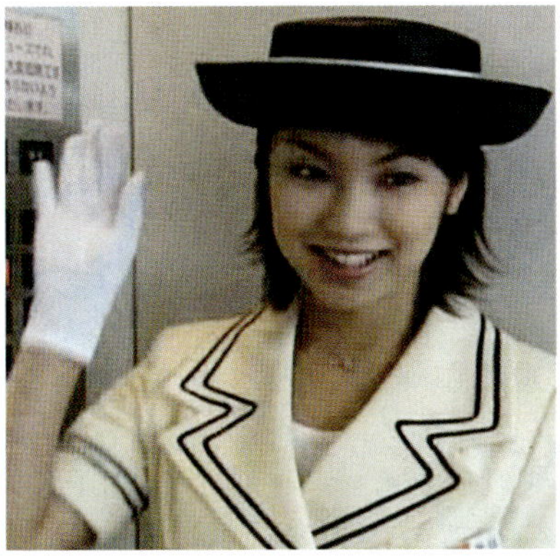

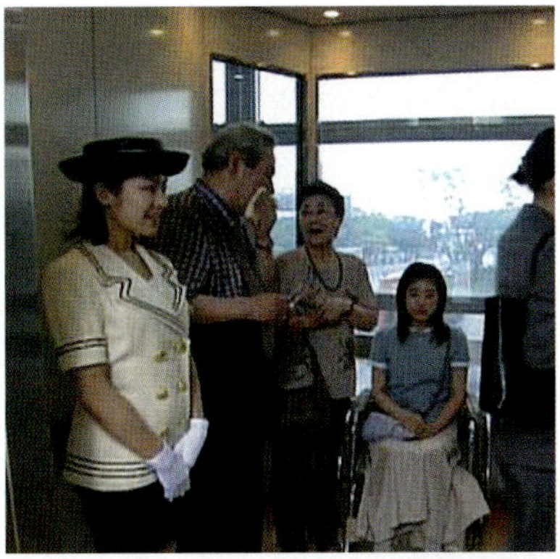

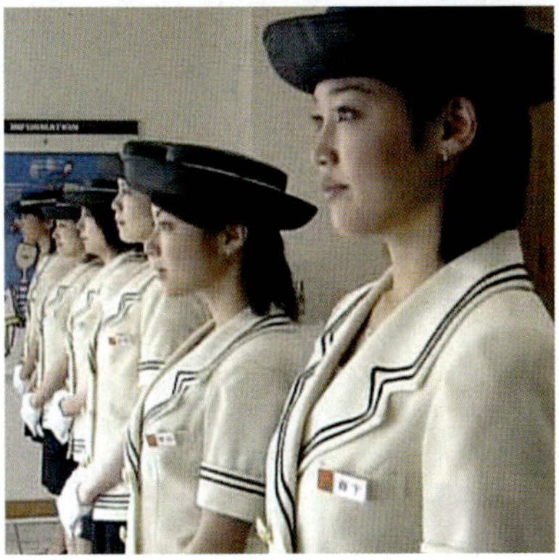

Fig. 44 Filmstills of the TV drama *Moto kare* (Ex-boyfriend) (2003) (00:07:45 and 00:07:39 of episode 2 and 00:06:09 of episode 1) with the elevator girl Hayakawa Nao (Uchiyama Rina).

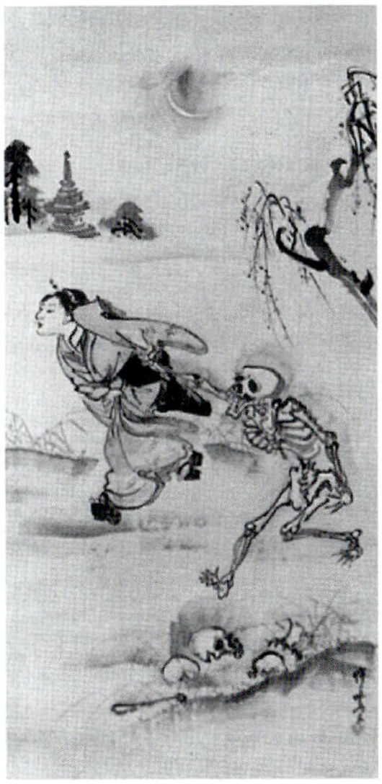

Fig. 45 Kawanabe Kyôsai, Untitled Hanging Scroll (1871). Ink and Light Colour on Silk, 137.7 x 63 cm, Linden-Museum, Stuttgart.

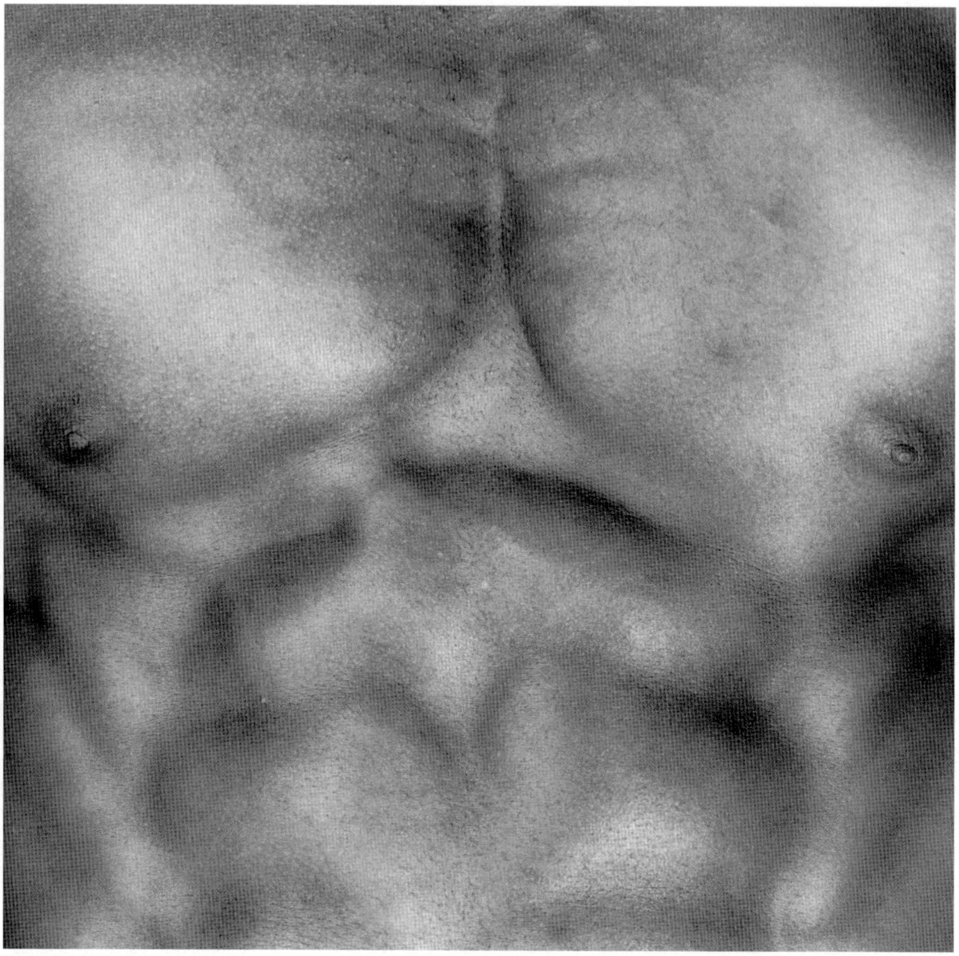

Fig. 46 Robert Mapplethorpe, *Chest* (1986). Gelatin Silver Print, 48.5 x 48.5 cm (edition of ten).

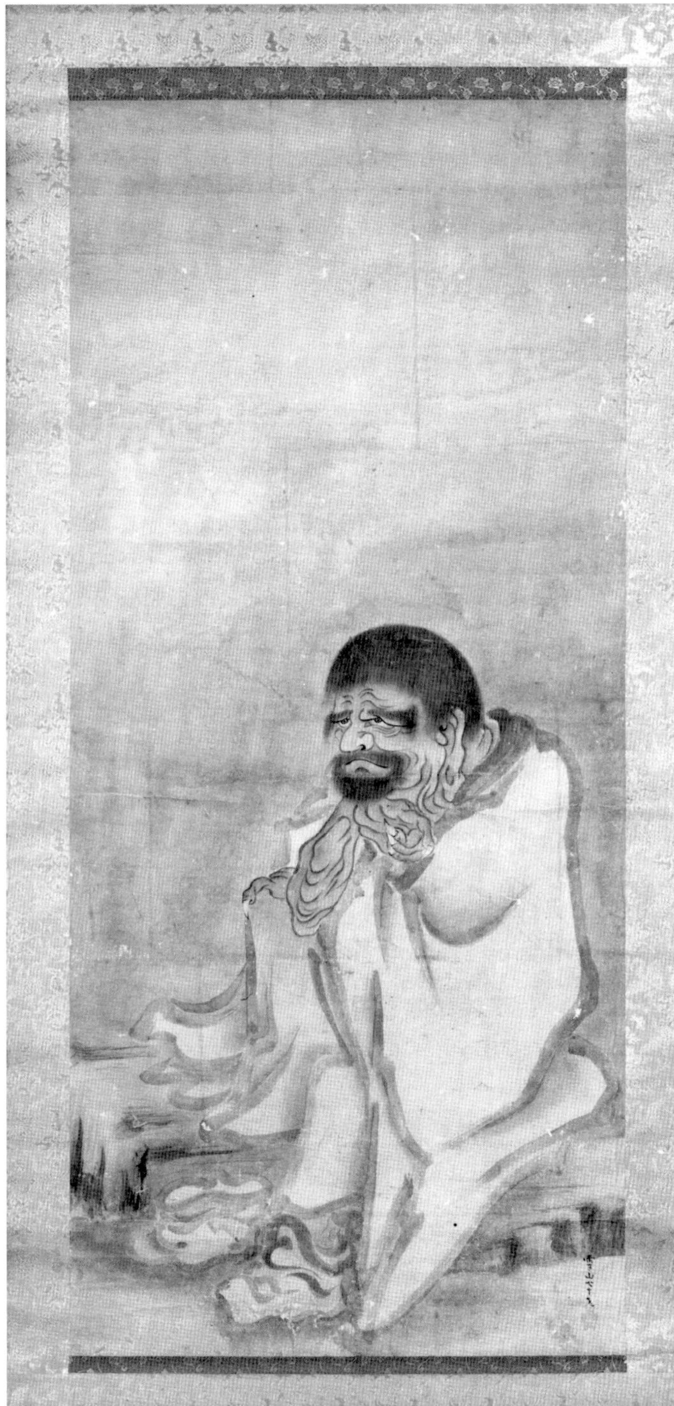

Fig. 47
Setsuzan, *Rakanzu*
(17th century).
Ink on paper,
119. 4 x 52.4 cm,
Museum of Fine Arts,
Boston.

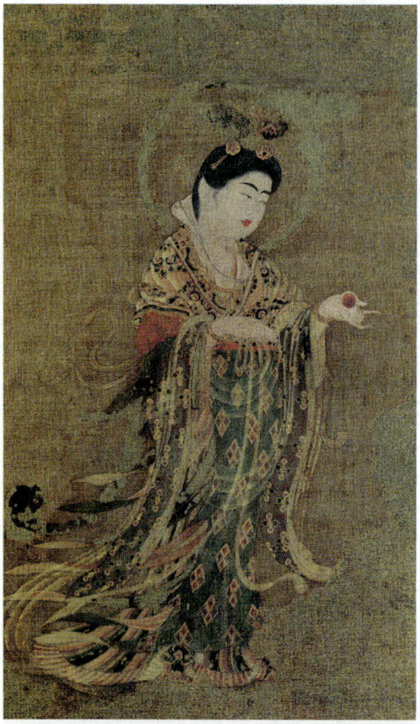

Fig. 48 *Kichijôten* (8th century).
Hanging Scroll, Colour on Hemp, 53 x 31.7 cm
Yakushi-ji Temple, Nara.

Fig. 49 Amida Nyôrai in front of a relief with fifty-two Bodhisattvas (Apsaras) (1053). Phoenix hall, Byôdô-in Temple, Kyoto.

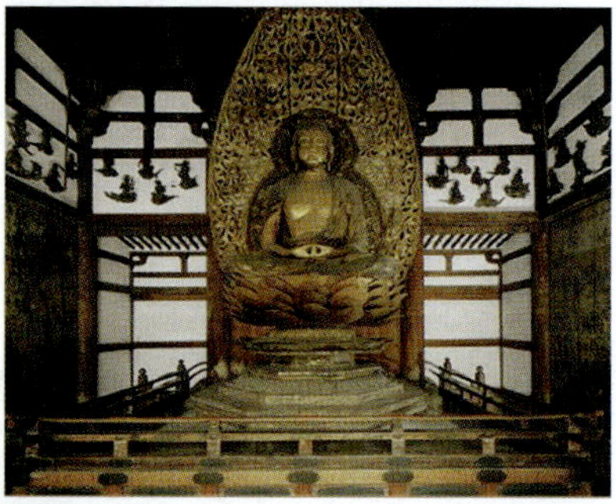

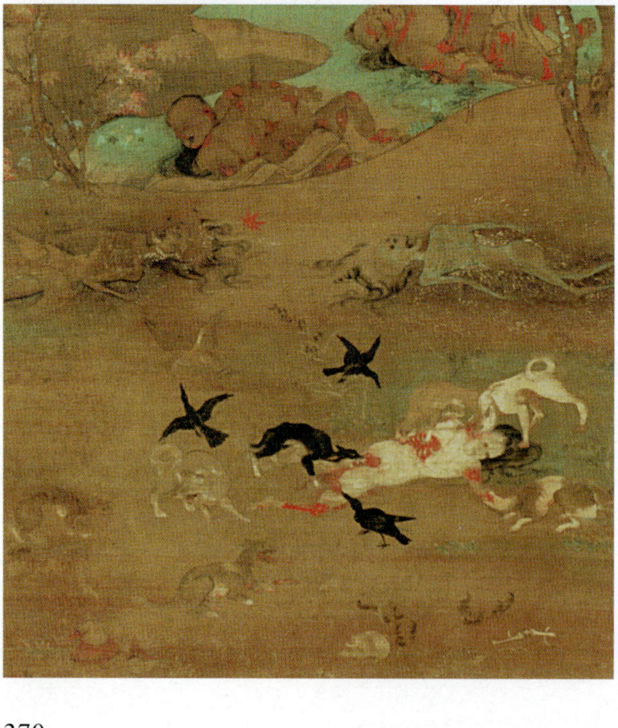

Fig. 50 Detail *Rikudôe, nindô fujô sôzu* (Painting of the Six Paths, Signs of the Impurity of the Human Path), (late 13th century). Hanging Scroll, 155.5 x 65 cm, Shôju Raigô-ji Temple, Shiga.

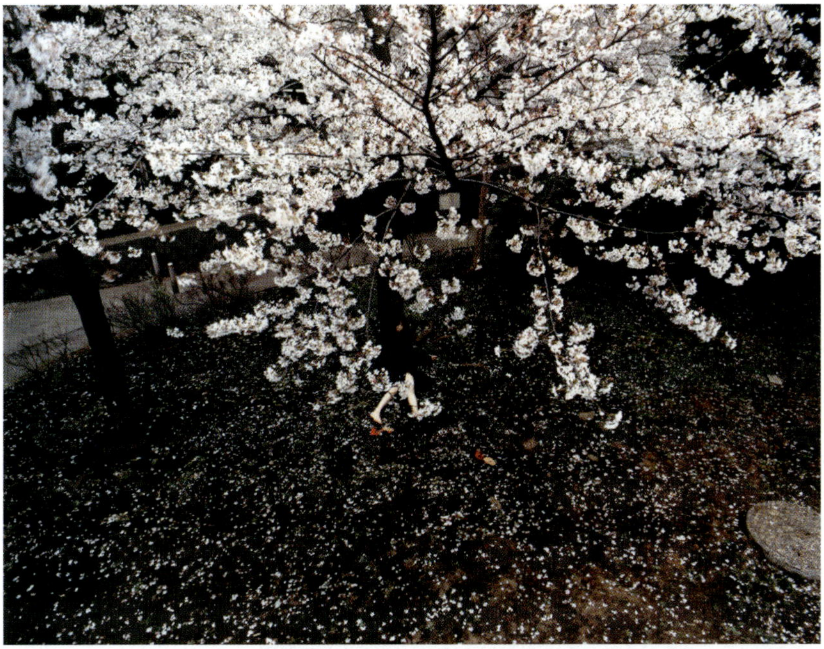

Fig. 51–53 Izima Kaoru, *Nagasaku Hiromi Wears Louis Vuitton # 221–223* (1999). C-Prints, **Fig. 51:** 100 x 127 cm (edition of five) and 40 x 50 cm (edition of ten).

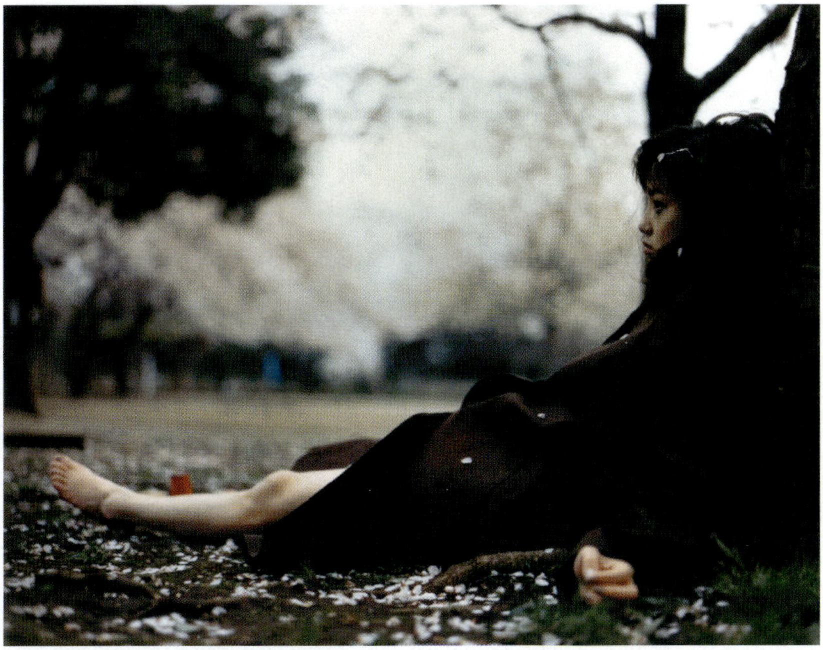

Fig. 52: 100 x 127 cm (edition of five) and 40 x 50 cm (edition of ten).

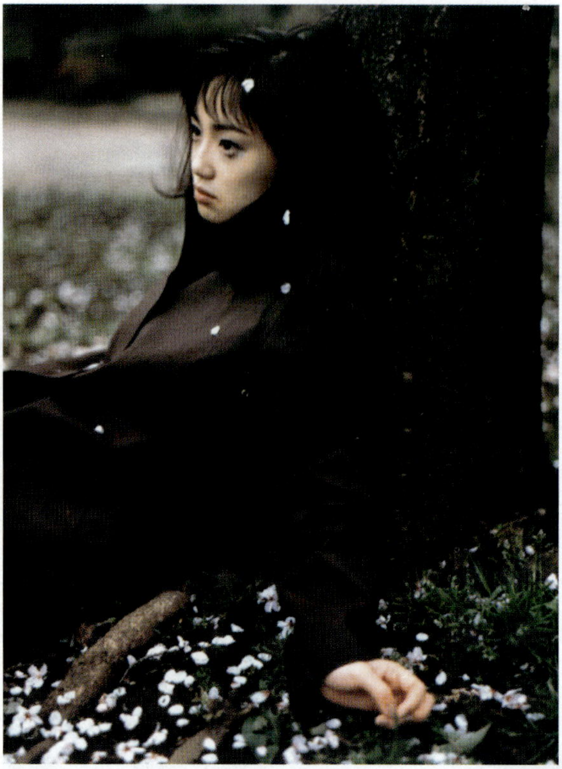

Fig. 53: 100 x 79 cm (edition of five) and 40 x 50 cm (edition of ten).

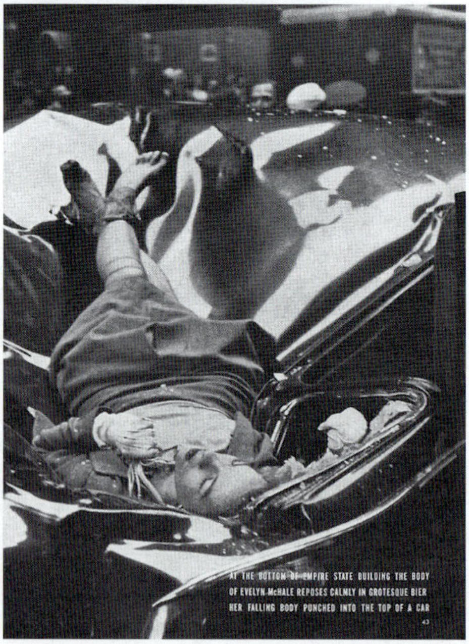

Fig. 54 Robert Wiles, Photograph of Evelyn Mchale in LIFE magazine (1947).